Reading Instruction for Students Who Are at Risk or Have Disabilities

William D. Bursuck
University of North Carolina–Greensboro

Mary Damer
Ohio State University

PEARSON

Boston   New York   San Francisco
Mexico City   Montreal   Toronto   London   Madrid   Munich   Paris
Hong Kong   Singapore   Tokyo   Cape Town   Sydney

KH

1/22/07

Executive Editor: Virginia Lanigan
Editorial Assistant: Matthew Buchholz
Senior Marketing Manager: Kris Ellis-Levy
Production Editor: Janet Domingo
Editorial Production Service: Omegatype Typography, Inc.
Composition Buyer: Linda Cox
Manufacturing Buyer: Linda Morris
Electronic Composition: Omegatype Typography, Inc.
Interior Design: Omegatype Typography, Inc.
Cover Administrator: Kristina Mose-Libon

For related titles and support materials, visit our online catalog at www.ablongman.com.

Between the time website information is gathered and then published, it is not unusual for some sites to have closed. Also, the transcription of URLs can result in unintended typographical errors. The publisher would appreciate notification where these errors occur so that they may be corrected in subsequent editions.

Library of Congress Cataloging-in-Publication Data

Bursuck, William D.
    Reading instruction for students who are at risk or have disabilities / William Bursuck, Mary Damer.
        p. cm.
    Includes bibliographical references and index.
    ISBN 0-205-40404-9
        1. Reading—Remedial teaching.   I. Damer, Mary. II. Title.

LB1050.5.B87 2007
372.43—dc22

2006048575

Printed in the United States of America.

10 9 8 7 6 5 4 3 2 1   10 09 08 07 06

To Beth and Stephen for allowing us the immense professional space required to bring this project to fruition. Without your patience, love, and support this book would not have been possible.

Contents

Chapter 4   Advanced Word-Reading   131

| **Chapter 5** | **Reading Fluency** | **168** |

Chapter 6	**Vocabulary Instruction**	**209**

Chapter 7   Comprehension   251

Preface

Between 2000 and 2004 we implemented Project PRIDE, a four-year federal model demonstration project that employed evidence-based practices to prevent reading problems in children who are at risk in three diverse, high-poverty urban schools in Rockford, Illinois. The principals of these schools opted to reverse their course from a more naturalistic reading program and make the commitment to retraining their staff because of a history of chronic reading problems and a teaching environment permeated by failure. Failure rates on the Illinois State Achievement Test (ISAT) for PRIDE schools ranged from 50% to 78%. Over the course of the project, through ongoing student achievement data and a close working relationship with the Rockford educators, we had the opportunity to fine-tune instructional strategies to a degree that would not have been possible without that collaboration.

During the four years of Project PRIDE we gained an even greater appreciation for Louisa Moats' expression, *Teaching Reading is Rocket Science.* On a daily basis we observed that as the human mind acquires the intellectual muscle to learn to read, the teacher must not only know how to carefully teach the sequence of small steps needed for reading at grade level, but also to recognize the missteps that can thwart those efforts. Whether students came to school from high-poverty backgrounds, with no parental support, with learning disabilities or behavior disorders, with medical conditions, from backgrounds of abuse, or without English-speaking skills, most of them were able to learn to read. The research in reading, as described in The Report of the National Reading Panel (2000), provides a clear guide for the use of systematic and explicit instruction to teach the largest number of students to read. In this book we have translated that guide into a detailed blueprint based on 1) explicit, systematic instruction, 2) a multi-tiered teaching approach, 3) data-based decision making, and 4) ongoing professional development.

Project PRIDE was based on the idea that in order to implement effective reading instruction "one size does not fit all." Therefore, we offered student support along a continuum of intensities or instructional tiers. These tiers allowed for maximum access to the general education reading program while providing more intensive instruction on an as-needed basis. The focus in each of those tiers was on skills in the five key areas identified by the National Reading Panel (2000) as essential for learning to read. These key areas include phonemic awareness, alphabetic principle, reading fluency, vocabulary, and reading comprehension.

In the PRIDE model, Tier 1 was delivered by the general education teacher using a whole-class grouping arrangement. Tier 1 instruction was based on the general education beginning reading programs that were used in the project schools including *Harcourt* (Farr, Strickland, & Beck, 2001) in two of our schools and *Open Court* (Bereiter et al., 1995) in one. We added several research-based teaching enhancements that help children who are at risk learn more efficiently and effectively (Kameenui et al., 2002). These teaching enhancements included the use of advance organizers; unison responses; appropriate level of teacher talk; a perky teaching pace; support for new learning using modeling, guided, and independent practice; careful, systematic correction of student errors; teaching to success; and a student motivational system.

Tier 2 consisted of booster or tutoring sessions that provided extra practice for small groups of two to eight students, working on essential reading skills covered in the school reading series. Students entered Tier 2 when their performance dipped below mastery on monthly or bimonthly curriculum-based assessments, but they still remained in the general education reading program. Tier 2 teachers used the same enhancements used in Tier 1 (e.g., unison response and systematic error correction), but at a different time of day in separate pull-out settings with smaller instructional groups. Tier 2 sessions were carried out by a variety of staff, including general education teachers, Title 1 teachers, special education teachers, and paraprofessionals.

Tier 3 was an intensive alternative reading program (*Reading Mastery*) conducted daily in separate pull-out settings with small, skill-based groups of two to six students. Students placed in Tier 3 had failed to make substantial progress on PRIDE assessments despite extra daily help in Tier 2 booster groups. *Reading Mastery* (Engelmann & Bruner, 1995) was designed specifically for at-risk children in need of a more intensive beginning reading program. The phonetically based *Reading Mastery* curriculum is characterized by a carefully designed instructional sequence as well as multiple scaffolds to facilitate student learning. Tier 3 was taught by Title 1, foreign language, and special education teachers plus a few highly skilled paraprofessionals. Children in Tier 3 received their general education classes either during reading when the rest of the students were involved in reading activities that were at a frustration level for these students, or during a subject matter class such as science or social studies. Children in Tier 3 did participate in general education reading activities, such as vocabulary (done orally) and comprehension (as a listening activity).

Students were assigned to the PRIDE multi-tiered system based on their performance on monthly or bimonthly assessments. The assessment results were summarized by the project coordinator, who then convened a meeting of the teachers to discuss tier placements for the subsequent intervention period.

Early literacy performance was measured primarily using the Dynamic Indicators of Basic Early Literacy Skills (DIBELS; Kaminski & Good, 1996). DIBELS assessments (Good, Gruba, & Kaminski, 2002) have been shown to be an accurate way of identifying children at risk for reading problems and monitoring their progress in phonemic awareness, attainment of the alphabetic principle, and reading fluency. A hallmark of the DIBELS assessments is efficiency, with each measure taking fewer than 5 minutes to give. At a time when the school calendar is increasingly taken up with high-stakes testing, efficiency was an essential quality for us.

Professional development and coaching for teachers and staff who carried out instruction in Tiers 1, 2, and 3 was provided by the two authors of this text. All teachers attended after-school workshops and a series of summer institutes, and received on-site coaching. The after-school workshops and summer institutes were used to introduce various teaching and assessment strategies, allow teachers to observe taped or live models of the strategies, and provide practice for the teachers in small groups using simulated experiences. During on-site coaching visits, data on tier implementation were gathered directly in the classroom; teachers were given feedback on their instruction until they demonstrated competence.

The impetus for writing this text came from the results attained during our four years of PRIDE implementation. Our results showed that all children could make progress toward learning to read when a system of assessments guided staff to identify children who were not responding to instruction, allowing them to meet their individual needs using evidence-based instructional options of varying intensities. The assessment and teaching strategies that were successful in PRIDE are those that occupy the pages of this text. The data shown in Table 1 from one project school and a control school reflect the percentage of children meeting or exceeding standard on the Illinois State Achievement Test.

Note the significant increases from 1999–2000 to 2003–2004, the latter being scores for our first PRIDE cohort. It is interesting that the ISAT scores for our PRIDE school began improving for the 2002–2003 school year, despite the fact that these were students who

TABLE 1 Percentage of Children Meeting or Exceeding Standard on the Illinois State Achievement Test

Third Grade Reading	1999–2000	2000–20001	2001–2002	2002–2003	2003–2004
School 1	31	22	15.2	55.2	68.2
Control	39	40	36.4	28.6	39

were not officially part of the project. We believe that at least part of that increase resulted because the school, seeing that PRIDE was working so well in the early grades, began to implement some of the same practices in the later grades that were not part of the PRIDE project. Note the rise in achievement at the control school for the 2003–2004 school year. This school began to implement the PRIDE model during that year and provided SRA Reading Mastery to all of its students in Grade 3.

It is clear from these results that more children met state standards in reading as a result of Project PRIDE. It is also true that about 30% of the students did not meet state standards. These were largely students who were receiving support in either Tier 2 or Tier 3. Nonetheless, our results showed that even though many Tier 2 and 3 students did not meet standards, they did make significant gains on all of the DIBELS measures (Bursuck, Smith, Munk, Damer, Mehlig, & Perry, 2004).We knew that grouping according to common skill needs had been criticized for exacerbating achievement differences by lowering expectations and watering down instruction, yet our results indicated that children can make progress in small, heterogeneous pull-out groups if the instruction delivered in those groups is evidence-based and delivered with integrity. Systematic, explicit instruction in our Tier 2 and Tier 3 small groups ensured significant progress for students in both of these groups. For example, effect sizes for all three tiers on all of our early literacy measures were all well over .40, the level at which an effect size is considered significant (Forness, Kavale, Blum, & Lloyd, 1997). Small, skill-based groups are not a dead end, if done appropriately.

Another common drawback of having different instructional options for children is that racial minorities tend to be overrepresented in the groups of children who are not responding to instruction. In PRIDE, children were assessed five to six times per year using highly efficient assessments directly tied to curricular goals and objectives. These assessments allowed us to make decisions in the best interest of individual children without being influenced by potentially biasing factors such as race. Our results showed that the proportion of African American children served in Tiers 2 and 3 has been no greater than could be expected given their proportion in our school population at large.

Whatever disagreements exist in the field about how to teach reading, few would argue with the overarching goal of a nation of life-long learners who enjoy reading for information as well as pleasure. We are troubled when educational strategies such as skill-based grouping, pull-out, and drill-practice-and-review are viewed as antithetical to the enjoyment of reading. That criticism is why we surveyed the attitudes of our Tier 1, 2, and 3 children at the end of grades 1 and 2 (McKenna & Kearn, 1990). The results showed that children receiving Tier 2 and Tier 3 instruction had positive attitudes toward both academic and recreational reading and that their attitudes were not significantly different from their Tier 1 counterparts. As shown in Figures 1 and 2, all three tiers averaged about 3 on a 4-point scale, with 4 indicating a high positive attitude. Child success, more than where instruction takes place, is what truly matters when it comes to students' attitudes toward reading. We believe we have also demonstrated that drill is one ingredient of an effective reading program for students who are at risk and, if done effectively, can *thrill*—not *kill*.

We know that however positive the results, it is often teacher acceptance of an instructional approach that determines the likelihood that it will continue to be used over time (Polloway, Bursuck, Jayanthi, Epstein, & Nelson, 1996). At the end of each year of the project, we surveyed our teachers to find out their feedback on all aspects of the

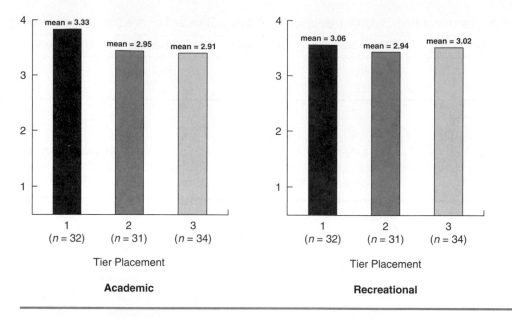

FIGURE 1   Attitude Toward Reading Scores by Tier Academic and Recreational Reading PRIDE, Grade 1

PRIDE model. Satisfaction was of particular interest to us because of our emphasis on teacher accountability for the reading achievement of each and every student. Our teacher satisfaction results, shown in Figure 3, have been very encouraging, with acceptance ratings after the first year for all parts of the model being consistently rated over 3 on a 4-point scale, with 4 representing the highest satisfaction. In the words of one of our principals, "It is interesting to watch the teachers' perceptions of Project PRIDE transition from fear and distrust to such high levels of satisfaction now that they are held

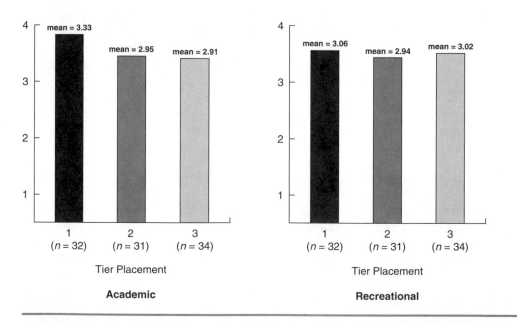

FIGURE 2   Attitude Toward Reading Scores by Tier Academic and Recreational Reading PRIDE, Grade 2

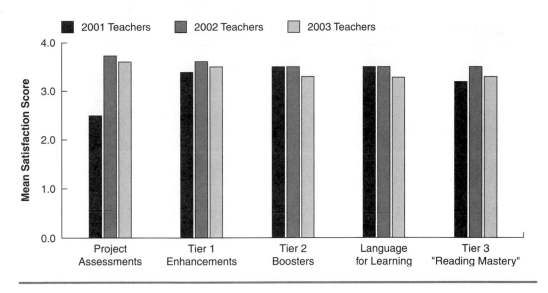

FIGURE 3   Teacher Satisfaction

directly accountable for student growth. I've watched them quickly develop their capacities to serve all of the learning needs within their classrooms after systematic professional development."

At the conclusion of the project, we asked teachers whether they thought their school should continue to implement Project PRIDE the following year. Twenty-nine, or 85%, of our project teachers responded to the question. Of the 29 teachers who responded, 28 (97%) wanted the project to continue.

Project PRIDE, with its emphases on regular progress monitoring of all students and the provision of a range of instructional supports based on need, is consistent with the provisions of the recent No Child Left Behind Act (NCLB). The results for children in all three of our tiers showed that 95% of the children made reading progress, and that their attitudes toward reading were positive. Our Title 1, general education, and special education teachers found the model acceptable and the model has been continued beyond the funding period. All of these results have encouraged us to write this book so that other teachers can become empowered to teach children to read who have traditionally been left behind.

DVD of Teaching Formats Included with this Book

In our work with teachers, the following concern was repeatedly raised: "Everyone talks and writes about how I should teach reading, but it would be such a help to actually see these skills being taught to children." That concern provided the impetus for producing this companion DVD. The video footage shows a teacher using the reading formats from the book to teach critical reading skills to students in a small group classroom situation. Viewers can refer to the text as they watch phonemic awareness, letter-sound correspondence, word reading, vocabulary and passage reading with comprehension being taught. For easy reference, menus on the DVD identify each format and reference the specific table in the book in which the teaching skill is introduced.

Acknowledgments

Over the years we have had the good fortune of working with and learning from a talented group of educators firmly committed to the proposition that every child can learn to read. Without the contributions of these dedicated professionals, writing *Reading Instruction for Students Who Are at Risk or Have Disabilities* would have been impossible. First, we owe a huge debt of gratitude to all of the people who have provided us as well as our field with a blueprint for success that will continue to have a positive impact on children for many generations to come. Particular thanks are offered here to Doug Carnine and Jerry Silbert for writing our "bible," and to Diane Kinder for inspiring us to prepare teachers with integrity and passion. We would also like to thank Louisa Moats for impressing on us the importance of foundational information in language to any teacher change effort in reading. Our thanks also to Roland Good for developing a sound, practical set of measures and who, in an act of educational philanthropy of historic proportions, made them available free on the Internet so that the data-based decision making so essential to a multi-tier model could be accomplished. Many thanks to Debbie Holderness and Sonia Martin for their invaluable assistance with the preparation of the manuscript.

We also wish to thank the colleagues who were instrumental in helping with the development and refinement of the many aspects of the multi-tier model, including Shirley Dickson, Rolanda O'Connor, Kelly Bolas, Dennis Munk, Missy Moreno, Libby Noel, and Sara Long. Thanks also to Val Bresnahan and Sue Grisco for their help with the Tier 3 tables.

We are indebted to the federal government for funding Project PRIDE through a Model-Demonstration grant (CFDA 84.324.T; H324T990024). We also owe a great debt of gratitude to the Rockford Public Schools, in particular Kishwaukee School, Lewis Lemon Academy, and the John Nelson School, whose conscientious effort to implement multi-tier instruction showed that we could have a positive impact on children who had previously fallen through the cracks. A particular note of thanks goes to these talented, committed teachers whose belief in the model and commitment to children sustained us: Paula Larson, Nancy Dornbush, Michele Dettman, Sharon Bramel, Sheri Hayes, Carol Gibbs, Joanne Robertson, Mixay Phonthibsvads, Marcia Carlstrom, Susan Vetrano, and Linda Oshita.

Special thanks go to the reviewers of the book whose careful, constructive attention to the manuscript gave us the confidence to proceed while at the same time improving the final product. The reviewers included: Shirley V. Dickson, California State University at Fullerton; Kathleen J. Marshall, University of South Carolina; Pam Matlock, Murray State College; Melinda R. Pierson, California State University at Fullerton; Darren Smith, Arkansas State University; and Vicki Snider, University of Wisconsin. Thanks also to Kurt Lazarof and Kazuko Matsuda for their invaluable help with the final preparation of the manuscript.

A final thanks to teachers everywhere who are willing to do whatever it takes to deliver effective, evidence-based reading instruction to their students. Your efforts will always teach and inspire us as we continue to pursue the vision of helping every child learn to read.

DVD Acknowledgments

Portraying the teaching formats discussed throughout the book would not have been possible without the skill of our master teacher Kelly Bolas, the children of Bluford Communications Magnet school in Greensboro, North Carolina (Brianna Lorrick, Christina Brown, Kamari Purvis, Jaquin Miller, and Paul Gaurdin), and their principal, LaToy Kennedy. Tom Lipscomb and Associates grasped the goals of the video immediately and captured on video everything we wanted and more.

1

An Introduction to Systematic, Explicit Reading Instruction

Key Terms

Alphabetic principle

At risk

Blending

Continuous sounds

Cumulative review

Differentiated instruction

Explicit instruction

Expressive vocabulary

Fluency-based assessments

Phonemic awareness

Phonics

Reading fluency

Receptive vocabulary

Segmenting

Stop sounds

Systematic error correction

Systematic instruction

Voiced sounds

Unvoiced sounds

Objectives

After reading this chapter, you will be able to:

1. Provide a rationale for using:
   a. differentiated instruction to teach students to read
   b. a prevention-based approach to reading
   c. explicit systematic phonics instruction to teach students who are at risk to read

2. Identify and describe five key skill areas that should comprise a reading curriculum for students who are at risk.

3. Describe a three-tier system for providing differentiated instruction for students who are at risk.

4. Identify and describe ways to enhance reading instruction for students who are at risk.

"Some people there are who, being grown forget the horrible task of learning to read. It is perhaps the greatest single effort that the human undertakes, and he must do it as a child."

John Steinbeck (1976)

No other skill learned by school children is more important than reading, described as the gateway to all other knowledge by the American Federation of Teachers (2003–2004). Yet, despite its critical importance for success in our society, millions of school children in the United States are failing to learn to read. The National Assessment of Educational Progress Report indicated that 50% or more of the fourth and eighth graders in the nation's largest urban areas were below the basic level in reading, unable to demonstrate even partial mastery of fundamental knowledge and skills (Kennedy-Manzo, 2003). The rate among African American and Hispanic children is even higher; 70% of young African American children and 65–70% of Hispanic children are unable to read. These reading problems do not just reside among school children but pervade our entire society. Experts estimate that more than 90 million adults lack a foundation of basic literacy skills necessary to function in society, losing over 200 billion dollars a year in income (Whitehurst, 2003–2004). Given these statistics, it is not surprising to hear the current epidemic of literacy problems referred to as a national health problem (Lyon, 1998).

In response to public concerns about unacceptably high rates of illiteracy and demands for increased accountability, the U.S. Congress passed the *No Child Left Behind Act (NCLB)* in 2001. A central provision of this act was the mandate that all of our nation's children be reading at grade level by the school year 2013–2014. While the goals of *NCLB* are laudable, this bold legislation has rightfully raised many questions among teachers trying to meet those goals. For example, which children have more trouble learning to read and why? How can we identify them? Are there effective methods available to teach these children to read? When is the most opportune time to teach children to read? Do all children learn to read the same way? Can we really teach all children to read? Teachers need practical answers to these and other questions if they are to make a legitimate attempt to teach all children to read.

Explanations about why large percentages of students do not attain minimum literacy levels echo the reasons that students are at risk in the first place:

- These students were raised in poverty.
- Their parents never read to them as children.
- These students have learning disabilities.
- English is not their first language.
- These students were premature babies.

Although educators agree that students who come to school with some or all of these factors present greater challenges, effective reading teachers believe that there are no excuses. These teachers can and will teach every student to read. Yes, John's mother took cocaine before he was born, but he will learn to read. Yes, Marissa has an exceptionally difficult time hearing the individual sounds in words, but she will learn to read. Yes, Shyron's mother has been married three times and amidst a blended family of eight kids he's lost in the shuffle. But he will learn to read. This tenacious attitude is necessary for teachers who get all or most of their students who are at risk to read at grade level.

A tenacious attitude alone isn't sufficient for success. Because of the greater challenges teaching students who are at risk to read, teachers need effective teaching techniques and curriculum that have a proven track record of success with these students. Students who are at risk for reading failure require more carefully coordinated curriculum and skill instruction than other students. Fortunately for today's teachers, the *Report of the National Reading Panel* (2000) helps translate research into practice. The National Reading Panel—which included leading reading researchers, college professors, teachers, administrators, and parents—spent almost two years identifying those research studies that met the highest empirical standards of scientific investigation out of a larger pool of 100,000 studies conducted over the past 34 years. Selected studies used to determine the most effective ways of teaching reading to the greatest number of students included students who were at risk, disabled, or underachieving.

Who Are the Students at Risk for Reading Problems?

The strategies for teaching early literacy described in this text are based on the idea that when it comes to reading instruction, "one size does not fit all." Figure 1.1 shows how many children in a typical first-grade classroom are likely to struggle learning to read. These figures are based on research sponsored by the National Institute of Child and Health and Development (NICHD; Lyon, 1998).

Looking at the chart, you can see that:

- About 5% of students come to school already able to read. These children learn to read naturally without any formal instruction.
- Another 20–30% of students learn to read with ease, regardless of the approach to reading instruction used.
- For 20–30% of students, learning to read will take hard work, with some extra support needed. If parents work with these students every night, reviewing books read in class and serving as tutors, the students may learn to break the code. Extra practice with a volunteer tutor may be enough to help them break the code
- An additional 30% of students will only learn to read if they are given intensive support. These students require explicit systematic phonics instruction and extensive practice reading the new words they are learning until they are at least able to read second-grade text accurately and fluently. If they do not receive appropriate support before second grade, many of these students will have a reading level significantly behind their peers and never catch up. Some may be incorrectly diagnosed as having learning disabilities.
- The remaining 5% of students have serious, pervasive reading disabilities and are served in special education.

In high-poverty schools, the number of children who need extra or intensive support may be even higher. This book refers to any students who require extra support to learn as **at risk.** Regardless of the cause, these students will not learn to read if a systematic, supportive approach is not in place.

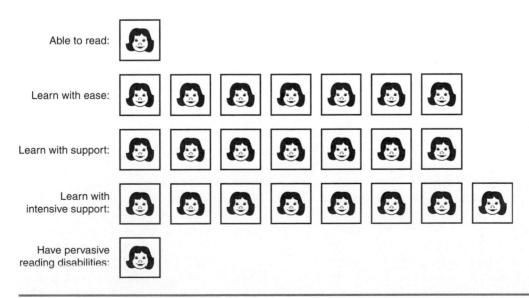

FIGURE 1.1 Typical First-Grade Classroom

When Is the Best Time to Begin Reading Instruction for Children Who Are at Risk?

Years ago educators believed that reading skills developed naturally and that as long as children were immersed in a literature-rich environment, they would eventually learn to read when they were "ready." In a system based on this belief, struggling readers were often not given extra support until second or even third grade. Since then, educators have been confronted by a large body of research that has emphasized the importance of early identification. Educators now recognize that many children who are at risk will never develop reading skills naturally. Even more disturbing is evidence that once they are behind in reading, most of these students do not catch up. For example, Juel (1988) found that only one in eight readers who were behind at the end of first grade would catch up by fourth grade. In another study, Francis and colleagues (1996) followed 407 children who were classified as poor readers in third grade. They found that fully 74% of these students remained poor readers when they reached ninth grade. Why is later reading intervention so ineffective for students who are at risk? One key reason for the low catch-up rate is that once students get behind it takes a significant expenditure of time and resources to catch them up, resources that budget-strapped schools may not have available. According to the NICHD, it takes four times as much assistance to improve a child's reading skills if help is provided in fourth grade versus starting the help in the middle of kindergarten (Hall & Moats, 1999). Not only do older students have to relearn ineffective habits they have acquired, they also must overcome pervasive feelings of failure and stress related to reading. Clearly, the best course of action is to identify children as early as possible and provide them with the supports they need to prevent reading problems in the first place. Although the teaching strategies described in this text are effective for students of all ages, they are most effective when used early.

Which Students Are Likely to Struggle When Learning to Read? How Can I Set Goals for Them and Monitor Their Progress?

Early identification of students who are at risk requires that teachers give assessments that accurately measure essential early reading skills, are easy to use, take up little classroom time, predict later reading problems, and readily enable teachers to monitor student progress. Most of the assessments described in this text meet these five criteria. You'll find that the majority of these assessments used to predict and monitor are part of the Dynamic Indicators of Basic Early Literacy Skills (DIBELS) series. The DIBELS are **fluency-based assessments** that measure early reading skills in areas deemed essential by the National Reading Panel (2000). They include phonemic awareness, alphabetic principle, reading fluency, vocabulary, and comprehension. All of the DIBELS measures are fluency-based, which means that they measure how quickly students answer or read, as well as how accurately. Measuring skill fluency has a number of important advantages. First, students who are so proficient at a skill that they can fluently apply it are more likely to remember the skill, even if they do not use it very often. If these students forget the skill, they need less time to relearn it. In addition, fluency with a basic skill helps students become proficient at more advanced skills. For example, students who can sound out nonsense words quickly in their heads are more fluent in figuring out new words that they encounter in passages. Finally, students who are more fluent in basic skills are freed up to perform cognitive strategies for understanding what they read. Students who can read a passage accurately and fluently are much more likely to also understand what they are reading (Deno & Markell, 1997).

Another advantage in using the DIBELS is that the authors have conducted extensive research establishing benchmarks of performance that are helpful not only for identifying students who are at risk, but also for setting concrete performance goals for them (Good, Gruba, & Kaminski, 2002). For example, in September Mr. Thomas gave his third-grade class the DIBELS measure of oral reading fluency, which shows the number of correct words per minute in third-grade passages that students read correctly. One student, Thomaniece, read 76 words per minute. According to DIBELS guidelines, her score indicates that without some support, she will fail to meet the year-end benchmark of 110 words correct per minute. Because the assessment showed that Thomaniece needed support, Mr. Thomas was able to get immediate Title 1 help for her. Knowing that research has shown that setting concrete goals for students leads to more focused assistance and improved performance, Mr. Thomas and the Title 1 teacher agreed on an end-of-the-year goal of 110 words correct per minute. They were determined that Thomaniece would read at grade level by June. For the rest of the year the Title 1 teacher designed instruction that would help Thomaniece meet that goal.

Teachers appreciate that the DIBELS measures are easy to give and score because they take very little class time away from instruction. When given to an entire class, DIBELS results allow teachers to chart the progress of every child and arrange for more supports as needed. In this way, DIBELS helps teachers monitor the progress of all students as well as meet the accountability demands of today's schools.

What Essential Skills Do Students Need, to Become Mature Readers?

The National Reading Panel (2000) identified key skill areas that should comprise the reading curriculum for students who are at risk. These areas include phonemic awareness, alphabetic principle, reading fluency, vocabulary, and reading comprehension. The key skills comprising each of these areas are shown in Figure 1.2 and described in this section. The time frame information in Figure 1.2 is intended to represent when each skill area is emphasized as part of a developmental reading program. These skills are also essential for remedial readers. The only difference is that remedial readers will learn these skills later than their peers.

> Publications from the National Reading Panel report are free and available for downloading: **http://www.nationalreadingpanel.org/Publications/publications.htm.**

Phonemic Awareness

Phonemic awareness is the ability to hear the smallest units of sound in spoken language and to manipulate them. Students who are at risk are less likely to develop this important foundational skill naturally. Word play activities and language games often do not provide enough support. Because phonemic awareness is a critical foundational skill for learning to read, researchers examined whether teaching phonemic awareness skills to students who are at risk was effective. As a result of these studies, a considerable body of research now provides guidance for teachers informing them that teaching phonemic awareness skills to students who are at risk within a language-rich environment makes it easier for them to learn to read (Armbruster, Lehr, & Osborn, 2001). Although there are many different phonemic awareness skills, this book stresses the two that researchers have concluded have the most value in a beginning reading program: segmenting and blending. **Segmenting** is

	Kinder Fall	Kinder Spring	First Fall	First Spring	Second All Year	Third All Year
Phonemic Awareness						
Segmenting	X	X	X			
Blending	X	X	X			
Alphabetic Principle						
LS Correspondence	X	X	X	X	X	X
Regular Word Reading		X	X	X	X	X
Irregular Words		X	X	X	X	X
Spelling	X	X	X	X	X	X
Reading Fluency				X	X	X
Vocabulary	*	X	X	X	X	X
Reading Comprehension	*	X	X	X	X	X
*Orally taught						

FIGURE 1.2   Scientifically Based Reading Curriculum

the ability to break apart words into their individual phonemes or sounds. A student who can segment says /f/-/i/-/sh/ when asked to say the sounds in *fish*. The ability to segment helps students strategically attack words they will be reading in text and break words into phonemes when spelling. **Blending,** the opposite of segmenting, is the ability to say a spoken word when its individual phonemes are said slowly. A student who can blend can say the word *fish* after the teacher slowly says the individual sounds /f/-/i/-/sh/. Blending enables students to read unfamiliar text by combining single sounds into new words. You will learn more about phonemic awareness and how to teach it to students who are at risk in Chapter 2.

Alphabetic Principle

Alphabetic principle is the understanding that there are systematic and predictable relationships between written letters and spoken sounds. Students who have attained alphabetic principle can identify and remember words accurately and automatically. The teaching strategy described in this text to teach the alphabetic principle is based on **phonics.** Phonics instruction teaches students the relationships between written letters, or graphemes, and the sounds of language, or phonemes. Although some would argue otherwise (see The Reflective Teacher on p. 7), the English language has more than enough regularity to merit the teaching of phonics.

The utility of teaching phonics has been clearly established, but not all phonics approaches are created equal. After identifying more than 100,000 research studies and submitting them to rigorous review, the National Reading Panel (2000) concluded that phonics programs that are both systematic and explicit are most effective for teaching students to read, particularly students who are at risk. In *Put Reading First,* Armbruster, Lehr, and Osborn (2001) summarized the key differences between systematic and non-systematic phonics programs. These differences are shown in Figure 1.3. The phonics strategies described in this book are designed to be both systematic and explicit, to ensure the success of students who are at risk.

The Reflective Teacher

Does Teaching Phonics Make Sense?

1. We must *polish* the *Polish* furniture.
2. "Tom, go around the corner and come to me now."

Judging from these examples, teaching students to read would be much easier if there were only one symbol for each of the 41 phonemes or sounds in our speech. In that case, the letter *o* would have the same sound regardless of context or what letter it happened to be positioned next to in a word. Unfortunately, as these examples show, that consistency is not always the case. In the first example, the letter *o* either says its name (as in *Polish*) or sound (as in *polish*), depending on the meaning of the words surrounding it. In the second sentence, seven of the words contain the letter *o*, and *o* makes a different sound in each word, depending in large part on the adjacent letters. The question is, given all of this irregularity, does teaching phonics still make sense? The truth is only about 13% of English words are classified as sight words with highly unpredictable letter–sound relations, whereas 50% of English language words are very predictable and can be decoded by a reader who has developed the alphabetic principle. The remaining words consist of more complex spelling patterns that can be explicitly taught (Foorman, Fletcher, & Francis, 2004). Many of the sight words, such as *said* and *where,* are easier to remember when some of their sounds are taken into account. Research also shows that context clues may only be helpful 10 to 20% of the time (Gough et al., 1981). Add to this over 30 years of research evidence in support of teaching phonics, and the inescapable conclusion is that the teaching of phonics is definitely justified.

Examples

Systematic programs that teach phonics effectively . . .

- help teachers explicitly and systematically instruct students in how to relate letters and sounds, how to break spoken words into sounds, and how to blend sounds to form words.

- help students understand why they are learning the relationships between letters and sounds.

- help students apply their knowledge of phonics as they read words, sentences, and text.

- can be adapted to the needs of individual students, based on assessment.

- include alphabetic knowledge, phonemic awareness, vocabulary development, and the reading of text, as well as systematic phonics instruction.

Nonexamples

Nonsystematic programs that do not teach phonics effectively include . . .

- **Literature-based programs** that emphasize reading and writing activities. Phonics instruction is embedded in these activities, but letter–sound relationships are taught incidentally, usually based on key letters that appear in student reading materials

- **Basal reading programs** that focus on whole-word or meaning-based activities. These programs pay only limited attention to letter–sound relationships and provide little or no instruction in how to blend letters to pronounce words.

- **Sight-word programs** that begin by teaching children a sight-word reading vocabulary of from 50 to 100 words. After children learn to read these words they receive instruction in the alphabetic principle.

FIGURE 1.3 Evaluating Programs of Phonics Instruction

Source: Armbruster, B., Lehr, F., & Osborn, J. (2001). *Put Reading First: The Research Building Blocks for Teaching Children to Read* (pp. 16–17). Washington, DC: Partnership for Reading.

To attain the alphabetic principle, students need to acquire skills in the following areas: identifying letter–sound correspondences, sounding out words containing letter sounds previously taught, and identifying words at sight. Spelling is also included here because of the benefits of having students spell words they are also learning to read. Chapters 3 to 5 explain how learning these skills will make your students fluent readers. Teaching students the alphabetic principle involves some of the most difficult, precise teaching you will do. The aim of these chapters is to provide you with information and guides so that you can teach all of your students to break the code and move into more advanced reading.

Reading Fluency

Reading fluency is the ability to read text accurately, quickly, and with expression. Students who are able to read fluently can focus their energy on finding out what the text means. Conversely, students who read in a choppy, word-by-word fashion are so focused on getting the words right that they have little energy left for deciphering their meaning. Reading fluency is an important part of the reading curriculum for students who are at risk because they may not develop it naturally, even if they have attained the alphabetic principle. Unfortunately, teachers often omit teaching and assessing this skill, which prevents many students who are at risk from transitioning into fluid, expressive readers. Fortunately, there is a large body of research showing that assessing and teaching fluency improve students' reading (Fuchs, Fuchs, Hosp, & Jenkins, 2001; Wolf & Katzir-Cohen, 2001). In Chapter 5 you will learn to do both.

Vocabulary

Vocabulary is the fourth key component of effective early literacy programs for students who are at risk. As shown in Table 1.1, vocabulary can be either receptive or expressive and oral or written. Oral **receptive vocabulary** involves understanding the meaning of words when people speak; written receptive vocabulary concerns understanding the meaning of words that are read. Oral **expressive vocabulary** means using words in speaking so that other people understand you; written expressive vocabulary is communicating meaningfully through writing. Whether students are reading, writing, or speaking, knowledge of the meanings of a wide variety of words is essential. Students who are at risk, including those in poverty, those having disabilities, or those who speak a second language, are likely to lag behind their peers in vocabulary development (Hart & Risley, 1995). Equally disturbing is that these vocabulary differences grow larger over time (Baker, Simmons, & Kame'enui,

TABLE 1.1   Vocabulary in Oral and Written Communication

	Oral Communication	Written Communication
Receptive Vocabulary	listening comprehension Example: The student knows the meaning of a vocabulary word in a story that the teacher reads aloud.	reading comprehension Example: The student knows the meaning of a vocabulary word in a story that she reads.
Expressive Vocabulary	meaningful speech Example: Correctly using the vocabulary from a story, the student describes the sequence of events in the story that he read or that was read aloud.	meaningful writing Example: Correctly using the vocabulary from a story, the student writes a description of the events that took place in a story that she read or that was read aloud.

1997), due to a lack of exposure at home and failure to teach vocabulary extensively at school (Beck, McKeown, & Kucan, 2002; Biemiller, 2001). Hart & Risley (1995) estimate the gap in words learned per year between students who are at risk and their peers who are not at risk amounts to more than 2,000 words per year.

The extent of students' vocabulary knowledge can have a significant impact on their early reading achievement. For one thing, reading is infinitely more meaningful and rewarding when students understand the meaning of the words they are decoding. Imagine what reading would be like if you were only reading nonsense words! A knowledge of vocabulary is also essential for reading connected text for meaning, the ultimate goal of reading instruction.

It is widely believed that most vocabulary is learned indirectly—either through speaking with others, being read to, or reading independently. However, many students who are at risk come to school with significantly less exposure to these naturalistic experiences. Clearly, for students who are at risk, vocabulary instruction is an essential part of teaching them to speak, read, and write adequately. Vocabulary instruction should have two key emphases: direct teaching of the meanings of important, useful, and difficult words; and strategies for figuring out the meaning of words independently using context, meanings of word parts, and the dictionary. In Chapter 6 you will learn how to teach vocabulary so that students have the opportunity to extensively use new words in their oral language, reading, and writing.

Reading Comprehension

One area on which reading experts agree is that reading comprehension is the ultimate goal of reading instruction. Students who understand what they read are able to decode connected text accurately and fluently, and know the meanings of a variety of vocabulary words. Good comprehenders have two additional qualities: they have a clear purpose for reading, and they think actively as they read (Armbruster, Lehr, & Osborn, 2000). The National Reading Panel (2000) identified a number of strategies that help students derive meaning from text. These strategies comprise our comprehension curriculum and are as follows:

- Activate background knowledge and use it to make meaning out of text
- Generate and ask questions while reading
- Evaluate or draw conclusions from information in a text
- Get meaning by making informed predictions
- Summarize information by explaining in own their words what the text is about
- Monitor comprehension including knowing when they understand and do not understand, and using additional strategies to improve when understanding is blocked
- Derive meaning of narrative and expository text by being able to identify relevant text structures

Chapter 7 explains teaching techniques that help students who are at risk to consistently use these strategies.

What Is the Most Effective Way to Teach Essential Reading Skills to Children Who Are at Risk?

The evidence is clear that students who are at risk benefit from reading instruction that is explicit and systematic. **Explicit instruction** is the clear, direct teaching of reading skills and strategies and includes:

- Clear instructional outcomes (what you want the student to do with the information you've taught)
- Clear purpose for learning
- Clear and understandable directions and explanations
- Adequate modeling/demonstration, guided practice, and independent practice as part of the teaching process
- Clear, consistent corrective feedback on student success and student errors

The second grade teachers at Fourth Avenue School use an explicit reading curriculum to teach reading. They expect their students to read at least 90 words per minute by the end of the year and to apply that skill when reading books of different genres for school assignments and for enjoyment. If the students are taking turns reading a play, the teachers explain the directions beforehand and tell students the procedure for rotating turns and for correcting errors. Because the teachers are so clear, the students have, after misreading a word, formed the habit of immediately starting again at the beginning of the sentence and rereading. The teachers always introduce new concepts by first showing the students how to do them and then supporting their learning until independence. Because the two- and three-syllable words introduced last week were difficult for many of the students, the teachers spent an extra day reviewing them so students had more practice. Whenever students make mistakes, the teachers follow the systematic error correction procedures that you will read about later in this chapter. By correcting errors using these procedures, teachers make sure that students know how to perform the skill correctly the next time they are called on to do it.

Systematic instruction is teaching that clearly identifies a carefully selected and useful set of skills and then organizes those skills into a logical sequence of instruction. For example, Mr. Prince decides to teach his students to sound out regular words because there is not enough time for them to memorize all the words with which they come in contact. Before he works on sounding out words, Mr. Prince teaches his students to say the sounds in words they hear and to blend sounds into whole words. Gradually, he begins teaching his students letter sounds. By the time his students begin sounding out words, they will have all the skills they need to be successful.

Students vary in the amount of explicit, systematic instruction they need for learning to read. Reflect back on the typical first grade class (Figure 1.1) with its wide range of learners. In a typical class, some students learn new material as fast as the teacher can teach it; other students need extra practice before they learn it; and a third group needs very deliberate teaching that slowly moves from easier skills to more difficult concepts. Because of these differences, schools need a range of instructional options to meet the diverse needs of their students. Teaching that provides this broader range of options is known as **differentiated instruction** (Tomlinson, 2000). Throughout this book, we will show you how to provide differentiated instruction through a three-tiered system where students receive the level of support necessary for them to read at or above grade level. These tiers are shown in Figure 1.4.

Tier 1 Instruction

Tier 1 is the least intensive, first level of instruction and consists of the current reading program used in the classroom whether it is a basal, strictly literature-based, or a combination of the two. Throughout Chapters 2 through 8 we will teach you ways to enhance regular Tier 1 instruction so that you can meet the needs of as many of your students who are at risk as possible. These Tier 1 teaching enhancements are explained in the next section. Of course, more students who are at risk will learn to successfully read with the additional Tier 1 enhancements if the regular education reading program reflects effective reading instruction, as described in the *Report of the National Reading Panel* (2000).

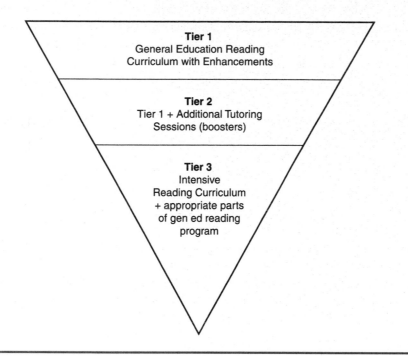

FIGURE 1.4   Multi-Tiered Model of Differentiated Instruction

Tier 2 Instruction

Tier 2 consists of Tier 1 instruction plus additional daily small-group practice sessions. These sessions are usually 10 minutes in kindergarten, and 30–40 minutes in the later grades. Tier 2 instruction ensures that students become fluent, accurate readers by providing extra practice on essential word reading skills. Many students who are at risk fail to comprehend what they are reading because they cannot read connected text accurately and fluently. Their comprehension will not mature until their word reading improves, enabling them to focus more attention on the meaning of the text. Students enter Tier 2 when their performance dips below mastery on the monthly or bimonthly assessments introduced earlier in this chapter. Tier 2 teachers use the same enhancements used in Tier 1, but in smaller groups of between three and six students. Tier 2 sessions are carried out by a variety of staff, including general education teachers, Title 1 teachers, special education teachers, and paraprofessionals.

Tier 3 Instruction

Tier 3 is more intensive instruction using an alternative reading program conducted daily for 30–90 minutes in separate pull-out settings with small, skill-based groups of two to five students. Students placed in Tier 3 have failed to make substantial progress despite a Tier 1 enhanced general education reading program and extra help in Tier 2 booster groups. Tier 3 includes all of the enhancements that are in Tiers 1 and 2 plus a more systematically designed and explicitly taught reading curriculum. Some teachers work with older students on a remedial basis as either Title 1 teachers or Special Education teachers. By the time they receive these students, they are significantly behind their classmates. Although difficult, their job is one of catching up these students so they are reading at grade level. As stated earlier, catching up students is difficult due to limits in district time and resources. Because of these factors, older students should be taught for at least 60 minutes a day with a well-designed Tier 3 program.

Although the focus of this text is on making sure that you can teach most children using Tiers 1 and 2, experience shows that, depending on where you are teaching, at least a third of your children may need Tier 3 instruction. The ultimate purpose of Tier 3 is to catch students up with their peers, which means that students need instruction that is well-designed, and efficiently and competently taught. Otherwise, Tier 3 groups can become a dumping ground with an irrelevant, watered-down curriculum, in which students fall further behind and become highly at risk for dropping out of school. Too often in the past, pull-out programs have become such dead end options. Because of potential risks associated with alternative pull-out programs, choosing an alternative reading program for Tier 3 instruction is a crucial decision. How can you determine which alternative reading program will have the most success with the largest number of your students? How do you know whether the alternative program has an adequate phonemic awareness emphasis? How can you tell if the alternative program is a systematic phonics program? These questions are confusing for many educators who are faced with testimonials defending reading curricula. To assist you or your school in deciding on a Tier 3 program, toward the end of each chapter we have listed key characteristics to look for in alternative reading programs. These key characteristics include the skill focus, design, and instructional approach as it relates to students who are at risk or who have disabilities. In addition, we have analyzed some commonly used alternative reading programs to determine which ones include these characteristics.

All three tiers use instructional strategies that a large body of research has shown make learning to read easier for students who are at risk (Rosenshine, 1986; Ellis, Worthington, & Larkin, 1994). The manner and extent that you use these instructional strategies depends on where you teach. Because Mr. Ranier teaches in an urban area where 90% of the children are living in poverty and high percentages of students struggle to meet state standards in reading, he uses the instructional enhancements with all of his students during Tier 1 reading instruction. Ms. Helmsley teaches in a more affluent area, where 70 to 80% of the students meet state standards in reading using her current reading approach. She differentiates her instruction by using some enhancement strategies in her large-group instruction, but relies on them mainly for the Tier 2 small-group instruction that helps her students who are struggling to keep up.

What Are the Instructional Enhancements for Students Who Are at Risk?

The instructional enhancements for students who are at risk include advance organizers, unison responses through the use of effective signals, perky pace, efficient use of teacher talk, increased practice, support for new learning using a My Turn–Together–Your Turn format, systematic error correction, cumulative review, teaching to success, and motivational strategies. Each of these enhancements is described in this section, and throughout this book we provide ways for you to integrate them into your teaching.

Advance Organizers

When students are easily distractible or come from chaotic home environments, they want and need structure and predictability in their environment. Disorganized students often do not automatically draw connections from one part of a learning task to another. Unless the teacher has told students that the words they are reading on the board will be in that day's story, some of the students who are more disorganized will not make the connection to those words when they open the new book and begin to read. Teachers establish a comfortable level of predictability when they use advance organizers at the start of each lesson by telling students what they are learning, why they are learning it, and what the behavioral expectations are during the lesson. When these advance organizers provide the beginning organization for each day's lesson, students learn to anticipate connections between what they are learning and how they will apply the new learning to other situations. By briefly describing the sequence of activities covered during the reading lesson and checking each one off after it is completed, teachers also motivate students who are likely to tune out or act out in a part of the lesson that they find difficult. For example, reading the new long-vowel words might be difficult for Debra, but if she knows that word practice is followed by an interesting story about a lizard who bakes cakes, she will pay closer attention and work harder. Advance organizers should include a graphic depiction along with a brief verbal description, especially for younger students. A sample visually presented advance organizer for a kindergarten lesson is shown in Figure 1.5. It includes the comments the teacher makes to prepare the students to learn.

Unison Responding

Students who are at risk need more practice of the key skills they are learning than their peers who are not at risk. They need to be actively engaged with many opportunities to orally practice the new sounds, read the new words, read the longer stories, and use new vocabulary words in increasingly longer sentences. In a class of 20 or 30 students, teachers can only provide that amount of practice by having all of the students answer in unison. Rather than ask one student to say the sound of the new letter *l,* the teacher increases academic learning time for everyone by asking all of the students to answer at the same time.

As an added benefit, students who are actively participating are more likely to pay attention to instruction and follow classroom rules. Students who are constantly answering and reading have little time to be off task, staring out the window, or disrupting the class. Since students who are at risk also need to have their answers carefully monitored to make sure that they are acquiring the skills that are taught, teachers are more effective if they follow each section of the lesson with a few quick, individual questions. These quick checkouts enable the teacher to provide more practice if some students still are making errors.

Effective Signals

Effective signals help a teacher get all of the students to answer together, speaking in one voice as if in a choir. If students answer too early or too late, reading instruction will not be as effective. One or two students who immediately grasp the concept may answer ahead of everyone else, creating the illusion that the class does not need any more practice. Students who are at risk may answer after everyone else, relying on other students' answers and not sounding out the words by themselves. The parts of an effectively delivered signal that will get all students to answer together are described in Table 1.2.

Note that the teacher first focuses the students' attention to the question. Questions that teachers ask in beginning reading instruction include:

- Asking students to name letter sounds
- Asking students to sound out words
- Asking students to say all of the sounds in the words they hear
- Asking students to read simple sentences

Next the teacher provides thinking time, which varies depending on the question. For new or more difficult questions the think time is longer than for easier or review ones. Following the thinking pause, the teacher asks the question, pauses one second, and then

1. Segmenting Lesson—"Let's pull some words apart!"

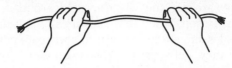

2. Blending—"Next we'll put some sounds together to make words."

3. Letter Sounds—"Then we'll work with the letter **d** and its buddies."

Working with the letter. . . **d** and its buddies.

4. Reading Words—"Then we'll read some words."

5. Spelling—"Then we'll spell some words."

During the lesson today I would like you to. . .
- Sit up nice and tall in your seats.
- Listen very closely.
- And answer on my signal.

FIGURE 1.5   Advance Organizer—Letter and Sounds Lesson

Source: Hicks, A. (2006). *Model advance organizer.* Unpublished manuscript, University of North Carolina at Greensboro.

gives the signal. The type of signal used depends on the nature of the question that students are asked. For example, when students are asked to sound out words listed on the board, the teacher points to the letters in the word signaling for students to sound them out. When

TABLE 1.2   Effective Signals

Component	Description
1. FOCUS students to pay attention, then ask your question	The teacher gains students' attention by focusing them to the word they will read or to an oral question. ■ When asking an oral question, hold up a hand to gain students' attention and tell students what they will do. Example: Hold up a hand and say, "You are going to take some words apart. First word is *mat.*" ■ If asking students to read, tell students what they will do and point a finger to the left of the first word. Example: Tell students, "Get ready to read the word when I touch it," and point to the left of the word.
2. THINK Time	A brief pause of no more than three seconds that provides students with time to formulate an answer. If the questions are easy or review, the teacher gives a very short thinking pause. If the questions are difficult or new, the teacher gives a longer thinking pause.
3. SIGNAL	The teacher gives the signal that indicates everyone should answer at that very instant. The signal always comes **after** the directions, never at the same time. Thus a teacher never talks and signals at the same time. Chapters 2 and 3 describe specific signals including: ■ Hand-drop ■ Hand-clap ■ Finger-raise ■ Loop signal

asking students to orally take apart words ("What are the sounds in *fish:* /f/ /i/ /s/ /h/") the teacher either snaps two fingers, claps hands together, or drops a hand as the signal. Specific strategies for using signals are covered in the chapters that follow.

Efficient Use of Teacher Talk

The clarity with which teachers present information to students at risk has a strong influence on their learning. Students in classrooms where teachers present material in concise statements, using language the students understand, are more likely to be on task than students whose teachers provide lengthy explanations and present information unrelated to the task at hand.

Perky Pace

Teachers can also increase student attention and learning by employing a perky pace throughout every lesson (Englert et al., 1992). Teachers who use a perky pace start with a brief advance organizer and minimize the transition time between activities, as well as between each student answer and the teacher's next question. Students give more of their attention to a teacher who uses an animated teaching style, conveying her enthusiasm for what they are learning. They are less likely to waste time, be uncooperative, or tune out when a theatrical teacher uses exaggerated affect, enthusiastic voice tones, and dramatic gestures

My Turn–Together–Your Turn Format

All students require support when they are learning new skills or content. Think about the frustration you felt when a math or physics teacher introduced a new concept and then, without adequately giving you practice using the new concept, expected you to apply it on that night's homework problems. As you tried to solve problems that depended on your knowledge of the new concept, your frustration and tension level increased as you stared at the work. Unless you could find a better teacher in the form of a friend, a tutor, or a detailed book, your learning was at a standstill.

Students who are at risk require even more support when they are learning to read and write. An effective way to support their new learning is to use the My Turn–Together–Your Turn strategy used in explicit instruction (Archer, 1995). In this approach:

- **My Turn:** The teacher first demonstrates how to do the new skill so that students have no difficulty understanding exactly what the new skill looks like.
- **Together:** The teacher practices the skill with his students until they are able to do it without him. Students experience a higher level of success and less frustration if they first have the opportunity to practice with the teacher. In this way students are prevented from practicing the errors and acquiring habits that, once learned, are difficult to break.
- **Your Turn:** The teacher monitors students as they do the skill independently. By closely monitoring his students, the teacher can correct any errors and prevent them from acquiring habits that, once learned, are difficult to break.

Teachers who use a My Turn–Together–Your Turn format for teaching new critical skills are explicitly teaching so that students are successful from the start. These teachers know that when students inadvertently learn errors such as saying /sh/ for the /th/ sound, valuable time will be wasted reteaching. Jerry Ameis cautions, "Reteaching is a significant waste of time for students and teachers. It is far better to spend the needed time on trying "*to get it right*" the first time than to bore and/or frustrate students (and yourself) by reteaching and reteaching . . ." (Ameis, 2003). Eventually teachers move to using "Your Turns" as students' accuracy shows they have learned the new skill.

Cumulative Review

Teachers who work with students who are at risk often observe that these students have difficulty retaining new information or skills. Just when it seems that they have learned something new, the very next day they have already forgotten it. In addition to problems with retention, students who are at risk also have trouble discriminating between new information and information previously learned. For example, Delarnes learned the sound of /b/ several weeks ago, but since learning other sounds has practiced it only once or twice. This week, he learned the new /d/ sound on Thursday. On Friday, he read all of the *b* words in his decodable book as if they contained the letter *d*. If Delarnes' teacher had continued to practice the /b/ sound every day after he learned it, he would have been less likely to confuse it with the /d/ sound. **Cumulative review** is a method of selecting teaching examples where the teacher adds previously learned material to examples of newly learned material. Cumulative review increases student retention and helps students discriminate between new and old learning. To use cumulative review, simply add examples of previously learned material to examples of newly learned material.

Systematic Error Correction

No matter how systematic and explicit the reading instruction, students will always make some errors. Research shows that in an effective lesson, students answer at least eight out of every ten answers correctly (McEwan & Damer, 2000). This minimum level of success instills confidence and reduces frustration for at-risk students. The way that teachers correct student errors is critical. If errors are not corrected appropriately, students continue to make the same errors and develop habits that can seriously undermine the goal of fluent, accurate reading with comprehension.

In making a **systematic error correction,** the teacher corrects the students immediately after they make the error by modeling the correct answer/skill ("My Turn"), guiding the students to correct the error as needed ("Together"), and then re-asking the same question so students have the opportunity to independently answer the question correctly ("Your Turn"). Later in the lesson, the teacher provides even more practice by asking students to answer the same question again. If students answer correctly, the teacher knows that she can move ahead in the lesson.

Teachers who use systematic error correction provide high levels of feedback to their students, an important component of explicit instruction. According to Fisher and colleagues (1980), academic feedback should be provided as often as possible to students. When more frequent feedback is given, students pay closer attention and learn more. In their research, academic feedback was more strongly and consistently related to learning than any of the other teaching behaviors.

Teaching to Success

Children who are at risk or have disabilities often require more time to learn to read. When teaching reading to students who are at risk, teachers often need to spend more time on a given skill, continuing instruction and not moving on to the next skill until students have clearly learned the one currently being taught. Research shows that if instruction is evidence-based, most children can learn, given the right amount of time (Ornstein & Lasley, 2004). For example, Mr. Lazaro's class was struggling to correctly identify the short sound for the letter a. While he had originally planned to introduce the sound for the letter p on the following day, Mr. Lazaro decided he would continue working on the sound of a, not introducing a new sound until his students could correctly identify the first one. Mr. Lazaro knew that if his students could not automatically identify the sound for the letter a, they would struggle with the many words they would subsequently be reading that contained it. Another teacher using this strategy was Ms. Gentry. Her class was orally reading the latest story in their reader. Ms. Gentry, who was keeping track of the number of words her students missed, found that they were missing more than two words per page and that their accuracy was below 90%. Before Ms. Gentry moved to the next story, she had her students practice reading the words they misread, and had them reread the current story until they could read it with 97% accuracy. In the past, when Ms. Gentry had moved her students to the next story regardless of their accuracy, she found that they made more errors.

Student Motivational System

Students who are at risk often enter school with a more limited repertoire of appropriate social and academic behaviors. As a result, learning can initially be quite difficult for them, even when the instruction provided by the teacher is systematic and explicit. Once students experience the success that comes of well-designed instruction, success alone may be enough to keep them motivated and working hard. Until then, teachers often need to use a student motivational system to maintain a positive classroom atmosphere and to strengthen key academic and social behaviors that students who are at risk often lack. When Pressley and colleagues (2001) investigated what types of teachers were most effective in teaching primary-level literacy, they found that the most effective teachers had classrooms that were positive learning environments. The authors found that these teachers frequently praised students' work and their behavior, in contrast to criticizing them.

Motivating Your Students to Do Their Best

Using the Teacher–Class Game

Getting a classroom of students to pay attention to the reading lesson, follow the classroom rules and procedures, and answer in unison can be challenging, especially when some students come to school without these basic behavior skills needed for learning:

- Wait for a turn to speak or act
- Understand and follow directions
- Actively listen
- Work independently
- Accept consequences of behavior

When students are not answering in unison or when misbehavior is interfering with learning time, the Teacher–Class game teaches students these skills while enabling the teacher to maintain a positive classroom environment. To organize the game before class starts, the teacher writes a T-grid on the board so he can easily award points to the class or to himself. A sample completed grid at the end of class looks like Figure 1.6.

Teacher	Class
~~IIII~~ III	~~IIII~~ ~~IIII~~
	~~IIII~~ ~~IIII~~
7	20

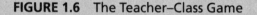

FIGURE 1.6   The Teacher–Class Game

During the lesson introduction, the teacher informs students that they will be playing the Teacher–Class game and reminds them how they can earn points. Periodically throughout the lesson when students are following the rules, the teacher awards the class points. Whenever a student does not follow the rules, the teacher gives himself a point. The more frequently the teacher gives the class a point and compliments students on their behavior, the more motivating the lesson becomes. As students work hard to get more points than the teacher, they learn successful school behaviors in the process. On Friday during the advance organizers for reading class, Mr. Setinz introduced the game to his class sitting on the rug by saying:

> "Remember to pay attention to my signals, to keep your hands and feet to yourself, and to do your best work. We are going to play the Teacher–Class game again today. Every day this week you have earned more points than I have (exaggerated sigh of exasperation). If you beat me today that is five days in a row and so everyone earns an extra recess at the end of the day. You'll need to pay close attention, because I am going to try my hardest to win today. I would like to win at least one day, but this class is hard to beat."

Without interrupting the flow of his teaching during the lesson, Mr. Setinz juggled paying attention to students' answers along with closely monitoring their behavior. He provided some of the following feedback as he gave or took away respective points:

> "Everyone followed my signal and read those first six words, so the class gets a point."

> "That's my point. Tanya and Robert, I need you to answer with everyone."

> "You took out your books so quickly that I just have to give you a point."

Whether a behavior strategy succeeds or fails depends on how effectively the teacher uses it. In order to teach positive behaviors with this game the following guidelines are recommended:

- **Do not give warnings about potential points lost.** If your rules are that no one gets out of his seat or talks out of turn, you need to immediately give yourself a point when a student does either of those behaviors. If you warn students by saying, "Next time I'm going to give myself a point," you are actually encouraging higher rates of misbehavior, since students recognize that sometimes they get away with breaking the rules.

- **Remember to notice positive student behaviors and give points for them.** "Row 3 has been working so hard and listening to my instructions that they've earned a point for the class." The game helps teachers maintain a positive classroom by frequently giving feedback on the positive actions of their students.
- **Put thought into selecting rewards.** Students should want the reward they will earn so they will be motivated to do their best work. Avoid using the same award every week because it will lose its impact as students become bored with it. Some rewards that Project PRIDE teachers used included:
  - the opportunity for a drawing period using the white boards
  - the opportunity to go to the music room and play some instruments
  - a special cartoon sticker choice
  - the opportunity to have extra computer lab time
  - a small box of crayons to bring home
  - the opportunity to use stamping markers or to earn one to bring home
  - the opportunity to fly paper airplanes
  - the opportunity to earn books that the teacher had purchased at garage sales the summer before
  Note: This game is as successful with older students as it is with younger ones, as long as the rewards are adjusted for that age level.
- **Give students frequent points in the beginning** so they experience success and win the game the majority of the time. Otherwise the game will not be effective.
- **Always give feedback with the points,** describing the reason why students earned or didn't earn points. Younger students require more enthusiastic, animated feedback than older ones when they earn a point. Your positive feedback will be effective if accompanied by a change in voice or facial expression that indicates you are genuinely pleased with their success. Feedback for teacher points should be explained in a matter-of-fact, no-nonsense voice tone: "Some students forgot to follow with their finger so I get a point. Remember to use your reading finger."

The Teacher–Class game has many variations. Some teachers will call the game Ms. Garvey vs. the Raptors, or Mr. Wood = St. Louis Cardinals vs. Class = Chicago Cubs. Teachers can give students several points when they see more effort than usual, "We worked so hard that we finished the lesson by 10:00 and can move on to another one. This class deserves five points." As student behaviors improve, the game should become more challenging. The teacher can tell the class that in order to win they cannot let him win more than 5 points during the entire class; or that they must earn twice as many points as he has earned to win. Another variation that is more complicated but commonly used is dividing the class into rows or teams. The teacher draws a grid for each team and for himself. Feedback might sound like this: "Teams 1, 3, and 4 were listening and have earned points." "I've earned a point on Teams 2 and 4's grid because some people did not remember to follow with their fingers." In the beginning, the teacher needs to give frequent feedback, awarding points after every one or two answers. Later, when students are accustomed to answering together and rarely cause disruptions that interfere with work, the teacher can award points after an entire section of the lesson.

In classrooms that are positive learning environments, teachers make three or four positive comments about students' work or behavior to every one criticism (McEwan & Damer, 2000). When this ratio is reversed, the teacher is caught in a criticism trap and students learn less and actually increase their misbehavior. If students come to school uncooperative and without school readiness skills, a teacher needs to consistently praise social behaviors such as staying in seat, answering on the teacher's signal, and keeping hands to self as well as correct answers or effort put into school work. If that praise alone is not enough to maintain the necessary 3:1 ratio of positive to negative teacher comments, the teacher needs to develop a student motivational system. If only one or two students need the additional motivation in order to be successful, the teacher can plan a motivational system just for them. Otherwise, the teacher can plan a class- or group-wide strategy for injecting positive motivation. Some teachers will find that extra motivation is only necessary in order to diminish frustration when students are first learning new skills or when they are practicing difficult ones. Strategies for motivating students who are at risk are described throughout this book. Table 1.3 shows what to do and what not to do when using the teaching enhancements just described.

What Letter Sounds Do Teachers Need to Know for Teaching Phonemic Awareness and Phonics Skills to Students Who Are at Risk?

Before teaching phonemic awareness (Chapter 2) or beginning word reading (Chapter 3), you need to know how to clearly pronounce the basic letter sounds as well as teach them to your students. Too often teachers mispronounce or incorrectly articulate the individual letter sounds with an extra /uh/ at the end. This extra phoneme is called a schwa and sometimes prevents students who are at risk from learning to blend, segment, or sound out words. If the teacher adds schwas to the end of letter sounds, even though she intends to ask students to blend the three sounds /p/-/a/-/t/ into the word *pat,* she is instead asking them to blend /puh/-/a/-/tuh/. Rather then simply blending these three sounds into a word, now the student must first take off the two /uh/ endings before saying the word *pat.*

Using the Chart of Letter Sounds

The letter–sounds chart in Table 1.4 (pp. 24–27) lists information about phonemes that will help you say and teach them. You should study this chart and become fully familiar with it. Exercises at the end of this chapter will help you get started. Here are some pointers to orient you:

1. The Phonetic Pronunciation column lists a word or words that contain the letter sound.

2. Sounds that are produced when the vocal cords are vibrating are called **voiced sounds.** Sounds that are produced when the vocal cords do not vibrate are called **unvoiced sounds.** If you put your fingertips on your throat, you can feel the vibration for voiced sounds. Often when students can not hear the difference between two sounds, the sounds are identical with the exception that one is voiced and the other unvoiced. Say the sounds for /b/ and /p/. Notice that when you say each one, both of your lips pop open and the sound pops out of your mouth with a burst of air. But when you put your hand to your throat while saying /b/, you feel the vocal chord vibration, whereas you do not feel it when you say /p/. Other pairs include: /k/ and /g/; /t/ and /d/; /f/ and /v/; th and <u>th</u>; /ch/ and /j/; and /s/ and /z/. When students have difficulty hearing the difference between a similar voiced and unvoiced sound, an effective teaching technique is to have them feel the vibration or lack of it for themselves.

3. The Articulation column provides information about how the sound is produced. Knowing how each sound is articulated will help you work with students who are not able to reproduce the sound after you introduce it. If Treena cannot reproduce /n/, using a small hand mirror you can show her how the front of your tongue rests behind your upper teeth toward

TABLE 1.3   Instructional Enhancements—What to Do and Not Do

	Examples What to do	Nonexamples What not to do
Advance Organizers	The teacher starts the lesson by saying, "Today we are going to learn a new letter sound and read words the fast way. This will help you learn how to read so you can decide what kind of ice cream you want when you read the Dairy Queen menu." The teacher places symbols for activities on the board as she describes them. "First we will practice a new tiger-roaring letter sound, then you will read some words that will be in our story. Today's story is about a red rabbit who gets mixed up about everything! Remember to sit up tall, keep your hands and feet to yourself, and answer when I signal."	The teacher begins the lesson by saying "I'll sound out a word very slowly, then you read the whole word fast, like we've done before." When the teacher says "/m/-/a/-/n/," one student shouts, "man." The teacher tells the students to start over and wait for her to clap her hands before they answer.
Unison Responding	The teacher asks all of the students in the group to sound out a word by saying the sound of each letter in the word when she touches under it. The teacher asks all of the students in the group to say the first sound in the spelling word *ran* when she drops her hand.	Individual students take turns coming to the board to sound out regular words The teacher doesn't use a visual signal when students in unison read words that are on the word wall. Some hesitant students in the group consistently answer late, reading the words a second after the more fluent readers.
Efficient Use of Teacher Talk	Wanting students to read a row of words written on the board, the teacher points to the first word and says, "Sound it out. Get ready." The teacher then signals by touching under each letter as students sound out the word. The teacher points to the letter combination *sh* and asks, "What sound?"	Wanting students to read a row of words, the teacher points to the first word and says, "Let's sound out this word. It's one we've worked on before. See if you can remember it. Careful now. Don't forget. This word is a weird one." The teacher points to the letter combination *sh* and says, "Let's read the sound of these two letters. Remember the rhyme we always say every morning about them. Tanya, that is always your favorite rhyme! What is the sound these two letters make when they come together in a word?"
Perky Pace	The teacher points to the first sight word on the list, asks, "What word?" and then when students read it correctly moves immediately to the next word. The teacher writes the letters for the letter–sounds activity on the board before the daily reading lesson begins.	The teacher points to the first sight word on the list and asks, "What word?" The students answer correctly. The teacher pauses at least 5 seconds between the student answer and the next sight word. The delay could be due to the teacher's excessive talking, a slow reaction time, or the time required to put the next word on the board. The teacher writes the *ch* combination on the board and asks students what sound it makes. The teacher then says, "Let's try another one," and writes the next letter–sound combination on the board. The teacher continues this pattern of asking a question and writing the next letter–sound combination for the rest of the lesson.

Continued

TABLE 1.3 Continued

	Examples What to do	Nonexamples What not to do
My Turn–Together–Your Turn Format	The teacher says, "Today we are going to sound out some words for the first time," and models sounding out /m/-/a/-/n/ = *man*. Then the teacher has students sound out the word twice with him before having them sound it out on their own. The teacher provides this support for the first four new words on the list and then asks students to read the rest of the new words on their own.	The teacher says, "Today we are going to sound out some words for the first time. Then the teacher asks students to sound out /m/-/a/-/n/ = *man* one time. About 60% of the students loudly answer and the teacher moves on to the next word.
	The teacher points to a new letter combination, *ar,* which is written on the board and says "These letters say /ar/. Listen again: /ar/." The students then say /ar/. The teacher continues, "When I touch, you say the sound." The teacher points then touches under /ar/. "What sound?" Note that this task does not require a Together step unless students have trouble articulating the /ar/ sound.	The teacher points to a new letter combination *ar* on the board and says, "This is the sound you hear in *park*. What sound do these letters make?" The teacher then moves on to another letter sound.
Cumulative Review	The teacher just introduced regular words that begin with *s* blends such as *stop* and *slow*. When the students are able to correctly read the *s* blend words, the teacher has the students read a list of words containing *s* blends plus other previously learned words beginning with *sh* and *th*.	The teacher just introduced regular words that begin with *s* blends, such as *stop* and *slow*. When the students are able to read a list of words beginning with *s* blends, the teacher introduces words with *p* blends.
	The teacher included two more difficult words from last week's spelling list on the spelling list for this week.	The teacher's spelling list this week has fifteen new words and no review words from previous lessons.
Systematic Error Correction	During a letter–sound teaching activity, the teacher touches the letter combination *ch* and says, "What sound?" The student says /sh/. The teacher responds, "These letters say /ch/. What sound?" The teacher then provides extra practice by alternately asking the student to say the sound for *sh* and six other sounds previously learned. Later in the lesson, she asks the student one more time to tell the sound for *sh*.	During a letter–sound teaching activity, the student says /sh/ when the teacher points to *ch*. The teacher says, "No, think about something good to eat." After the student names foods, the teacher says, "Chocolate is good to eat. What letters does chocolate begin with? Do you see those letters on the board? What sound do they make?" When the students says /ch/, the teacher moves on to the next word.
	During a sight word reading, the teacher points to the word *ghost* and says, "What word?" Several students pronounce the word incorrectly. The teacher says, "The word is *ghost*. What is this word?" When students answer correctly, the teacher returns to the top of the list of five words and has the students read all five words again including the word *ghost*.	During a sight word reading activity, the students say *gets* when they see the word *ghost*. The teacher says, "The word is *ghost*. Let's try the next word."
Teaching to Success	The teacher introduced the *ou* sound to her students for the first time. The next day she tested her students to see if they could identify the *ou* sound when it was mixed in with the previously	The teacher introduced the *ou* sound to her students for the first time. The next day she tested her students to see if they could identify the *ou* sound when it was mixed in with the previously learned

TABLE 1.3 Continued

	Examples What to do	Nonexamples What not to do
Teaching to Success (continued)	learned combinations of *sh, ea, ow,* and *th.* Her students made repeated errors on the *ou* sound, and missed *th* and *sh* as well. The following day, the teacher decided to provide more practice on all of the sounds from the day before. She would only introduce *ar* when the students were able to identify these other sounds correctly.	letter combinations of *sh, ea, ow,* and *th.* Her students made repeated errors on the *ou* sound, and missed *th* and *sh* as well. The following day the teacher introduced a new letter combination: *ar.*
	The teacher had her students read today's story orally. The group made 20 errors, reading the story with about 88% accuracy. The following day the teacher provided drill for the students on the words missed the previous day. She also had the students reread the story until they read it with 97% accuracy.	The teacher had her students read today's story orally. The group made 20 errors, reading the story with about 88% accuracy. The following day the teacher moved to the next story in the book.
Student Motivational System	During small group instruction, Billy often leaves his seat. The teacher frequently praises Billy for staying in his seat and working so hard. She also praises other students for staying in their seats. The teacher seldom has to tell Billy to come back to his seat.	During small-group instruction, Billy often leaves his seat. Often when Billy leaves his seat, the teacher says, "Billy, if you can't pay attention, I'll have to call your mom." The teacher does not praise Billy when he is in his seat.
	While sight-reading a list of words, students continue to miss a number of them. Before reading through the list again, the teacher tells the students that their goal is reading every word correctly. This time, she praises the students immediately after each of the sight words is read correctly. When the list is finished, she smiles and exclaims, "I knew you could do it. Every one right! Give yourself a pat on the back!"	While sight-reading a list of words, students continue to miss a number of them. Each time they miss a word, the teacher makes a comment like, "This sure is a bad day," or "I don't know what you are all thinking about." When students continue to make mistakes, the teacher ends the lesson saying, "Maybe tomorrow you will all be awake."

the front of your mouth while the air is expelled through your nose. Treena can then hold the mirror and practice as you help her reproduce the sound.

4. Knowing whether a sound is a stop or a continuous sound will also help you correctly articulate the sound. With **stop sounds,** the air is completely blocked before it is expelled either because the lips come together as with /p/ or because the tongue touches the upper mouth as when saying /d/. This air blockage accounts for the higher level of difficulty in learning to read words that begin with stop sounds. Avoiding schwa endings is also more difficult with stop sounds. With **continuous sounds,** also known as continuants, the airflow does not stop as the sound is pronounced, so the sound can be held as long as some air remains in the lungs. When first teaching a continuous letter sound, the teacher holds the sound for several seconds.

5. The last column in Table 1.4 is a list of tips that teachers use to help students who have difficulty reproducing the sound when it is first introduced.

We recommend that you use each letter sound's phonetic pronunciation that reflects how the phoneme sounds when it is blended into words. The three letter sounds that

TABLE 1.4 Using the Correct Sounds in Effective Phonics Instruction

Letter Sound	Phonetic Pronunciation	Voiced or Unvoiced	Articulation	Stop or Continuous Sound? ⚠ = don't add a schwa	When Students Have Difficulty Saying the New Letter Sound:
/ă/	as in *sat*	voiced	Widely spread smiling mouth position; tongue low in mouth.	continuous	Ask students to cry like a baby as they say the sound. If students have difficulty distinguishing /ă/ from /ĕ/, ask them to put their hand on their jaw as they say *bed* and *bat*. They will feel their jaw lower when they say /ă/.
/ā/	as in *bake*	voiced	More open smiling mouth position; tongue in middle of mouth; increased mouth tension.	continuous	Ask students to make a big smile as they say the sound, /ā ā ā/.
/b/	as in *bell, baby,* and *tab*	voiced	Both lips pop open; sound pops out of mouth with a burst of air.	stop ⚠	Show students how their lips pop open when they say the sound.
/k/	as in *cat, maker,* and *tack*	unvoiced	Back part of tongue in contact with the soft palate toward the back of the mouth; loud burst of air is expelled.	stop ⚠	Ask students to touch the back of the roof of their mouth the first time they say /k/. Have them hold their hand in front of their mouth and feel the pop of air.
/d/	as in *dog, sudden,* and *bad*	voiced	Tongue taps behind upper teeth; sound pops out of mouth with a burst of air.	stop ⚠	Model how the tip of your tongue goes up and down as you say the sound. Ask them to make the hard popping sound of /d/, overemphasizing the sound to clearly differentiate it from /t/.
/ĕ/	as in *pen*	voiced	Smiling mouth position; tongue centered in the mid front.	continuous	Recognize that this is often the most difficult vowel to pronounce. See the last tip for /ă/. Ask students first to say easy words with /ĕ/, before saying just the sound: (*pen, /ĕ/; help, /ĕ/*).
/ē/	as in *feet*	voiced	Smiling mouth position with lips open wide; tongue high in mouth near front; increased mouth tension.	continuous	Ask students to smile as if for a picture and say /ē ē ē ē/. Exaggerate the tense spread of lips.
/f/	as in *fish, safer,* and *calf*	unvoiced	Upper front teeth on lower lip: air gust expelled.	continuous	Show students how the top teeth rest on the bottom lip. Ask students to put their fingers right in front of their lips to feel the air as they say the sound.

TABLE 1.4 Continued

Letter Sound	Phonetic Pronunciation	Voiced or Unvoiced	Articulation	Stop or Continuous Sound? ⚠ = don't add a schwa	When Students Have Difficulty Saying the New Letter Sound:
/g/	as in *go, hugging,* and *tag.*	voiced	Back part of the tongue in contact with the soft palate toward the back of the mouth; sound pops out of mouth with a burst of air.	stop ⚠	Ask students to grab the top part of their neck as they say the sound, feeling the vibration.
/h/	as in *hat* and *enhance*	unvoiced	Air gust quickly expelled; tongue and mouth assume position of vowel following /h/.	stop ⚠	Have students silently blow air on their upraised hand or on a feather.
/ĭ/	as in *pin*	voiced	Lips are parted and spread; tongue is high.	continuous	Emphasize how relaxed the face feels. Have students make the icky sound they would say after seeing something disgusting.
/ī/	as in *like*	voiced	Smiley face; tongue and jaw raise to a high position.	continuous	Ask students to first say words with /ī/, then to say /ī/ (*ice,* /ī/; *mice,* /ī/.)
/j/	as in *jet* and *enjoy*	voiced	Tip of tongue briefly contacts the roof of mouth; a burst of air is expelled with sound.	stop ⚠	Ask students to make the sound a large train engine makes: /j/ /j/ /j/.
/l/	as in *lip, mailing,* and *fill*	voiced	Tongue lifts behind upper teeth; air passes over sides of tongue.	continuous	Practice saying "la-la" to watch the tongue move.
/m/	as in *man, summer,* and *same*	voiced	Lips pressed together: air expelled through nose.	nasal: continuous	Have students imagine that they smell a pizza and ask them to press their lips together saying /mmmm/.
/n/	as in *nap, sunny,* and *in*	voiced	Front of tongue behind upper teeth toward front of mouth: air expelled through nose.	nasal: continuous	Have students pinch their nostrils as they say the sound of a mosquito.
/ŏ/	as in *pop*	voiced	Lips are tightly rounded; back part of tongue is low in mouth; jaw is open wide.	continuous	Ask students to pretend they are at the doctor's office and must open their mouths to say /ŏŏŏ/.

Continued

TABLE 1.4　Continued

Letter Sound	Phonetic Pronunciation	Voiced or Unvoiced	Articulation	Stop or Continuous Sound? ⚠ = don't add a schwa	When Students Have Difficulty Saying the New Letter Sound:
/ō/	as in *rope*	voiced	Rounded mouth that shuts like a camera shutter; tongue in middle; increased mouth tension.	continuous	Have students form their mouth into a circle just like the letter *o*.
/p/	as in *pet, hippo,* and *lip*	unvoiced	Both lips pop open and air blows out.	stop ⚠	In a whisper voice, ask students to make a very quiet motor boat sound as they feel the air when their lips silently pop open.
/q/ = /kw/	as in *queen*	unvoiced	/qu/ sounds like /kw/ and is comprised of two phonemes. Refer to the description of those letter sounds and say this sound, quickly blending them together into one sound. Immediately pronounce the next vowel sound after the *u*.	continuous	Ask students to make the sound of a cuckoo clock: "kwoo-kwoo."
/r/	as in *rip, marry,* and *star*	voiced	Tongue slightly bunches behind upper teeth toward front of mouth, not touching anything; mouth puckers.	continuous	Ask students to make the sound of a lion roaring.
/s/	as in *sad, missing,* and *fuss.*	unvoiced	Tongue behind upper teeth toward front of mouth; air blowing out.	continuous	Ask students to put their fingers in front of their mouths to feel the air as they say the sound. Ask students to make a long hissing snake sound /sssss/ or the sound of air coming out of a balloon.
/t/	as in *tub, bottom,* and *hat*	unvoiced	Tongue taps behind upper teeth.	stop ⚠	Ask students to make the sound of a ticking watch. Have them look at or feel the tip of their tongues going up and down. Ask them to feel the pop of air on their hand.
/ŭ/	as in *mud*	voiced	Lips slightly parted; tongue at rest in center of mouth.	continuous	Ask students to make the sound they would make if punched in the stomach or the sound they make when they don't know an answer.

TABLE 1.4   Continued

Letter Sound	Phonetic Pronunciation	Voiced or Unvoiced	Articulation	Stop or Continuous Sound? ⚠ = don't add a schwa	When Students Have Difficulty Saying the New Letter Sound:
/ū/	as in *use*	voiced	Sounds like /y/ + /oo/; refer to those letter sounds.	continuous	Have students point an index finger at other students and in a scolding voice say, "you, you, you."
/v/	as in *vest, heavy,* and *save.*	voiced	Upper front teeth on lower lip.	continuous	Ask students to make the sound of a big flying insect.
/w/	as in *well* and *sandwich*	voiced	Round your lips as if you are going to pronounce /ū/; vibrate your vocal cords for a very short /woo/ sound, then open your lips to pronounce the next sound in the word.	continuous	Ask students to pucker their lips as if about to kiss and then push the sound out. Ask students to hoot like owls in the forest at night. Be sure to keep your lips in a circle and don't overpronounce the /oo/.
/x/	as in *fox* and *mixer*	unvoiced	/x/ sounds like /ks/; refer to the description of those letter sounds.		Say the word *box*, exaggerating the /ks/ sound. Then ask the students to repeat the /ks/ sound. Repeat several familiar words ending in /x/, repeating the /ks/ letter sound after each word (*box, /x/; fix, /x/*).
/y/	as in *yes* and *yo-yo.*	voiced	Blade of tongue in middle of mouth; sounds like /yee/. Immediately pronounce the next vowel sound in the word.	continuous	Tell your students to make their lips smile as they say this sound. Be sure that you and they are not saying /ē/ for this sound.
/z/	as in *zoo, gazing,* and *fuzz*	voiced	Tongue behind upper teeth toward front of mouth; air blowing out.	continuous	Tell your students to feel the tickle when they make the buzzing bee sound: /zzzz/.

Sources: Avery, P., & Ehrlich, S. (2002); Celce-Murcia, M., et al. (1996); Edelen-Smith, P., & Frimmer, B. (1986); Ladefoged, P. (1975); McCormick, C., et al. (2002); Singh, S., & Singh K. (1976).

may surprise you are /qu/, /w/, and /y/, but if you take apart words that contain those sounds, you can clearly hear the phonetic pronunciation. Try this test with /qu/, which the chart indicates is pronounced like /kwoo/. First say the word *quick*. Then say each sound slowly (/kwoo/ +/i/ +/ck/). Now blend those sounds together faster; and finally as fast as you can say them as you once again hear the word *quick*. Do this same exercise for /w/ = /woo/ and the word *will*; repeat the exercise a final time for /y/ = /yee/ and the word *yak*.

Fact or Fiction

Circle the research-based answer and then check your answer. Investigate one of the research references in this chapter to determine how it supports this position. Be prepared to defend your position in class using the research reference.

1. Intensive phonics instruction should be an important option in a balanced literacy program.

Fact   **Fiction**

Fact: Intensive phonics instruction is explicit systematic teaching of beginning word reading skills that takes place in small groups, has a carefully designed instructional sequence with frequent opportunities for practice and review, and has multiple supports to make learning new skills easier. The National Institute of Child Health and Development estimates that as many as 30% of school children may need intensive phonics instruction to learn to read. Our experience shows that in urban schools, that figure may be even higher (Bursuck, Smith, Munk, Damer, Mehlig, & Perry, 2004). This need for the option of intensive instruction in phonics was validated by Groff (1998), who stated that, "much experimental evidence indicates that considerable time should be devoted in reading lessons to explicit and comprehensive development of beginning readers' phonics skills" (p. 139). While not a needed option for all, intensive phonics instruction is clearly a necessary option for some, especially children who are at risk due to poverty, learning disabilities, or not having English as their primary language. It is equally clear that students who are at risk also need explicit, systematic instruction in reading fluency, vocabulary, and comprehension. A balanced literacy program for students who are at risk should include these elements in addition to intensive phonics instruction.

APPLIED ACTIVITIES

1. Using a hand-held mirror, say each letter sound and observe how the sound is reproduced. Compare what you see to the description in the Articulation column of Table 1.4.
2. Ms. Garcia is a new kindergarten teacher. In unison as a group, tell her how to say these letter sounds without adding schwas: $q\ w\ b\ h\ o\ e\ i\ p$ and y.
3. Explain what is wrong about each nonexample in Table 1.3.
4. Think of the most difficult class you had this past year. If the teacher used a My Turn–Together–Your Turn strategy to support your success in learning the material, describe how that teaching strategy was used. If the teacher did not use a My Turn–Together–Your Turn strategy, describe how that strategy could have been used to help you more successfully learn the course material.
5. Have you worked for a boss who maintained a 3:1 ratio of positive comments to critical comments? Have you worked for a boss who had a ratio of 3:1 critical comments to positive comments? How did you feel about each of these individuals for whom you worked? Who was more motivating and why? How did you behave differently for each of these individuals?

6. Describe your experience as a student with a teacher who used unison responses as part of his or her teaching technique. How did the teacher get everyone to answer and how well did you learn the material?
7. Use Table 1.4, which lists the basic letter sounds, to complete the following tasks:
   a. Circle each of the phonemes that are stop sounds:

      b   e   f   c   d   l   m

   b. Circle each voiced phoneme in the following pairs:

      f   v
      b   p
      k   g
      t   d
      h   u

   c. Which letter sounds are nasal (air expelled through nose)?
   d. Which letter sounds are formed by the tongue tapping behind the front teeth?
   e. Show how you would help a child who was unable to say /h/ learn to articulate that phoneme.

REFERENCES

Ameis, J. (2003). *Early years e-text book: Three stages of teaching* [Electronic version]. Retrieved October 6, 2005 from University of Winnipeg Department of Education: http://io.uwinnipeg.ca/~jameis/New%20Pages/EYR5.html.

Archer, A. (Speaker). (1995). *The time is now* (Cassette recording). Eugene, OR: World Association of Direct Instruction 21st Annual Conference.

Armbruster, B., Lehr, F., & Osborn, J. (2001). *Put reading first: The research building blocks for teaching children to read.* Washington, DC: Partnership for Reading.

Avery, P., & Ehrlich, S. (1992). *Teaching American English pronunciation.* New York: Oxford Press.

Baker, S., Simmons, D., & Kame'enui, E. J. (1997). Vocabulary acquisition: Research bases. In D.C. Simmons & E. J. Kame'enui (Eds.), *What reading research tells us about children with diverse learning needs: Bases and basics* (pp. 183–217). Mahwah, NJ: Erlbaum.

Beck, I., McKeown, M., & Kucan, L. (2002). *Bringing words to life: Robust vocabulary instruction.* New York: The Guilford Press.

Biemiller, A. (2001). Teaching vocabulary: Early, direct, and sequential. *The American Educator, 25*(1), 24–28.

Bursuck, B., Smith, T., Munk, D., Damer, M., Mehlig, L., & Perry, J. (2004). Evaluating the impact of a prevention-based model of reading on children who are at risk. *Remedial and Special Education, 25,* 303–313

Celce-Murcia, M., et al. (1996). *Teaching pronunciation: A reference for teachers of English to speakers of other languages.* New York: Cambridge University Press.

Deno, S., & Markell, M. (1997). Effects of increasing oral reading: Generalization across reading tasks. *Journal of Special Education, 31,* 233–250.

Edelen-Smith, P. (1997). How now brown cow: Phoneme awareness activities for collaborative classrooms. *Intervention in School and Clinic, 33,* 103–111.

Ellis, E. S., Worthington, L., & Larkin, M. (1994). Oregon Univ., Eugene. Coll. of Education. [BBB14997], National Center To Improve the Tools of Educators, Eugene, OR. [BBB32952], Special Education Programs (ED/OSERS), Washington, DC. [EDD00017], Research Synthesis on Effective Teaching Principles and the Design of Quality Tools for Educators. Technical Report No. 5. ED386853.

Englert, C., Tarrant, K., & Mariage, T. (1992). Defining and redefining instructional practice in special education: Perspectives on good teaching. *Teacher Education and Special Education, 15*(2), 62–86.

Fisher, C., Berliner, D., Filby, N., Marliave, R., Cahen, L., & Dishaw, M. (1980). Teaching behaviors, academic learning time, and student achievement: An overview. In C. Denham & A. Lierberman (Eds.), *Time to learn: A review of the Beginning Teacher Evaluation Study* (pp. 7–32). Washington, DC: Department of Health, Education, and Welfare.

Foorman, B., Fletcher, J., & Francis, D. (2004). *Preventing Reading Failure* [Electronic version]. Retrieved from: http://teacher.scholastic.com/professional/teachstrat/preventing.htm#bio.

Francis, D. J., Shaywitz, S. E., Stuebing, K. K., Fletcher, J. M., & Shaywitz, B. A. (1996). Developmental lag vs. deficit models of reading disability: A longitudinal individual growth curves analysis. *Journal of Educational Psychology, 1,* 3–17.

Frimmer, B. (1986). *Sounds and language: A work/play approach.* Danville, IL: The Interstate Printers & Publishers.

Fuchs, L., Fuchs, D., Hosp, M., & Jenkins, J. (2001). Oral reading fluency as an indicator of reading competence: A theoretical, empirical, and historical analysis. *Scientific Studies of Reading, 5,* 239–256.

Good, R. H., Gruba, J., & Kaminski, R. A. (2002). Best practices in using dynamic indicators of basic emerging literacy skills (DIBELS) in an outcomes-driven model. In A. Thomas & J. Grimes (Eds.), *Best practices in school psychology IV* (pp. 699–720). Bethesda, MD: National Association of School Psychologists.

Gough, P. (1983). Context, form, and interaction. In K. Rayner (Ed.), *Eye movements in reading* (pp. 331–358). Cambridge, MA: MIT Press.

Groff, P. (1998). *Preventing reading failure.* Portland, OR: Halcyon House.

Hall, S., & Moats, L. (1999). *Straight talk about reading.* Chicago: Contemporary Books.

Hart, B., & Risley, T. (1995). *Meaningful differences.* Baltimore: Brookes.

Juel, C. (1988) Retention and non-retention of at-risk readers in first grade and their subsequent reading achievement. *Journal of Learning Disabilities, 21,* 571–580.

Kennedy-Manzo, K. (2003, December 17). Urban Minority Students Performing On Par With Suburban Counterparts [Electronic version]. *Education Week, 23*(15). Retrieved from: www.edweek.org/ew/ewstory.cfm?slug=15naep_web.h23.

Ladefoged, P. (1975). *A course in phonetics* (pp. 1–57). New York: Harcourt Brace Jovanovich.

Lyon, R. (1998). Why reading is not a natural activity. *Educational Leadership, 3,* 14–18.

McEwan, E., & Damer, M. (2000) *Managing unmanageable students.* Thousand Oaks, CA: Corwin Press.

McCormick, C., Throneburg, R., & Smitley, J. (2002). *A sound start: Phonemic awareness lessons for reading success.* New York: The Guilford Press.

Moats, L. C. (2000). *Speech to print: Language essentials for teachers.* Baltimore, MD: Paul H. Brookes Publishing.

National Reading Panel. (2000). *Teaching children to read: An evidence-based assessment of the scientific research literature on reading and its implications for reading instruction.* Washington, DC: National Institute of Child Health and Human Development.

Pressley, M., Wharton-McDonald, R., Allington, R., Block, C., Morrow, L., Tracey, D., Baker, K., Brooks, G., Cronin, J., Nelson, E., & Woo, D. (2001). A study of effective first-grade literacy instruction. *Scientific Studies of Reading, 5*(1), 35–58.

Rosenshine, B. (1986). Synthesis of research on explicit teaching. *Educational Leadership, 43*(7), 60–69.

Singh, S., & Singh, K. (1976). *Phonetics principles and practices.* Baltimore, MD: University Park Press.

Steinbeck, J. (1976). *The Acts of King Arthur and His Noble Knights: Introduction to his translation of Morte d'Arthur.* In *The Winchester Manuscripts of Thomas Malory & Other Sources* (pp. 3–4). Portsmouth, New Hampshire: Heinemann Publishing Company.

Tomlinson, C. (2000). Differentiated instruction: Can it work? *The Education Digest, 65*(5), 25–31.

Whitehurst, G. (2003, September 10) Interview: *Evidence-Based Education Science and the Challenge of Learning to Read.* Interviewer: David Boulton. [Electronic version] Retrieved from: www.childrenofthecode.org/interviews/whitehurst.htm.

Wolf, M., & Katzir-Cohen, T. (2001). Reading fluency and its intervention. *Scientific Studies of Reading, 5,* 211–238.

2 Phonemic Awareness

Key Terms

Acquisition stage of learning

Fluency stage of learning

Onset

Phoneme

Progress-monitoring assessments

Rime

Scripted lessons

Objectives

After reading this chapter, you will be able to:

1. Identify and describe the sequence of the essential phonemic awareness skills of segmenting and blending

2. Identify and describe key assessments for measuring segmenting and blending skills

3. Use assessment data to identify children at risk, diagnose skill deficits, and monitor instructional progress

4. Implement teaching strategies to enhance phonemic awareness instruction

5. Implement teaching strategies to provide extra booster help to students for whom large-group instruction is not sufficient

6. Adapt phonemic awareness activities from general education commercial reading programs

7. Describe the characteristics of students requiring an alternative, intensive reading program in Tier 3

8. Identify and describe the phonemic awareness component of five commonly used intensive reading programs

9. Explain how instruction in phonemic awareness can be carried out with English language learners and older students

What Skills Do I Need to Teach?

Words in the English language are made up of approximately 41 to 44 individual sounds called **phonemes** that are conventionally represented between slash marks. Phonemic awareness is the ability to hear these smallest units of sounds in spoken language and to manipulate them. The word *cat* has three phonemes (/c/ /a/ /t/), as does the word *shut* (/sh/ /u/ /t/), and the word *hope* (/h/ /ō/ /p/). Word-play activities such as identifying a new rhyming word to fit into a song or changing the first sound in a word to create another word involve hearing and manipulating phonemes.

Phonemic awareness is a critical foundational skill for learning to read, but children who are at risk are much less likely to develop phonemic awareness skills naturally. Rhyming games, word-play books, and songs requiring students to manipulate language will not provide enough practice opportunities or feedback for many students who are at risk. Fortunately, phonemic awareness skills can be taught. The National Reading Panel reported that phonemic awareness training not only developed phonemic awareness skills but also improved the reading and spelling performance of students who are at risk. A teacher's first important decision involves determining which phonemic awareness skills to teach. Figure 2.1 shows all of the possible choices. Notice that all of these skills rely on students hearing individual phonemes, not seeing them. As one of our teachers told us recently, "You can do phonemic awareness activities in the dark."

As stressed in Chapter 1, teachers can ill afford to spend time on skills that may be only marginally related to reading. Researchers have concluded that two skills have the most value when teaching children to read and that instruction directly teaching these phonemic awareness skills is more effective than instruction covering three or more. These two critical skills are segmenting and blending (National Reading Panel, 2000). Segmenting is the ability to break apart spoken words into their individual phonemes. A student who can segment says /f/ /i/ /sh/ when asked to say the sounds in *fish*. The ability to segment helps students strategically attack words they will be reading in text and break words into phonemes when spelling. Blending, the opposite of segmenting, is the ability to say a spoken word when its individual phonemes are said slowly. A student who can blend says the word *fish* after the teacher slowly says the individual sounds, /f/-/i/-/sh/. Blending enables students to read unfamiliar text by combining single sounds into any new word.

Effective instruction for students who are at risk is careful and deliberate, and a successful teacher needs to break down larger skills into their more basic components. The following list of blending and segmenting skills will help you guide students from the earliest, most basic segmenting and blending skills through more difficult ones.

- **Rhyming:** What word rhymes with *can*?
- **Phoneme deletion:** What word would be left if the /k/ sound were taken away from *cat*?
- **Word to word matching:** Do *pen* and *pipe* begin with the same sound?
- **Blending:** What word would we have if you put these sounds together: /s/-/ă/-/t/?
- **Sound isolation:** What is the first sound in *rose*?
- **Phoneme segmentation:** What sounds do you hear in the word *hot*?
- **Phoneme counting:** How many sounds do you hear in the word *cake*?
- **Deleting phonemes:** What sound do you hear in *meat* that is missing in *eat*?
- **Odd word out:** What word starts with a different sound: *bag, nine, beach, bike*?
- **Sound to word matching:** Is there a /k/ in *bike*?

FIGURE 2.1 Examples of Phonemic Awareness Tasks

Source: Stanovich, K. (1994). Romance and reality. *The Reading Teacher, 47*(4), 280–291.

Segmenting and Blending Sequence

1. Segmenting: First Sound

    Description: After hearing the teacher say a whole word, students identify the first sound in a word.

    Example skills: teacher: "What's the first sound in *cat*?"
    students: "/k/"
    teacher: "What's the first sound in *end*?"
    students: "/ĕ/"

2. Blending: Onset-Rime

    Description: After hearing the teacher slowly say the **onset** [the beginning sound(s) that precedes the vowel in a syllable] and the **rime** [the rest of the syllable that contains the vowel and all that follows it], students say the whole word.

    Example skills: teacher: "/s/-/ĕll/. What word?"
    students: "sell"
    teacher: "/m/-/āke/. What word?"
    students: "make"

3. Segmenting: Onset-Rime

    Description: After hearing the teacher say the whole word, students say the onset and the rime.

    Example skills: teacher: "Take apart /pit/."
    students: "/p/-/ĭt/"
    teacher: "Take apart /home/."
    students: "/h/-/ōme/"

4. Blending: Individual Sounds

    Description: After hearing the teacher slowly say the individual sounds in the word, students say the whole word.

    Example skills: teacher: "/n/-/ă/-/p/. What word?"
    students: "nap"
    teacher: "/ă/-/s/-/k/. What word?"
    students: "ask"

5. Segmenting: Individual Sounds

    Description: After hearing the teacher say the whole word, students say the individual sounds in the word.

    Example skills: teacher: "Take apart /leg/."
    students: "/l/-/ĕ/-/g/"
    teacher: "Take apart /stop/."
    students: "/s/-/t/-/ŏ/-/p/"

Phonemic awareness instruction for children just beginning kindergarten should start at segmenting first sound. Once the majority of students have learned to segment first sound for each of the sounds you have taught in your classroom, begin teaching blending onset-rime. Gradually move through the skill sequence until students in your classroom are able to segment

> Reading research conducted during the past decade highlights how well-designed kindergarten curriculum can provide necessary prereading skills so that kindergarteners who are at risk are on track for reading in first grade. *What Kids Should Know Before Entering First Grade* describes key skills kindergarteners should have by the end of the year. **www.readingrockets.org/articles/381.**

individual sounds. For first grade students and older beginning readers, simply start blending and segmenting instruction at the individual sound level.

How Can I Efficiently Assess and Monitor the Progress in Phonemic Awareness Skills?

Because segmenting and blending are important foundational skills for reading, teachers must first assess these skills to determine which skills students already know and which skills students still need to learn. Once teachers begin teaching phonemic awareness, brief monthly assessments called **progress-monitoring assessments** help monitor the progress of students learning how to segment and blend.

Mr. Glenn is a kindergarten teacher who uses monthly assessments to help guide his teaching. The October progress monitoring assessment that he gave his students showed that almost everyone in the class has learned to segment first sounds and blend at the onset-rime level. Mr. Glenn is delighted that his instruction has been so effective because he has been teaching these skills every day. During November he moves to the next skill and teaches his students to segment onset-rimes. If the assessment Mr. Glenn gives his students at the end of November shows that students have learned that skill, he will begin teaching blending individual sounds.

The following three phonemic awareness assessments are appropriate for kindergarten teachers to monitor the effectiveness of their teaching and determine when to move to the next skill. Teachers of older students give their students the DIBELS Phonemic Segmentation assessment and the informal blending assessment to determine whether they have learned these skills.

Segmenting First Sound: DIBELS Initial Sound Fluency Assessment

When is it given? Fall of kindergarten year is when this skill is ordinarily introduced.
What score indicates success? Eight or more sounds per minute at the beginning of kindergarten; 25 or more sounds per minute at the middle of kindergarten.

Students who are at risk often come to school unable to identify the first sounds in words. Even when teachers teach the letter-sounds, unless they give direct, explicit instruction, many students cannot identify the first sounds of words. During the first few months of kindergarten, check whether students are gaining competence in this early phonemic awareness skill.

> At the official DIBELS website (**http:// dibels.uoregon.edu/dibels_what. php**), you can watch a teacher giving the Initial Sounds Fluency assessment to a student. Directions to administer and score the test are available at the same website, as are copies that can be downloaded at no charge.

When giving this timed assessment, the teacher presents four pictures to the student, names each picture, and then asks the student to identify by pointing to, or saying the picture that begins with the sound, said orally by the teacher. For example, the teacher says, "This is *sink, cat, gloves,* and *hat.* Which picture begins with /s/?" In response, the student points to the correct picture. The student is also asked to say the beginning sound for an orally presented word that matches one of the given pictures.

At the official DIBELS website, you can watch a teacher giving the Initial Sounds Fluency assessment to a student. Directions to administer and score the test (Figure 2.2) are available at the same website, as are copies (Figure 2.3 on page 36) that can be downloaded at no charge.

DIBELS™ Initial Sound Fluency
Short Form Directions

Make sure you have reviewed the long form of the directions and have them available. Say these specific directions to the student:

> This is *mouse, flowers, pillow, letters* (point to each picture while saying its name). *Mouse* (point to *mouse*) begins with the sound /m/. Listen, /m/ *mouse*. Which one begins with the sounds /fl/?

Correct Response	Incorrect Response
Student points to flowers, you say	If student gives any other response, you say
Good. *Flowers* begins with the sounds /fl/.	*Flowers* (point to flowers) begins with the sounds /fl/. Listen, /fl/ *flowers*. Let's try it again. Which one begins with the sounds /fl/?

> *Pillow* (point to pillow) begins with the sound /p/. Listen, /p/ *pillow*. What sound does *letters* (point to letters) begin with?

Correct Response	Incorrect Response
Student says /l/, you say	If student gives any other response, you say
Good. *Letters* begins with the sound /l/.	*Letters* (point to letters) begins with the sound /l/. Listen, /l/ *letters*. Let's try it again. What sound does *letters* (point to letters) begin with?

> Here are some more pictures. Listen carefully to the words.

FIGURE 2.2   DIBELS Initial Sound Fluency Assessment Direction Sheet

Source: Official DIBELS home page: http://dibels.uoregon.edu/2002–2004.

Extensive research enabled the test developers of the DIBELS to establish benchmark levels for students in kindergarten. These benchmarks, shown in Table 2.1, enable a teacher to determine whether a student is on track for reading at grade level.

Blending Individual Phonemes: Informal Assessments

When is it given? The blending individual phonemes assessment is usually given starting in kindergarten.

What score indicates success? Four out of five words correct (80% accuracy)

TABLE 2.1   Benchmarkes for DIBELS Initial Sound Fluency

Beginning of Kindergarten		Middle of Kindergarten	
If score is . . .	*Diagnosis*	*If score is . . .*	*Diagnosis*
Less than 4	At risk	Less than 10	Deficit
4–7	Some risk	10–24	Emerging
8 or more	Low risk	25 or more	Established

Benchmark K–1
DIBELS™ Initial Sound Fluency

This is tomato, cub, plate, doughnut (point to pictures).

1.	Which picture begins with /d/?	0	1
2.	Which picture begins with /t/?	0	1
3.	Which picture begins with /k/?	0	1
4.	What sound does "plate" begin with?	0	1

This is bump, insect, refrigerator, skate (point to pictures).

5.	Which picture begins with /sk/?	0	1
6.	Which picture begins with /r/?	0	1
7.	Which picture begins with /b/?	0	1
8.	What sound does "insect" begin with?	0	1

This is rooster, mule, fly, soap (point to pictures).

9.	Which picture begins with /r/?	0	
10.	Which picture begins with /fl/?	0	
11.	Which picture begins with /s/?	0	
12.	What sound does "mule" begin with?	0	1

This is pliers, doctor, quilt, beetle (point to pictures).

13.	Which picture begins with /b/?	0	
14.	Which picture begins with /pl/?	0	
15.	Which picture begins with /d/?	0	1
16.	What sound does "quilt" begin with?	0	1

Time: _____ Seconds   Total Correct: _____

60 × Total Correct = _____   Correct Initial Sounds per Minute

---

FIGURE 2.3   DIBELS Initial Sound Fluency Score Sheet

Source: Official DIBELS home page: http://dibels.uoregon.edu/2002–2004.

Blending Individual Phonemes Assessment   Teachers can develop a brief test to assess whether their students are learning how to blend individual phoneme into words. By selecting five words similar to words practiced every day during blending instruction, a teacher can write a test similar to the one shown in Figure 2.4. As blending lessons begin to include more difficult words such as those containing short /e/ or those beginning with the /h/ sound, words used for this assessment should reflect that level of difficulty.

When giving students this informal blending assessment, the teacher:

1. says the individual phonemes of the word
2. asks the student to say the whole word
3. records whether the student said the correct word

This informal assessment is not timed. When the majority of students are blending four of the five words said by the teacher, blending activities become integrated with instruction in word reading. Students who do not show that success level require extra practice. If a student's performance in this and other areas such as letter sounds and segmenting does

Date: _____   Student Name: _____

Directions Teacher says, "I am going to say a word very slowly and then I'm going to say the word fast. If I say /s/-/ĭ/-/t/, the word is *sit*. Let's try one: /k/-/ă/-/t/. What's the word?"

After the student responds, continue with the administration of the assessment.

Scoring: Score 1 for each correct word given and 0 for an incorrect response. Calculate and record the total score.

Blending Individual Phonemes	Score (0,1)
1. /b/ - /a /- /t/ [bat]	_____
2. /m/ - /u/ - /d/ [mud]	_____
3. /p/ - /a/ - /n/ [pan]	_____
4. /s/ - /i/ - /k/ [sick]	_____
5. /h/ - /a/ - /n/ - /d/ [hand]	_____
Total Correct	_____

FIGURE 2.4   Blending Individual Phonemes: Informal Assessment

not improve, even with extra daily practice, he or she may require a more intensive reading curriculum such as those described at the end of this chapter.

Segmenting: DIBELS Phonemic Segmentation Assessment

When is it given? After the first semester of kindergarten at the earliest.
What score indicates success? Thirty-five phonemes per minute or more by the end of kindergarten.

In addition to blending sounds into spoken words, students must also know how to do the opposite: take apart spoken words into individual sounds. In the DIBELS Phonemic Segmentation Fluency (PSF) measure, students are presented with a series of spoken words and asked to say the phonemes or sounds in each word. The teacher presents words for one minute and records the number of correct phonemes the student is able to identify in a minute. Directions to administer and score the DIBELS PSF assessment, downloaded from the official website, are shown in Figure 2.5. Samples of completed scoresheets are in Figures

Make sure you have reviewed the long form of the directions and have them available. Say these specific directions to the student:

> I am going to say a word. After I say it, you tell me all the sounds in the word. So, if I say, "sam," you would say /s/ /a/ /m/. Let's try one. (one second pause) Tell me the sounds in "mop."

Correct Response	Incorrect Response
If student says, /m/ /o/ /p/, you say	If student gives any other response, you say
Very good. The sounds in "mop" are /m/ /o/ /p/.	The sounds in "mop" are /m/ /o/ /p/. Your turn. Tell me the sounds in "mop."

> OK. Here is your first word.

FIGURE 2.5   DIBELS Phonemic Segmentation Fluency Short Form Directions
Source: Official DIBELS home page: http://dibels.uoregon.edu/2002–2004.

```
Name: Darrell
Date: May 21

bad      /b/ /a/ /d/          lock     /l/ /o/ /k/          6 / 6
that     /th/ /a/ /t/         pick     /p/ /i/ /ck/         6 / 6
mine     /m/ /ie/ /n/         noise    /n/ /oi/ /z/         5 / 6
coat     /c/ /oa/ /t/         spin     /s/ /p/ /i/ /n/      7 / 7
meet     /m/ /ea/ /t/         ran      /r/ /a/ /n/          6 / 6
wild     /w/ /ie/ /l/ /d/     dawn     /d/ /o/ /n/          6 / 7
woke     /w/ /oa/ /k/         sign     /s/ /ie/ /n/         6 / 6
fat      /f/ /a/ /t/          wait     /w/ ] /ai/ /t/       4 / 6
side     /s/ /ie/ /d/         yell     /y/ /e/ /l/          _ / 6
jet      /j/ /e/ /t/          of       /o/ /v/              _ / 5
land     /l/ /a/ /n/ /d/      wheel    /w/ /ea/ /l/         _ / 7
beach    /b/ /ea/ /ch/        globe    /g/ /l/ /oa/ /b/     _ / 7

                                               Total    46 / 75
```

FIGURE 2.6 Darrell's DIBELS Phonemic Segmentation Fluency Score Sheet

```
Name: Mose
Date: May 21

bad      /b/ /a/ /d/          lock     /l/ /o/ /k/          1 / 6
that     /th/ /a/ /t/         pick     /p/ /i/ /k/          1 / 6
mine     /m/ /i/ /n/          noise    /n/ /oi/ /z/         2 / 6
coat     /c/ /oa/ /t/         spin     /s/ /p/ /i/ /n/      1 / 7
meet     /m/ /ea/ /t/         ran      /r/ /a/ /n/ ]        2 / 6
wild     /w/ /ie/ / l/ /d/    dawn     /d/ /o/ /n/          _ / 7
woke     /w/ /oa/ /k/         sign     /s/ /ie/ /n/         _ / 6
fat      /f/ /a/ /t/          wait     /w/ /ai/ /t/         _ / 6
side     /s/ /ie/ /d/         yell     /y/ /e/ /l/          _ / 6
jet      /j/ /e/ /t/          of       /o/ /v/              _ / 5
land     /l/ /a/ /n/ /d/      wheel    /w/ /ea/ /l/         _ / 7
beach    /b/ /ea/ /ch/        globe    /g/ /l/ /oa/ /b/     _ / 7

                                               Total    7 / 75
```

FIGURE 2.7 Mose's DIBELS Phonemic Segmentation Fluency Score Sheet

At the official DIBELS website (**http://dibels.uoregon.edu/dibels_what.php**), you can watch a teacher giving the Phonemic Segmentation Fluency assessment to a student. Directions to administer and score the test are available at the same website, as are copies that can be downloaded at no charge.

2.6 and 2. 7. The benchmarks for kindergarten and Grade 1 shown in Table 2.2 enable a teacher to determine whether a student is on track for reading at grade level.

Note that the benchmark for the end of kindergarten is reported as a range from 35–45 segments correct per minute. Teachers should set high expectations and aim to get as many students as possible to this benchmark by the end of the year. Students who are at benchmark have achieved grade-level performance on the area tested. Our recommendation is that the higher figure of 45 should be used in situations where children have received systematic, explicit instruction in phonemic

TABLE 2.2   Benchmarks for DIBELS Phonemic Segmentation Fluency Assessment

Middle of Kindergarten		End of Kindergarten–Middle of Grade 1	
If score is . . .	*Diagnosis*	*If score is . . .*	*Diagnosis*
Less than 7	At risk	Less than 10	Deficit
7–17	Some risk	10–34	Emerging
18 or more	Low risk	35–45	Established

Source: Good, Kaminski, & Howe (2005, June).

> Although DIBELS assessments can be used with older students, the benchmarks may not be applicable. For a norm-referenced measure of phonological processing that can be used with older students, use the Comprehensive Test of Phonological processing (CTOPP). For more information go to **www.earobics.com/products/ctopp.cfm.**

segmentation. An example of how a teacher can use the results of DIBELS Phoneme Segmentation Fluency to make instructional decisions is described in Effective Teachers at Work on page 40.

How Do I Teach Children to Segment and Blend?

In Chapter 1, the diagram of a typical first-grade classroom showed that some children learn to read with relative ease while children who are at risk or have learning disabilities require a more explicit, systematic approach. The multi-tiered approach described in this text allows teachers to accommodate a range of students when teaching students to segment and blend. Teaching strategies for segmenting and blending are described within the context of this multi-tiered model. Enhancements to large-group Tier 1 instruction are elaborated in this section.

Enhancements to Large-Group Tier 1 Instruction

The needs of many children can be met when large-group instruction in early reading is carried out effectively. Sample scripts for presenting blending and segmenting to students are shown in Tables 2.3, 2.4 (p. 42), and 2.5 (p. 43). These scripts are based on ones originally developed and field-tested by Carnine and colleagues (2004). Using **scripted lessons** will help you present information clearly while staying focused on the essentials. In this next section, you will learn how to use the scripts to enhance your students' success in learning phonemic awareness skills. The strategies introduced in Chapter 1 and expanded here enable teachers to increase student responding and attention, provide support for new learning, correct errors consistently, increase skill retention through cumulative review, increase student motivation, and teach to success. Depending on the percentage of students who are at risk in the community where you teach, the effective use of these strategies can ensure that the needs of one-half to two-thirds of students are met.

> The *Tampa Reads* website, which contains a number of phonemic awareness worksheets, explains: "the most difficult sounds to learn are—h - l - m - n - q - r - w (at the beginning) and y (at the beginning of words). It will take 3–5 times more practice for a child to memorize these sounds in comparison to other consonant sounds, so please give special attention to their mastery." **www.tampareads.com/phonics/whereis/index.htm.**

Increase Student Responding and Attention   Providing an advance organizer is the first thing teachers can do to

Effective Teachers at Work

Frequent Assessment

The following account demonstrates how student scores from the DIBELS Phonemic Segmentation can help guide a teacher's phonemic awareness instruction.

At the end of kindergarten, in addition to an assessment of individual sound blending and letter sounds, Ms. Lee gave the one-minute DIBELS Phonemic Segmentation Fluency assessment to every student in her class. She tested half of her class during rest time, when she could easily ask individual children to sit across from her at a table in a well-lit corner of the room. The other students were assessed at a small desk just outside her classroom during a playtime supervised by the paraprofessional in her room. In both testing situations, she sat in a position facing her classroom in case she needed to intervene in any sudden disruptions. The small magnetic kitchen timer Ms. Lee had purchased at a hardware store ensured that she stopped each test after one minute.

Ms. Lee knew that, based on segmenting benchmarks for this assessment, children who score 35 phonemes per minute or more at the end of kindergarten are more likely to have success with beginning word reading in grade 1; children scoring between 10 and 34 are at some risk for having difficulty with word reading in grade 1; and children scoring below 10 are at risk for having problems learning to read in grade 1. Ms. Lee also knew that her students' scores in blending and letter sounds would also help her identify children at risk for future reading problems.

Later, when Ms. Lee examined the assessment results, she reflected on the different needs of two students in her class and the recommendations she was making to the first grade teachers based on the test results. Darrell, who broke apart the words said by his teacher into 46 phonemes correct per minute, attained a score above benchmark levels. Darrell's assessment is shown in Figure 2.6. Notice that the teacher scores correct segments by underlining the corresponding phonemes. In the word bad, Darrell correctly said all three phonemes. Therefore, all three phonemes are underlined. In the word spin, Darrell only identified three out of the four phonemes, failing to separate the /s/ and /p/. As a result, Ms. Lee underlined the /s/ and /p/ together. This assessment showed that Darrell was able to fluently break most of the spoken words into individual sounds. He also knew how to blend and could identify the sounds of individual letters in isolation without error. With effective instruction, Darrell should be able to apply his skills to reading written words. Ms. Lee knew that he was on track to read in first grade.

Mose, on the other hand, earned a score of 7 correct phonemes per minute. Only first sounds of the phonemes are underlined on the scoresheet in Figure 2.7 because Mose still identifies only the first sound in words. Also, Mose only knew 50% of his sounds, and had yet to reach mastery level in blending individual sounds. Ms. Lee knew that Mose needed extensive help in first grade if he was to be able to meet benchmark levels and move out of the at-risk category. She found it helpful to discuss the assessment with Mose's parents when they met to talk about the intensive reading program he would participate in during first grade.

increase student responding and attention. As discussed in Chapter 1, advance organizers make clear to students what is being covered, why it is being taught, and what behavioral expectations are in place during instruction. Such clarity helps students focus on the task at hand and sets the occasion for active student answering and attentive behavior. For example, before she starts her phonemic awareness lesson, Ms. Grenaldi tells her students, "Today we will take apart ten words. Learning how to take apart words will help you learn to spell so that you can write a story about your favorite TV show. Remember to answer on signal, keep your hands and feet to yourself, and look at me."

TABLE 2.3 Segmenting 1: Format for Segmenting First Sound

Outcome	After hearing a three-phoneme word (*cat*), students say the first sound: /k/.
Materials Needed	List of three-phoneme words starting with letter sounds that the students have already learned in class. At least 25% of the words should begin with the new letter sound of the week.
Signaling	Extend your index finger, fingersnap, or hand drop as you say the first sound.
Time	3–5 minutes for 10 words
Rationale	Segmenting words helps students separate words into sounds. Segmenting first sound is the first step in learning to segment longer words.
Tips	■ When presenting words containing a new letter sound, use steps 2–5 for the first three or four words. Then if students are accurately segmenting first sound, use steps 4–5 (Your Turn and Individual Student Checkout) for the remaining words. ■ Students who have most difficulty with segmenting first sound need more turns during individual student checkouts. ■ When conducting a review session, use steps 4–5 (Your Turn and Individual Student Checkout) for all of the words.

Instructions	**Teacher**	**Students**
	1. Advance Organizer	
	2. My Turn **"It's time to play the *first-sound* game. I'm going to say a word, and you'll say the first sound in the word. My turn. First sound in *sat* is "/s/."**	
	3. Together: The teacher answers with students this time: **"First sound in *sat*?"** (signal) **"/s/. Yes, /s/."**	/s/
	4. Your Turn **"Your turn. First sound in *sat*?"** (answer) **"Yes, /s/."**	/s/
	5. Individual Student Checkout **"Individual turns. First sound in *sat*? Jontrell."** (signal) (answer) **"Yes, /s/."** **"First sound in *mop*? Corinne."** (signal) (answer) **"Yes, /m/."** Call on several individual students to check accuracy.	/s/ /m/

Error Correction	If students make an error, immediately return to a My Turn–Together–Your Turn pattern. Later present the word that was missed two more times during the lesson.
Perk up Your Drill	■ Hold up pictures matching the words on the day's list. ■ Use an animal puppet to say the words and signal.
Adaptations	■ Inattentive students should sit next to you so their attention can be refocused to your mouth. For extra emphasis during the first week, overemphasize the first sound as you say each word. ■ When students reach criteria, begin segmenting first sound of classmate's names, funny animals, or favorite holidays. ■ Hold continuous sounds for two seconds as you say them so students clearly hear the sound.

Increasing student responding and attention also involves the judicious use of teacher talk. Keeping teacher talk to a minimum helps attain a lively teaching pace that, in turn, increases student attention. Students learning to identify first sounds or to blend sounds into words need to maintain all of their attention on the word or sounds in the words. A teacher

TABLE 2.4   Blending 2: Format for Blending Individual Phonemes

Outcome	After hearing a three-phoneme word broken into individual phonemes (/n/-/ă/-/p/), students say the word at a normal speed (*nap*).
Materials Needed	List of three-phoneme words starting with letter sounds that the students have already learned in class. At least 25% of the words should begin with the new letter sound of the week.
Signaling	Choose one signal:
	Signal 1: Extend your index finger as you say the first sound, extend your middle finger as you say the second sound, extend your ring finger as you say the third sound, and signal that students should say the entire word by arching your other hand in a rainbow motion over all three fingers. Be careful how you position your hand when showing students how to do this. You want them to read your fingers left to right, just as they would read text. (See Figure 2.8.)
	Signal 2: Use a fingersnap/handclap for each sound and for the entire word.
Time	3–5 minutes for 10 words
Rationale	Blending sounds into words helps students use their phonics to read printed words.
Tips	■ When presenting words containing a new letter sound, use steps 2–5 for the first three or four words. Then if students are accurately blending the words, use steps 4–5 (Your Turn and Individual Student Checkout) for the remaining words.
	■ Students who have most difficulty with blending individual phonemes need more turns during individual student checkouts.
	■ When conducting a review session use steps 4–5 (Your Turn and Individual Student Checkout) for all of the words.
	■ Remember, this and all of the phonemic awareness formats in this chapter are strictly oral; no written words are involved. In the words of one wise teacher, "If you can do it in the dark, it's phonemic awareness."

Instructions	**Teacher**	**Students**
	1. Advance Organizer	
	2. My Turn	
	"Today we're going to play *Say It Fast*. I'm going to say a word slowly, and then fast. My turn. /n/-/ ă /-/p/. The word is *nap*."	
	3. Together: The teacher answers with students this time:	
	"Together." (extend fingers) **"/n/-/ ă /-/p/. What word?"** (arch palm) **"nap. Yes, *nap*."**	nap
	4. Your Turn	
	"Your turn." (extend fingers) **"/n/-/ ă /-/p/. What word?"** (arch palm) (answer) **"Yes, *nap*."**	nap
	5. Individual Student Checkout	
	"Individual turns." (extend fingers) **"/m/-/ ŏ /-/p/. What word? Mary."** (arch palm) (answer) **"Yes, *mop*."**	mop
	(extend fingers) **"/r/-/ ŭ /-/n/. What word? Telly."** (arch palm) (answer) **"Yes, *run*."**	run
	Call on several individual students to check accuracy.	

Error Correction	If students make an error, immediately return to a My Turn–Together–Your Turn pattern. Later present the word that was missed two more times during the lesson.
Perk up Your Drill	■ Say the sounds using "robot talk" and get your class to answer in the same monotone.
	■ Draw a map of your school on the board with steps leading from your class to the playground. Every time students get a word correct, move a Velcro-backed student cut-out closer to the playground. When the student cut-out reaches the playground, it is recess time.
Adaptations	■ Use manipulatives to help make this task more concrete. You can use blocks, magnetic letters, cardboard letters, letter blocks, etc. Since manipulatives add extra challenges in a large group, work in a small group with a few students whose test results indicate that they are not blending.
	■ Once students can easily blend three phonemes, provide practice blending more difficult four-phoneme words, and words containing long vowels. Students are now ready to move into reading words and sentences containing three-phoneme words.
	■ For students who have trouble holding words in their short-term memory, avoid using the oral cue "What word" and just go straight to the arch signal.

Source: This script is based on one originally developed and field tested by Carnine, Silbert, Kame'enui, & Tarver (2004), *Direct Instruction Reading: 4th ed.* New Jersey: Merrill Prentice Hall.

TABLE 2.5 Segmenting 2: Format for Segmenting Individual Phonemes:

Outcome	After hearing a three-phoneme word spoken at a normal rate (*rap*), students say the individual sounds in the word (/r/-/ă/-/p/).
Materials Needed	List of three-phoneme words starting with letter sounds that the students have already learned in class. At least 25% of the words should begin with the new letter sound of the week.
Signaling	Choose one signal:
	Signal 1: Extend your index finger as you say the first sound, extend your middle finger as you say the second sound, extend your ring finger as you say the third sound. Be careful how you position your hand when showing students how to do this. You want them to read your fingers left to right, just as they would read text.
	Signal 2: Use a fingersnap/handclap for each sound and for the entire word.
Time	3–5 minutes for 10 words
Rationale	Segmenting words helps students separate words into sounds. Learning how to segment words will help at-risk students who do not have disabilities learn to spell (National Reading Panel, 2000).
Tips	■ When presenting words containing a new letter sound, use steps 2–5 for the first three or four words. Then if students are accurately segmenting all of the phonemes, use steps 4–5 (Your Turn and Individual Student Checkout) for the remaining words.
	■ Students who have most difficulty with segmenting individual phonemes need more turns during individual student checkouts.
	■ When conducting a review session, use steps 4–5 (Your Turn and Individual Student Checkout) for all of the words.
	■ Remember, this and all of the phonemic awareness formats in this chapter are strictly oral; no written words are involved.

Instructions	Teacher	Students
	1. Advance Organizer	
	2. My Turn: **"I'm going to say a word, and you'll say all the sounds in the word. My turn. Take apart *leg*. /l/-/ĕ/-/g/. The sounds in *leg* are /l/-/ĕ/-/g/.**"	
	3. Together: The teacher answers with students this time: **"Together. Take apart *leg*."** (extend finger) **"/l/"** (extend finger) **"/ĕ/"** (extend finger) **"/g/. Yes, the sounds in *leg* are /l/-/ĕ/-/g/."**	/l/-/ĕ/-/g/
	4. Your Turn: **"Your turn. Take apart *leg*."** (extend finger) (answer) (extend finger) (answer) (extend finger) (answer) **"Yes, the sounds in *leg* are /l/-/ĕ/-/g/."**	/l/-/ĕ/-/g/
	5. Individual Student Checkout	
	"Individual turns. Take apart *men*. Sharnicca." (extend finger) (answer) (extend finger) (answer) (extend finger) (answer) **"Yes, the sounds in *men* are /m/-/ĕ/-/n/."**	/m/-/ĕ/-/n/
	"Take apart *win*. Bryan." (extend finger) (answer) (extend finger) (answer) (extend finger) (answer) **"Yes, the sounds in win are /w/-/i/-/n/."**	/w/-/i/-/n/
	Call on several individual students to check accuracy.	

Error Correction	If students make an error, immediately return to a My Turn–Together–Your Turn pattern. Later present the word that was missed two more times during the lesson.
Perk up Your Drill	■ Tell your students they are cheerleaders and have them cheer the segments, using right arm out, both arms up, left arm out motions.
	■ Ask parents to come in with younger sisters and brothers and watch students successfully segment.
	■ Have students do imaginary karate chops for every phoneme.
Adaptations	■ As long as you remember My Turn–Together–Your Turn, the more students practice sound/word spelling (see Chapter 3), the better they will become at segmenting. Everyone should do daily sound/word spelling.
	■ Once students can easily segment three phonemes, provide practice segmenting words with more phonemes and difficult letter sound patterns.

Source: This script is based on one originally developed and field tested by Carnine, Silbert, Kame'enui, and Tarver and published in *Direct Instruction Reading (4th ed.).* New Jersey: Merrill Prentice Hall.

who provides unnecessary details about a word risks losing the focus of students with short attention spans. If, after asking students to tell her the sounds in *mop,* Ms. Grenaldi talks about how she hates to mop floors, Tan may be unable to say /m/-/ŏ/-/p/ because he is thinking about how funny she would look mopping the classroom floor.

Require Answering in Unison   Requiring students to answer in unison also helps keep the attention of students who are at risk. When students are required to respond frequently, they are so busy answering questions that they do not have time for distractions. Unison responses also guarantee that children who are at risk receive the practice manipulating sounds that they need to reach mastery on all essential phonemic awareness skills by the end of kindergarten. For example, students who do not hear the first sound in words beginning with /h/ or /a/ need to practice saying the first sound in many words that begin with those phonemes. A teacher's quandary is how to provide that practice yet keep the phonemic awareness section of the lesson from taking more than 10 minutes of class time and running the risk of boring the students. When every student gets practice segmenting all ten words beginning with /h/ or /a/, the lesson moves faster and more students experience success with a difficult skill. The key to getting unison responses from students during phonemic awareness instruction is using a clear and consistent system of signaling for answers.

Signaling for Segmenting   Use the following steps to establish effective signaling for segmenting instruction.

1. Focus students' attention, making sure that everyone is looking directly at you.
2. Let students know that a question will be asked by holding up the palm of your hand towards the class.
3. Begin segmenting instruction by turning the hand, holding up a closed fist with fingers towards your face.
4. Say the word and ask students to segment the word.
5. Signal by raising one finger at a time for each sound that is said. Extend the index finger as you say the first sound, extend the middle finger as you say the second sound, and extend the ring finger as you say the third sound.
6. When introducing segmenting for the first time, practice with students and model the signals as well as the expected answers.

Signaling for Blending   Figure 2.8 shows a teacher's view as she signals her students to say the sounds in *sat.* Although other signals such as finger-snapping or clapping can be used, an advantage of the fingers-up format is that children raise their own fingers when

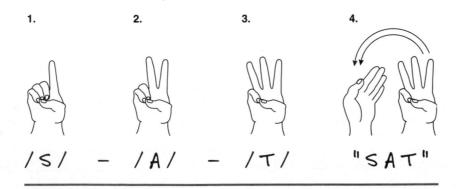

1.   2.   3.   4.

/ S /   —   / A /   —   / T /   " S A T "

FIGURE 2.8   Hand Signals for Blending Sounds

Research to Practice

Blending

Project PRIDE teachers discovered that students who were unable to learn how to blend onset-rimes needed to have that blending activity broken into even smaller steps. Many students learned how to blend onset-rimes after the teacher went back a half-step and asked them to blend compound words for several days or weeks. Instead of saying onset-rimes, the teachers slowly said the two parts of compound words, requiring students to say the whole word fast: *cow + boy = cowboy, tooth + brush = toothbrush, snow + man = snowman, cough + drop = cough-drop, play + ground = playground, cheese + burgers = cheeseburgers.*

Once the students were blending compound words, the teacher next practiced onset-rimes with students' names. Students easily blended their classmates' names such as /v/-/ictoria/, /l/-/atoya/, or /s/-/kyler/.

saying the sounds in words, providing them with a multisensory cue. Fingers-up signals are also helpful when students say the sounds in words before spelling them.

Use these steps to establish effective signals for blending instruction.

1. Focus students' attention, making sure that everyone is looking directly at you.
2. Let students know that a question will be asked by holding up the palm of your hand toward the class.
3. Say the sounds slowly: extend your index finger as you say the first sound, extend your middle finger as you say the second sound, and extend your ring finger as you say the third sound.
4. Ask students to say the word the fast way and signal by arching your palm in a rainbow motion over all three fingers as you and/or your students say the entire word. Be careful how you position your hand when showing students how to do this sequence. You want them to read your fingers left to right, just as they would read text.
5. Model the signals and expected responses when introducing blending for the first time.

Another way to gain student attention and provide the most practice is to maintain a perky pace by minimizing the transition time between questions or activities. Mr. Williams always conducted a lively, fast-paced class. His students sat criss-cross on the rug during his animated segmenting instruction. When he taught students to segment the following four words—*run, mat, sit,* and *fun*—he thrust out his fingers with a staccato rhythm which students copied as they segmented the words. After the students had segmented *run* correctly, Mr. Williams immediately presented the word *mat*. He knew that an effective teacher is also an actor and that quick transitions were essential to keeping the attention of his audience. After his students had segmented all of the words, Mr. Williams moved quickly to the next part of the lesson: letter sounds.

Increase Support for New Learning

Segmenting and blending spoken words are often difficult skills for students to learn. You can increase support for children as they learn these skills by first carefully demonstrating the new skill, then performing the skill with the students, and finally having students perform the skill on their own. Let's take a look at how Ms. Ortez ensured her students' success on the first day she taught blending consonant–vowel–consonant words beginning with continuous sounds such as /m/ and /r/.

Step 1: My Turn   Ms. Ortez introduced the first new word by saying the three sounds (/m/ /a/ /n/) before quickly blending them into the new word *man*. "All eyes up here. Today we're going to play *Say It Fast*. I'm going to say a word slowly, and you'll say the word fast. **My turn. /m/ - /ă/ - /n/. man.**"

Step 2: Together   Ms. Ortez then repeated the same learning activity with her students saying, **"Together. /m/-/ă/-/n/. What word?"** (signal) **"*man*. Yes, the word is 'man.'"** If students blended the correct word with her, she moved on to the next step.

Step 3: Your Turn   Finally, Ms. Ortez asked the students to blend the word on their own. **"Your turn. /m/-/ă/-/n/. What word?"** (signal). **"Yes, the word is 'man.'"** When students blended all of the words correctly, Ms. Ortez called on two or three students individually to blend the word. She usually called on students whose test results showed that they were having more difficulty blending so that she could provide extra help on the spot. Since students still had difficulty blending some of the words, Ms. Ortez introduced the next word with a My Turn.

The number of Togethers that a teacher uses during a lesson depends on the difficulty of the skill. Students usually catch on to blending more quickly and require fewer questions asking them to answer with the teacher. After the first two words, Ms. Ortez would probably begin to skip Step 2 in her instruction. As long as the students are correctly answering, this step would not be necessary. In contrast, segmenting sounds is more difficult than blending, often requiring that a teacher say the sounds with the students for most or all of the lesson. Students have more difficulty articulating /ĕ/ in *pen* or splitting the word *hat* into /h/-/ă/-/t/. How do you know precisely the right time to move from Togethers to Your Turns? Student accuracy is the only way to make this determination. Move on when students respond firmly and seem to anticipate your response before you make it.

The end goal of instruction is getting students to answer independently. Teachers know their students have acquired a new skill when instruction begins with Step 3, Your Turn, and the class correctly answers every question. Our teacher, Ms. Ortez, knew that her students were ready to move on to a new skill when she could ask them Your Turn questions for blending consonant–vowel–consonant words beginning with continuous sounds, and they would rapidly blend the words without help. The next day Ms. Ortez began asking her students to blend more difficult words, beginning with stop sounds. Because she was teaching a new skill, Ms. Ortez again started her instruction with My Turn examples for the new words.

Stretch and Connect Sounds   In the approach for teaching segmenting described thus far, children are taught to pause between each of the segmented sounds. This approach is the most common one used in beginning reading programs and works well for a majority of students (Bursuck et al., 2004). However, pausing between the sounds may make blending the sounds into spoken words more difficult for students who are at risk (Weisberg & Savard, 1993). For example, while Mr. Halpern's students were able to say each of the individual sounds in *mat*, when asked to blend the sounds together, many students said *at*, leaving out the first letter. Chard and Osborne (1999) suggest that many children who are at risk benefit from teachers modifying the segmenting task by stretching out and connecting the sounds, such as saying the sounds in *Sam* as /sssăăămmm/. By not pausing or stopping between the sounds, children are less likely to make blending errors. As all children who are at risk do not need this stretch approach, teachers might want to use it as extra support as part of Tier 2 or Tier 3 instruction. On the other hand, making stretch blending/segmenting a part of your Tier 1 instruction may allow you to meet the needs of more of your students within the larger instructional group.

The Reflective Teacher

Always Analyzing Students' Answers

Even though Ms. Ortez structured her teaching to ensure the most success, her students still made errors during instruction. For example, after Ms. Ortez said /l/-/ă/-/p/, a number of students answered *map*. Rather than blending the word, these students had rhymed. In order to correct errors consistently each time the students answered incorrectly, Ms. Ortez remembered that she must return to the procedure that she used when first teaching the blending skill—namely, My Turn–Together–Your Turn.

"My turn. /l/-/ă/-/p/. *lap.*"

"Together. /l/-/ă/-/p/. What word?" (signal) "*lap.*"

"All by yourselves. /l/-/ă/-/p/. What word?" (signal) "*lap.*"

After Ms. Ortez took students through these three steps for the missed word *lap,* she asked the students to blend another word. If the students correctly blended it, she then asked them to once again blend /l-/ă/-/p/. She made sure that she asked the missed word two or three more times during her blending instruction. By asking her students to blend the missed word several times, she reduced the probability that students would miss the same word the next day.

After correcting the students' error, Ms. Ortez quickly analyzed the mistake. She asked herself whether the students blended incorrectly because of something she had done. Did she use an effective signal, had she praised the students, was her pace perky, did she get the students' attention before she asked the question? If her teaching was the problem, she knew she must immediately change what she was doing.

Because Ms. Ortez's students were enthusiastically answering and she had praised students at her normal rate of about once a minute, she immediately asked herself whether the error occurred because she started asking Your Turn questions before students were ready for them. Thinking back to her instruction during the past two weeks, Ms. Ortez reflected that students routinely answered eight or more of the blending questions during her Your Turn instruction. She knew that she waited to begin omitting the My Turn–Together–Your Turn steps of instruction until students no longer needed that more intensive support. Thus, Ms. Ortez had not left the Your Turn phase of instruction too early. In the space of a few seconds, without slowing down her instruction, Ms. Ortez analyzed the students' error, determining that they were still occasionally answering with a rime rather than the blended word. Ms. Ortez reasoned that even though this error did not occur often, she would not move on to more difficult words beginning with stop sounds until student success increased for blending words with continuous sounds. She concluded that her class needed more practice and that tomorrow they would practice blending more consonant–vowel–consonant words beginning with continuous sounds. At the end of blending practice when students moved to their tables for another activity, Ms. Ortez quickly made a note of the blending error on the clipboard she always had at her side. She wanted to remember the errors and provide more practice by asking students to blend sounds in the word *lap* while they were waiting in the stalled lunch line outside of the cafeteria.

Provide Ongoing Review   Phonemic awareness skills build on themselves, so ongoing review is automatic as long as students move through the skills according to the sequence described in the text. For example, segmenting at the onset-rime level (*mat* = /m/-/ăt/) automatically incorporates first sound segmenting, so a student who is segmenting onset-rime does not need to also practice that earlier skill.

Since phonemic awareness skills are sequential, teachers who teach to success, checking out whether students are at mastery before moving on to more difficult skills, have more students in their class meet DIBELS benchmarks. When Mr. Halpern's students were struggling with blending individual sounds, he did not move on to the more difficult format of segmenting individual sounds. Instead, he provided more support for blending, conducting blending activities at the My Turn level, increasing the time students spent in booster sessions, and using opportunities throughout the day to provide short practice sessions. He knew that if he moved on too quickly to individual sound segmenting, some of his students would be so confused that they would not learn either blending or segmenting. Even though a few other teachers at his grade level were several lessons ahead of his class, Mr. Halpern knew that the extra time taken to teach this important skill to his students would pay off.

Increase the Motivation   When students first move to the next phonemic awareness skill or when the words used for that skill are more difficult, teachers who recognize the increased difficulty level and integrate more motivation into the lesson keep students working their hardest. Teachers can raise the motivation level by increasing their animated teaching level, by increasing the number of times they praise students for their hard work, and by telling students that if they work their hardest during the phonemic awareness activity, they will be able to play a favorite sound game after the lesson. Students may need increased motivation during these more difficult phonemic awareness activities:

- Blending or segmenting words that contain more sounds
- Blending or segmenting words that begin with stop sounds
- Blending or segmenting words that begin with or contain consonant blends such as /tr/ or /st/
- Blending or segmenting words that contain the /ĕ/ sound

On a long Monday, some teachers vary their inflection as they blend sounds to create novelty. Using "turtle talk" or "whisper talk," teachers and students slowly and quietly enunciate the sounds for the day's words. On school picture day when students are excitable and increased motivation helps maintain a perky pace, these teachers tell their students that it is "robot talk" day and everyone will segment and blend in a robotic monotone.

During her planning period, Ms. Orton decided that the next day when she asked her students to blend several words starting with the /l/ sound, she would teach to success by telling her class that if they did their best work and put together all of their new words correctly, Toby the Tiger would come out of his box and sing a song about his favorite roaring sounds.

Providing Differentiated Instruction

Often the teaching activities suggested in commercial reading programs are not systematic and explicit enough for your students who are at risk. Shown below is a phonemic awareness activity similar to ones that often appear in commercial general education reading programs. The objective for the activity is to segment the three-phoneme words *bat, tap,* and *rat.*

> Using a puppet, have the puppet show the children a picture of a man. After the children say the picture name out loud, have the puppet ask the children to say the word *man* slowly— that is, to segment the sounds. If necessary, have the puppet say /m/-/ă/-/n/. Once the children grasp the idea, have them segment other words such as *bat, tap,* and *rat.*

As written, this lesson may not provide enough support for new learning. Consider the following ways to differentiate instruction for your students who are at risk by using the Tier 1 enhancements described in the text.

To increase student responding and attention, use the puppet's clapping as a signal for the students' unison answers. Each time the puppet's hands come together, the children should say the next sound in the word. To set a perky pace, keep your talk to minimum as you emphatically tell students: "Today Mr. Puppet will teach you to say words the slow way. Every time Mr. Puppet claps, say a sound." To further increase the number of answers students make per minute, have the list of words accessible so you can move quickly from one word to the next.

If segmenting represents new learning for the children, do a My Turn–Together–Your Turn as follows:

"Listen to Mr. Puppet take apart the word *man.* /m/ /ă/ /n/."

"Together with Mr. Puppet. Take apart *man.*" (extend finger) "/m/" (extend finger) "/ă/" (extend finger) "/n/. Yes. The sounds in man are /m/ /ă/ /n/."

"Your turn. Take apart *man.*" (extend finger) "/m/" (extend finger) "/ă/" (extend finger) "/n/. Yes. The sounds in man are /m/ /ă/ /n/."

If students are struggling with segmenting, teach to success by continuing with the Together step until students are able to segment accurately on their own. When students have learned to segment sounds and are applying that new learning, have Mr. Puppet provide the signal for a series of Your Turn questions.

When students make an error while segmenting with Mr. Puppet, consistently correct by having the puppet demonstrate and say the word slowly. Next ask students to say the word slowly with the puppet before asking them to say the word slowly by themselves. Remember to ask students to segment a missed word at least two more times during the lesson as well as later in the day.

If the students do not respond on signal or start making a number or errors, integrate increased motivation into the activity. Tell your students that they will have a contest with Mr. Puppet to see who can get more points. The puppet will get a point every time students do not answer to the signal or when they make an error segmenting a word. Students get points for answering to the puppet's claps and for saying the correct sounds in a word.

Because segmenting individual sounds incorporates all of the earlier segmenting skills, you do not have to add segmenting review. Blending individual sounds is not included in the lesson, so you need to provide review by having Mr. Puppet ask the students to say some words the fast way.

Seize the Teachable Moment

All Day Long

Teaching phonemic awareness takes place all day—not just during reading block. When you are discussing the afternoon assembly that was about "birds of prey," ask students to tell you the first sound they hear in the word *falcon.* If some students do not answer, go into a My Turn–Together–Your Turn pattern and immediately teach on the spot. Ask them to take apart the word *eagle.*

After a fire drill, ask students to tell you what sound they hear at the beginning of *fire.* You will probably get giggles when you ask for the sound at the start of the word *bathroom,* just before you walk down to that room. After morning announcements ask the students to tell you the first sound in *morning.* Do not forget to ask about the word *music* before your students trot down to music class. Try to catch important words that start with the sounds your students are learning.

How Can I Help Students Who Still Are Not Learning to Segment and Blend, Even with Enhancements?

Depending on where you teach, as many as one- to two-thirds of your students may need extra practice learning to segment and blend despite enhanced instruction carried out in the large group. Tier 2 booster sessions conducted in small groups or one-to-one provide extra practice before or after your large-group phonemic awareness instruction.

Tier 2 Booster Sessions

These booster sessions typically involve more practice with the skills covered that day in Tier 1 and can be taught by the classroom teacher or by paraprofessionals or even peer or cross-age tutors, provided they are appropriately trained. A relatively quiet corner in the hallway or in a corner of the library can be more effective than a noisy classroom. Teachers who have booster sessions often pull students during quiet time. Sometimes teachers will work with a small group in the hallway during computer lab, pulling out the students who need extra time. Given the time and personnel constraints involved, the key to having an effective system of boosters is efficiency. You want to teach as effectively as possible in the smallest amount of time. If you use unison responses during the booster sessions, the formats shown in Tables 2.3 to 2.5 can be delivered in approximately 10 minutes.

After each progress-monitoring assessment, you can form your booster groups for the month. Refer to the tables and select the format(s) that represent(s) the earliest sequential skill that the student hasn't mastered. Trina and Craig are in Ms. Glendell's class, which is now working on segmenting onset-rime. Because Trina and Craig still cannot segment first sound, Ms. Glendell will practice segmenting first sound during their booster sessions. If Terri's and Javon's assessments show that they cannot blend onset-rime, Ms. Glendell will practice those formats with them during boosters. Later in the month if they have success blending onset-rime, Ms. Glendell will use the booster time to work on segmenting onset-rime with these two students. When next month's assessment is given, Terri and Javon, having caught up to the group, may no longer need boosters, but two or three other students may now need to start them. Trina and Craig may finally have mastered first sound so they can practice blending onset-rime during boosters. These extra practice sessions ensure that students immediately get the extra help they need when their continuous progress comes to a halt.

How Can I Help Students Who Still Are Not Learning to Segment and Blend, Even with Daily Tier 2 Booster Sessions?

The decision to place a student into an alternative, more intensive reading program is an important, yet difficult, one. On the one hand, you want all students to succeed in the general education reading program. On the other hand, given the poor catchup rate for students who get behind, you don't want to prolong their placement in a more intensive program. Because of the importance of the Tier 3 placement decision, it is recommended that performance in multiple areas be considered, including phonemic awareness as well as letter–sound identification and letter naming fluency. DIBELS Letter Naming Fluency is a valid indicator of linguistic processing speed and a good predictor of future reading

Research to Practice

What We Learned about Booster Sessions

Kindergarten teachers and school staff working in Project PRIDE conducted daily 5- to 10-minute booster sessions for students whose monthly phonemic awareness test scores indicated that they were not successful with that skill. The number of booster groups in a classroom depended on the needs of the students and how effectively skills were taught that month. During January, Ms. Grayson had four new students move into her class, requiring her to add two new booster groups. That same month, Ms. Winters doubled the amount of time she was teaching blending in the large group and substantially reduced the number of daily booster groups. Some students needed the support they gained in booster groups all year; others attended boosters for only a month or two when their progress stalled on one of the phonemic awareness skills. Here are some tips on how to conduct booster sessions based on our PRIDE experience.

Because research indicates that instruction in small groups of three is as effective as one-to-one instruction (Vaughn et al., 2003), booster groups were typically comprised of three students. Some PRIDE teachers who did not have many students needing booster support preferred to conduct individual one-on-one booster instruction, claiming that their most inattentive students were more on task. In one-on-one instruction, teachers could repeatedly refocus these students' attention to their mouths. Teachers found that larger groups of between three and five students worked better with students who were almost at mastery. The teachers learned that students who were struggling with acquiring phonemic awareness skills often needed to use hand-held mirrors and combine articulation practice with blending or segmenting. One-on-one booster instruction made this intensive support easier.

In addition to using mirrors, PRIDE teachers found that when a student's progress was stalled at the blending stage, sometimes adding three-dimensional letters spurred progress. Pushing together interlocking blocks with letters matching the blended word was an adaptation that worked for some students. When students were not hearing a sound during segmenting, the teachers stretched out the sound. For example, when Johnette had trouble hearing the /l/ in *flap*, Mr. Dirksen had her stretch out the /l/ sound for two seconds so that she could distinctly hear it.

All of the PRIDE teachers reported that they found it more beneficial to conduct booster groups in relatively quiet locations. Some teachers found that sitting on the floor in the corridor just outside the classroom door was more effective than working in the classroom. Other teachers conducted boosters during rest time or had school staff work with their students in a hall alcove.

Teachers found that if their classroom paraprofessionals or other school staff conducted the booster groups, careful, coordinated training was essential. Student progress stalled unless booster teachers used the same Tier 1 enhancements as the classroom teachers (e.g., My Turn–Together–Your Turn, increased motivational strategies, and perky pace).

Results from the first two years of Project PRIDE showed that in November of kindergarten, children who continued to perform at low levels in blending onset-rimes and letter sounds despite daily boosters were most likely to experience reading problems at the end of grade 1. For this reason a more intensive, alternative reading curriculum was recommended for these children beginning in December.

Summary of Booster Tips

- Form groups containing between one and three students.
- Place students having the most difficulty in the smallest groups.
- Conduct instruction in a relatively quiet location so students can clearly hear the sounds.
- Keep focusing distractible students' attention to your mouth.
- Stretch out difficult sounds that students have difficulty hearing.
- Use manipulatives to jumpstart blending and segmenting for students who are not progressing.
- Use mirrors to help provide visual feedback for students who have difficulty saying a new sound.
- Carefully train anyone teaching booster groups so that they are consistent in teaching the phonemic awareness formats.
- Remember that students who do not make adequate progress in booster sessions despite these adaptations may require a more intensive alternative Tier 3 reading curriculum.

problems. In this assessment, which is described in more detail in Chapter 3, students are shown a randomized list of upper and lower case letters and are asked to name as many letters as they can in 1 minute. Benchmarks for this test are shown in Table 3.2 (p. 78). Scores in the at-risk range in Letter Naming Fluency help strengthen the case for Tier 3 instruction, particularly in borderline cases.

Tier 3 Placement Rules

The decision to place a student in Tier 3 is made according to the following research-based decision rules.

In January of kindergarten the student scores less than 10 segments per minute on the DIBELS Phonemic Segmentation Fluency Assessment and/or less than 10 on the DIBELS Initial Sound Fluency Assessment and/or less than 15 on the DIBELS Letter Naming Fluency Assessment. Although these assessments are not part of the formal criteria for Tier 3 placement, a score of 40% or lower in blending (see p. 36) and/or less than 60% in letter sounds (see p. 73) represent additional at-risk factors.

In May of kindergarten the student scores less than 10 on the DIBELS Phonemic Segmentation Fluency Assessment and/or less than 29 on the DIBELS Letter Naming Fluency Assessment and/or less than 15 letters per minute on the DIBELS Nonsense Word Fluency Assessment (see p. 78). As described above, scores of below 40% in blending and below 60% in letter sounds represent additional at-risk factors.

Intensive, Alternative Reading Programs for Tier 3

Table 2.6 lists and compares five reading programs (*Reading Mastery, Lindamood®: LiPS, Reading Recovery, Wilson Reading System,* and *Language!*) that are frequently used by school districts in different parts of the country for students requiring intensive intervention. These programs represent different approaches to beginning reading, differing substantially in their emphases on phonemic awareness and phonics, how those skills are taught, and how they are connected to word and story reading. Subsequent chapters will include an analysis of how these reading programs teach the critical reading skill addressed in that chapter. Additional reading programs that could be used for Tier 3 instruction, but weren't included because of space constraints are: *Read Well, REWARDS, Corrective Reading, Orton-Gillingham,* and the *Spalding Method.*

How Can I Teach Phonemic Awareness to English Language Learners?

More than six million students in the United States live in households where English is not the primary language. About 45% of these English language learners come to school with extremely limited English proficiency. Adding to the challenges posed by language differences, three-fourths of these six million students come from high-poverty households (National Research Council, 2000). Language and poverty provide a double challenge for reading educators, and far too often these students are over-identified as needing special education services. Equally problematic is the high proportion of secondary-level English language learners whose frustration with school and the reading demands of the higher grades leads them to drop out before the twelfth grade.

TABLE 2.6 Comparison of Commonly Used Tier 3 Approaches

	Direct Instruction: Reading Mastery	Lindamood®: LiPS	Reading Recovery	Wilson Reading System	Language!
What phonemic awareness skills are explicitly taught?	Blending Segmenting Rhyming	Blending Segmenting Phoneme deletion Counting phonemes Phoneme manipulation	Segmenting and blending	Segmenting and blending are not taught as separate skills, but in context of phonics.	Blending Segmenting Rhyming Phoneme deletion Phoneme substitution Phoneme reversals
How much time is spent on phonemic awareness instruction?	Beginning 30- to 60-minute lessons are split between phonemic awareness and letter-sound identification and writing.	Beginning 45- to 60-minute lessons are split between phonemic awareness, letter-sound identification, and writing.	Segmenting and blending instruction comprises a small part of the 30-minute lessons that cover seven activities each day.	Students finger-tap sounds (segmentation) when decoding words (approximately 30% of lesson)	5 to 10 minutes of the lesson
What is the instructional setting?	One-to-one instruction, small group, or large classroom	One-to-one instruction, small group, or large classroom	One-to-one instruction	One-to-one, unless with a Wilson certified teacher, who works with small groups of 3 to 5 students. Wilson group certification enables teacher to work with 10 to 12 students.	One-to-one instruction, small group, or large classroom
What determines students' placement in curriculum?	Current achievement level placement test	Current achievement level All students start at beginning of program. Some students will move more quickly through curriculum.	No grouping	All students must begin in Step 1. Some students will move more quickly through curriculum.	Current achievement level, based on placement test.
Are students required to know letter sounds of words they are orally blending or segmenting?	No	Yes	No	Yes	Yes

Continued

53

TABLE 2.6 Continued

	Direct Instruction: Reading Mastery	Lindamood®: LiPS®	Reading Recovery	Wilson Reading System	Language!
Are words taught during phonemic awareness specifically coordinated with first words read in isolation and later in stories?	Yes	Yes	No	Coordination of first sounds, first words read in isolation, and later in stories.	Yes
Do lessons move from simpler phonemic awareness skills to ones that are more difficult?	Yes	Yes	No	No. Phonemic awareness (blending and segmenting) is taught in context of reading.	Yes
What multi-sensory activities are included as part of beginning phonemic awareness/letter-sound recognition instruction?	Lessons include student action requiring students to hold up fingers for sounds that they segment, and move fingers as they blend sounds into words. Visual feedback (pictures) is provided after some blending activities.	Lessons include moving lip pictures, moving blocks, moving counters, moving letter tiles, use of mirrors to provide feedback on phoneme production, and the manipulation of syllable cards.	Lessons include placing counters or letters into sound boxes.	Finger tapping (each finger is tapped to the thumb) while the student says the separate sounds of the word, moving magnetic letters to form words, repeating sounds and locating appropriate graphemes, moving graphemes to form words.	Fingers are raised for each separate sound in a word. Various activities in which students move markers or letters. Sound and letter cards are manipulated.
Are continuous sounds stretched longer for emphasis in phonemic awareness instruction?	Stretched sounds are used throughout the curriculum, both in phonemic awareness activities and later in decoding words.	Stretched sounds are sometimes used when the student has difficulty with phonemic awareness tasks.	No	No	No
What other intensive supports are used to teach phonemic awareness?	Scripted lessons follow a carefully designed sequence of instruction. Students move from teacher-guided instruction to independent student-guided instruction	Use of Socratic questioning throughout lessons develops the student's ability to evaluate his own thinking and to self-monitor. Choice and contrast questioning is used as	Teacher-student conversations are emphasized as a technique to assist student in problem solving. Students move from teacher-guided instruction to independent	None	An extensive resource binder includes numerous activities for developing phonemic awareness. There is a separate book titled *Sounds and letters for readers and spellers: Phonemic*

	awareness drills for teachers and speech–language pathologists. The book contains a variety of sequenced phonemic awareness drills to be used with each lesson. Use of counters, stickies and other manipulatives is encouraged. Various templates aid listening to sounds in words.	student-guided instruction through modeling and questioning.	Mastery tests at the end of each unit include a section on phoneme segmentation. However, this is tied in with decoding. There is no separate purely auditory phonemic awareness assessment.
	through careful implementation of the My Turn–Together–Your Turn strategy. Coordinated correction procedures are used for student errors.	correction procedure for student errors, allowing student to discover errors and correct them.	No separate assessment for phonemic awareness. Sound segmentation through finger tapping is a basic part of each lesson. Students must be able to correctly tap (segment) each word before moving to the next sub-step.
What assessments are conducted?	Brief placement test assesses how much teacher support a student will need for success. Students begin the curriculum at the lesson designated by the assessment. Short mastery tests given to students approximately every five lessons determine whether students are ready to move to the next lesson or should move to a faster- or slower-paced group.	The Lindamood Auditory Conceptualization (LAC) Test, which contains a variety of phonemic awareness measures paralleling skills taught in the program, is given to determine appropriate groups for instruction. Although some groups may move through lessons more quickly, all students start at the beginning of the program. Ongoing observation of the student's daily performance on phonemic awareness tasks during lessons provides the foundation for decisions on how quickly to move the student through the program.	The phonemic awareness section of the initial battery of observational assessments requires students to write a sentence or two dictated by the teacher, who then analyzes the number of written phonemes. Ongoing observation of writing helps the teacher determine words to use for segmenting.

Bridging the Gap

Should I Use Manipulatives to Teach Phonemic Awareness?

Many beginning reading programs recommend the use of manipulatives to teach phonemic awareness. The purpose of the manipulatives is to make the abstract concept of sounds within spoken words more concrete. The types of manipulatives used varies. Some programs use interlocking plastic blocks. Students say a sound for each block and then lock all the blocks together to make a word. Other programs have students place plastic counters on a row of empty boxes appearing on a page as they say the sounds in a word and then blend the sounds together.

Unfortunately, only three studies have looked directly at the relationship between manipulatives and student learning of phonemic awareness skills (Elkonin, 1973; Lewkowicz & Low, 1979; Young, 1999). The results of these studies are mixed. Elkonin and Lewkowicz and Low found that students who were taught to segment using manipulatives performed better than children who were not. Elkonin also found that the various types of manipulatives were equally effective. Young (1999), on the other hand, found that direct instruction formats with and without manipulatives were equally effective.

Given the mixed results of the research, as well as our own classroom experience, the following approach to the use of manipulatives is recommended.

- Use manipulatives only after less-intrusive strategies such as the ones recommended in this chapter (See Tables 2.3–2.5) have been attempted first.
- Use manipulatives when working with students in small groups or one-to-one. Using manipulatives in larger groups can be difficult to manage and monitor.
- Once students are able to segment or blend using manipulatives, gradually fade them out.

The connection between phonemic awareness and reading has been demonstrated in both alphabetic and nonalphabetic languages. Research studies with Spanish-speaking students have shown that phonemic awareness in Spanish skills predicts later word recognition in English. More than IQ or language ability, phonemic awareness assessment provides a way for schools to identify who will need additional early, intensive support in reading (Quiroga, Lemos-Britton, Mostafapour, Abbott, & Berninger, 2002).

As with native English speakers, phonemic awareness training improves later reading performance in English language learners, even when the student receiving the phonemic awareness training is not proficient in English (Roberts & Corbett, 1997). When phonemic awareness training is paired with sound spelling and decoding instruction, word reading shows significant growth (Durgunoğlu & Öney, 1999).

Increase Connections to the First-Language Culture

When teaching phonemic awareness in English to second language learners, you can increase your effectiveness by increasing the cross-connections you make to the first language culture (Gersten, Baker, & Marks, 1998).

1. Once students have mastered a blending or segmenting stage, ask them to blend or segment words in their first language.
2. During story time, ask students to segment key words from a book you've selected about their culture.

3. Find a speaker of the student's first language and train him to teach short phonemic awareness drills. Supplement English phonemic awareness training with training in the native language.
4. Since modeling is critical for English language learners, stay longer at the My Turn phase of instruction.
5. Maintain consistent language and avoid metaphors and idioms that might be confusing.
6. Speak at a slower pace, teaching from a script such as the ones shown in Tables 2.3–2.5.

Research to Practice

Intercultural "Blending"

Three months before Project PRIDE started, our staff assessed the phonemic awareness skills of the Laotian and Vietnamese children in the bilingual kindergarten class at one of our three schools. Although these students recognized common sight words and knew their letter sounds, only 17% could blend simple consonant–vowel–consonant words. The K–5th grade Laotian, Thai, and Vietnamese teachers taught in English for the majority of the day, but students learned to read in both languages, with an emphasis on English. Some teachers described their frustration teaching reading to students who came from Laotian hill tribes without established written languages.

During the teacher training sessions, we wondered if it was realistic to expect the Laotian teachers to use the precise letter–sound articulation for blending and segmenting, a skill the other teachers learned in the first two sessions. Lao and Vietnamese are monosyllabic and tonal languages in which five or six tones determine the meaning of single syllables. When we visited the Laotian classes we observed that students and teachers:

- pronounce /f/ as /th/
- omitted the final /d/ in words or pronounced it as /t/
- did not use plurals
- often pronounced /s/ and /j/ as /sh/
- pronounced /ā/ as /ĕ/; pronounced /ĭ/ as /ē/

Our decision about whether to conduct phonemic awareness training in Lao or English was resolved by the bilingual teachers who wanted to use the same Midwestern pronunciation as their peers. Using audio tapes to practice at home and practicing with the teaching coach at school, the teachers learned to articulate the precise Midwestern phonemes for their blending and segmenting instruction with the exception of /ĭ/. Because even with extended practice, teachers and students continued to pronounce /ĭ/ as /ē/, everyone agreed to accept that substitution. When a student in the bilingual class was given the DIBELS segmenting assessment, credit was given for three phonemes when *pig* was segmented as /p/-/ē/-/g/.

Another issue that arose during the initial training sessions was more quickly resolved. During the first practice session of the training, a distraught Thai teacher approached us and said that she could not snap her fingers as a signal for unison answers, a signal we were modeling during training. She explained that in her culture snapping fingers indicated that a woman was a prostitute. Assuring us that she was not offended when Westerners snapped our fingers, she said, "We understand that Americans do not understand this. Anything you do is okay. We just cannot do." The Thai teacher was visibly relieved when we told her that alternative signals such as clapping were just as effective as finger snapping.

Student success in learning to blend and segment in the bilingual classes was accelerated through the teaching style of the Asian teachers. Accustomed to integrating more drill and memorization activities into daily lesson plans than their American counterparts, the teachers often extended the recommended 10-minute time period for phonemic awareness skills so that

Continued

their students had more time to practice articulating the precise phonemes. Maintaining the expectation that every student in their class would honor them by doing well on the assessment, teachers gave more turns to students having the most difficulty.

The teachers honored their students by praising their good work at least once every minute. Correct answers for difficult words were often followed by praise in the form of group applause. Routinely, the teachers praised their students ten or eleven times for each time they corrected their work or their behavior.

Some cultural differences presented new challenges to teaching a three-tiered model. Bilingual teachers wanted to continue teaching all their students the same material in a large group in order not to isolate any student. Thus, instead of forming small booster groups, the teachers conducted booster groups for the entire class. Because some of the younger students would only learn to segment and blend if they received instruction in a small group, the team decided to have the Title 1 teacher instruct the small booster groups. The Title 1 teacher came into the classroom every afternoon and pulled out two small groups of three children for extra practice in the relatively quiet hallway outside the classroom. As the bilingual teachers observed their students in boosters catching up to the rest of the class, they began to feel more comfortable about the concept of small practice groups. They continued to push their students to correctly answer all the questions on the monthly assessments so that very few students needed to leave for the 5-minute booster sessions.

After being taught phonemic awareness skills since the beginning of the school year, the new group of kindergarten bilingual students were tested in March to see if teaching phonemic awareness had made a difference. This time 80% of the students blended words successfully. Explicit practice ensured that almost everyone had learned a key phonemic awareness skill needed to successfully meet the challenges of first grade.

How Important Is Phonemic Awareness Instruction for Older Learners?

Although the National Reading Panel indicated that studies with older readers with disabilities showed that phonemic awareness training improved reading skills in students from second to sixth grade, the relatively few studies with older students leave more questions than answers. Phonemic awareness instruction for older students does not lead to the same improvement in spelling that is observed in younger students. Meanwhile, debate continues about whether valuable classroom time spent in actual decoding instruction with written text, when students are blending letters into words, will more efficiently accelerate the older learners' progress in catching up to their peers.

When assessment shows that older students are still not fluently blending or segmenting and you believe they would benefit from 5 minutes of practice each day, use the individual sound formats: "Say the sounds in shake. /sh/-/ā/-/k/." Be sure that students verbally segment words before they write them. When students make mistakes segmenting, use the explicit teaching strategies My Turn–Together–Your Turn by immediately modeling the correct phonemes and then asking students to repeat them. A few minutes later, ask the students to segment the same troublesome word. Using a rap rhythm to segment motivates some older students, as does holding a microphone. Add a karaoke machine for additional motivation.

How Can I Use Games to Reinforce the Phonemic Awareness Skills That Students Have Learned?

During the **acquisition stage of learning** when students are first learning to accurately blend or segment, teachers should avoid games and minimize the amount of errors that

Technology

Phonemic Awareness

Although research has demonstrated that computer-assisted instruction can lead to student growth in phonemic awareness, teacher instruction is still more effective. Educators hope that as increasingly sophisticated computer programs are developed, the gap between instruction presented by a teacher versus a computer will be reduced. To date, the inability of computers to recognize phonemes and words pronounced by students remains the greatest drawback of computer-assisted instruction in teaching phonemic awareness. A teacher hears that a student said /n/ instead of /m/ and provides immediate feedback, first pronouncing the correct phoneme and then saying it with the student. Computer-assisted instruction is still unable to incorporate this type of feedback.

Despite this major drawback, computer-assisted instruction teaching phonemic awareness has improved substantially over the past decade. High-quality graphics and improved digitized speech accompany programs using game formats. These instructional games will predictably lead to growth for students who can quickly learn phonemic awareness through a My Turn instructional format. Students receiving computer instruction have increased their phonemic awareness, and this increase has led to improvement in reading. Some teachers attempt to lessen the disadvantages of computer-assisted instruction by training paraprofessionals or volunteers to provide feedback and immediate corrections as they sit with students working at the computer. Questions to ask when selecting a computer-assisted training program include:

1. Does the pronunciation of the phonemes match what I teach during classroom phonemic awareness instruction? Are the stop sounds articulated without schwas?

2. Does the program allow the teacher to determine a sequence of sounds? If I have taught the following sounds, /a/, /i/, /b/, /m/, /s/, /t/, /f/, can I adjust the program to have students only segment words that contain those phonemes?

3. Is the game format distracting to the instruction? Will students continue their adventure quest even though they make errors?

4. Does the program keep a record that I can later use to identify the accuracy rate for an individual student's work?

students who are at risk make in order to avoid spending unnecessary time reteaching. After students acquire the new skill and move into the second stage of learning, the **fluency stage,** they will continue to need practice with the new skill in order to become more fluent. Once students are accurate and fluent with the new skill, instruction can then focus on assisting them to generalize the skill to new situations. A student who has just learned to segment individual sounds with a high level of accuracy will still score below 35 phonemes per minute on the DIBELS Phonemic Segmentation Fluency Assessment because she has not yet developed the speed needed to effortlessly apply this skill at a rapid rate. Gradually increasing the pace of teaching during the Your Turn phase of your instruction develops students' fluency through expanded opportunities for practice. A teacher conducting challenging drill sessions using the segmenting individual sounds format uses rapid-fire questions as she asks the students, "Take apart *bat*," "Take apart *bun*," "Take apart *cake*."

At the *Phonemic Awareness in Young Children* website, reading experts discuss phonemic awareness and provide ideas for related phonemic awareness game activities. **www.readingrockets.org/articles/408.**

In addition to more challenging drill, structured games providing additional practice also provide opportunities to extend learning after students have accurately acquired a skill. After Mr. Jeffries' class was successful segmenting first sound, his class went outside and played *Spiderweb*. When everyone was sitting in a circle, Mr. Jeffries asked one of the students to name the first sound in *cat*. As soon as the student answered, Mr. Jeffries held on to one end of a yarn ball and tossed it to her. Once again he quickly called out another word, and a spider web began taking form after the second correct answer and another throw of the yarn ball. For the next few weeks, Mr. Jeffries would play a number of different games requiring students to segment first sound. In another month, when the class was successful with blending onset-rime, he would start playing the *I Have a Secret* game, asking students to blend the secret words he was making with the onset-rimes he said (/g/-/ōld/).

Games can help or hinder your goal to develop fluency with a newly learned skill depending on how well you structure the game. Games can trigger increased behavior problems if they require long waiting times, have infrequent student turns, last too long, involve rules the students do not fully understand, are perceived by the students as being unfair, or involve manipulatives that the teacher cannot monitor. You can avoid these problems by:

- Preteaching the rules to the game and asking students to practice them before actually playing the game
- Avoiding unnecessary manipulatives
- Using team games where ⅓ to ½ of the students are responding together
- Keeping the game time limited to no longer than 10 or 15 minutes

The selection of games you use will depend on the maturity level and behavioral skills your students have. This year Mr. Jeffries' class is able to play the *Spiderweb* game without students yanking the string out of another student's hand and having the ball roll into the middle of the circle. His class last year was less mature, with more behaviorally challenging students. Last year within 4 or 5 minutes, this *Spiderweb* game would have collapsed into chaos. The extended time it would take to walk outside was not worth the lost learning time. Thus last year, Mr. Jeffries adapted the game into an indoor *Frog Hopping* game, to include more turns and structure. He divided his class into four teams and had each team sit on a line that was part of a larger square. Then Mr. Jeffries called out, "Team 1, what's the first sound in *cat?*" If Team 1 answered by yelling out /c/, he gave a thumbs up and called out a number. All the students on team one then had the opportunity to jump up and down like frogs the specified number of times. Anyone who did not follow the rules and started pushing over the other frogs in his line had to leave the game and sit by Mr. Jeffries' side. Since student turns occurred at least once every one or two minutes, students rarely were called out to the sidelines. After 5 minutes of much-needed exercise, the class was ready to listen to a story.

What Activities Help Students Apply Their New Phonemic Awareness Skills to Reading Words?

Despite its importance to early reading, student acquisition of phonemic awareness skills alone does not guarantee reading achievement. The Report of the National Reading Panel (2000) indicates that the effectiveness of phonemic awareness instruction is significantly enhanced if, at some point during the instruction, children are helped to apply their newly acquired phonological awareness skills directly to simple reading and spelling tasks. As you have probably already noticed, the chapters in this text are organized around key clusters of skills needed to become a mature reader, such as phonemic awareness, phonics, reading fluency, and so forth. While this organizational framework makes conceptual sense, it is not intended to imply that skills within each area are taught in isolation from each other and/or at different times. Therefore, it is critical to integrate letter sounds and beginning word reading and spelling as soon as possible into your phonemic awareness instruction.

Motivating Your Students to Do Their Best

Teaching Classroom Routines and Procedures

Structure and routines provide the predictability so many students who are at risk need to learn. Teachers who preplan rules and procedures, teach them, consistently follow them, and in turn praise students for following them are able to spend more time teaching because their students have fewer disruptive behaviors. These teachers can focus the majority of their attention toward acknowledging student success.

"Everyone in Team 4 is listening to Corisha talk about the dragonfly she saw. Good listening, Team 4."

"Class, give yourselves a pat on the back. We were so quiet walking down the hallway today that no other class was interrupted."

"Two days in a row where everyone remembered to turn in their homework. Way to go."

Transition times between one activity and the next will take less time when students are accustomed to following the classroom procedures, knowing what materials are needed and where to go. During the first week of class a teacher of a more challenging class can teach students to go to their individual work groups by following this procedure:

- Tell students the procedure for breaking into their groups. For example, students should walk quickly and quietly to the designated area when their name or row is called, sit down, and start working on the assigned task.
- Explain that you will always tell the students what materials they need to bring to their groups so they will need to listen carefully.
- Explain that you will set the timer for 3 minutes, which is how long they will have to move into their groups and start working.
- Give the students an easy task so they can practice the transition. Set the timer and monitor the students by walking around and providing redirection if necessary.
- When the timer rings, praise students and give team points for making a smooth transition. If students don't meet the time limit, explain the rules and practice again.
- Once students are following the procedures, discontinue using the timer.

By midyear, kindergarten students are ready to apply their phonemic awareness skills and blend the letter sounds they have learned into words. Wanting to avoid errors during this acquisition stage of learning, the teacher writes large consonant–vowel–consonant words on the board and asks the class to say each letter sound in unison before blending the sounds into a word. Some teachers use large magnetic letters for this early word reading; others have large magnetic word cards they put on the board. Large flip books with three columns of letters that flip over (with vowels in the middle column) allow a teacher to change letters easily so students can read the next word. Early word reading when the class is sounding out novel words without the teacher's assistance should be celebrated by the teacher and communicated to students and parents. Young children have no greater thrill than reading a word all by themselves for the first time. Teachers who help their at-risk students make the connections between these words and interesting books that they will soon be reading increase motivation for learning to read. "Wow! You read the words, *cat, Sam,* and *hat.* The library has some funny books about cats, and you are learning to read some of the words that will be in those books." Once students are easily reading three-letter words, the teacher can move into simple sentences. The use of large sentence strips connected with a ring enables the teacher to have the entire class read the sentence in unison. After students read a sentence, the teacher then asks comprehension questions to connect meaning to the sentences. Even a simple sentence such as "Sam has a hat," allows a teacher to ask, "Who has a hat?" "What is Sam wearing?" "What kind of animal do you think Sam is?" "Why do you think Sam is wearing a hat?" By learning individual letter sounds and blending skills, students rapidly move into independent reading and comprehension connected to that reading. Formats for doing these early reading activities are described in Chapter 3.

The effectiveness of segmenting instruction is also enhanced by connecting segmenting and letter–sound recognition to spelling. From the day when they learn their first letter sound, students should learn to write the letter when their teacher says the sound, "Write /t/." "Write /s/." If you have taught students to write the sounds they have learned each week, students can write readable words as soon as they learn to segment. When students first begin to apply their segmenting to spelling, use large magnetic letters on the board, asking individual students to spell a word the class has just segmented. The other students are then instructed to give a "thumbs up" if the word is spelled correctly, a task which requires everyone's active thinking. Before Ms. Jones asks her class to write *jam,* she first asks them to segment the sounds, /j/-/ă/-/m/. After they have orally segmented the sounds, she asks her students to write the word on the small chalkboards they are holding. In order to immediately correct any mistakes, Ms. Jones has the students hold up their chalkboards facing her as soon as they have written the word. During center times, in addition to writing practice, many teachers use magnetic letters with small groups of students who are segmenting and spelling. Some teachers use more structured sound boxes, requiring students to put sounds of the specified word into each box. Once students are using interchangeable magnets to spell words after segmenting them, the teacher can introduce phoneme manipulation. "You read the word *jam* on the board. Now turn *jam* into *Pam."* Chapters 3 and 4 will provide more ideas on how to move your students into independent reading and spelling.

Table 2.7 lists other classroom procedures teachers need to establish before they start teaching their first reading class. Only by actively monitoring are teachers aware of

TABLE 2.7   Classroom Procedures for Reading Classes

Question	Elaboration
1. How do students participate during class discussions?	Are students supposed to silently raise their hands until called upon? How is this behavior taught? What happens when it is not followed?
2. How do students learn to answer in unison?	How are students taught to follow a signal? What happens when everyone does not answer?
3. What are the procedures for completing assignments?	Do students have a special folder or book for assignments? Is there a designated place in the classroom for them? Are students reminded at the end of the day about materials they need to bring home? How are parents involved in homework completion? What are the consequences for homework that is not completed?
4. What are individual seatwork procedures?	Is quiet talk allowed or are students expected to work silently? Is there a cue such as a raised hand to indicate when the noise level is too high? What is the procedure for interrupting? How do students indicate that they need help when the teacher is walking around and monitoring the class? How do students indicate that they need help when the teacher is working with another group?
5. How are books and materials passed out?	How are students selected to help with these tasks? Have students learned what behaviors are expected while they wait for their materials? Are materials organized so that waiting time is minimized?
6. What are the procedures for students turning in work?	Are there shelves or folders where students turn in completed assignments? What do students do when they have completed their assignments before the allotted time?
7. What are the out of seat policies?	When do students need permission to be out of their seats? What do they do if their pencil breaks? What do they do if they need a drink of water or have to go to the bathroom?

students who are and who are not following the rules and procedures. Whether directly teaching, supervising independent work, or coordinating a transition to another room, a teacher can minimize behavior problems by establishing a feeling of "with-itness" in the classroom (Gunter, Shores, & Rasmussen, 1995). Teachers who are effectively monitoring move around to all corners of the classroom, use their eyes to scan other sections of the classroom than the one they are in, expect eye contact from students in their group, and give feedback on positive as well as off-task behavior.

Fact or Fiction

Two questions about teaching phonemic awareness to students who are at risk are included in this chapter's fact or fiction questions.

Pair up with a partner and take turns defending your position for one of these questions using references from research sources cited in the chapter or from information on the website resources listed in the sidebars.

1. **Teaching skills in phonemic awareness is not sufficient for helping students who are at risk for become successful readers.**

      Fact   Fiction

   Fact: While there is much research that shows that teaching phonemic awareness makes it easier for children to learn to read (Blachman, 2000), it is equally clear that teaching phonemic awareness alone is not enough (Armbruster et al., 2001; National Reading Panel, 2000).
      Children must also develop phonics concepts and apply these skills fluently in text (Lyon, 1998, p. 17). In fact, there is evidence to suggest that learning in both phonemic awareness and word reading are enhanced when phonics and phonemic awareness are taught together (National Reading Panel, 2000), which is the approach taken in this text.

2. **Teaching children using scripted lessons is boring for both the teacher and students.**

      Fact   Fiction

   Fiction. Scripted lessons are teaching formats that specify what the teacher says when presenting information or skills to students. The purpose of the scripts is to ensure that instruction is uniformly clear, efficient, and effective. In this text, scripts are presented for key skill areas to help you present information to your students who are in need of instruction that is presented very carefully. Scripts are also used in *Reading Mastery,* one of the Tier 3 programs described in the text. Scripts can help you be more successful when you are using systematic, explicit reading instruction for the first time. Being successful from the start is important in today's atmosphere of accountability, where beginning teachers cannot afford to improvise. If you follow the scripts faithfully, you can be successful with your children who are at risk from the start of the school year.
      There are those who say that teaching scripts stifle teacher creativity and lead to bored teachers and students. Fleetwood (personal communication, December 9, 2003) offers an analogy in the field of acting in response to this oft-heard criticism.

I ask them if they think actors are creative. And, of course, it's hard to deny that. Then I bring up the point that actors, too, follow a script and very specific directions—what to say, how to say it, where to stand, how to look, how to turn, etc. **but,** it's what they bring to those directions that makes a good actor and a good performance and that is what the audience is looking for. Anyone can stand there and read Shakespeare or Arthur Miller, but it's how you present it that grabs people.

So, you can follow the script, yet still interject your own personalities and styles into the presentations. Of course there is also the fun of teaching students to read who most everyone else has given up on.

Project PRIDE used scripted formats in its Tier 2 kindergarten boosters as well as in its Tier 3 *Reading Mastery* instruction. The results of our yearly teacher satisfaction surveys show uniformly high teacher satisfaction with the scripted materials (see the Preface for specific results). Our teachers have been successful with students whom they had previously given up on, and this success has been very satisfying.

APPLIED ACTIVITIES

1. Listed below are key blending and segmenting skills. Number each skill in the list in the order in which you would teach it.
   a. Blending–Individual Sounds _____
   b. Segmenting–Onset-Rime _____
   c. Blending–Onset-Rime _____
   d. Segmenting–First Sound _____
   e. Segmenting–Individual Sounds _____
2. By November, most students in Ms. Gregg's kindergarten class can tell her the first sound in words that begin with any of the seven sounds taught during the first two months of school. The children can also blend words if she says the word's onset and rime. Describe what skills Ms. Gregg should teach next and in what order she should teach them.
3. During the third week of May, Ms. Harvey gave her kindergarten class the DIBELS test of phonemic segmentation fluency and an informal test of letter sounds and blending individual sounds. Ms. Harvey wanted to identify the students who were at risk for not reading at grade level so that the first grade teacher could provide them with intensive support from the first day of school. Her students' scores on both assessments are shown in Table 2.8. Place each child into one of the following categories based on their performance in phonemic segmentation fluency: *low risk; some risk; at risk.* How did children in each of these categories perform in blending and letter sounds?
4. Figure 2.9 shows a DIBELS phonemic segmentation fluency score sheet for Damien. Based on his answers, identify Damien's current skill level in segmenting, and describe what skills you will now teach him.
5. Orally segment the following four phoneme words into their smallest phonemes without adding any schwas. Count the number of letters in each word.

For each word, determine whether the number of letters equals the number of phonemes. Explain.

Fred   dump   black   stop   gags   help   spray

6. Blend each group of phonemes into a word and write your answer in the blank:
   - /k/ /r/ /ă/ /k/ /s/ _____
   - /b/ /r/ /ĕ/ /d/ _____
   - /t/ /ē/ /m/ _____
   - /l/ /ū/ /v/ /d/ _____
7. Identify the first and final letter–sounds in each of the following words.

	First letter–sound	Final letter–sound
• try	_____	_____
• bride	_____	_____
• fudge	_____	_____
• camp	_____	_____

8. Map the phonemes in each of the following words. The first three have been completed for you:

close	k	l	/ŏ/	z		
greet	g	r	/ē/	t		
temple	t	/ĕ/	m	p	l	
grand						
drain						
sell						
famed						
handed						
mass						
fanned						
sprig						
spill						

TABLE 2.8 Classroom Score Sheet for May

Names	May Blending Score	May Blending Score Percent Correct	May DIBELS Segmenting Score	May Letter Sounds	May Letter Sounds Percent Correct
Allison Cooke	5	100%	57	23	88%
Ben Bradley	5	100%	61	24	92%
Benito Valancia	4	80%	16	10	38%
Carla Gartyn	4	80%	39	26	100%
Dayrone Carton	3	60%	24	25	96%
Garret Crane	5	100%	37	19	73%
Jordan Morris	5	100%	16	26	100%
Juan Menesia	5	100%	40	26	100%
Kendra Thomas	5	100%	36	26	100%
Kent Gray	5	100%	48	20	77%
Kent Schrock	5	100%	37	25	96%
Kissick Bailey	5	100%	47	24	92%
Maria Gomez	5	100%	51	26	100%
Mia Mantos	5	100%	43	26	100%
Monikee Green	5	100%	48	25	96%
Shayleen Sanders	3	60%	5	22	85%
Shireel Brown	4	80%	57	26	100%
Simone Ashton	5	100%	56	25	96%
Tan Lee	5	100%	41	24	92%
Tan Souveythong	4	80%	49	24	92%
Tricia Wilson	5	100%	14	26	100%
Tyrell Jordan	5	100%	46	25	96%

Name: Damien
Date: May 25

bad	/b/ /a/ /d/	lock	/l/ /o/ /k/	3 / 6
that	/th/ /a/ /t/	pick	/p/ /i/ /ck/	3 / 6
mine	/m/ /ie/ /n/	noise	/n/ /oi/ /z/	4 / 6
coat	/c/ /oa/ /t/	spin	/s/ /p/ /i/ /n/	4 / 7
meet	/m/ /ea/ /t/	ran	/r/ /a/ /n/	4 / 6
wild	/w/ /ie/ /l/ /d/	dawn	/d/ /o/ /n/	5 / 7
woke	/w/ /oa/ /k/]	sign	/s/ /ie/ /n/	1 / 6
fat	/f/ /a/ /t/	wait	/w/ /ai/ /t/	_ / 6
side	/s/ /ie/ /d/	yell	/y/ /e/ /l/	_ / 6
jet	/j/ /e/ /t/	of	/o/ /v/	_ / 5
land	/l/ /a/ /n/ /d/	wheel	/w/ /ea/ /l/	_ / 7
beach	/b/ /ea/ /ch/	globe	/g/ /l/ /oa/ /b/	_ / 7

Total 24 / 75

FIGURE 2.9 Damien's DIBELS Phonemic Segmentation Fluency Score Sheet

9. Every day Ms. Hextel asks her class to segment the first sound of words. Demonstrate how you would instruct Ms. Hextel's class using the format in Table 2.3 to teach segmenting first sounds using the following words as examples:

   sat   man   bell   fit   sip

10. By January the kindergartners at Davis Elementary School are ready to begin blending individual phonemes. You are working in one of the classrooms as a substitute teacher. Use the format in Table 2.4 to teach blending individual phonemes using the words listed below as examples. Remember to articulate the phonemes without adding schwas.

    cat   mill   big   win   yes

11. The following blending activity resembles activities included in general education reading programs. Read the activity and then tell how you would enhance it to increase student responding and attention, provide support for new learning, correct errors consistently, include continual review and practice, add motivation, and teach to success.

    "Tell students they are going to play a guessing game with some words. Ask them to listen as you say the word *cat* slowly, separating the three sounds: /k/ /ă/ /t/. Segment the word several times, each time blending the sounds a little more. Then say the word *cat* in a normal way."

    Now ask the students to say other words that you will say in the same way. Encourage them to blend the sounds to say the words.

/k/-/ă/-/p/	cap	/k/-/ŏ/-/p/	cop
/k/-/ō/-/ch/	coach	/k/-/ŭ/-/p/	cup
/k/-/a/-/r/	car	/k/-/ŭ/-/t/	cut

12. Ms. Ortez, who was featured in the "Reflective Teacher" section (p. 47), had to think on her feet as she taught her students to blend phonemes into words. Answer the following questions about her flexible decision making:
    - How did Mrs. Ortez minimize the number of errors her students made?
    - Describe all of the questions that Mrs. Ortez asked herself after her students made an error.

    Select words that Mrs. Ortez can ask her students to blend tomorrow. Demonstrate how she will teach the first two words.

13. Mr. Mixay is teaching his bilingual class how to segment words into individual sounds. On Tuesday, he segmented ten words with his class, and students made errors on four of the ten words presented. Acquisition of this skill has been difficult for the class, and Mr. Mixay noticed that the interest level of a number of students was waning. To get the students motivated, he decided to have them play a board game on Wednesday. In small groups, students moved around the board by segmenting words into individual sounds.

    What do you think of Mr. Mixay's decision to introduce the board game on Wednesday? What else could he have done in this situation to help his students meet the challenge of segmenting words into individual sounds?

14. Carmen is an English language learner in Mr. Bartez's class. When segmenting the word *tape,* she said /d/-/ā/-/p. What should Mr. Bartez do?

15. If you are currently involved in the schools, examine the literacy curriculum used for struggling readers in kindergarten and first grade. Select six of the areas listed in the left-hand column of Table 2.6 and describe how that curriculum addresses each one.

REFERENCES

Armbruster, B., Lehr, F., & Osborn, J. (2001). *Put reading first: The research building blocks for teaching children to read.* Washington, DC: Partnership for Reading.

Blachman, B. (2000). Phonological awareness. In M. Kamil, P. Mosenthal, P. D. Pearson, & R. Barr (Eds.), *Handbook of Reading Research Volume III* (pp. 483–502). Mahwah, NJ: Lawrence Erlbaum.

Bursuck, B., Smith, T., Munk, D., Damer, M., Mehlig, L., & Perry, J. (2004). Evaluating the impact of a prevention-based model of reading on children who are at-risk. *Remedial and Special Education, 25,* 303–313.

Carnine, D. W., Silbert, J., Kame'enui, E. J., & Tarver, S. (2004). *Direct instruction reading* (4th ed.). New Jersey: Merrill Prentice Hall.

Chard, D. J., & Osborn, J. (1999). Phonics and word recognition instruction in early reading programs: Guidelines for accessibility. *Learning Disabilities Research & Practice, 14*(2), 107–117.

Durgunoğlu, A., & Öney, B. (1999). A cross-linguistic comparison of phonological awareness and word recognition. *Reading and Writing: An Interdisciplinary Journal,* (11), 281–299.

Elkonin, D. B. (1973). U.S.S.R.: Methods of teaching reading. In J. Downing (Ed.), *Comparative reading: Cross-national studies of behavior processes in reading and writing* (pp. 551–580). New York: MacMillan.

Gersten, R., Baker, S. K., & Marks, S. U. (1998). Strategies for teaching English-language learners. In K. R.

Harris, S. Graham, & D. Deshler (Eds.), *Teaching every child every day: Learning in diverse schools and classrooms* (pp. 208–249). Cambridge, MA: Brookline Books.

Good, R. H., Kaminski, R. A., & Howe, D. (2005, June). *What data tells us about children and how to support their success.* Presented at AZ Reading First Conference, Phoenix, AZ.

Lewkowicz, N. K., & Low, L. Y. (1979). Effects of visual aids and word structure on phonemic segmentation. *Contemporary Educational Psychology, 4,* 238–252.

Lindamood, P., & Lindamood, P. (1998). *The Lindamood® Phoneme sequencing program for reading, spelling, and speech: LiPS® teacher's manual for the classroom and clinic* (3rd ed.). Austin, TX: Pro-Ed.

Lyon, R. (1998).Why reading is not a natural process. *Educational Leadership, 55*(6), 14–18.

Miller-Young, R. (1999). *The impact of concrete phonemic representations on phonological awareness acquisition of at-risk kindergartners.* Unpublished dissertation. DeKalb: Northern Illinois University.

National Reading Panel. (2000). *Teaching children to read: An evidence-based assessment of the scientific research literature on reading and its implications for reading instruction.* Washington, DC: National Institute of Child Health and Human Development.

National Research Council. (2000). *Testing English Language Learners in U.S. Schools: Report and Workshop Summary.* Committee on Educational Excellence and Testing Equity. Hakuta, K., & Beatty, A. (Eds.), Board on Testing and Assessment, Center for Education. National Academy Press, Washington DC, 12–13.

Quiroga, T., Lemos-Britton, Z., Mostafapour, E., Abbott, R. D., & Berninger V. W. (2002). Phonological awareness and beginning reading in Spanish-speaking ESL first graders: Research into practice. *Journal of School Psychology, 40,* 85–111.

Roberts, T., & Corbett, C. (1997). *Efficacy of explicit English instruction in phonemic awareness and the alphabetic principle for English learners and English proficient kindergarten children in relationship to oral language proficiency, primary language and verbal memory.* (ERIC Document Reproduction Service No. ED 417 403.)

Stanovich, K. (1994). Romance and reality. *The Reading Teacher, 47,* 280–291.

Vaughn, S., Linan-Thompson, S., Bryant, D. P., Dickson, S., & Blozis, S. A.(2003). Reading instruction grouping for students with reading difficulties. *Remedial and Special Education, 24,* 301–315.

Weisberg, P., Savard, P., & Christopher, F. (1993). Teaching preschoolers to read: Don't stop between the sounds when segmenting words. *Education and Treatment of Children, 16*(1), 1–18.

CHAPTER

3 Alphabetic Principle

Key Terms

Automatic word recognition

Consonant Blends

CVC variants

Decodable books

Digraphs

Diphthongs

Grapheme

High-frequency words

Irregular words, also called sight words

Lexical retrieval

Regular words

Sight words

Sound out

Synthetic phonics

Subvocal sounding-out

Objectives

After reading this chapter you will be able to:

1. Identify and describe the sequence of skills needed for students to attain the alphabetic principle.

2. Adapt letter–sound and word reading lessons in general education reading curricula for students who are at risk or who have disabilities.

3. Use assessment data to identify students who are at risk of not attaining the alphabetic principle, diagnose specific letter–sound and word-reading difficulties, and monitor student progress in beginning word reading.

4. Implement strategies for teaching letter sounds and beginning word reading that maximize the probability of students attaining the alphabetic principle.

5. Implement strategies to provide extra help for students for whom the regular classroom reading time is not sufficient.

6. Identify and describe the beginning letter–sound and word-reading components of five commonly used intensive reading programs.

7. Identify and describe ways to help older students attain the alphabetic principle.

8. Explain how beginning letter–sound and word reading instruction can be adapted for English language learners.

What Skills Do I Need to Teach?

Chapter 2 emphasized the importance of assessing and systematically teaching phonemic awareness to students who are at risk, explaining how an understanding of the sound system of spoken language relates to reading. Although this knowledge of our system of spoken language is essential, phonemic awareness is only one component needed for developing accurate and fluent reading. An effective reading program for students who are at risk must also help them attain alphabetic principle, another key component that comprises the focus for this chapter. Alphabetic principle is "the understanding that there are systematic and predictable relationships between written letters and spoken sounds" (Armbruster, Lehr, & Osborn, 2001, p. 12). Students who have alphabetic principle have moved from the earliest stage of reading where they first must sound out individual phonemes before blending them into a word (/k/ + /a/ + /t/ = *cat*) to a more efficient stage where they automatically read words as whole words (*cat*). These students decipher new and familiar regular words accurately and automatically. They also acquire and remember sight words more readily. "In short, knowledge of the alphabetic principle contributes greatly to children's ability to read words both in isolation and connected text." (Armbruster, Lehr, & Osborn, 2001, p. 12). Most importantly, the fluent decoding that results when readers have developed alphabetic principle enables them to focus more thought on the meaning of the text they are reading.

> Learn more about alphabetic principle and the role it plays in decoding: **http://reading.uoregon.edu/au/index.php.**

The purpose of phonics instruction is to establish the alphabetic principle by teaching students the relationship between written letters or **graphemes** and the 41 to 44 sounds of spoken language or phonemes. Educators who minimize the role of phonics in teaching reading argue that the English language does not incorporate a one-to-one relationship between the 41 to 44 sounds and 26 letter symbols. For example, sometimes the sound of /ĕ/ as in *red,* also appears as *ea* as in *bread.* The sound /ā/ can be written *ay* as in *may, a_e* as in *made* or *ai* as in *maid.* These critics ignore the large proportion of regularity in English that justifies the teaching of phonics and is supported by an extensive research literature validating its effectiveness, particularly with children who are at risk or who have disabilities.

The foundation of our book is based on a systematic and explicit phonics approach called **synthetic phonics,** in which student success and independence is emphasized through the use of carefully supported teaching strategies and curriculum. A teacher using a synthetic phonics approach first teaches the most common letter–sound associations in isolation using a logical, success-oriented sequence. With carefully supported teacher instruction, students learn to apply their phonemic awareness skills and knowledge of letter–sound correspondences to sounding out words in lists and sentences as well as spelling from dictation. The teacher provides substantial practice so students apply their decoding skills to reading and writing. Beginning reading books and written assignments are carefully coordinated with those skills.

Synthetic phonics is not the only explicit and systematic way of teaching phonics. Other systematic and explicit phonics programs include analytic phonics, analogy phonics, and phonics through spelling. Analytic phonics emphasizes first teaching the whole word before analyzing letter–sound relationships. In this approach, students learn letter–sound relationships using words they already know. Letter sounds are not introduced in isolation. Analogy-based phonics emphasizes using known word family patterns to identify unknown words. Phonics through spelling emphasizes phonetic spelling as the foundation for word reading. In this approach, students learn to break apart words into phonemes and to spell words by translating the phonemes into letters. Although the many varied systematic and explicit phonics programs are primarily based on one of these categories, realistically most of the programs incorporate strategies from some or all of these approaches. In this book, when we describe how to effectively teach synthetic phonics, we also include recommendations that come from the phonics through spelling approach, analytic phonics approach, and analogy phonics approach.

The systematic and explicit phonics approach described in this text follows a logical sequence of skills needed to read **regular words** accurately and fluently. The first words taught contain the most common sounds of individual letters. Once the student can decode some basic consonant–vowel–consonant (CVC) words, a relatively small number of irregular or sight words are introduced. A list of skills in a typical systematic phonics program is shown in Figure 3.1 and described in the following section. Note the first group of words are likely to appear in beginning phonics programs prior to students attaining the alphabetic principle. Students at this level are reading at the individual letter-sound level with a focus on the most common letter sounds including the short vowels. The second group of words mainly appears after students have reached alphabetic principle and are beginning to decode clusters as opposed to individual sounds.

Sequence for Teaching Alphabetic Principle

Identify the Most Common Sounds of Individual Letters in Isolation   All systematic phonics programs identify a planned sequence for teaching letter–sound correspondences. The most common letter sounds are stressed because they lend more predictability to the beginning reading process and also lead to the eventual identification of more words. A list of the most common letter sounds was shown in Table 1.4. Note that teaching the sounds of letters is recommended before teaching letter names. Students who are at risk are more likely to come to school unable to identify the letters of the alphabet by name. Since these students may have difficulty learning the letter names and sounds at the same time, letter sounds should be taught first because they lead more directly to reading words. Systematic and explicit phonics programs are designed to start instruction in word reading as soon as student success is assured.

An often neglected key to teaching phonics effectively is the careful pronunciation of letter sounds. In the approach to sounds recommended here, great care is taken when teaching students to pronounce consonants without adding an *uh* or schwa sound to each. For example, the sound for the letter *t* is pronounced /t/, rather than /tuh/; the sound for *d* is pronounced /d/, not /duh/, the sound for *p* is pronounced /p/, not /puh/. Saying the consonants without adding schwa sounds makes the blending of sounds into words easier. If Corvon has been taught letter sounds with sloppy schwa endings, he may logically sound out the word *bat* as /buh/ + /a/ + /tuh/ or *buhatuh*. In order to read this word correctly, Corvon must add an extra step and delete the two /u/ sounds contained within the blended word. Teaching letter sounds correctly from the beginning eliminates this problem.

Each systematic phonics program presents its own rationale for the sequence of letter sounds that are introduced. Although the National Panel Report (2000) didn't address the issue, the order in which the letter sounds are taught can influence how quickly students acquire them during instruction (Carnine et al., 2004). Bridging the Gap beginning on page 72 summarizes the rationale behind the order in which letter sounds are taught in two systematic phonics programs.

Read CVC Words   Orally **sound out** lists of single-syllable words that contain letter sounds previously taught. When they sound out, students say each sound in succession, moving from left to right. Students then blend the sounds together to quickly say a word. The first words students read are often referred to as short vowel words or consonant–vowel–consonant (CVC) words, such as *mat* or *sit*. Words beginning with stop sounds (*t, d, b*) are more difficult to read than those beginning with continuous sounds (*m, s, f*). Words with stop sounds in the middle are also more difficult. CVC words are regular words, meaning that they can be sounded out.

Pre-Alphabetic Principle*

1. CVC words beginning with a continuous sound:
   mad, mop, red, rig, sun
2. CVC words beginning with a stop sound:
   bad, did, gun, hot, jet
3. CVCC words ending with a consonant blend or double consonants:
   band, pond, jump, miss, kept
4. CCVC words beginning with a consonant blend:
   clam, frog, glad, skin, step
5. CCVCC, CCCVC, and CCCVCC words beginning and/or ending with a consonant blend:
   blink, glass, slump, split, struck

Post-Alphabetic Principle

1. VCe (silent e) pattern words in which the vowel is long (VCV rule)
   - Words beginning with a single consonant (CVCe):
     hope, cute, Pete, mile, tape
   - Words beginning with a consonant blend (CCVCe):
     skate, spoke, froze, bride, stripe
   - Multisyllable words with a VCe syllable:
     hopeless, excuse, likely, stampede, grateful
2. Letter combinations:
   *ra**i**n, h**ar**m, g**ree**n, cl**ou**d, **sh**ed*
3. Suffixes:
   *miss**ed**, cheer**ful**, midd**le**, ac**tion**, grump**y***
4. Prefixes:
   *amount, **con**duct, **mis**lead, **pro**test, **trans**late, **under**go*
5. CVCe derivative words:
   - Words with *s* endings:
     *bite**s**, cube**s**, mope**s**, plane**s**, time**s***
   - Words with *er* endings:
     *lat**er**, smok**er**, us**er**, brav**er**, tim**er***
   - Words with *ed* endings:
     *hop**ed**, nam**ed**, smil**ed**, smok**ed**, glid**ed***
   - Words with *ing* endings (VCV rule):
     *nam**ing**, rid**ing**, clos**ing**, shad**ing**, bit**ing***
   - Words with *y* endings:
     *grav**y**, spic**y**, bon**y**, shin**y**, wav**y***
   - Words with *est* endings:
     *cut**est**, lat**est**, wis**est**, saf**est**, wid**est***
6. Y-derivative words:
   *fogg**iest** (foggy), funn**ier** (funny), part**ies** (party), bab**ied** (baby)*

* Pre-alphabetic words can be used as oral examples in phonemic awareness activities.

FIGURE 3.1   Phonics Word Types Pre- and Post-Alphabetic Stages

Read CVC-Variant Words   Orally sound out and read lists of single-syllable **CVC-variant** words that contain blends comprised of letter sounds previously taught. Single-syllable words that begin or end with consonant blends are more difficult to read than regular CVC words. **Consonant blends** are two or more successive consonants sounded out in sequence without losing their identity. Examples of consonant blends include *st* as in *stop, nd* as in s*and,* and *st* and *nd* as in *stand.* CVC words containing blends are described by their consonant–vowel pattern and termed CVC-variant words. *Stop* is a CCVC word, s*and* is a CVCC word, and *stand* is a CCVCC word.

Bridging the Gap

Rationales for Introducing Letter Sounds in Two Systematic Phonics Programs

The order in which letter sounds are introduced can have a big impact on how easily the letters are learned. Described below are two different strategies for sequencing letter sounds used in reading programs shown to be successful with students who have great difficulty learning to read: *Reading Mastery* and *Lindamood®: LiPS.* Even if you don't use these programs, the rules they use for sequencing letters can be applied to adapt other programs, or, at least, give you clues to where your students might experience difficulty. As you read the descriptions of the way that letter sounds are introduced in the two programs, determine the strengths and weaknesses of each.

Rationale 1: Direct Instruction

Reduce confusion when learning letters with similar sounds or appearance.
Letters that have a similar sound or are similar in appearance should be separated by at least three letters from each other. Letters that have both a similar sound and appearance should be separated by at least six letters. Carnine and colleagues (2004) further suggest that all the vowels be separated by at least three letters, and that /ĭ/ and /ĕ/ be separated by six letters. Table 3.1 lists specific letters that students are likely to confuse and are in need of separating when teaching.

TABLE 3.1   Letter Characteristics

Letters with smilar sound	Letters with similar appearance	Letters with similar sound and appearance
b and *d*	*b* and *d*	*b* and *d*
b and *p*	*b* and *p*	*m* and *n*
m and *n*	*m* and *n*	*b* and *p*
ĭ and ĕ	*q* and *p*	
k and *g*	*h* and *n*	
t and *d*	*v* and *w*	
ŏ and ŭ	*n* and *r*	
f and *v*		

Move into story reading earlier by teaching high-frequency letter sounds
Introduce more-useful letter sounds (consonant sounds such as /m/, /n/, /s/, /t/; all of the vowel sounds) before less-useful letter sounds (/x/, /z/, /q/).

Teach lower-case letters before upper-case letters
Most upper-case letters are not identical to their lower-case counterparts, and learning both at the same time can place an undue burden on a student who is at risk. Since beginning reading passages contain mostly lower-case letters, these are the letters that should be taught first.

Rationale 2: *Lindamood®: LiPS*

Choose Your Approach
Depending on the needs of the students, teachers can opt for Path 1, in which all of the consonant sounds are taught before the vowel sounds. These sounds are then applied to manipulating phonemes, spelling, and reading. Path 1 is typically used for older students. On Path 2, three

consonant pairs or a total of six sounds and three vowel sounds are taught and then used in manipulating phonemes, spelling, and reading. When students have success applying those letters to reading and spelling, the other consonants and vowels are taught. Path 2 is more appropriate for younger children and remedial students who have experienced consistent failure (Lindamood & Lindamood, 1998).

Teach the Brothers

Teach consonant pairs called *brothers.* Each consonant pair represents a voiced and unvoiced consonant formed with the same mouth movements. Examples of consonant pairs are:

- /p/ and /b/
- /t/ and /d/
- /k/ and /g/

Teach the Cousins

After students know the brothers, teach the groups of consonants called *the cousins.* Nose sounds (/m/, /n/, /ng/), wind sounds (/w/, /wh/, /h/), and lifters (/l/, /r/) fall under this category.

Teach the Borrowers

Next teach the last group of consonants, called the *borrowers* because they borrow the sounds of other letters (/c/, /x/, /qu/, /y/).

Teach the Vowel Circle

Fifteen long and short vowels are categorized into four distinct groups according to the way they are formed by the mouth and tongue. Students discover where the vowel sounds are articulated, using sensory information to organize them into the following categories: round, smile, sliders, and open. Students learn to organize the vowels into a linguistic vowel circle depicted in Figure 3.2, organized by tongue placement and shape of the mouth for each vowel.

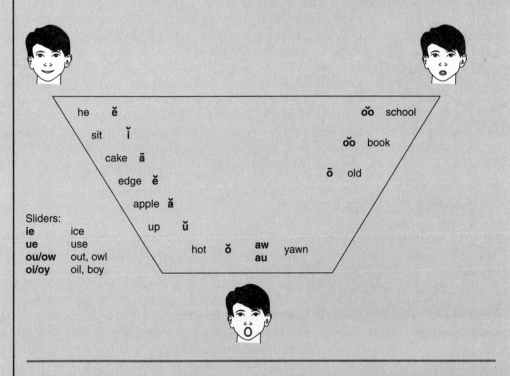

FIGURE 3.2 Vowel Circle Map

Source: Gildroy, P. G., & Francis, S. (1999). Learning about phonemes (Module 1, Lesson 2). In B. K. Lenz & P. G. Gildroy (Eds.). Beginning word reading [Online]. Lawrence, KS: University of Kansas, Center for Research on Learning. Available online at www.academy.org.

Read Single Syllable Words Containing Letter Combinations   Sometimes students are introduced to more complex phonic patterns before they have attained the alphabetic principle. These phonic patterns include combinations of letters called:

- **digraphs:** two successive letters articulated as a single phoneme. Examples of digraphs include *ch* as in *chop,* *th* as in *this,* and *oo* as in *book.*
- **diphthongs:** vowel blends in which the first sound appears to glide into the second sound. Examples of diphthongs include *ou* as in *mouse* and *oi* as in *boil.*

Read a Small Number of High-Frequency Sight Words Needed to Read Passages   By teaching students a limited number of **high-frequency** or common sight words required for reading beginning text (for example, *a, the, I, is,* and *to*), teachers can focus student attention on critical sounding-out strategies.

Sound Out Previously Taught One-Syllable Words in Sentences and Passages
Include CVC words, CVC variants, and words containing letter combinations. Books in which at least 70% of the text is comprised of words that can be sounded out mixed in with a relatively small proportion of previously taught high-frequency sight words are called **decodable books.** Passage reading differs from reading lists of individual words in that students are reading connected text, scanning each word from left to right, moving from word to word, learning how punctuation marks affect meaning, and answering comprehension questions. In passage reading, students are required to sound out words by independently moving their fingers from letter to letter as they sound out the words. Requiring students to move from letter to letter while pointing to each letter reinforces left-to-right reading and keeps the reader focused on each letter in the words.

Read One-Syllable Words and Passages the Fast Way   When students have ample opportunities to read word lists and text coordinated with letter sounds they have learned, they begin *subvocal sounding out* by silently moving their lips or silently reading the sounds before blending. Since some students will not make this leap on their own, teachers of students who are at risk will be more effective if they explicitly teach subvocal sounding out and provide practice for their students to use the new strategy. Begin by having your students read words the fast way by first sounding out words subvocally, without making an audible sound, and then reading the words out loud. Students then learn to read words the fast way in lists followed by passages or connected text. Students who begin to use subvocal sounding-out are close to reaching fully developed alphabetic principle. Gradually, with more practice they will *automatic word recognition.*

Build on Previous Skills

Once students have attained the alphabetic principle, a more advanced sequence of letter combinations and structural analysis skills is taught to prepare students to read multisyllable words. Chapter 4 describes strategies to teach these more complex words.

Although this chapter describes how to teach the letter–sound relationships needed to develop alphabetic principle, many systematic phonics programs also incorporate spelling and writing as soon as the students learn their first letter sound. After learning to say letter sounds, students learn to write those same sounds. As students learn to read words, they are taught to spell those same words and incorporate them into their writing.

Following a skill sequence such as the letter sounds and word reading ones described in the text does not mean that each skill is taught by itself and then dropped when the next skill in the sequence is introduced. In a systematic phonics program, newly introduced skills remain in play even as other newer skills are introduced. For example, once students have learned a few common letter sounds, carefully planned instruction bounces between applying these new sounds to reading words in lists and passages, and applying them to spelling and written expression. The following description chronicles a typical day's instruction in the classroom of a teacher using a systematic and explicit phonics program. Notice how Mr. Hohnberger incorporates multiple skills from the *Sequence For Teaching Alphabetic Principle* hierarchy as he works to develop alphabetic principle with his class.

By the end of October, Mr. Hohnberger's first grade class had learned 23 letter sounds and could sound out basic CVC and CVCC words. Since /x/ was the next letter sound presented in the curriculum, Mr. Hohnberger took a few minutes to directly teach his students the /x/ sound. In late fall, Mr. Hohnberger's goal was to take all of his students from the slower sub-vocal sounding-out most of them were using to more automatic word decoding. Thus he had his students silently sound out and read 15 CVC and CVCC words the fast way. These words contained the 23 letter sounds he had previously taught. Later in the week, he planned to add words containing the /x/ sound to the word list.

After reading the word lists, three of Mr. Hohnberger's students passed out a two-page story about two cats who were pals. The students placed the story in front of them and put their reading finger to the left of the first word so they were ready to silently sound out the words, before saying them. By the second reading, his students were ready to answer the comprehension questions he asked about the story and its accompanying picture. When he discovered that a number of students did not know the meaning of *pal*, he directly taught the meaning of that vocabulary word. Mr. Hohnberger was pleased to note that his students were automatically decoding and reading at a normal pace by their third reading. He knew that this carefully coordinated practice was essential for some of his students who were at risk. Mr. Hohnberger was eager for his students to automatically decode on a first read, because that would signal they had fully acquired and were applying alphabetic principle.

After passage reading, Mr. Hohnberger taught his students how to print the letter for the /x/ sound, which students practiced on their chalkboards. Next, Mr. Hohnberger asked the students to segment and write some CVC words that were in the cat story. Before students moved on to the next language arts activity, identifying action verbs, Mr. Hohnberger taught the sight word *would,* which would be in the next week's story about a fox. Just before Mr. Hohnberger began to teach action verbs, the two students in his class who entered school reading at a second-grade level returned from the second grade class where they went for a large portion of their reading instruction.

How Do I Efficiently Assess and Monitor Students' Progress with the Alphabetic Principle?

Teachers need to asses two key skills until their students have attained alphabetic principle: individual letter–sound correspondences and sounding out words. Careful assessment of the individual letter sounds informs a teacher when to introduce regular word sounding out. For example, when Ms. Remick assessed her students to determine whether they knew the six letter sounds she taught during the first three weeks of school, almost every student in her class correctly identified the /a/, /m/, /t/, /r/, /s/, and /l/ letter sounds. Because previous assessments in phonemic awareness showed that her students could also segment and blend at the individual sound level, Ms. Remick knew that her students were ready to learn how to sound out CVC words beginning with continuous sounds. After giving the letter–sound assessment Ms. Remick selected a decodable book that had only regular words containing the /a/, /m/, /r/, /s/, and /l/ sounds in addition to three sight words her students knew.

While not a skill that is useful in sounding out words, the ability to name letters of the alphabet rapidly is useful in identifying students who are at risk for future reading problems. The reason for this is that rapid letter naming appears to measure **lexical retrieval,** or the efficiency with which a reader can locate and apply to reading previously learned information about letters and words stored in long-term memory. Lexical retrieval is an early indicator of fluency and is highly predictive of later reading ability (O'Connor & Jenkins, 1999; Speece, Mills, Ritchey, & Hillman, 2003). That is why DIBELS Letter Naming Fluency is also described in this section.

Teachers also need to directly assess word sounding out to determine whether students are making progress toward attaining alphabetic principle and to determine when students have fully acquired it. Once the alphabetic principle is attained and students are accurately and automatically sounding out words, teachers can begin to introduce more complex combinations of letters, multisyllable words, and passage reading fluency exercises. Letter–sound, letter-naming and word-sounding-out assessments are described in the next section.

Letter–Sound Correspondence: Informal Measure

When Is It Given?   Ideally these assessments are given six times during kindergarten or preschool as soon as letters are introduced. If students are first learning letter sounds in higher grades, teachers should coordinate these assessments with the sequence of letters they are teaching, giving the letter–sound assessments after every four or five letters taught in the phonics program. This assessment should always include all of the letter sounds taught from the beginning of the year until the time of the current assessment.

What Score Indicates Success?   One-hundred percent accuracy is required. By the end of October, Ms. Bolas taught her class letter sounds for the following letters: *a, h, m, d,* and *s.* Then in order to determine whether her instruction was effective, for two days during center time, she worked with one student at a time giving them a brief letter–sound assessment. The student test sheet, score sheet, and directions for the letter–sound assessment she gave are shown in Figures 3.3 and 3.4.

Note that in the measure, only the letters Ms. Bolas taught until the end of October were assessed. Note also that Ms. Bolas taught her students the sounds for both upper- and lower-case letters. If you are teaching your students the sounds for lower-case letters first, then your assessment should only include lower-case letters. Although some teachers will add a column for letter names, the score for this assessment is based only on the student's accurate identification of letter sounds so necessary for word reading.

H	h
T	t
A	a
M	m
D	d
O	o
S	s

FIGURE 3.3   Letter–Sound Assessment: Student Test Sheet

When giving the letter–sounds assessment Ms. Bolas put a student test sheet in front of the student. Letters on the test sheet were typed in a large font matching the font used in classroom instruction. While the example above uses manuscript letters, if you are teaching D'Nealian, fonts in that script are available for your classroom computer.

Lexical Retrieval: DIBELS Letter Naming Fluency

When Is It given?   DIBELS Letter Naming Fluency (LNF) is given at the earliest in September of kindergarten and then three times thereafter in winter and spring of kinder-

Student Name: *Caryn*   Date: *Oct. 31*

Directions: Place the Test Sheet in front of the student and hold the Record Sheet on a clipboard so that the student can not see the scores you record. Point to the letters and say, "Look at these upper- and lower-case alphabet letters. I want you to tell me the sound that each letter makes." Cover all the letters except the first one with a sheet of paper, point to that first letter and say, "What sound does this letter make?" If the student says the correct letter sound, write the score, slide the paper down one row, point to the next letter and ask the same question. If the student says the letter name, say, "___ is the name of this letter. Now tell me what sound this letter makes." Uncover one letter at a time, until you have asked for the sound of every letter on the sheet. If the student says the long vowel sound, say, "That's one sound this letter makes. What is another sound this letter makes?"

Scoring: Score 1 point for every correct letter sound. Score 0 for every incorrect letter sound.

Testing Tips: The child either knows a letter sound or does not know a letter sound. Do not prompt any answers by giving hints. If a child cannot say just the letter sound, but has to say a keyword jingle that matches it ("/ă/ - apple - /ă/") or has to say the letter sound three or four times in succession (/h/, /h/, /h/), count the answer as incorrect. In order to accurately decode words, a student must be able to say the letter sound once and continue decoding.

Letter	Letter Sound
1. H h	/
2. T t	/
3. A a	0
4. M m	/
5. D d	/
6. O o	/
7. S s	/
Total Correct	6
Percent	86%

FIGURE 3.4 Letter–Sound Assessment: Teacher's Directions and Score Sheet

garten and fall of grade 1. Because the ability to name letters of the alphabet is not directly needed to read beginning words, we recommend that it be used strictly as a screening measure and/or diagnostic measure and not as an outcome or progress monitoring measure. Note also that the validity of this assessment depends on some initial exposure or knowledge of the alphabet. Therefore, when students enter kindergarten without this exposure or knowledge, the measure should be given in winter of kindergarten at the earliest.

What Score Indicates Success? Benchmark levels for DIBELS LNF are shown in Table 3.2. Research shows that students who are not at benchmark on DIBELS LNF are more likely to have difficulties in fluently reading text (Wolf et al., 1986). Students are given a minute to name as many of the upper- and lower-case letters of the alphabet as they can. Directions are shown in Figure 3.5 and a sample teacher score sheet is shown in Figure 3.6. A more detailed explanation of scoring procedures can be found at the DIBELS website: http://dibels.uoregon.edu.

TABLE 3.2 Benchmarks for DIBELS Letter Naming Fluency (LNF) Assessment

Beginning of Kindergarten		Middle of Kindergarten	
If score is . . .	*Diagnosis*	*If score is . . .*	*Diagnosis*
Less than 2	At risk	Less than 15	At risk
2 to 7	Some risk	15 to 26	Some risk
8 or more	Low risk	27 or more	Low risk

End of Kindergarten		Beginning of First Grade	
If score is . . .	*Diagnosis*	*If score is . . .*	*Diagnosis*
Less than 29	At risk	Less than 25	At risk
29 to 39	Some risk	25 to 36	Some risk
40 or more	Low risk	37 or more	Low risk

Source: R. H. Good, D. Simmons, E. A. Kame'enui, and J. Wallin (2002). *Summary of decision rules for intensive, strategic, and benchmark instruction recommendations in kindergarten through third grade* (Technical Report No. 11). Eugene, OR: University of Oregon.

In scoring the DIBELS LNF assessment, give students credit for every letter identified correctly. Note that Desmon, the student in Figure 3.6, identified 28 letters correctly per minute in May of his kindergarten year. This score indicates he is at risk for future reading difficulties. Depending on Desmon's scores in other areas such as letter sounds, DIBELS Phonemic Segmentation Fluency, and Nonsense Word Fluency, Desmon's teachers might decide to place him in a Tier 3 intensive reading program.

Directions for Administration:

1. Place the student copy of probe in front of the student.
2. Place the examiner copy on clipboard and position so that the student cannot see what you record.
3. Say these specific directions to the student:

   Here are some letters (point). Tell me the names of as many letters as you can. When I say "begin," start here (point to first letter), and go across the page (point). Point to each letter and tell me the name of that letter. If you come to a letter you don't know I'll tell it to you. Put your finger on the first letter. Ready, begin.

4. Start your stop watch.
5. Follow along on the screening probe. Put a slash (/) through letters named incorrectly (see score sheet in Figure 3.6).
6. If the student provides the letter sound rather than the letter name, say, "Remember to tell me the letter name, not the sound it makes." This prompt may be provided once during the administration. If the student continues providing letter sounds, mark each letter as incorrect and indicate what the student did at the bottom of the page.
7. At the end of *1 minute,* place a bracket (]) after the last letter named and say "Stop."

FIGURE 3.5 DIBELS Letter Naming Fluency (LNF) Assessment Directions

Source: Official DIBELS home page: http://dibels.uoregon.edu/2002–2004.

Benchmark 1
DIBELS™ Letter Naming Fluency

Name: *Desmon*   Date: *May 10*

V	I	h	g	S	y	Z	~~W~~	L	N
I	K	T	D	K	T	q	d	~~z~~	w
h	w	~~z~~	m	U	r	j	G	X	u
g	R	B	Q	I	f	I	Z	s	r
S	n	C	B	p	Y	F	c	a	E
y	s	Q	P	M	v	O	t	n	P
Z	A	e	x	f	F	h	u	A	t
W	G	H	b	S	I	g	m	i	i
L	L	o	o	X	N	E	Y	p	x
N	k	c	D	d	y	b	j	R	v
V	M	W	q	V	I	h	g	S	y

Total: *28*

FIGURE 3.6   Sample DIBELS LNF Score Sheet (for Desmon)

Source: Official DIBELS home page: http://dibels.uoregon.edu/2002–2004.

Alphabetic Principle: DIBELS Nonsense Word Fluency

When Is It Given?   The DIBELS Nonsense Word Fluency Assessment (NWF) is given at least three times per year when students are first learning to sound out words. Since the Report of the National Reading Panel clearly indicated that phonics instruction taught before the end of first grade is more effective than phonics instruction introduced later, the DIBELS NWF is typically given from the middle of kindergarten until the beginning of grade 2. Because teachers need to regularly monitor student progress towards attaining alphabetic principle, ideally the DIBELS NWF assessment should be given at least every month or more frequently. Once students meet the benchmark score, they do not need to be monitored as closely. A sample student test sheet, score sheet, and directions for the assessment are shown in Figures 3.7 and 3.8 (pp. 80 and 81).

> At the official DIBELS website (**http://dibels.uoregon.edu/measures.nwf.php**), you can watch a teacher giving the Nonsense Word Fluency assessment to a student. Directions to administer and score the test are available at the same website, as are copies that can be downloaded at no charge.

What Score Indicates Success?   Benchmark levels for the DIBELS NWF are shown in Table 3.3 (p. 81). Note that a score of 50 to 60 letter sounds correct per minute with at least 15 words read as whole words shows that students have attained the alphabetic principle. These children are more likely to meet grade-level benchmarks on future assessments of oral passage reading fluency (Good et al., 2002).

As the name suggests, in the DIBELS Nonsense Word Reading assessment students are given 1 minute to read a series of make-believe words, all having the most common sounds of letters arranged according to the CVC word pattern. The advantage of using nonsense words to measure the alphabetic principle is that nonsense words can only be decoded by accurate sounding out. Nonsense words control for context as well as sight word memorization and are therefore a relatively pristine measure of a student's ability to sound out. Students who

**Nonsense Word Fluency
Short Form Directions**

Make sure you have reviewed the long form of the directions in the Administration and Scoring Guide and have them available. Say these specific directions to the student:

> Look at this word (point to the first word on the practice probe). It's a make-believe word. Watch me read the word: /s/ /i/ /m/ "sim" (point to each letter then run your finger fast beneath the whole word). I can say the sounds of the letters, /s/ /i/ /m/ (point to each letter), or I can read the whole word "sim" (run your finger fast beneath the whole word).
>
> Your turn to read a make-believe word. Read this word the best you can (point to the word "lut"). Make sure you say any sounds you know.

Correct Response:	Incorrect or No Response:
If the child responds "lut" or with some or all of the sounds, say	If the child does not respond within <u>3 seconds</u> or responds incorrectly, say
That's right. The sounds are /l/ /u/ /t/ or "lut"	Remember, you can say the sounds or you can say the whole word. Watch me: the sounds are /l/ /u/ /t/ (point to each letter) or "lut" (run your finger fast through the whole word). Let's try again. Read this word the best you can (point to the word "lut").

Place the student copy of the probe in front of the cihld.

> Here are some more make-believe words (point to the student probe). Start here (point to the first word) and go across the page (point across the page). When I say "begin," read the words the best you can. Point to each letter and tell me the sound <u>or</u> read the whole word. Read the words the best you can. Put your finger on the first word. Ready, begin.

FIGURE 3.7   DIBELS Nonsense Word Fluency (NWF) Directions

Source: Official DIBELS home page: http://dibels.uoregon.edu/2002–2004.

---

can read enough nonsense words within a minute to achieve a score of 50–60 letter sounds correct per minute by winter of first grade are automatically decoding. The DIBELS score of 50–60, with at least 15 words read as whole words, indicates that you can predict that students will be reading at grade level by the end of first grade. If first-grade students whose scores are below 50 do not show continuous progress from testing period to testing period, you know that they need additional support immediately in order to read at grade level by the end of the year. In situations in which students have already been exposed to systematic, explicit phonics, you may want to use the higher figure of 60 as your benchmark cutoff.

In scoring the DIBELS NWF assessment, give students credit for every letter–sound correspondence identified correctly, regardless of whether the sounds are identified individually or as a part of a whole word. For example, when Jamarius came to the nonsense word *bif,* he read it as three separate sounds, /b/-/i/-/f/. He received a score of 3 for three letter sounds identified correctly. When Matoria came to the same word, she said *bif* accurately, decoding the entire nonsense word as a whole word. Although Matoria also received 3 points, one for each letter sound in the word, her final score was higher because by reading the nonsense words as whole words she rapidly moved through the nonsense words, receiving credit for more letter sounds than Jamarius. This example shows how students' nonsense scores increase and eventually reach the benchmark of 50–60 letter sounds correct per minute once they begin to read nonsense words at the word level, where sounding is automatic and internal. In the event students score 50–60

f a p	b o s	f i c	d i f	v i m	____/15
l o m	o v	v e f	h i z	b e j	____/14
r i z	m a g	v e g	f e v	u b	____/14
y u f	h o z	w u c	m i d	m e z	____/15
n a k	y i p	w u l	f e c	k a l	____/15
k u d	z u t	j u b	s u p	a d	____/14
t o f	n e z	l a l	d o c	b u j	____/15
r u d	p e s	s i g	n u d	z u r	____/15
a c	r i s	w o v	b o l	t a j	____/14
m o d	r o g	m o z	w u c	r o m	____/15

Total: ____

Error Pattern:

FIGURE 3.8   DIBELS NWF Assessment and Score Sheet (Blank)

Source: Official DIBELS home page: http://dibels.uoregon.edu/2002–2004.

TABLE 3.3   Benchmarks for DIBELS NWF Assessment

Middle of Kindergarten		End of Kindergarten	
If score is . . .	*Diagnosis*	*If score is . . .*	*Diagnosis*
Less than 5	At risk	Less than 5	At risk
5 to 12	Some risk	5 to 25	Some risk
13 or more	Low risk	25 or more	Low risk

Beginning of First Grade		Middle of First Grade		End of First Grade	
If score is . . .	*Diagnosis*	*If score is . . .*	*Diagnosis*	*If score is . . .*	*Diagnosis*
Less than 13	At risk	Less than 30	Deficit	Less than 30	Deficit
13 to 23	Some risk	30 to 49	Emerging	30 to 49	Emerging
24 or more	Low risk	50 to 60 with 15 words read as whole words	Established	50 to 60 with 15 words read as whole words	Established

Source: Good, R. H., Kaminski, R. A., & Howe, D. (2005, June). What data tell us about children and how to support their success. Presented at AZ Reading First Conference, Phoenix, AZ.

Sounding-Out Stage
Student #1 : Jervon

l̲i̲n̲   m̲u̲s̲   u̲k̲   d̲o̲v̲   o̲v̲

Transition Sounding-Out Stage
Student #2: Tori

l̲i̲n̲   m̲u̲s̲   u̲k̲   d̲o̲v̲   o̲v̲

Onset Rime Sounding-Out Stage
Student #3: Yolanda

l̲i̲n   m̲u̲s̲   u̲k   d̲o̲v   o̲v

Fully Developed Alphabetic Principle
Student #4: Katina

l̲i̲n   m̲u̲s̲   u̲k   d̲o̲v   o̲v

FIGURE 3.9   Sample DIBELS Scoring Patterns

by reading single letters only, Good has added the following criterion for meeting benchmark: students must also read at least 15 words as whole words (Good, Kaminski, & Howe, 2005).

The *Woodcock Reading Mastery Test Revised* (WRMT-R) Word Attack subtest requires students to sound out a series of nonsense words of increasing complexity. While this measure lacks the important fluency component of DIBELS Nonsense Word Fluency, its use of nonsense words of types other than basic CVC words can provide teachers with more diagnostic information. Also, the norms are helpful for older students for whom the DIBELS benchmark may not be relevant. For more information, go to **http://ags. pearsonassessments.com/group. asp?nGroupInfoID=a16640.**

The *Test of Word Reading Efficiency* (TOWRE) also measures students' word attack skills as well as the ability to read high frequency sight words. TOWRE is fluency-based and the norming group includes adolescents. For more information go to: **http://69.41.181.153/Scripts/ prodView.asp?idProduct=1608.**

By looking at individual student answer patterns as well as the cumulative score, you can tell how to adapt your instruction to reflect where students are in relation to fully developed alphabetic principle. Students go through four definite sounding phases on their way to attaining the alphabetic principle. These phases are shown in Figure 3.9. Note that student 1, Jervon, is still reading at the individual sound level, as indicated by the scoring of his nonsense word reading. Every letter is marked because he only said the individual letter sounds as he read through the test. Student 2, Tori, is at a transitional sounding-out stage; she is still saying the individual sounds for each word, but she is also blending them together into whole words. The third student, Yolanda, is sounding out many words as onset rime before reading them as whole words. She is beginning to read many two-letter words automatically as one word without needing to sound out. At this stage, students' scores begin to increase substantially as they near alphabetic principle. Finally, the fourth student, Katina, represents a student who has attained alphabetic principle. Of the four students, only Katina will score at benchmark levels. She is ready to sound out more complex words and work on fluency in grade-level text. Jervon needs more practice sounding out and blending basic CVC words. Tori needs to transition to subvocally sounding out words so she begins to read words the fast way or more automatically. Yolanda is almost there. Continued daily practice with word and passage reading will help Yolanda go that extra step and move into fully developed alphabetic principle.

Effective Teachers at Work

Use the DIBELS NWF to Identify Students for Tutoring

The following account demonstrates how student scores from the DIBELS Nonsense Word Fluency assessment helped a first-grade teacher determine which students would benefit the most from working with the volunteer reading tutor.

During the first week of November, the principal told the first-grade teacher, Mr. Graham, that the district curriculum director had started to train volunteer reading tutors who would start coming to elementary schools next week. First grade was a priority for the principal, who told Mr. Graham that the reading tutor would be available for tutoring in the afternoon twice a week. During their training, the tutors had learned all of the skills necessary to conduct one-on-one tutoring sessions helping students read decodable or regular text books. Mr. Graham's responsibility was to assign students to the tutor and to provide appropriate reading books.

As Mr. Graham thought about how he would use the tutor, he looked at the October DIBELS Nonsense Word Scores and decided that his lowest-scoring Tier 2 students would most benefit from additional time reading decodable books. Since the majority of students in his class were scoring 35 phonemes per minute or more, they were on track to reach 50 by January 1. Currently Mr. Graham was concerned about Rachel, Tony, and Karissa, whose DIBELS Nonsense Word Scores were still in the 20s despite Tier 2 tutoring. At this rate they would not acquire alphabetic principle by January when long vowels would be introduced.

From past experience, Mr. Graham knew that the reading of students without alphabetic principle could take a nose dive when they moved into reading words with long vowels. In order to recognize that a vowel is long, a reader must automatically decode, seeing the word in its entirety. Students who were still slowly sounding out and then blending the words often read the long vowels as short vowels or began to read all vowels as long vowels. The resulting confusion usually led to a halt in their reading progress and eventually a move into the more intensive Tier 3 program. Mr. Graham needed to provide even more support to these three students to try and jumpstart their acquisition of alphabetic principle. But what to do about squeezing extra time out of a hectic classroom schedule?

Because a trained tutor was the perfect answer, Mr. Graham arranged a time for each of the three students. He selected some decodable books that Rachel, Tony, and Karissa hadn't read, but that contained letter sounds and sound patterns taught in class. Twice a week they would go to the tutor to practice reading the CVC variant words. The next DIBELS Nonsense Words Assessment would show whether the extra tutoring time provided enough support or whether these three students needed to move into a more intensive reading program.

How Do I Teach Students So That They Attain the Alphabetic Principle?

As emphasized in Chapters 1 and 2, the multi-tiered approach described in this text allows teachers to accommodate a range of learners. The teaching enhancements described in those chapters also apply for each of the key skill areas that comprise the alphabetic principle. The general education reading program for children who are at risk is enhanced through the use of advance organizers, unison responding, perky pace, support for new learning using My Turn–Together–Your Turn systematic error corrections, cumulative review, integrated motivational strategies, and teaching to success. The following formats for teaching letter sounds, word reading, and text reading are used for large-group Tier 1 instruction and also small-group, Tier 2 booster sessions. In addition, descriptions of more intensive programs appropriate for Tier 3 are provided along with special strategies for English language learners and older students.

Identifying Letter–Sound Correspondences

Even when students can segment and blend, before learning to sound out words they must be able to automatically identify some letter-sounds in isolation. For example, Carnine and colleagues (2004) recommend that at least six to eight letter–sound correspondences, including one or two vowels, be taught prior to the introduction of sounding out words. Failure to work on letter sounds in isolation prior to sounding out words can result in problems shown in the following example:

> Keionda's teacher showed her how to sound out the word *man* but Keionda had not learned /ǎ/, the most common sound of the letter *a*. Keionda's teacher had to stop the sounding out instruction temporarily in order to practice the /ǎ/ sound. Stopping to work on a letter sound that should have been learned previously slowed the pace of the lesson and diverted Keionda's attention from learning the sounding-out strategy. This spur of the moment instruction on the letter sound did not provide enough practice for Keionda to predictably remember /ǎ/ the next day.

Many programs teach sounds using an indirect approach. Instead of introducing sounds in isolation, teachers write a list of words that begin with the new letter on the board. After asking the students what sound is the same in all of these words, the teacher has the students say the sound of the new letter. For students with disabilities or who are at risk this approach is clearly not explicit enough. Such an approach does not provide enough practice of the new sound or review of previously introduced sounds. The format in Table 3.4 directly teaches letter–sound correspondences and provides extensive student practice and review. This format is based on ones originally developed by Carnine and colleagues (2004). The first part of this format introduces the new letter sound using the My Turn–Together–Your Turn strategy shown in steps 2–5 in Table 3.4. In Part B of this format, the teacher provides practice of the new letter sound in combination with six or seven other previously introduced sounds. In Part B, the teacher first tests the group (Your Turn) on the new and review sounds before checking student mastery by calling on individual students to say the sounds.

Figure 3.10 shows the LOOP signal used by the teacher to elicit unison answers from the group. As shown, the teacher first points to the left of the letter, provides a thinking pause, asks "what sound," and then loops his finger to touch underneath the letter. He pauses under the letter two to three seconds for continuous sounds and immediately bounces out for stop sounds. When he bounces off to return to the starting point or loops back to the starting point, students stop saying the letter sound. In this way, the teacher can calibrate the length of time students say the sound.

FIGURE 3.10 LOOP Signal

Four Best Practices for Teaching Letter Sounds   Let's look at how Mrs. Nguyen taught letter sounds to her class, using the following four effective teaching strategies.

Use Classroom Time Efficiently   Since many of Mrs. Nguyen's students came to school with limited language skills, she started teaching letter sounds by the second week of school. Although the regular curriculum was designed to teach one letter sound a week, she knew that she could not waste any time because many of her kindergartners would need two weeks on each vowel and the more difficult consonants. Every morning after calendar time, she immediately started her language arts instruction by following the letter sound format in Table 3.4 for 3 to 5 minutes. If a morning assembly was scheduled so that it coincided with letter–sound practice time, she either skipped calendar time and inserted letter–sound practice or went through the drill exercises immediately after the assembly.

TABLE 3.4 Format for Introducing New Letter Sounds in the General Curriculum: Part A

Outcome	After seeing a new letter, students say its sound with 100% accuracy.
Materials Needed	Board, chart paper, or overhead transparency and writing implement
Signaling	Before starting letter–sound drill, students should practice responding to your loop signal, so they learn to say the sound of the letter as long as your finger stays on the letter. Place your finger to the left of the letter. **"What sound?"** initiates the signal for unison answers.
	Signal for continuous sounds: After looping to the letter, hold your finger under it for 2 seconds as students say the sound before looping your finger back to the starting point.
	Signal for stop sounds: After looping to the letter, immediately bounce your finger out as students say the sound and return to the starting point.
Time	3–5 minutes

Instructions	**Teacher**	**Students**
	1. Advance Organizer	
	2. My Turn (examples given for continuous and stop sounds)	
	Write a lower case letter *s* on the board and point to the letter:	
	Signal for *continuous sounds:* (finger to the left of letter) **"Here's our new sound for today."** (loop signal) **"/s/."** (loop back to starting point) **"This letter says"** (loop signal) **"/s/"** (end signal).	
	Write a lower case letter *t* on the board and point to the letter:	
	Signal for *stop sounds:* (finger to the left of letter) **"Here's our new sound for today."** (loop signal and bounce out) **"/t/."** (back to starting point) **"This letter says"** (loop signal and bounce out) **"/t/"** (end signal).	
	3. Together	
	The teacher answers with students this time.	
	Signal for *continuous sounds:* (finger to the left of letter) **"Together. What sound?"** (loop signal) **"/s/."** (loop back to starting point) **"Yes, /s/."**	/s/
	Signal for *stop sounds:* (finger to the left of letter) **"Together. What sound?"** (loop signal and bounce out) **"/t/."** (back to starting point) **"Yes, /t/."**	/t/
	Repeat this sequence several times.	
	4. Your Turn	
	Signal for *continuous sounds:* (finger to the left of letter) **"Your turn. What sound?"** (loop signal) (answer) (loop back to starting point) **"Yes, /s/."**	/s/
	Signal for *stop sounds:* (finger to the left of letter) **"Your turn. What sound?"** (loop signal and bounce out) (answer) (back to starting point) **"Yes, /t/."**	/t/
	Repeat several times.	
	5. Individual Student Checkout	
	Signal for *continuous sounds:* (finger to the left of letter) **"Individual turns. What sound? Marissa."** (loop signal) (answer) (loop back to starting point) **"Yes, /s/."**	/s/
	Signal for *stop sounds:* (finger to the left of letter) **"Individual turns. What sound? Tonia."** (loop signal and bounce out) (answer) (back to starting point) **"Yes, /t/."**	/t/
	Call on several individual students and check accuracy.	

Error Correction	If students make an error, immediately return to a My Turn–Together–Your Turn pattern. You may need to refocus students to your mouth position as you say the letter.
Perk up Your Drill	■ Occasionally signal using an unusual pointer such a puppet's hand, a wand, or a baton. Decorate a pointer to fit the occasion; dress it up with ribbons and glitter or an appropriate theme for the time of year.

Continued

TABLE 3.4   Continued

Perk up Your Drill (continued)	■ Some teachers teach their students to fingerspell the new letter as they say it. Other teachers add easier hand signals for the more difficult letters. For example, when students say /p/, the teacher has them point their finger down; when students say /i/ the teacher holds up a pretend antenna to represent an *insect*. Signals can provide extra motivation as long as teachers eventually fade them out. Signals should not interfere with the pace of instruction.
Adaptations	■ Before teaching the new letter sound, see if students in the class can repeat the new sound after they hear you say it. Some students may need articulation practice. For example, if students have difficulty saying /p/, put your fingers to your lips and show the students how your lips pop when you say the /p/ sound. Next ask the students to put their fingers on their lips and make the same lip-popping sound. If some of the students are vocalizing the /b/ sound instead of /p/ sound, ask students to put their hands on their neck in order to feel the difference between a voiced sound and an unvoiced sound.
	■ In the beginning some students may need to look into a small hand-held mirror in order to make the new letter sound.
	■ Refer to the letter–sound chart in Table 1.4 for more introductory tips for teaching letter sounds.

Format for Introducing New Letter Sounds in the General Curriculum: Part B

On the second day you teach a new letter sound, add Part B to your lesson.

Outcome	After seeing 26 letters, students say their sounds with 100% accuracy.
Materials Needed	Board, chart paper, or overhead transparency, a writing implement, and a list of letter sounds learned to date.
Signaling	Before starting letter–sound drill, students should practice responding to your loop signal, so they learn to say the sound of the letter as long as your finger stays on the letter. Place your finger to the left of the letter. **"What sound?"** initiates the signal for unison answers.
	Signal for *continuous sounds:* After looping to the letter, hold your finger under it for 2 seconds as students say the sound before looping your finger back to the starting point.
	Signal for *stop sounds:* After looping to the letter, bounce your finger out as students say the sound and return to the starting point.
Time	3–5 minutes

Instructions	**Teacher**	**Students**
	1. Advance Organizer	
	2. Your Turn	
	The teacher uses an alternating pattern to teach the new letter sound by writing the new lower-case letter on the board followed by one previously taught letter, followed by the new letter, followed by two previously taught letters. This pattern is continued until five letters separate the last two new letters (for example, **s** t **s** a t **s** m t a **s** h m t a **s** a t h m f **s**). The teacher provides more practice identifying the more difficult previously taught letters and vowels by including them in the list every day.	
	Signal for *continuous sounds:* (finger to the left of letter) **"Your turn. What sound?"** (loop signal) (answer) (loop back to starting point) **"Yes, /s/."**	/s/, /t/, /s/, /a/, /t/,
	Signal for *stop sounds:* (finger to the left of letter) **"Your turn. What sound?"** (loop signal and bounce out) (answer) (back to starting point) **"Yes, /t/."**	/s/, /m/, /t/ /s/ . . . .
	3. Individual Student Checkout	
	Signal for *continuous sounds:* (finger to the left of letter) **"Individual turns. What sound? Kyle."** (loop signal) (answer) (loop back to starting point) **"Yes, /s/."**	/s/

TABLE 3.4 Continued

	Signal for *stop sounds:* (finger to the left of letter) **"Individual turns. What sound? Lynnette."** (loop signal and bounce out) (answer) (back to starting point) **"Yes, /ă/."** Call on several individual students to check accuracy.	/ă/ . . . .
Error Correction	If students make an error, immediately return to a My Turn–Together–Your Turn pattern. Then alternate between the missed letter and familiar letters until students identify the missed letter correctly three times. For example, if you are working on *a, m, r, s,* and *i,* and the students missed *s,* say, (finger to the left of letter) **"This sound is /s/"** before asking, **"What sound?"** (loop signal and end) **"Yes, /s/."** Then ask the students to identify letter sounds using the following alternating pattern: a **s** m i **s** r i m **s.**	
Perk up Your Drill	■ Vary the color of the letters. ■ Hold your pointer finger on a continuous sound letter for an extra second or two and praise everyone who had enough air to hold it the entire time. ■ Occasionally tell students that they will say the sounds in booming lion voices, in squeaky mouse voices, or in robot voices. ■ Tell the students that later in the day, you will suddenly stop what you are doing and ask them to say the sound of the new letter. Challenge students to surprise you and remember the sound. ■ Present a challenge. When students are at mastery on the letter-sounds, tell students you will try to trick them by going at a speedy "Road Runner" pace.	
Adaptations	■ When students have reached 100% accuracy on Part B, you can begin to use a combination of upper-case and lower-case letters.	

Source: This script is based on one originally developed and field tested by Carnine, Silbert, Kame'enui, and Tarver, (2004). *Direct Instruction Reading* (4th ed.). New Jersey, Merrill Prentice Hall.

For New Letter Sounds, Use Part A Steps 1–5 When teaching a new letter sound, Mrs. Nguyen used the format in Table 3.4 Part A: Steps 1–5 for the first two or three days. If students said the new sound accurately, she moved to Steps 4–5 (Your Turn) before asking individual student checkouts. Thus, last week when introducing /b/, Mrs. Nguyen first checked that all of her students could articulate the explosive lip-popping sound. Then she spent the first two days carefully moving her teaching from Step 2 (My Turn) through Step 5 until the individual checkouts assured her that all of the students were saying /b/ when she pointed to the letter. By Wednesday her students were so solid on the /b/ sound that they no longer needed all of the My Turn–Together steps and so her instruction on /b/ began at Part A: Step 4. By this time, she could easily move to the Part B review after a minute.

When Reviewing Letter Sounds with the Format in Table 3.4 Part B, Use Steps 2–3 for All of the Letter Sounds Every day after teaching the new sound of the week, Mrs. Nguyen reviewed the previous letters. Immediately after practicing the new /b/ sound, Mrs. Nguyen used the format in Table 3.4 Part B, reviewing the /f/, /s/, /a/, and /m/ sounds that she had taught the first month and a half of school.

Give More Individual Turns to Students Who Have the Most Difficulty Shoshana, Greg, and Tracy's scores on last month's letter–sound assessment showed that they had learned the fewest sounds, so Mrs. Nguyen asked them more questions during individual student checkouts.

Sound Spelling Activity: Children write /t/ and /r/.

Teacher: "You're going to write some letter sounds."
"First sound /t/. What sound?" (signal) (answer) **"Yes, /t/."**
"Write /t/." Check children's answers and give feedback.
"Next sound /r/. What sound?" (signal) (answer) **"Yes, /r/."**
"Write /r/." Check children's answers and give feedback.

FIGURE 3.11   Sound Writing Format

Source: This script was adapted from *Reading Mastery* (Engelmann & Bruner, 1995) by Kinder (1990).

Writing Letter–Sound Correspondences

> The Word Identification and Spelling Test (WIST) provides in-depth assessment of word attack, word identification, and spelling skills that can be helpful in planning pre-alphabetic reading lessons for students. Norms are provided for ages 7 through 18. For more information, go to: **http://69.41.181.153/Scripts/prodView.asp?idProduct=2031.**

Students' learning of letter sounds is enhanced when they are required to write or spell what they are reading. Therefore, when you are teaching the letter sounds in isolation, students should also write as well as say the sounds. For example, Ms. Chapelle's students can identify the most common sounds for the following letters: *s, r, m, t, a,* and *d*. After practicing these sounds with the letter–sound format, Ms. Chapelle has her students take out their white boards and write the same sounds from dictation using the format shown in Figure 3.11.

Providing Differentiated Instruction

The following lesson introducing the most common sound for the letter *u* is a typical lesson from a modern reading curriculum:

> Say *us* and *under* slowly, focusing on the /u/ sound. Ask the students what sound they hear at the beginning of both words. Write a large upper case *U* and lower case *u* on the blackboard and say, "This is upper-case *U* and this is lower-case *u*." Tell the students that a vowel can stand for several sounds. Call on volunteers to identify words on a rhyme printed on a chart that begin with the letter *u*.
>
> Write *us* and *under* on the chart and have the students tell you other words that begin with the /u/ sound. Add these words to the chart and read them all together with the students.

This activity is likely to create several problems for children who are at risk. First, and most importantly, the lesson doesn't provide adequate practice and support by introducing the letter sound using a My Turn–Together–Your Turn strategy. Students never directly hear what sound the letter *u* makes, nor are they given any direct practice on saying the sound while the teacher points to the letter. Pointing to *u* words in the rhyme and volunteering words that begin with *u* can all be done without knowing the letter sound of the written letter *u*. If the teacher has called on individual students to answer these questions, adequate practice for everyone is not provided. Students who are at risk will be unlikely to be able to identify the *u* sound when they come to a word.

> More than 30 years of reading research conducted by the National Institute of Child Health and Human Development (NICHD) demonstrated the importance of explicitly taught phonics and phonological awareness. Learn about major findings from the NICHD research: **www.nichd.nih.gov/crmc/cdb/approach.pdf.**

Another problem with this lesson is that the words on the chart that students read are not in any way coordinated with the sounds and skills they have already learned. During the previous week students may have learned the difficult letter sound /j/, which still needs daily practice. When words on the chart do not incorporate cumulative review, prior learning is

Seize the Teachable Moment

Help Your Students Articulate and Differentiate Sounds

The *b* vs *d* Conundrum

When your daily teaching shows that some of the first graders are still mixing lower case *b's* with *d's*, they will benefit from practicing reading words with these sounds. The key to this practice is focusing on accuracy. Make a list of four three- or four-phoneme words containing *d's* or *b's* and give a point for every word read correctly. Tell the student that 10 points wins the game.

Getting Students to Hear *j*

These tips about the production of /j/ should make your task easier if students are saying a different sound for this letter. According to the *Lindamood-Bell LIPS Program*, /j/ is a "Noisy Fat-Pushed Air" sound (Lindamood & Lindamood, 1998).

Why Is /j/ Noisy????

If you put your hand on your throat as you say /j/, you can feel the vibration. With quiet sounds such as /s/ and /p/, you will not feel this vibration. Help your children feel their neck vibrate as they make the /j/ sound.

What Is "Fat-Pushed Air?"

As you say the /j/ sound, hold the back of your hand in front of your mouth and feel the air push out. Unlike /s/ or /sh/, where one's air comes out in a smooth flow, the /j/ sound requires a fat-push of air that sprays all over.

What Else Can I Do to Help My Students Hear This Sound?

Practice the "segmenting first-sound" phonemic awareness drill exercises from Chapter 2. Compose a list of /j/ words that are familiar to your students with words like *jet, jump, jelly,* and *jellybean.* Following the script, say, "My turn, *jet.* First sound? /j/." Follow this with a Together and Your Turn until the children begin to produce a clear /j/ sound. Remember to loudly and clearly say the /j/ sound, overaccentuating it. You will have to work at saying /j/ loud and clear so that your children distinctly hear it.

The Elusive /ĕ/

Frequently some first graders and kindergartners will confuse the sounds of /ĕ/ and /ă/. For example, when asked to blend /p/-/ĕ/-/n/ , students confusing these two phonemes reply *pan.* They are likely to make the same mistake when reading the word *pan.* When asked what the new word means, they proudly explain that it is something to write with. Slipping the following activities into your day will help end the confusion:

- These students would benefit from 5 to 10 minutes every day of practice blending, segmenting, and spelling words with these two sounds.
- Play a short game where the children hold up one "man" if you say *man,* and two "men" if you say *men.*
- Ask students to say *cook* if you say *pan,* and *write* if you say *pen.*
- Make sure that students can write *e* when you say that sound. Expect students to sound-write all the vowels.
- Write the vowels in a circle on the board and have the students "say the vowel circle," as you point to the letters. Listen to be certain they are accurately saying each sound. Be sure that your voice and jaw go down when you say /ă/, overaccentuating the dip.
- Line up with a vowel focus: As you call students to line up, instead of saying, "Table 1 Line Up," ask Table 1 to first say the sound for /ĕ/ before lining up. Locate your students at Table 1 who still have vowel confusion and ask them to individually tell you the difficult letter sound. Example: "Table 1, tell me the sound of short e before you line up." (signal) "Good. Jessie and Dustin, let me hear you say the short a sound one more time." (signal) "Table 2. . . . ."

frequently forgotten. Students are encouraged to memorize the words, thus promoting the idea that reading words involves memorization, not sounding out.

Adapting this lesson for students who are at risk includes adding more My Turn–Together–Your Turn opportunities so everyone gets enough practice. The format for introducing new letter sounds in the general curriculum, which is detailed in Table 3.4 beginning on page 85, can be used by teachers to instruct any new letter sound. Once students receive more directed instruction and practice the new sound by itself, teachers build in practice of the new sound along with previously introduced sounds using Part B of the same format. Any teacher using a reading curriculum containing lessons similar to the example /u/ lesson can modify letter–sound activities by starting lessons using the formats included in Table 3.4. Although it is important that students directly see how the letter sounds and phonemic awareness they are learning relate to word reading, having students read these words as sight words can undermine their acquisition of the alphabetic principle. Instead of having students read the words, ask the students to say the first letter sound when you point to and read the words on the chart.

Reading Regular Words Is a Three-Part Process

The ultimate goal of instruction in reading regular words is helping your students attain the alphabetic principle; this means obtaining a score of 50 or greater on DIBELS Nonsense Word Fluency while reading at least 15 of the nonsense words as whole words. When students reach alphabetic principle they move beyond the individual sound level and automatically decode groups of letter sounds as chunks. There are three parts to the format for reading regular words. In Part 1, students sound out each word orally, receiving added support from the teacher using My Turn–Together–Your Turn as needed. In Part 2, students continue to sound out the words, but do so in their heads. In Part 3 student sounding out is at an automatic level; students read each regular word the fast way, without any conscious sounding out. In this section a description of each of these parts, including when to use them based on students' DIBELS NWF scores, will be provided.

Part 1: Sounding Out Orally   Sounding out regular words should begin as soon as possible, because phonemic awareness and knowledge of letter sounds are not sufficient for students who are at risk. Systematic, explicit instruction in sounding out words is a third component for learning to read. Students who are at risk require extensive practice sounding out words before they attain the alphabetic principle. Solid sounding out and blending of regular words is a key prerequisite to the automatic recognition of words necessary for fluent reading. When students sound out loud, the teacher can closely monitor their accuracy, providing corrections and additional teaching when needed.

You can begin teaching students to sound out words as soon as they have learned between six and eight letter sounds, including one or two common vowel sounds, and have met benchmark levels in oral segmenting and blending (see Chapter 2). Beginning sounding out is most effectively taught when word selection is first confined to the CVC variants. As described earlier, these are one-syllable words formed using the most common sounds of all single consonants and vowels. Some teachers may want to follow the easy-to-hard sequence of CVC words shown in Figure 3.1 (p. 71), starting with CVC words that begin with continuous sounds, because these are the words easiest to blend.

In Part 1 of regular word reading, students orally sound out regular words. This teaching procedure, which is shown in Table 3.5, is most helpful for students at the sounding-out stage as represented by a score of less than 30 on DIBELS NWF, with few if any nonsense words read as whole words. Part 1 stresses several critical skills required to sound out words: sounding out words from left to right and attending to every letter in the word before reading the whole word. Note that students are first taught to sound out words

TABLE 3.5 Format for Reading Regular Words—Part 1: Oral Sounding-Out

Outcome	After seeing a regular word, students orally sound out the letter sounds before saying the word.
Materials Needed	Board, chart paper, or overhead transparency and writing implement. Write the regular words that students will read in rows on the board. For example, if students are reading eight words, write two rows of four words.
Signaling	Three-part signal: Finger is in starting position to the left of the word. **"Sound out,"** or **"What word"** initiates the signal for unison answers.
	1. Use loop signal for orally sounding out the letter sounds in the words.
	2. As students are saying the final letter sound, immediately loop finger back to the starting point.
	3. Pause for a moment of think time before asking students **"What word?"** and side-slash to the end of the word.
Time	Depends on number of new words and difficulty level. Kindergarten students often work on this skill between 5 and 15 minutes each day. First grade students may need to work on this skill for up to 20 minutes if the curriculum has introduced many new words or a new letter–sound pattern. Older students with alphabetic principle may only have a few new one-syllable words that are appropriate for this format.

Instructions	**Teacher**	**Students**
	1. Advance Organizer	
	2. My Turn (Note: See Ms. Elizondo's fourth tip on page 93 in the text to determine whether to start at Step 2, 3, or 4.)	
	(finger to the left of the first letter) **"My turn sounding out this word."** (loop from letter to letter) **"/f/-/ă/-/n/"** (loop back to starting point) **"What word?"** (side-slash signal) ***"fan."***	
	3. Together	
	The teacher answers with students this time:	
	(finger to the left of the first letter) **"Together, sound out this word."** (loop from letter to letter) **"/f/-/ă/-/n/."** (loop back to starting point) **"What word?"** (side-slash signal) ***"fan."*** (loop to starting point) **"Yes, *fan."***	/f/-/ă/-/n/ fan
	4. Your Turn	
	(finger to the left of the first letter) **"Your turn to sound out this word."** (loop from letter to letter) (answer) (loop back to starting point) **"What word?"** (side-slash signal) (answer) (loop to starting point) **"Yes, *fan."*** Repeat step 4 for every word in the row.	/f/-/ă/-/n/ fan
	5. Individual Student Checkout:	
	Point to the first regular word written on the board (*fan*) and place your finger slightly to the left of the word.	
	"Individual turns. Sound out this word. Grant." (loop from letter to letter) (answer) (loop back to starting point) **"What word?"** (side-slash signal) (answer) (loop to starting point) **"Yes, *fan."***	/f/-/ă/-/n/ fan
	"Sound out this word. Leila." (loop from letter to letter) (answer) (loop back to starting point) **"What word?"** (side-slash signal) (answer) (loop to starting point) **"Yes, *sip."***	/s/-/ĭ/-/p/ sip
	Call on several students to check for accuracy. When students' correct answers show you that they know all of the words in the row, move to the second row of words. Be sure to move to using mainly Your Turns as soon as possible.	
Error Correction	If students make an error, immediately return to a My Turn–Together–Your Turn pattern, always requiring them to sound out the word. Then return to the beginning of the row and have students reread words the fast way.	

Continued

TABLE 3.5   Continued

Perk up Your Drill	■ Do not assume that students are connecting word reading to story reading, even when you do both activities each day. In addition to providing the rationale for word reading at the beginning of the lesson, at least once or twice during the lesson explain to your students how learning to read words will enable them to read books about interesting topics: "You just read the word *sip* all by yourself. When you read books about birthday parties, you might see the word *sip* used when everyone in the story sips some pop before eating the cake." Telling students that the words they are reading on the board will later appear in the story motivates them to do their best.
	■ When students are at this beginning pre-alphabetic principle stage and need to slowly sound out before blending words, you may find following this format tedious and slow going. Be assured that this is the most important drill that you can do and if you carefully follow the scripts allowing students to practice their sounding out, your class will soon acquire alphabetic principle and move on to faster word reading.
Adaptations	■ Although you may have readers in your class, you cannot assume that they have learned alphabetic principle, since they may have originally learned the beginning regular words as sight words. Thus, they will benefit from practice with decoding these words. If any readers in your class appear to be reading one or two grade levels above your other students, work with your school team to determine whether it is appropriate for them to participate in a higher grade-level reading group. Use a higher grade-level DIBELS Oral Reading Fluency assessment (Chapter 5) to determine whether the student(s) in question should move up to another reading group or a reading class in a higher grade.
	■ Some students can automatically read new words after one or two times of sounding them out and blending the letter sounds. Before the end of the lesson, ask these students to read the words the fast way.

Source: This script is based on one originally developed and field tested by Carnine, Silbert, Kame'enui, and Tarver, (2004). *Direct Instruction Reading* (4th ed.). New Jersey, Merrill Prentice Hall.

in lists, so that they avoid the use of picture and context cues. Picture and context cues can undermine student acquisition of the alphabetic principle by encouraging guessing and are not recommended when teaching beginning students who are at risk to read. Reading cues will be discussed at length later in this chapter and in Chapter 4. Students should remain at Part 1 of regular word reading until they are able to sound out lists of CVC words with 100% accuracy, and without the teacher having to provide support in the form of My Turn–Together–Your Turn.

The signaling procedure for Part 1 of reading regular words is shown in Figure 3.12. First the teacher points to the left of the word to show that sounding always begins on the left side of a word and that sounding is about to begin. The teacher then uses a looping motion as she moves from letter to letter in the word. Students say the letter sound as the

FIGURE 3.12   Signal for Sounding Out Regular Words

teacher's finger rests underneath the letter for one or two seconds. As students are saying the final letter sound, the teacher immediately loops her finger back to the first letter sound. After a pause, the teacher asks students, 'What word?" and side-slashes to the end of the word.

Five Best Practices for Teaching Oral Sounding-Out   Let's look at how Ms. Elizondo used Part 1 of regular word reading with her students at the sounding stage using the following five best practices:

Provide more time as needed for teaching difficult skills to mastery.   Most of Ms. Elizondo's students came to first grade knowing their letter sounds. Many of them still needed more practice blending because they slowly and often inaccurately sounded out words. In order to make sure that her students had fully developed alphabetic principle by January, she spent more time than the general education reading curriculum recommended on word reading, including the sounding out comprising Part 1. Every day before class, she wrote the new words in the regular curriculum on the board and started by using the Part 1 format listed in Table 3.5 to teach them. Although the curriculum recommended a lesson a day, when the words were especially difficult, she spent two or even three days on the problematic lesson. Because the principal had decided that morning language arts instruction was sacred and that all assemblies or other activities would always be scheduled in the afternoon, she was more confident moving through the curriculum at a slower pace. With nothing interfering in the morning, she had gained more teaching days.

Avoid adding schwas to stop sounds.   Ms. Elizondo was careful to avoid adding schwas to her sounds when using the My Turn strategy the first time through the word list. Although she had learned the correct pronunciation of letter sounds, the teaching coach had pointed out that when Ms. Elizondo was blending words, she sometimes added those cumbersome schwas. While the coach was observing her, she had actually blended *pal* as /puh/+/a/+/luh/. Sometimes bad habits pop up at the most embarrassing times. Ms. Elizondo was careful so that situation never happened again.

Calibrate think time to difficulty of the task.   Once Ms. Elizondo moved from the My Turn step, she was careful to calibrate the amount of think time that she provided students before asking "What word?" If she didn't pause between the time when students said the letter sounds and when they said the entire word, only her best students would answer. Ms. Elizondo knew that when those three or four louder readers answered at lightening speed, she could easily be fooled into believing that the entire class knew the new words taught that day. The first time she had students read the words on a new list, she gave more think time than on the second or third time, because her goal was having students read the words faster.

When students are successful sounding out new words, start teaching at Step 4.   *Continue using the entire My Turn–Together–Your Turn sequence for more difficult new words.* Although during the first and sometimes the second time reading the word list Ms. Elizondo carefully progressed through all of the steps in Table 3.5, when her students were more proficient and orally sounding out the words independently she phased out the My Turn and Together steps and started teaching at Step 4 (Your Turn). As soon as Ms. Elizondo noticed that her students were reading new CVC words accurately and more rapidly the first time they saw them, she began encouraging independence by also starting at Step 4 for the new word lists. After all, Ms. Elizondo knew that readers must develop confidence when sounding out new words they are seeing for the first time. When a more difficult word was on the new list that she anticipated her students would miss, she continued to use the entire My Turn–Together–Your Turn sequence for that word.

Use assessment information to determine individual turns.   Every day Ms. Elizondo gave more turns during individual checkouts to her students who received the lowest scores on the DIBELS Nonsense Word Assessment. She knew that they would receive extra practice reading the words in the afternoon during booster sessions, but she also wanted to provide extra practice during her morning teaching session. When her students were able to sound out words accurately without her help Ms. Elizondo added Part 2 of regular word reading to her daily instruction in reading regular words.

Providing Differentiated Instruction

Typical Activity.   A typical reading curriculum details an early word reading lesson in which the purpose of the activity is blending sounds into words using the new letter sound /n/ and several other letter sounds previously introduced. The teacher is instructed to give each student the following letter cards: *n, i, a, p,* and *t* and tell everyone to place each letter into their mini pocket chart. As each letter is placed in the chart, the students are to say its sound.

Next the teacher is advised to place the letters *a* and *n* in her large pocket chart and direct the students to do the same in their small ones. Instructions in the curriculum guide indicate that the teacher should demonstrate blending the word *an* by sliding her hand under the letters as she slowly stretches the sounds /ăăănnn/. She is supposed to say the word *an* naturally before asking her students to do the same.

Finally, the teacher is instructed to give the following directions before students blend sounds to read new words:

"Put *p* at the beginning. What word did you make?" (*pan*)
"Change the *a* in *pan* to *i*. What word did you make?" (*pin*)
"Make the *p* and *n* change places. What word did you make?" (*nip*)

Weaknesses of the Activity.   The major problem with this activity is that the teacher doesn't provide enough support for blending sounds into words. She does one My Turn when she blends the word *an* before immediately moving into a Your Turn. Usually multiple My Turns and Togethers are necessary when teaching students to blend sounds for the first time. More confusion is introduced when the teacher follows this one example with a series of Your Turns, expecting students to form new words by moving letters around. Evidently, the teacher assumes that with no guided practice, after one example, students will learn to blend the sounds in these new words automatically and independently. Unless modified, this activity does not provide the support and practice that many students who are at risk need to learn blending. A final problem with this activity is that students are asked to respond individually with their own letters. Managing students' behavior and monitoring their work under these conditions present additional challenges in many classrooms.

Enhancing the Activity.   This activity described above could be adapted in a number of ways. First, to avoid the behavior management and monitoring problems that can occur when using manipulatives in a large group, the teacher could have students respond in unison as she manipulates the letters on her large pocket chart. The teacher could also use the format in Table 3.5, injecting My Turn–Together–Your Turn for each of the words the first time the students blend them. The second time through the list, the teacher could switch to Your Turns for these same words, first asking students to sound out each word before reading it the fast way. The teacher could also use individual turns with some of her lowest performers to make sure that all of the students acquire the emphasized word reading skill.

Part 2: Sounding Out Words Subvocally   A key goal of reading instruction is the accurate, fluent reading of connected text. Once students can orally sound out words independently with a high degree of accuracy, teachers need to prepare them for the next phase in attaining the alphabetic principle by adding Part 2 to their daily regular word reading instruction: sounding out words in their heads, or **subvocal sounding-out.** It was once thought that fluent adult readers relied mainly on context and background knowledge to figure out words, engaging in what was often called a guessing game as they made their way through connected text. More recent research shows just the opposite; while mature readers are fluent, they still attend to the letters in words, but at an automatic level. Pausing to look at pictures or use word attack strategies that focus on the middle or the end of the word interrupts the reading process. Consider this description by Shaywitz (2003) of a mature reader encountering a new word.

> She sees a word and scans all the letters. Do any of the letters fall into a familiar pattern? Do they resemble letter groups—parts of words—that she has stored? If so, she is able to take these letter patterns and connect them to a known pronunciation. For example, if she sees the unfamiliar printed word *architect,* meaning a designer of buildings, she may know that the letters t-e-c-t- go together and how they are pronounced. She may also know from experience that the letters a-r-c-h are often grouped together and that arch sounds either like arch of your foot or Noah's ark. She tries to pronounce the unknown word both ways, architect or ar-ki- tect, and uses the surrounding text to judge which pronunciation fits. From the context, she realizes that the word is *architect,* meaning a designer of buildings, and is pronounced like ark (ar-ki-tect). Once she has successfully decoded this word, it joins the other words stored in her lexicon. (p. 104)

Note that in this example, the reader first scans the word from left to right looking for graphophonemic cues. Only after the reader looks at the letters does she use context cues to make her final decoding decision. This example demonstrates the importance of the alphabetic principle and why it needs to be established first, before other decoding cues such as using the context are introduced.

Teachers cannot assume that most students who are at risk will make a successful transition from oral sounding out to silently reading words the fast way without adding a transition step that provides subvocal sounding-out practice. Once students no longer need to say each sound aloud, their speed with word reading will increase. Part 2 of regular word reading is a format for helping students make the transition from sounding out loud to sounding out words in their heads. This teaching procedure is especially effective for students who are still scoring below 30 on the DIBELS NWF but are at the transition sounding-out stage described earlier in the chapter. The transition sounding-out stage means that they are still saying the individual sounds in words but are blending them into whole words as well. The format for Part 2 of regular word reading is shown in Table 3.6.

The signals used for subvocal sounding-out are the same as those used for sounding out words aloud. The only difference is that when the teacher engages in the looping motion from letter to letter, students are mouthing the sounds without saying them out loud. The only time the students answer out loud is when the teacher asks them to identify the word.

Three Best Practices for Teaching Subvocal Sounding-Out   Ms. Elizondo was delighted when she was able to add Part 2, subvocal sounding-out, to her daily instruction in regular word reading. She used Part 2 when her students were able to first sound out the words for the day with 100% accuracy using Part 1. She then moved to Part 2 while using the following three best practices to help her students transition to subvocal sounding-out:

Carefully watch students' eye movements.   Ms. Elizondo carefully watched eye movement to check if students' eyes were moving from left to right as they directly looked at the words on the board. When she saw someone's eyes staring in the distance, she tapped their shoulder or called their name to redirect them to the reading work. Because Ms. Elizonda wanted to maintain a motivating classroom, she gave student points for paying attention to the words.

TABLE 3.6   Format for Reading Regular Words—Part 2: Subvocal Sounding-Out

Outcome	After seeing a regular word, student subvocally sounds out the letter sounds before saying the word.
Materials Needed	Board, chart paper, or overhead transparency and writing implement. Write the regular words that students will read in rows on the board. For example, if students are reading eight words, write two rows of four words.
Signaling	Three-part signal: Finger is in starting position to the left of the word. **"Ready,"** **"Sound out in your heads,"** or **"What word"** initiates the signal for unison answers.
	1. Use loop signal for orally sounding out the letter–sounds in the words.
	2. As students are saying the final letter sound, immediately loop finger back to the starting point.
	3. Pause for a moment of think time before asking students **"What word?"** and side-slash to the end of the word.
Time	Depends on number of new words and difficulty level. Kindergarten students often work on this skill for 5 minutes each day. First-grade students may need to work on this skill for up to 20 minutes if the curriculum has introduced many new words or a new letter–sound pattern.

Instructions	**Teacher**	**Student**
	1. Advance Organizer	
	2. My Turn (finger to the left of the first letter) **"My turn sounding out this word in my head."** (loop from letter to letter and silently mouth the letter sounds /f/-/ă/-/n/) (loop back to starting point) **"What word?"** (side-slash signal) **"fan."**	
	3. Together The teacher answers with students this time: (finger to the left of the first letter) **"Together, sound out this word in your heads."** (loop from letter to letter and silently mouth the letter sounds /f/-/ă/-/n/) (loop back to starting point) **"What word?"** (side-slash signal) **"fan."** (loop to starting point) **"Yes, fan."**	fan
	4. Your Turn (finger to the left of the first letter) **"Your turn. Sound out this word in your heads."** (loop from letter to letter) (students mouth sounds) (loop back to starting point) **"What word?"** (side-slash signal) (answer) (loop to starting point) **"Yes, fan."**	fan
	5. Individual Student Checkout (finger to the left of the first letter) **" Individual turns. Sound out this word in your head. Maria."** (loop from letter to letter) (student mouths sounds) (loop back to starting point) **"What word?"** (side-slash signal) (answer) (loop to starting point) **"Yes, fan."** Call on several individual students to check for accuracy.	fan
	6. Read the Row: Reading the row of words the fast way. Note: If you provide three seconds of think time before signaling for an answer, students should be ready to read the row of words the fast way. Use the Part 3 format for this section: **"Let's read all four words the fast way this time."**	
	(think time) **"What word?"** (side-slash signal) (answer) (loop to starting point) **"Yes, fan."**	fan
	(think time) **"What word?"** (side-slash signal) (answer) (loop to starting point) **"Yes, sip."**	sip
	(think time) **"What word?"** (side-slash signal) (answer) (loop to starting point) **"Yes, let."**	let
	(think time) **"What word?"** (side-slash signal) (answer) (loop to starting point) **"Yes, cat."**	cat
	Be sure to move to using mainly Your Turns as soon as possible.	

TABLE 3.6 Continued

Error Correction	If students make an error, immediately return to a My Turn–Together–Your Turn pattern requiring them to sound the word out loud. Then return to the beginning of the row and have students reread words the fast way.
Perk up Your Drill	■ Students love to reach a predetermined goal. Before reading all the words in a row, tell students that their goal is reading every single word in that row. If they read the words correctly, quickly draw a star next to the row and tell them that they just earned their first "starred" row.
	■ When students are reading with 100% accuracy, perk up the pace by giving less think time. As long as the accuracy remains high, you can comfortably move at this quicker pace.
Adaptations	■ As your students transition to Part 3, you will begin to switch between the Part 2 and Part 3 scripts depending on the difficulty of the word. If your students are solid on CVC words containing any vowel but /ĕ/, you will start asking them to read those easier CVC words the fast way from the beginning. When you come to a CVC word containing an /ē/, have the students subvocally sound out the word. If you anticipate that students will almost certainly make an error on a difficult word the first time they read the word, ask them to sound it out loud.

Source: This script is based on one originally developed and field tested by Carnine, Silbert, Kame'enui, and Tarver, (2004). *Direct Instruction Reading* (4th ed.). New Jersey, Merrill Prentice Hall.

When students are subvocally sounding out new words accurately with teacher support, start teaching at Step 4. Continue to use the entire My Turn–Together–Your Turn sequence for difficult new words.   When her students became more proficient at subvocal sounding-out, Ms. Elizondo again faded out the My Turn and Together steps and started teaching at Step 4, Your Turn. She continued to use the entire My Turn–Together–Your Turn sequence for difficult new words.

Once students can subvocally sound out words without help, add Part 3, reading words the fast way, to your daily regular word reading.   As her students moved through Part 2 reading and were able to subvocally sound out words accurately, without added teacher support, Ms. Elizondo added Part 3, reading words the fast way, to her daily instruction in reading regular words. It was at this point that Ms. Elizondo noticed that her students' DIBELS scores were beginning to approach 30, the point at which they could read word lists the fast way, using sounding-out only for more difficult words or for making error corrections.

Part 3: Reading Words the Fast Way   Once students are able to sound out words in their heads accurately, add Part 3 to your daily teaching, which is reading words the "fast way," a term used by Carnine and colleagues (2004) to represent sounding-out at an automatic level. It is important to make a distinction here between what is called reading the "fast way" and another frequently used term, *sight reading.* While interpretations of the meaning of sight reading vary, a common implication drawn from the term is that the words have been memorized first rather than sounded out. For the purposes of this text, "reading the fast way" is preferred, because, except for irregular words that can't be sounded out, reading the fast way is preceded by sounding-out, not memorization. When this part of reading regular words is introduced into your daily word reading exercises, students are beginning to say the words without pausing to sound out, because the process is becoming automatic. Table 3.7 describes Part 3, the format for teaching students to read words the fast way. When your students' DIBELS NWF scores are at 30 and above, they are beginning to see words in chunks, rather than as individual sounds. You can detect this when you notice that your students are reading at the onset-rime stage on their DIBELS NWF (starting to read dov as *d ov* rather than as *d o v*). They may also be reading the nonsense

TABLE 3.7   Format for Reading Regular Words—Part 3: The Fast Way

Outcome	After seeing a regular word, students orally read the word the fast way.
Materials Needed	Board, chart paper, or overhead transparency and writing implement. Write the regular words that students will read in rows on the board. For example, if students are reading eight words, write two rows of four words.
Signaling	Finger is in starting position to the left of the word. **"What word"** initiates the side-slash signal for unison answers.
Time	Depends on number of new words and difficulty level. First grade students may need to work on this skill for up to 20 minutes if the curriculum has introduced many new words or a new letter–sound pattern. Older students with alphabetic principle may only have a few new one-syllable words that are appropriate for this format.

Instructions	**Teacher**	**Student**
	1. Advance Organizer	
	2. My Turn (use for first word only, and only for the first day or two using this format)	
	(finger to the left of the first letter) **"My turn to read this word the fast way?"** (side-slash signal) ***"fan."***	
	3. Your Turn	
	Note: For new words that you anticipate your students misreading, use the Part 1 sounding out format the first time the word is introduced in the list.	
	"Your turn to read the rest of the words."	
	(point and pause) **"What word?"** (side-slash answer) (loop back to starting point) **"Yes, *fan.*"**	fan
	(point and pause) **"What word?"** (side-slash answer) (loop back to starting point) **"Yes, *hat.*"**	hat
	(point and pause) **"What word?"** (side-slash answer) (loop back to starting point) **"Yes, *sit.*"**	sit
	(point and pause) **"What word?"** (side-slash answer) (loop back to starting point) **"Yes, *Pam.*"**	Pam
	4. Individual Student Checkout	
	(point and pause) **"Individual turns. What word? Ali."** (side-slash answer) (loop back to starting point) **"Yes, *fan.*"**	fan
	(point and pause) **"What word? Toni."** (side-slash answer) (loop back to starting point) **"Yes, *sit.*"**	sit
	Call on several individual students to check for accuracy.	

Error Correction	If students make an error, immediately return to Part 1 sounding-out aloud using a My Turn–Together–Your Turn pattern. Then return to the beginning of the row and have students reread words the fast way.
Perk up Your Drill	■ Tell students that words they read correctly will go in their weekly dictionaries taken home to parents. Create a sense of drama about the large number of words that are going into the dictionary.
	■ Ask a student to lead the drill, signaling just as you do.
Adaptations	■ Many students who are at risk will not automatically know common vocabulary such as *snap, pal,* or *tap.* Connecting words to their usage or meaning will help students remember them while expanding their vocabulary. After students read a word for which they don't know the meaning, some teachers will connect the word to its meaning and use the word in a brief sentence, saying the key word louder for emphasis. **"A *pal* is a friend. In our story yesterday, Big Bear's *pal* was mouse."**

Source: This script is based on one originally developed and field tested by Carnine, Silbert, Kame'enui, and Tarver, (2004). *Direct Instruction Reading* (4th ed.). New Jersey, Merrill Prentice Hall.

words slowly, but as whole words. When students reach this point, use Part 3 exclusively for their daily regular word reading, except for particularly difficult words or when correcting student errors.

The signaling procedure for reading the fast way consists of touching to the left of the word, providing a thinking pause, saying, "What word?", and then giving the side slash signal. Tips for teaching students to read words the fast way are as follows.

Five Best Practices for Teaching Part 3, "The Fast Way"   Note how Ms. Elizondo used the following five best practices when she used Part 3 in teaching her students to read words the fast way:

Use assessment information to guide teaching.   Every morning, Ms. Elizondo wrote the new words from the daily lesson on the board and presented a brief advance organizer, telling her students that first they would read words that would later appear in the new elephant story. Since almost everyone in her class had scored 50 or higher on the DIBELS NWF Assessment, she only used Part 3 for her regular word reading unless the story had a particularly difficult word that needed to be sounded out or when her students made errors.

Gradually decrease your think time.   Ms. Elizondo knew that think time was critical during this stage of reading. The first time students read through the word list, Mrs. Elizondo paused for three seconds after asking, "What word," before giving the signal to read the word. This longer think time increased her students' success reading the words the first time. The second time she went through the list, she paused for only one or two seconds of think time.

Only begin with a My Turn when first introducing the Part 3 format.   Because Ms. Elizondo's students already understood what reading words the fast way meant, she skipped the My Turns in Steps 1 and 2, and began her Part 3 word reading with a Your Turn using Step 3.

Preplan by using the optional step for difficult words.   To prevent errors when a difficult new word was on the list, Ms. Elizondo used the "optional step" and asked students first to orally sound out the difficult word. For example, when /str/ was introduced in the new lesson, she returned to a My Turn–Together–Your Turn Part 1 sounding-out pattern to show students how to apply the new letter sounds to *strum*, *stream*, and *strict*. She knew that whenever students make errors reading a word, it takes much longer for them to learn it.

Use assessment information to determine individual turns.   As always, Ms. Elizondo gave students who received the lowest scores on the DIBELS NWF assessment more turns during individual student checkouts.

The process of helping students attain the alphabetic principle is critical, but important decisions about when to use which of the three word-reading formats, and with which students, can be complicated. A chart of how to match your students with the appropriate formats based on their scores on the DIBELS NWF measure is shown in Figure 3.13.

Writing Regular Words

Students benefit when they are writing or spelling the same regular words that they are learning to sound out and read. For example, Mr. Drake's students sounded out the following words in their daily lesson: *man*, *rap*, *top*, *pat*, *stop*, and *grab*. He then asked his students to spell each of these words using the format shown in Figure 3.14.

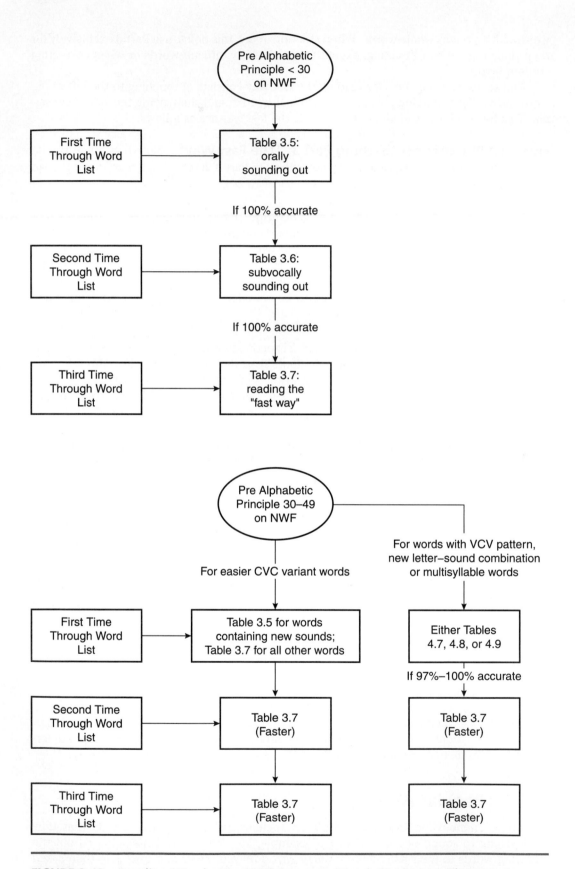

FIGURE 3.13   Reading Words: Use NWF Scores to Match Students with Formats

Spelling activity: Students write *in, pin, pat.*

Teacher: "You're going to write the word *in*. Listen. *In.* Say the sounds in *in*."
Signal for each sound by using a fingersnap, clap, or extended finger as the children say / ĭ ĭ ĭ / (pause) /nnn/. Repeat until firm.

Teacher: "Everybody, write the word (pause) ***in*."**
Check children's answers so you can give feedback.

Repeat for ***pin,*** and ***pat.***

FIGURE 3.14   Regular Word Spelling Format

Source: Adapted from *Reading Mastery* (Engelmann & Bruner, 1995) by Kinder (1990).

Reading Sight Words

Reading connected text, even when most of the words can be sounded out, requires recognition of the most frequently used sight words. For the purposes of this text, a sight word is defined as a word that either contains letters that don't say their most common sounds or letters that have yet to be taught to students in isolation. For example, the word *said* is irregular because the letters *a* and *i* do not represent their most common sounds. The

Bridging the Gap

Which Is the Best Way to Teach Beginning Readers?

Should I start instruction by teaching students to blend individual letter–sounds into words, or start with larger units or word-families and have students use them to read words?

Two of the most common beginning phonics approaches are letter–sound blending and word-family instruction (Wanzek & Hagger, 2003). In letter–sound blending, students are first taught the most common sounds of letters in isolation and are then taught to blend them into words. This is the approach used in this text that is referred to as synthetic phonics. For example, Mr. Ellis taught his students to identify the sounds /m/, /s/, /t/, and /a/ in isolation. Once these letter sounds were learned, and his students could orally segment and blend, Mr. Ellis taught them to read words such as *Sam, sat,* and *mast*. Another beginning phonics approach starts by using larger units of sounds such as word families. In this approach, called analogizing, students are typically taught a rime pattern and then taught to use that known word part to form new words. For example, Ms. Calhoun taught her students to read the rime /am/. She then taught her students to read related words such as *Sam, ham, mam,* and so on.

The National Reading Panel (1990) found that both letter–sound blending and analogizing were effective in teaching beginning word-reading to students. Which of these approaches should teachers use with their students who are at risk? Wanzek and Hagger (2003) suggest that both be used, with letter–sound blending coming first because it is a necessary preskill for word reading, and word-family instruction next because it helps students better generalize their decoding skills to more complex words. Once students have alphabetic principle, Wanzek and Haggar (2003) suggest the following guidelines for teaching analogizing.

- Select rimes that consist of previously taught letter–sound correspondences or letter combinations.
- Select words that progress from simple onsets (*man*), then blends (*Stan*), then multisyllable words (*panel*).
- Provide opportunities for students to find similar patterns in words and teach them to use words they know to read other words (p. 36).

TABLE 3.8 Format for Reading Sight Words

Outcome	After seeing a sight word, students orally read the word the fast way.
Materials Needed	Board, chart paper, or overhead transparency and writing implement. Teacher writes the new sight words in a column. The review sight words are written in another column.
Signaling	Two-part signal: **"What word?"** or **"Spell _____"** initiates the signal for unison answers. 1. After asking **"What word?"** use a side-slash signal and after students answer, loop back to the starting point before affirming the answer. 2. After saying **"Spell _____,"** point under each letter as students spell the word.
Time	3–5 minutes

Instructions	Teacher	Student
	1. Advance Organizer	
	Part 1: Introduction of new words.	
	2. Write the new sight words from the daily story in a column on the left side of the board: for example, *today, father, strange.* Write four review sight words in a column on the right side of the board: for example, *was, isn't, should, great.* Teach the first new sight word written on the board (*today*).	
	a. (finger to the left of the first letter) **"This word is"** (side-slash while saying **"today."**) (loop back to starting point)	
	b. **"What word?"** (side-slash-answer) (loop back to starting point) **"Yes, *today."***	today
	c. **"Spell *today."*** (point to each letter as students answer) (loop back to starting point)	t-o-d-a-y
	d. **"What word?"** (side-slash-answer) (loop back to starting point) **"Yes, *today."***	today
	e. (finger to the left of the first letter) **"This word is"** (side-slash while saying **"father."**) (loop back to starting point)	
	f. **"What word?"** (side-slash-answer) (loop back to starting point) **"Yes, *father."***	father
	g. **"Spell *father."*** (point to each letter as students answer) (loop back to starting point)	f-a-t-h-e-r
	h. **"What word?"** (side-slash-answer) (loop back to starting point) **"Yes, *father."***	father
	i. Return to the top of the list and point to the left of the first word. Pause and ask, **"What word?"** (side-slash-answer) (loop back to starting point) **"Yes, *today."***	today
	Quickly point to the left of the second word. Pause and ask, **"What word?"** (side-slash-answer) (loop back to starting point) **"Yes, *father."***	father
	j. Repeat steps e–i with the remaining words until students can read all of the words in the column without errors.	
	k. Individual Student Checkout: Call on between one and three students to check for accuracy.	
	Part 2: Students sight read new words and review words.	
	3. Point to words randomly.	
	a. **"When I signal, read the word."**	
	(finger to the left of the first letter) **"What word?"** (side-slash-answer) (loop back to starting point) **"Yes, *father."***	father
	(finger to the left of the first letter) **"What word?"** (side-slash-answer) (loop back to starting point) **"Yes, *was."***	was
	(finger to the left of the first letter) **"What word?"** (side-slash-answer) (loop back to starting point) **"Yes, *should."***	should
	b. Individual Student Checkout: Call on between one and three students to check for accuracy.	

TABLE 3.8 Continued

Error Correction	If students make an error, immediately return to a My Turn. Tell students the word, ask them to spell the word, and then ask them to read the sight word (Part 1: Steps a–d).
Perk up Your Drill	■ On the last section of the sight word script (Part 2), tell students that you will erase every word they read correctly. The goal is to have all words erased on the first read-through.
	■ If you are working with a smaller group, you can write each sight word on a large card to hold up. Construct a "we know that" box and on the last section of the sight word script (Part 2), dramatically throw each word that students read correctly into the box.
Adaptations	■ Many students who are at risk will not automatically put sight words such as *was, where, should,* and *couldn't* into context unless you briefly add that component at the start. Connecting words to their usage or meaning will help students remember them while expanding their vocabulary. The first time they introduce a new sight word, some teachers will use the sight word in a brief sentence, saying the sight word louder for emphasis, **"This word is *should.*" Your mom says, "It's late and you *should* go to bed."** Later in the lesson, if students make an error, the teacher will use another sentence to connect the word to its meaning.

Source: This script is based on one originally developed and field tested by Carnine, Silbert, Kame'enui, and Tarver, (2004). *Direct Instruction Reading* (4th ed.). New Jersey, Merrill Prentice Hall.

word *chin* would be irregular if students had yet to learn the /ch/ sound. Students who are at risk or who have disabilities need extra practice learning sight words, especially before the alphabetic principle has been established. When a new sight word is introduced, students are first told what the word is and are asked to repeat it. The students then spell the word as the teacher points to each individual letter. Lastly, the students say the word again. Requiring that students spell the word reinforces the important idea that even for words that can't be sounded, it is still important to look at all the letters of a word in a left-to-right sequence. Once sight words are introduced, they are thereafter read the fast way unless there is an error. In that case, the teacher returns to a My Turn, supplying the word and asking students to spell it, just as if the word was being introduced for the first time. The format for introducing sight words is shown in Table 3.8.

Two Tips for Teaching Sight Words   Try these two strategies to enhance your teaching of sight words:

Use thinking pauses to build student fluency in reading new sight words.   During Part 1, when first introducing the word, use longer think time and pause for 3 seconds before asking, "What word?" During Part 2, only pause for 1 or 2 seconds to build student fluency.

Avoid teaching similar sight words together, such as *where* and *were.*   Include similar sight words together only after students can automatically read each individual word when it is presented by itself.

Reading Decodable Sentences

Once students can sound out a number of regular words and know a few sight words, you can begin reading sentences. Sentence reading provides a good opportunity to explicitly teach students to read connected text. Using this format, students quickly learn to follow a line of print, recognize that spaces mark boundaries between words, automatically move from left to right, read word-by-word, recognize that sentences are composed of words, and recognize final punctuation marks. If your students' DIBELS NWF scores are under 30 and they are still learning new words by orally or subvocally sounding them out before reading

Bridging the Gap

Can I Still Use My Word Wall?

A Word Wall is a group of high-frequency written words displayed in alphabetical order on a bulletin board or a section of a classroom wall. The purpose of the wall is to make the words accessible so that students can find them when reading and writing and teachers can readily focus on them when providing practice in class (Cunningham, 2000). The Word Wall gives children extra practice reading, writing, and understanding the meaning of high-frequency regular words and sight words. This purpose is consistent with the objectives of the phonics approach described in this text. In addition, the "chanting" often used when reading from the Word Wall is very similar to the unison response formats used here. Problems with the Word Wall can occur when the words on the wall are not decodable; that is, they include regular words containing untaught sounds, untaught words, or too many irregular words. Here are four keys to using the Word Wall effectively with students who are at risk.

1. Only select regular words that contain sounds that have already been taught.
2. Select only irregular words that have already been taught.
3. For every five regular words, select one irregular word.
4. When asking your students to read the words, use teaching strategies that discourage student guessing. For example, have students sound out the regular words while they are chanting, rather than having them sight read the words. Try putting regular and irregular words in a separate color. Use signals so everyone answers together. Calibrate your think time for students' reading ability.

Seize the Teachable Moment

A Dozen Creative Suggestions

Killer Word Boost

If your class has a "killer word" for the week, wear a scarf one day and tape the difficult word on the scarf or pin the word to your lapel. Students' eyes will alight on the word every time they look at you. Tell students you will try to trick them throughout the day by asking them to read the word at moments when they least expect that question.

Beat the Clock

If you routinely write all new sight words on large cards, you can pull these cards out when your class is waiting to get their pictures taken or go to an assembly and you have 5 minutes to fill. Each new word should be written on three cards to play this game. Select a set of irregular words that students have already learned to correctly identify for the game (for example, *through, beautiful, where, enough, though*). Your goal is getting students to recognize these words more fluently.

- Include multiple cards of each word in the card deck.
- Set a goal such as 25 words correct per minute. Tell the students that you will play a game with them and that their goal is to correctly read at least 25 word cards in 1 minute.
- Start the timer or have an appointed student start it.
- Hold up the first word card so that all students can answer in unison.
- Provide quick corrective feedback whenever students make errors ("This word is *because*.")
- Continue presenting words until the timer rings.
- Words that are correctly identified go in the throwaway box.
- Words that are read incorrectly go in a pile next to you.
- At the end of 1 minute, count the number of words correct and let the class know whether they met the goal.
- Pick up the cards in the pile and review errors with the students before repeating the activity for another minute.

the whole word (Tables 3.5–3.6), use those same formats during sentence reading. When students come to a sight word, have them read it as a whole word.

Your students will quickly start reading the sentences in unison, but expect that the first few times, your pace will slow as you teach students to follow the signals when reading an entire sentence. If you maintain high expectations for students to read together, they will quickly adopt the habit during this part of instruction. If you do not start with a clear signal for each word ("What word?"), your best readers who do not need as much think time will jump ahead with the word and students who need an extra second or two will soon stop trying and coast by echoing the faster readers. You will be fooled into thinking that students are fluently reading, when in reality, three or four of the best readers are doing all the work for the rest of the class.

The curriculum that Ms. Elizondo was using in her class introduced sentence reading by the middle of September, so she wrote two or three sentences on the board each day underneath the reading words. When her students were still sounding out words (DIBELS NWF < 30), she had them sound out each word before reading it in the sentence: "Sound out." "What word?"; "Sound out." "What word?"; "Sound out." "What word?" If she didn't have students sound out the words on the first read, some students would not be able to apply their decoding skills. Although she sometimes felt like a broken record signaling across the sentence, she knew that with enough practice, the students would soon move into reading words the fast way. Then they would also start reading their sentences without sounding out each word. By the third time students read each sentence, Ms. Elizondo had students read the sentences the fast way using normal intonation.

Reading Decodable Passages– Prealphabetic Principle

Dr. Reid Lyon explains, "The average child needs between four and fourteen exposures to automatize the recognition of a new word. Therefore, in learning to read it is vital that children read a large amount of text at their independent reading level (95% accuracy) and that the text format provides specific practice in the skills being learned" (Lyon, 1998, p. 6). Students who are at risk often need even more opportunities to practice reading books that contain the words they have learned in class. One important component of explicit, systematic phonics instruction is the use of decodable books for passage-reading activities. Decodable books contain a high percentage of regular words comprised of sounds the students have learned plus a few high-frequency sight words. For example, Ms. Rodriguez's students had learned the most common sounds for *s, c, n, a, r, t, l, b,* and *i.* They also learned the sight words *the, a, said, were, to,* and *is.* The following sentence represents decodable text for her students:

Bill ran to the bin.

The students would be able to sound out the regular words *Bill, ran,* and *bin,* and read the sight or irregular words *to* and *the.*

The following sentence, while including high-frequency words, would not be decodable for the same group of students:

Come here, Bob.

In this sentence the sight words *come* and *here* haven't been learned yet. Students have also not learned the most common sound of the letter /o/ and would not be able to sound out the word *Bob.* This sentence is not decodable. For information on how to select decodable books for your students, see the feature on decodable books later in this chapter.

During the first half of first grade, before students typically score 50 on the DIBELS NWF Assessement, the teacher has students read in unison so they get the most practice

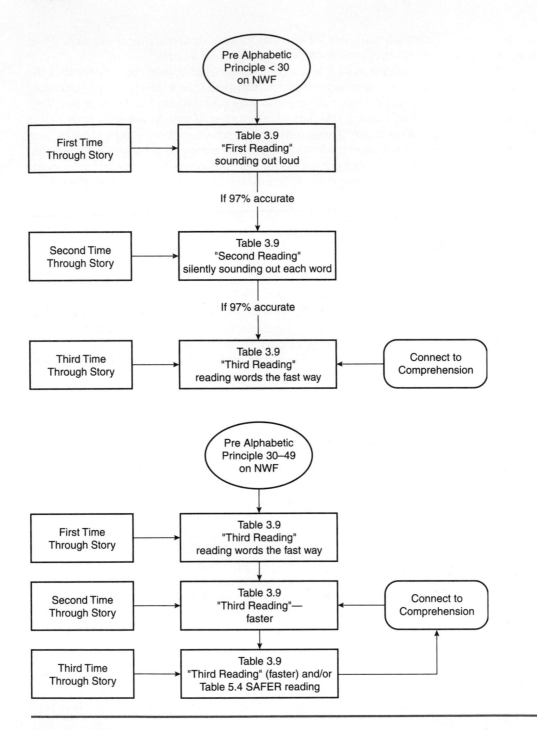

FIGURE 3.15a   Passage Reading: Use NWF Scores to Match Students with Formats

possible on sounding out and reading regular words, the heart of the alphabetic principle. When students are explicitly taught to read connected text, they quickly learn to follow a line of print, to recognize that spaces mark boundaries between words, to automatically move from left to right, to read word by word, to recognize that sentences are composed of words, and to recognize final punctuation marks. Figures 3.15a and b will help you decide which format a student needs, based on the DIBELS NWF score.

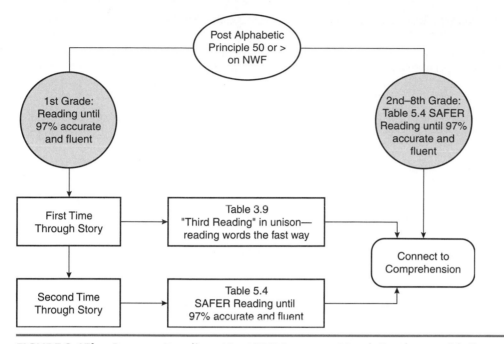

FIGURE 3.15b   Passage Reading: Use NWF Scores to Match Students with Formats

The actual steps of the format are described in Table 3.9 (pp. 108–109). For students whose scores on the DIBELS NWF are less than 30, the teacher uses all three readings described in the format, as follows. On the first reading the students sound out all words in unison except for sight words, which are read by the group as whole words. The teacher moves to the second reading when the first reading is performed with at least 97% accuracy. If students read below 97% accuracy, they sound out the story again, orally. During the second reading, the students subvocally sound out each word in the decodable text before saying it. For the third reading, students read each word in unison the fast way. If the teacher has selected a book that matches the students' word reading skills, this third reading is usually done accurately the first time through. As was done with the first reading, the second and third readings are repeated if performed with less than 97% accuracy. Check comprehension on the third reading.

You learned earlier that students whose scores on DIBELS NWF are between 30 and 49 are reading whole words in their list reading. Therefore, their passage reading begins with the third reading on Table 3.9, reading words the fast way in unison. The students read the story through two times in unison as a group, reading each word the fast way, with the teacher building fluency by gradually decreasing the thinking time required over the course of the two readings. If students perform fluently with 97% accuracy the second time through, take individual turns, with each student reading one sentence each. Check comprehension during this third reading. Once students reach benchmark levels on DIBELS NWF, they are ready to read stories in a more traditional fashion by taking individual turns as described in the SAFER oral-passage-reading format in Chapter 5 (see Table 5.4, p. 184).

Tips for the Transition from Words to Passages

A few tips will help you successfully move from word-reading to decodable-passage reading.

1. Although your students will quickly start reading the sentences in unison, expect that the first few times your pace will slow as you teach students to follow the signals while they follow with their fingers and turn pages of the book.

TABLE 3.9   Format for Reading Stories in the Curriculum and Decodable Books: Pre-Alphabetic Principle

Outcome	Students who have scored less than 30 letter sounds per minute on the DIBELS NWF assessment will read a book containing words or word patterns taught in class, sounding out the words before reading them with 100% accuracy. Students who score between 30 and 49 on DIBELS NWF will read words the fast way using the procedures described in the third reading.
Materials Needed	Use decodable text or text containing regular and sight words that the students are capable of reading with at least 90% accuracy.
Signaling	Finger snap or hand clap. **"What word?"** initiates the signal for unison answer.
Time	Between 15 and 30 minutes

Instructions	**Teacher**	**Students**
	Advance Organizer	
	Steps to reading stories and books (Pre-Alphabetic Principle):	
	First Reading(s)	
	1. Suggested wording for focusing students to follow along: **"We are first going to sound out each word and then we will read it the fast way. When I clap, say the sound of the first letter. When I clap again, move your finger and say the next sound. When you are at the end of the word, move your finger back to the beginning of the word so you can read it the fast way. Watch me do it first."** (You will need to use a finger snap with your nondominant hand as you show students how you follow along to the signal, sounding out and reading the words.) **"Everybody, put your finger under the first letter of the very first word."**	Students touch under the first letter of the first word.
	2. Focus students to accurate reading and tell them the goal you've set: **"Our goal is to miss no more than one word today."**	
	3. First Story Reading—Sounding-Out: Pause 1 second and then say, **"Sound it out"** and clap for the first sound. After 1 to 1½ seconds, clap for the next sound. After 1 to 1½ seconds later clap for the last sound. When students have said the last sound correctly, make sure that they move their finger back to the left of the word. Ask **"What word?"** and clap. Students side-slash their finger as they read the word the fast way. Then they immediately move their finger to the left of the next word.	Students say sounds, pointing under the letters as they say them; they move their finger back to the beginning of the word before orally reading the word at a normal rate.
	4. Pause 1 second and then say **"Sound it out"** and clap for the first sound. After 1 to 1½ seconds, clap for the next sound. After 1 to 1½ seconds later clap for the last sound. When students have said the last sound correctly, make sure that they move their finger back to the left of the word. Ask **"What word?"** and clap. Students side-slash their finger as they read the word the fast way. Then they immediately move their finger to the left of the next word.	
	5. For sight words, avoid sounding out. When students move their fingers to the left of a sight word, say, **"What word?"** and clap to signal students to say the word.	Students read the whole word without sounding it out.
	6. Continue using this format to the end of the story or to the end of the page.	
	7. Wrap Up: Have students reread the story, sounding out each word until the error limit is met. When the error limit is met give individual turns. Do not move on to the second reading format until the error limit is met.	

TABLE 3.9   Continued

Second Reading(s) 1. Repeat Steps 1–5, but have students subvocally sound out the words as in Stage 2 regular word reading (Table 3.6). At the end of the story have students practice reading any missed words. Do not move on to third reading format until the error limit is met.	Students subvocally sound out, before saying the word at a normal rate.
Third Reading(s) 1. Repeat Steps 1–5, but have students read words the fast way as in Stage 3 (Table 3.7) word reading. 2. Use individual checkouts to determine whether students are solid on reading the story. Have each student read one sentence.	Students read the words in the story the fast way.

Error Correction	■ When students make a sounding out error, immediately say, **"My Turn,"** and sound out the word correctly. Move into a Your Turn and ask students to sound out the word before always going back to the beginning of the sentence. Any error (missed word, plural ending left off, etc.) is treated as an error.
Perk up Your Drill	■ Approach each story with a high degree of enthusiasm. If you convey your interest in the characters and plot, no matter how simple the story, the students' interest level and motivation will be heightened. During the second reading of the story, you will need to model voice inflection to match punctuation and emphasis in the story. Then ask students to reread the same text using an appropriate tone of voice.
	■ If students grumble about reading a story one more time, reminding them that their accuracy will determine when they move to the next story empowers them and motivates them to do their best.
	■ The day that students take home the story they have learned to read, ask them to whom they will read it. Encourage them to think about reading to a younger sibling, a parent, a grandparent, or a cousin. At the start of the next day's lesson, be sure to ask students about their story reading at home.
Adaptations	■ Kindergartners and first graders who are still scoring under 30 on the DIBELS NWF assessment may need to repeat the first reading steps several times until they are ready to subvocally sound out the same words.
	■ If your students are at Part 2, subvocal regular word reading, begin the story with the second reading format. When your students come to a difficult word, move back into first reading sounding-out for that word.
	■ If your students are nearing alphabetic principle (DIBELS NWF scores in 30–49 range and non-sense words read as whole words) and they read most CVC-variant words as whole words, read new stories starting at the third reading procedure.

Source: This script is based on one originally developed and field tested by Carnine, Silbert, Kame'enui, and Tarver, (2004). *Direct Instruction Reading* (4th ed.). New Jersey, Merrill Prentice Hall.

2. Take time to teach students how to follow the text with the pointer finger of their dominant hand. When students are following along with their fingers, whether reading in unison or when another child is reading, you know they are paying attention. Since consistently following the text will be difficult for your most inattentive students, provide an incentive in the beginning for consistent finger pointing: "The class just earned another point because everyone remembered to follow with their fingers."

Bridging the Gap

Should I Use Pictures with My Beginning Readers?

Teachers are often confused about how to use pictures in their beginning reading programs. Some experts say that pictures are an important motivator for students and that they also help students with comprehension. Other experts warn that pictures can impede progress toward attaining the alphabetic principle by sending students the message that the text is not the primary source for decoding words. These experts say that such a mixed message can lead students to seek sources other than the letters in the word, such as picture and context cues, when confronted with a word they don't know (Solman et al., 1992). Can teachers resolve this dilemma, using pictures to motivate and clarify meaning, yet without the side effect of interfering with the teaching of systematic sounding-out? Yes—simply by having pictures follow text—rather than occurring on the same page. Pictures that are shown after text is read can function as a reward for accurate reading, as well as a stimulus for discussing the meaning of the text. Teachers further discourage guessing for early readers when they expect students to point to each word with their fingers and continually remind them to look at the letters in the word.

3. Some teachers will clarify key vocabulary when students first read words they do not know during the first read-through. Other teachers focus exclusively on sounding out words or reading during a first read and will wait until the second reading to ask comprehension questions and discuss vocabulary. Other teachers pre-teach the meaning of vocabulary words that they anticipate the children will not know. Chapter 6 will discuss strategies to teach vocabulary explicitly.

Selecting Decodable Books

The role of decodable books in beginning reading instruction remains one of the most contentious topics between phonics reading educators and literature-based reading educators. (See Bridging the Gap: Should I Use Predictable Books? on p. 113.) Unfortunately, the National Reading Panel Report provides no direct guidance and instead recommends that more research is needed to investigate this question (National Reading Panel, 2000). Meanwhile, since most explicit and systematic phonics curricula use decodable texts as a key part of beginning reading instruction, teachers of students who are at risk need to familiarize themselves with decodable materials and investigate the issues for themselves.

Why are decodable books such an integral component of so many systematic and explicit phonics programs? First, decodable books provide more practice opportunities for students who are learning to decode letter–sound patterns. As noted earlier in this chapter, the average child needs between 4 and 14 exposures to a new pattern before it is identified automatically. Students who are at risk are likely to need even more exposure. After Mr. Jerry's class successfully read the list of words starting with *st, tr,* and *d* consonant blends, he wanted to give his students more practice reading these same words in connected text. He knew that if the next story his students read contained only one or two words beginning with these new consonant blends, many students would not get enough practice and would be unable to identify the pattern successfully when it appeared in next week's story. For these early readers, albeit for a relatively short period of time, decodable books serve as "a bridge between phonics instruction and the reading of trade books" (Moats, 2000, p. 148).

Because decodable books incorporate words or sounds that students have already learned in class, students typically are highly successful reading decodable books even for the first time. Historically, many students who are at risk or have disabilities have experienced such high levels of failure while learning to read that by third grade they have already developed negative attitudes toward reading. By providing students with the opportunity to read successfully on their own, decodable books can help students develop confidence and a more positive attitude toward reading (Bursuck et al., 2004; Stanovich, 1993/1994).

When students are at the pre-alphabetic reading stage, most comprehension instruction is done through listening and discussing different genres of children's literature. If used correctly, decodable books can also provide opportunities for comprehension development. A creative teacher can draw out several questions even from a short decodable story. For example, after reading the decodable book *Frank the Fish Gets His Wish,* Mr. Jerry had his students identify main characters, explain why Frank was lonely, sequence events in the story, visualize how they would feel if they were the fish, and talk about the fantasy aspects of the book. When students reread the story the second time, they used fish voices and tried to express fear when knocked out of their fishbowl.

Teachers selecting supplementary decodable books need to systematically match the sequence of letter sounds and word patterns taught in their classroom with text in decodable books. Because some books selling as decodables include a relatively high percentage of sight words, teachers cannot assume that a book labeled as such is decodable. Put simply, many books advertised as decodables frequently are not. Table 3.10 lists a common sequence of increasingly difficult words that you can use as a guide for selecting decodable books.

When selecting additional books, consider these questions:

- Are the students beginning readers and able to follow only one or two lines of text on a page?
- Do flashy pictures interrupt the students' concentration when sounding out the words?
- Are the students older readers who need a decodable chapter book with fewer pictures?
- Are full pages of text needed because the students are ready to transition to chapter books?
- What letter sounds and types of words have the students learned to decode? What sight words do students know? Does this book match their skills?

> For specific information about how to teach decoding and use decodable readers, visit the *Teaching Decoding* website: **www.aft.org/pubs-reports/american_educator/spring_sum98/moats.pdf.**

TABLE 3.10 Selecting Decodable Books Based on Word Difficulty

Skill	Examples
VC and CVC words that begin with continuous sounds	*it, fan*
VCC and CVCC words that begin with a continuous sound	*lamp, ask*
CVC words that begin with a stop sound	*cup, tin*
CVCC words that begin with a stop sound	*dust, hand*
CCVC words	*crib, blend, snap, flat*
CCVCC, CCCVC, and CCCVCC words	*clamp, spent, scrap, scrimp*
Long vowels and short vowel combinations	*late, stand, stay, Pam*

Research to Practice

Decodable Reading

At the end of November, a team of three first-grade Project PRIDE teachers were concerned that eleven of their students in Tier 2 were still scoring between 20 and 30 on the DIBELS NWF assessment. Because these students had not yet developed alphabetic principle, they would not be ready to start learning long vowels after the Christmas break. Since this was the first year of enhancing the general curriculum with intensive phonics and most of the books in the general curriculum had less than 60% decodable text, the teachers wondered if these eleven students were failing to progress because they had not had enough practice reading connected decodable text. Half of these students had received extra language support in kindergarten because they entered school with considerable language deficits. Before moving the students to Tier 3, the teachers wanted to try and provide more support with decodable reading for a few weeks.

Once the school team determined that a student teacher and a building paraprofessional could be pulled for instruction, the students were divided into four groups. Each group met for a half-hour four times each week in order to read increasingly difficult decodable books. Every room in the school was full, so the groups met in the hall or in the back of the library. In the beginning, the students followed the pre-alphabetic format in Table 3.5, sounding out words before reading them. Since everyone was actively reading in unison for the entire 30 minutes, the teachers and the students stopped in the hall for a drink of water before and after the group. At first the reading groups slowly made their way through stories containing CVC words and short a vowels.

Besides focusing on accurate decoding, teachers conducting the decodable reading groups always asked comprehension questions during the second read-through. Gradually, the students moved to subvocal sounding-out, and by the end of January they were slowly reading words the fast way during their first reading of the stories. Whenever they finished reading a story with at least 97% accuracy, the students took home a photocopy of the story. The next day they reported to the group whether they had read the story to their younger siblings, their grandmother, or their parents. All of the students' DIBELS NWF Scores were now showing progress, and by the end of January the average score was 18 points higher. Classroom teachers noted substantial improvement during reading class for most of the students who were now able to read the day's unfamiliar words the fast way.

Eight of these original eleven students finished first grade at Tier 1 or Tier 2, solidly reading words with both short and long vowels. By April they no longer needed the daily practice reading decodables. The other three students had not solidly developed alphabetic principle and became so confused when long vowels were introduced that they never caught up with their peers. As these three boys fell further behind, the team decided they needed even more support and moved them into an intensive Tier 3 group.

At the beginning of the next school year these same first-grade teachers were determined to provide decodable reading support earlier in the fall. By the end of September any student who was not on track to reach 50 on the DIBELS NWF assessment started supplementary decodable reading.

Putting the Pieces Together: What Does Instruction Look Like for Tier 1 and Tier 2 Students?

Kindergarten

Every morning after circle time, Mr. Hicks uses the formats in Chapter 1 to teach his students how to blend onset-rime. As part of his advance organizer, he tells students that first they will blend some words together, then they will learn a new letter that they make with their

Bridging the Gap

Should I Use Predictable Books?

Problem readers often overuse the context to recognize unknown words. For example, students with reading problems tend to guess when they come to a word they don't know by using the context ("What word makes sense?") or by looking at the first letter of a word ("This word begins with *sss*"). Research shows that content words, those that are most important for text comprehension, can be predicted from the surrounding text only 10 to 20% of the time (Gough et al., 1981). Predictable books are designed to make guessing pay off, giving students the idea that they don't have to look at all parts of words when figuring them out. Students who are at risk need to develop a consistent sounding strategy before they are taught to use the context. This means that their early reading experiences should involve as little guessing as possible. If students are required to sound out words in one setting and guess in another, they are likely to be confused and may not learn a systematic sounding strategy altogether. Therefore, the use of predictable books with students who have yet to attain the alphabetic principle is not recommended. Decodable text based on the sounds the students are learning is much more likely to result in a strategic reader as opposed to a guesser.

If you must use predictable texts:

1. Avoid having students reread the texts if they are beginning to memorize the story.
2. Prior to reading the story, circle words that students can decode (either a regular word for which they know the sounds or a sight word). As you read the story, students can be responsible for reading the decodable words. If decodable words are missed, make sure you use sounding out as part of your correction procedure.
3. Occasionally model sounding out when reading predictable texts. Through your example, students see that reading is not all memorization.

Divide your class into two groups. Use predictable books with the higher groups and decodable books with your students who are below the DIBELS benchmarks.

lips together, and finally they will practice all of the letter sounds that they have learned. After 5 minutes of blending practice, he introduces the new letter for the week, *m*, by reading a mouse poem in the teacher's manual. After the poem, he asks everyone to put their lips together and make the /m/ sound. He individually calls on Jenny and Roxanne, who have speech difficulties, so he can check to see whether they are saying the correct sound. Jenny is articulating an /n/ so he instructs her to put her finger on her lips and press them together. Now she can make the sound. Next he directs all of the students' attention to the two mountains in the letter *m*. Finally, he is ready to use the letter–sound script and practice Part A. After students seem firm with saying /m/, he moves to Part B of the script and reviews the six letters learned in the past six weeks. Using a long pointer, Mr. Hicks asks everyone to say the letter sounds when he gives the signal. Since his students did not make any mistakes yesterday, he exaggerates his quick pointing from letter to letter, pretending that he is out of breath trying to keep up with them. The children enjoy making Mr. Hicks tired. Since every day his students write the new letter sound after saying it, he takes them through a 2-minute stretch break before asking them to return to their desks for writing practice.

First Grade

Ms. Matizza likes to begin reading right after morning announcements when her students are at a higher energy level. When she made her lessons plans last Friday, Ms. Matizza went through the reading curriculum teaching guide so that she knew all of the letter sounds, words, sentences, and stories for the week. Before students came in the room, Ms. Matizza wrote all of the letter sounds students would practice on one section of the board, all of the new words on another section of the board, and three sentences on the third section. Before class begins, four students leave to go to their intensive Tier 3 reading class. Ms. Matizza is pleased that these students have started to read two-phoneme words, although they still are blending at a slow rate and have only learned a few letter sounds.

When class starts, students know the letter sounds so well that after 2 minutes, Ms. Matizza moves on to the words. This part of the lesson moves more slowly, because most of her students do not have alphabetic principle and first need to sound out each word before saying it. She frequently calls on students in Tier 2, since they need more practice. Mr. Matizza draws a candle next to each row after students quickly read all the words in the row. Her students enjoy having her say that "It's a four-candle day" whenever they have fluently read every word. Sentence reading moves much more quickly, because students have already learned the words in the sentences. Everyone likes to read the question sentence, making their voice intonation rise at the end.

Ms. Matizza prefers conducting reading group on the carpet, so she asks her students to move to their circle. Two class helpers pass out the reading books about a swamp, and everyone turns to the first page, reading fingers ready. Because this is a new book and the *ir,* *er,* and *ur* words are more difficult, Ms. Matizza only plans to get through half of the book, saving the rest for tomorrow. The first time through the story, Ms. Matizza uses a unison response and has the group sound out the regular words in the story together. Ms. Matizza signals for every sound using a clap and then claps for the whole word. When the students come to a sight word, Ms. Matizza does not have them sound it out. She asks, "What word?" and then claps for them to say the whole word. By the second time through the story, students, with a little bit of think time, can say whole words without sounding them out first. In the middle of the reading group the students in Tier 3 return to class, take a book, and turn to the page everyone else is reading. Although still unable to read the words, they are able to stay on the same page as the rest of the class. During the third read-through, Ms. Matizza calls on two of the Tier 3 students to answer comprehension questions. After the story is finished, Ms. Matizza has everyone return to their desks to draw the water-soaked swamp land.

How Can I Help Students Who Still Can't Identify Letter Sounds or Read Regular Words or Longer Decodable Passages?

Students' scores on the letter–sound assessment let you know who needs extra Tier 2 booster practice reviewing those sounds. Student scores on the DIBELS NWF assessment inform you who needs extra Tier 2 booster practice with decoding skills. Booster sessions vary, depending on whether students are just working on letter sounds or are also learning to decode.

For students just learning letter sounds in kindergarten, small-group booster sessions last between 5 and 10 minutes. Students whose letter–sound assessment indicates that they know fewer than 90% of the letter sounds taught by the teacher should start booster practice immediately, so that they don't fall too far behind the class. Because many kindergarten students who need letter sound practice also need phonemic awareness boosters, you can combine the two skills into one short practice session. During the booster group, practice with the same letter–sound format (Table 3.4) that was used during large-group Tier 1 instruction. Each day students practice one letter, continuing to practice that same letter each day until mastery. The class may have learned sounds for the following letters, *s, t, a, m, f, b, i,* and *l,* but if Keivon does not know the sounds for *f, b,* and *l,* the teacher has him identify the sound of *f* every day until he knows it. Each day she also reviews the sounds he knows. After Keivon learns the sound for *f,* she begins working on the sound for *b.* Teaching more than one letter sound at a time to students who are not keeping up with the pace of the class is not effective because it is likely to be confusing.

Students learning to blend sounds into words need longer daily 30-minute booster sessions in which they can practice new letter sounds, regular and sight words, and passage reading. Some first-grade teachers like to schedule the boosters before reading class, so that the students in Tier 2 who just practiced the material can participate more fully with the class. Other first-grade teachers prefer to schedule booster practice just after lunch. These teachers like to have the students' practice spaced so that there are morning and afternoon practice sessions. Since beginning decoding Tier 2 booster sessions last longer, some schools elect to have another teacher or trained paraprofessional work with each small group, taking them to a relatively quiet location. Although small groups of three students are ideal, some schools with many students who are at risk do not have enough personnel for such small groups. In our project schools we found that having six or fewer students in each booster group worked well. Booster groups at our three schools were taught by a music teacher, a French teacher, a Spanish teacher, a former *Reading Recovery* teacher, a librarian, a special education teacher, a Title 1 teacher, or a paraprofessional. Each of these individuals first learned to teach the same scripts used by the classroom teacher so that they used the same signals and followed the same formats.

Some booster groups are able to keep up with the pace of the classroom and practice the same skills and words that were taught in class. Other booster groups fall behind when difficult new patterns such as *ch* are introduced. These groups continue to practice the earlier lessons until they have success. Because booster teachers can only fit in letter–sound practice, regular word reading, sight word reading, and sentence reading into the 30-minute sessions, often there isn't enough time for reading the longer decodable book. Some school teams will use tutors or paraprofessionals to provide additional time for Tier 2 students to read more decodable text.

What Can I Do for Students When Daily Tier 2 Booster Sessions Aren't Working?

In Chapter 2, the need for more intensive Tier 3 instruction for some students in kindergarten who are particularly at risk was discussed, and decision rules were provided to help you identify those students. However, not all students who need Tier 3 enter in kindergarten. Some enter in grade 1, as well. Later placements into Tier 3 can occur for a number of reasons. Some students manage to acquire enough segmenting, blending, and letter–sound skills to remain in Tier 2 in kindergarten, but exhibit much difficulty acquiring the alphabetic principle in grade 1. Other students may move into your school from a school that did not stress phonemic awareness and letter–sound skills in kindergarten.

The recommended decision rules for placement into Tier 3 in grade 1 as identified by Good and colleagues (2002) are as follows:

- In September of grade 1, student scores below 13 letter sounds per minute on DIBELS NWF, or less than 25 letters correct per minute on the DIBELS Letter Naming

Fluency, or less than 10 segments correct per minute in DIBELS Phonemic Segmentation Fluency.

■ In January of grade 1, student scores below 30 letter sounds correct per minute on the DIBELS NWF, or less than 20 words correct per minute on DIBELS Oral Reading Fluency (ORF is discussed in Chapter 5).

■ In May of grade 1, student scores less than 30 letter sounds correct per minute on the DIBELS NWF, or less than 20 words correct per minute on DIBELS Oral Reading Fluency. The DIBELS recommendation at less than 20 is based on an end-of-first-grade benchmark of 40. Chapter 5 provides discussion about why a year-end benchmark of 60 may be more desirable.

While the decision rules described are research-based and generally accurate, experience dictates that teacher judgment be part of the decision-making equation as well. For example, in some cases teachers have requested that the assessments be given again because the scores did not reflect students' performance in class. In other cases, students who have borderline scores and who also present behavior problems in class were placed into Tier 3 because their behavior and attention were improved in a small-group setting. Table 3.11 describes how alphabetic principle is taught in each of the five alternative programs described in Chapter 2.

How Can I Teach Alphabetic Principle to English Language Learners?

Systematic and explicit phonics benefits English language learners whether they are first taught to read in English or in their native language. Numerous research studies in the United States and England demonstrate that when young English language learners receive explicit teaching of the alphabetic principle, they outperform their peers in word recognition and comprehension (Stuart, 1999; Gunn et al., 2000; Foorman, 1998). Even when students are not yet fluent in English, explicit practice in sounding out words develops both English reading skills and English speaking skills, if explicit vocabulary instruction accompanies the phonics. Teachers who show pictures or use gestures to depict the meaning of unfamiliar words after students decode those words are teaching both alphabetic principle and comprehension. English language learners also require extra practice learning to articulate letter sounds that have no equivalent in their native language. The length of time learning explicit phonics may be crucial for grade-level reading, with many English language learners requiring two years to catch up to their English-speaking peers.

Fortunately, "cracking the code" in one language often expedites learning to read in a second language. If students first acquire alphabetic principle in their native language, their ability to decode can transfer to later English reading (Durgunoglu, 2002). This transference will be more difficult for students who had trouble learning to read in their native language, and these same students will be at high risk for reading failure in English unless they get intensive support (Gersten, 1996).

When you listen to an English language learner read, you may have difficulty determining whether a misread word is an actual error or just an articulation difference. Becoming aware of articulation patterns in students' native languages will help your analysis in these situations. Table 3.12 (p. 119) details pronunciation difficulties that native Spanish speakers may have when reading English text.

TABLE 3.11 Comparison of Five Common Tier 3 Approaches

	Direct Instruction: Reading Mastery	Lindamood® LiPS Program	Reading Recovery	Wilson Reading System	Language!
Do lessons introduce a predesigned sequence of letter sounds?	Yes	Yes	No	Yes. However, several sounds are introduced within one sub-step.	Yes
Does curriculum specifically coordinate letter sounds taught in isolation with first words read in isolation and later in passages?	Yes	Yes	No	Yes	Yes
Do students practice letter sounds and word reading, only moving to the next lesson after they are successful?	Yes	Yes	No	Yes	Yes
Are phonics cues encouraged as the primary method for reading unfamiliar words?	Yes	Yes	No	Yes; pictures are never used in this program.	Yes
Do lessons introduce a sequence of regular words that are increasingly difficult to decode? (Example: VC or CVC followed by CVC variants)	Yes	Yes	No	Yes	Yes
Are students discouraged to guess at words as one strategy for word reading?	Yes	Yes	No	Yes	Yes
Is decodable reading used to help students apply the letter–sound knowledge they have learned?	Yes. Program includes decodable reading books that are coordinated with letter sounds and words taught to students.	Yes. Teachers select decodable reading that is coordinated with letter sounds and words taught to students.	No. Program discourages decodable reading.	Yes. Decodable reading in sentences and passages is coordinated with letter sounds and words taught to students.	Yes. Program includes decodable reading books that are coordinated with letter sounds and words taught to students.

Continued

	Direct Instruction: Reading Mastery	Lindamood® LiPS Program	Reading Recovery	Wilson Reading System	Language!
What is the amount of time spent on development of learning letter sounds, sounding out words, writing them, and sounding out words in passages?	After first 30 lessons, almost the entire daily lesson is spent on learning these skills. Comprehension development is also included in lessons.	Beginning lessons are split between phonemic awareness and development of alphabetic principle.	The use of magnetic letters and word boxes to analyze words comprises a small proportion of the 30-minute lessons, which cover seven activities each day.	Between 66% to 90% of lesson is devoted to learning these skills. Some lessons also include listening comprehension development.	Each literacy lesson is divided into 10 sections and is designed to take 90 minutes. Of those 10 sections, 4 are devoted to these skills.
Are sight words pretaught before they appear in reading passages?	Yes	Yes	No	Teachers are encouraged to preteach.	Yes
Are the first sight words taught limited to high-frequency words necessary for story reading?	Yes	Yes	No	No. Both real and nonsense words are taught.	Yes
Is left-to-right blending stressed throughout all word- and passage-reading activities?	Yes	Yes	No	Yes	Yes
Do students write words that they are learning to read?	Yes	Yes	Yes	Yes	Yes
How are students assessed?	Short mastery tests of word or passage reading given to students approximately every five lessons determine whether students are ready to move to the next lesson or move to a faster- or slower-paced group.	Ongoing observation of the students' daily performance on reading tasks during lessons provides the foundation for decision-making about how quickly to move through the program.	Teachers keep daily running records, notating errors that students read in predictable books.	Specific criteria are set for reading and spelling per lesson/per substep. Students are post-tested at the end of every step. Assessment determines how quickly student moves through curriculum.	Each unit of 10 lessons contains mastery tasks for the skills presented in that unit. Students are expected to achieve 80% on all tasks to proceed to the next unit.

TABLE 3.12 Potential English Pronunciation Problems for Native Speakers of Spanish

Consonants	Vowels
/v/ is often pronounced as /b/ or a sound close to /w/; *vase* becomes *base.*	/ā/ is often confused with /ĕ/; *mat* becomes *met.*
At the beginning of a word, /p/ is often pronounced as /b/; *pet* becomes *bet.*	/ē/ is often pronounced as /ī/; *meet* becomes *mit.*
At the beginning of a word, /t/ is often pronounced as /d/; *tap* becomes *dap.*	/ā/ is often pronounced as /ĕ/; *make* becomes *mek.*
At the beginning of a word, /k/ is often pronounced as /g/; *kit* becomes *git.*	/oo/; is often pronounced as /o͞o/; *book* becomes *bo͞ok.*
/sh/ is usually pronounced as /ch/; *ship* becomes *chip.*	
/y/ is often pronounced as /j/; *yell* becomes *gell.*	
/z/ is often pronounced as /s/; *zig* becomes *sig.*	
/m/, /n/, and /ng/ may be substituted for each other; *ping* becomes *pin.*	
When words begin with consonant clusters (*pr, cl, pl, sl*), an extra vowel is often inserted at the beginning of the word; *speak* becomes *espeak.*	
When words end with consonant clusters, the final consonant sound is often omitted; *fast* becomes *fas.*	
When a voiced /th/ occurs in the middle or the end of a word, /d/ is often substituted; *mother* becomes *moder.*	

Source: Adapted from P. Avery and S. Ehrlich (1992): Teaching American English Pronunciation, pp. 149–153.

How Important Is Alphabetic Principle for Older Learners?

While systematic phonics instruction produces the biggest impact on growth in reading when it begins in kindergarten or grade 1 (National Reading Panel, 2001), teachers are responsible for bringing significant numbers of struggling older readers to proficient levels of reading. The National Assessment of Educational Progress 2003 Report indicated that 50% or more of the fourth- and eighth-graders in the nation's largest urban areas were below the basic level in reading, unable to demonstrate even partial mastery of the fundamental knowledge and skills. Nationally, about 24% of fourth-graders and 33% of eighth-graders fell below the basic level (Kennedy-Manzo, 2003).

Studies investigating older students and adults who have reading problems reveal that most have basic deficits in decoding skills. Of those older students with decoding deficits, there appear to be two groups (Archer, Gleason, & Vachon, 2003). Older students in one group, the smaller of the two groups, read at the first- and second-grade level. These students have yet to attain the alphabetic principle. The second group are those reading between the second- and fifth-grade levels. While these students can decode single-syllable words and read some high-frequency sight words, they struggle to decode multisyllable words and have considerable difficulty reading connected text fluently. The needs of the smaller group of students who have yet to attain the alphabetic principle are addressed in this chapter. The needs of the larger group of older students with decoding problems are discussed in Chapters 4 and 5.

As Share has aptly pointed out, it is tempting to focus reading instruction for older students on whole-word recognition because the phonics strategies needed to attain the alphabetic principle appear to be babyish (Share, 1995). In addition, progress in developing systematic word attack skills can be slow at first, as guessing habits acquired during many years of previous instruction are difficult to unlearn. Slow progress combined with student reluctance can act to weaken teachers' resolve to stay the alphabetic principle course. Nonetheless, teachers are urged to use curricula with these older readers that is aimed at systematically and explicitly developing an awareness of the alphabetic principle (Lerner, 1989). Otherwise these students will remain stuck in the word guessing mode for the rest of their lives.

The teacher's only productive option when teaching alphabetic principle to older learners is to step back and teach the phonemic awareness, letter–sound skills, regular word reading skills, and coordinated passage reading skills previously described in Chapters 2 and 3. However, doing so presents two challenges. The first is to find a text that is not only explicit and systematic but also has age-appropriate stories and doesn't look "baby-ish." Three evidence-based programs that have these features are *Corrective Reading* (Engelmann, Carnine, Johnson, Meyer, Becker, & Eisele, 1999), *Language!* (Greene, 2000), and *Wilson Reading System* (Wilson, 1996). The second challenge is to find enough instructional time during the school day. Programs such as the three identified here are designed for a minimum of an hour-and-a-half to two hours of intensive teaching each day.

> This article by Louisa C. Moats, "When Older Students Can't Read," explains some of the benefits that result from teaching phonics to older struggling readers: **www.cdl.org/resource-library/articles/older_read.html**

How Can I Use Games to Reinforce Students' Decoding Skills?

Once your students are decoding CVC and CVC-variant words, use every opportunity to take advantage of the school environment for more practice. Using the words your students can decode, make posters with short poems or captions describing a funny picture and display these posters in areas where your students routinely wait—outside of the bathroom, by the lunchroom waiting line, near the library. Draw your students' attention to the posters, asking them questions about content. You will help your students feel like readers, actively applying their reading to the outside world.

After students have successfully read a decodable book, play "Landing on Mars" with them. Ask your students to turn to a page in their book and hold up their index finger as the rocket. When you call out a word that is on the page, they are to launch their rocket into the air and land it on the word you named. Say, for example, "Find *shut*." (pause) "Find *"pigpen*." (pause) "Find *rack*." (pause) "Yes! This class landed on Mars all three times!" Students will work their hardest to find the words quickly, speeding up the rate at which they are decoding.

The Word Box Game

Put several clear word-building boxes on an accessible shelf so that students can play Word Box when they have completed other work.

Prepare the Game   Inside each box put:

- lower-case letters of only the letter sounds you have taught your students. All of the vowels should be a distinctive color or marked with a distinctive tape.

Technology

Alphabetic Principle

Because there is so little published research investigating the effectiveness of computer-assisted phonics instruction, the National Reading Panel could only conclude that computer technology "appears to hold promise" for reading instruction (National Reading Panel, 2000, 6–2). To date, computer software designed to improve reading instruction is still in its infancy and most appropriately used in classrooms to supplement or reinforce a systematic, explicit phonics program.

Teaching students who are at risk to move from letter sounds to alphabetic principle requires extremely careful, coordinated instruction. *More* instruction is not always *better* instruction, especially when poorly designed activities contribute to mistakes that the student will later have to unlearn. Teachers who are evaluating software to supplement their instruction in letter sounds, word-reading, or passage-reading should consider the following factors:

- How closely coordinated is the teaching of letter sounds with the students' daily reading curriculum? Check the order in which the letter sounds are introduced. If the order is different, reorder the sequence presented in the computer program. If the computer software program includes digitized speech, the letter sounds should match your articulation. For example, letter sounds should be articulated without schwas. Finally, check the intelligibility of the synthesized speech. Although the quality of synthesized speech continues to improve, the longer sentences are sometimes unintelligible.
- How well do the games and activities involving regular word reading reflect skills that students have learned? For example, if students have not yet learned to decode consonant blends, they should not be expected to read consonant blend words while playing a computer game. If the skills stressed in the games and activities do not match your reading curriculum, find out whether the design allows you to modify types of words and text that are read.
- Does the program introduce regular words comprised of letter sounds that the students can identify? Are those same words later in closed sentences, paragraphs, or stories? If not, the activities are likely to be of little benefit in strengthening skills covered in the daily reading curriculum.
- Is the phonics program systematic and explicit? Computer assisted instructional phonics programs may include nonsystematic phonics activities reminiscent of those in the most tedious workbooks of years past. Computer phonics programs may also undermine your systematic phonics program by encouraging students to guess at words and memorize too many whole words. Finally, since the student isn't using her finger while reading, monitoring left-to-right reading is difficult, if not impossible.
- Does the software program include performance checks to assure that students reach mastery before moving on to a more difficult skill?
- Does the program have a built-in monitoring system that allows you to evaluate how the student is progressing?

- a laminated grid that students use to make words, placing a letter on each square (Figure 3.16).
- a pencil
- a "rocket" sheet that students can use for writing their words (Figure 3.17).

Prepare the Students

1. Tell students to bring a pencil and piece of paper when they play Word Boxes.

FIGURE 3.16 Grid

FIGURE 3.17 Rocket Sheet

2. Teach the game to students, showing them how to put a letter in each box. Tell students to always put a marked vowel in the middle box.
3. After students put a letter into each box, ask them to say the letter sounds quietly before blending them into a word.
4. Tell students to write the word they read on their paper, reading it out loud one more time after they write it.
5. Show students how to write their grand total on the page. Enthusiastically describe how, as they learn more and more words, their total numbers will get bigger and bigger.
6. Monitor students carefully as they play the game during this teaching phase to assure that they will follow all of the steps when they independently take out the word boxes.

What Activities Help Students Apply Their Newly Acquired Alphabetic Principle?

By midyear of first grade, students on track to read at grade level should have developed alphabetic principle and be ready to read more difficult words containing long vowels, more advanced sound clusters such as *tch,* and multisyllable words. Students will advance more quickly if they have the opportunity to receive feedback and help when needed by reading aloud to the teacher, tutors, parents, or older siblings. Some classrooms have successfully used First-Grade Peer-Assisted Literacy Strategies (PALS) (grade 1–grade 2) to provide more oral reading practice of connected text. In these classrooms, a stronger reader is

---

Research to Practice

Attitudes of Students Who Are at Risk

Effective teaching for children who are at risk involves providing them with frequent opportunities to practice the skills they are learning. Practice activities are most successful when a teacher is animated, teaches at a perky pace, and challenges her students without frustrating them. Still, much controversy surrounds the issue of student practice, with repeated practice activities often being referred to as "drill and kill."

Prior to acquiring the alphabetic principle, Project PRIDE students spent many hours with teachers and staff identifying letter sounds, reading new words, and reading decodable passages. Particularly challenging for teachers and students alike was having to sound out words in both lists and passages before reading them the fast way. While our students seemed to enjoy the lively pace and the reading success brought by the practice, given the controversy in the field over the use of practice, we wanted to be certain that the daily drill and decodable reading was not dampening student interest in reading.

In order to investigate exactly how our students felt about reading, we assessed our first cohort of students at the end of grades 1 and 2 using the "Elementary Reading Attitude Survey" (McKenna & Kear, 1990). In this survey, student attitudes towards both academic and recreational reading are assessed. Students are asked to circle a picture of Garfield the cat that best depicts how they feel in response to items that are read aloud by the teacher. Ten of the items assess academic reading, while another ten assess recreational reading or reading for fun. To answer each question, students select either the "very happy" Garfield standing with a big smile, the "little bit happy" Garfield, the "little bit upset" Garfield, or the "very upset" Garfield, who had a distinctive scowl. Questions such as, "How do you feel about reading instead of playing?" assess students' attitudes towards recreational reading. Questions such as, "How do you feel about the stories you read in reading class?" assess academic reading.

Scores for all of the instructional tiers for both grades 1 and 2 were uniformly high; students enjoyed both academic and recreational reading, scoring an average of 3 out of 4 on both types of items. Despite the frequent presence of drill in the reading instruction, students in all of the tiers liked to read, confirming our strong belief that when practice is lively and geared to student needs on skills leading to important outcomes, practice will thrill, *not* kill.

---

paired with a weaker reader to coach him or her. Students are taught to cooperate with their partners, praise their partners, and work steadily at reading. Student coaches learn to teach and practice letter–sound identification, word-reading, and connected text reading. By the time they begin working independently with their partners, these students have even learned to give a My Turn–Your Turn response any time the weaker student makes an error. The positive feedback and effective error correction are critical elements in this process (Mathes & Babyak, 2001). A similar PALS strategy has also been effective with weaker high school readers (Fuchs et al., 1999).

Connecting reading to spelling further develops reading skills. Not only should students be able to read CVC and CVC variants by December, but they should also accurately spell those words that are regular, where the letters match the sounds exactly. Once students can read words that contain *sh*, they should also write words that contain that pattern. Rather than having to memorize words such as *shut, shed, sharp,* and *ship,* students are able to automatically spell them once they have learned to read the *sh* pattern. The teacher who then tells her students to write a story about a big red bug who lives in a *shag* rug is extending her students' new learning even further. Shortly after the beginning of first grade is also the time to begin teaching the spelling of a few of the most common sight words that

Motivating Your Students to Do Their Best

Strategies to Encourage Positive Behavior

- Ms. Larson used the Teacher's Rocking Chair game to teach self-control to her kindergartners and help them learn to sit quietly for short amounts of time. Before she started playing the game with her students, when a parent, the principal, or a special education teacher would walk into the kindergarten and need a minute to talk to Ms. Larson, a few students, noticing that the teacher was occupied, would become loud or misbehave to get her attention. Ms. Larson wanted to teach everyone to sit for a few quiet moments without interrupting. During the rocking chair game, all of the children sat in rows on the carpet. One student was selected to sit in the teacher's large rocking chair in front of the room. The selected student sat in the rocking chair surveying everyone else to determine the "quietest" student who would get the next turn to sit in the chair. When Ms. Larson said, "Your turn is up," the student in the chair picked another quiet student. Everyone wanted to be selected for the rocking chair. Students knew that if they talked during the transition when the next student was walking to the chair that they lost their chance to sit in the chair. After starting to use the game, Ms. Larson established the rule that "girls pick boys and boys pick girls," so that everyone would have a chance. Often Ms. Larson instructed students to "pick someone who hasn't had a turn," or "pick someone by the time you've counted to 20." Even after students had learned to quietly wait for short time periods, Ms. Larson continued to use the game because students asked for the opportunity to play it. Students learned self-control playing the game and applied these skills to other situations during the day such as waiting for their turn when answering questions about a story the teacher was reading.

- Ms. Buddin brought several large bowling trophies to her class to encourage students to follow the classroom rules when working at their tables. Quiet talking was allowed, but students were expected to finish their work or project and to ask permission if they needed to leave the table. When Ms. Buddin noticed everyone at a table following the rules, she put a bowling trophy on the surface. When someone didn't follow a rule, the trophy was removed. Gradually, working quietly became routine and the trophies were no longer needed.

- Ms. Gibbs wanted her students to become more aware of the impact their behavior had on other individuals in their community. She knew that some of her students had little experience receiving positive feedback from adults and needed to learn the feeling of pride for doing a good job which others appreciated. Thus Ms. Gibbs hung a "Compliments Chart" in the front of her classroom. Anytime the students, collectively or individually, received a compliment from anyone in the building—the principal, the custodian, another teacher, a parent—a tally mark was put on the compliment chart. When the hundredth tally mark was put on the chart, the class earned a special surprise, which might be a pizza party or the opportunity to have a picnic lunch outside. Students who left the classroom for reading group looked forward to earning points for the class on days when their reading teacher complimented them during the lesson.

- Ms. Foley set up an "office" space where Terrance, a distractible student, could go to do his best work. By having a student desk and chair surrounded on two sides by dividers in the quietest part of the room, she could redirect him to work in the office when he could not complete independent work in a larger group. She would redirect him, by saying, "Terry, take your journal to the office where you can do your best work." Rather than a punishment area, the "office" provided a quieter, less distracting work place to complete work. Ms. Foley's goal was to get Terrance to independently go to the office when he realized that he wasn't focused on a paper or project.

- Every teacher periodically used group clapping, pats on the back, and thumbs up to acknowledge effort, hard work, and rule-following during reading class.

  "Sharnicca, give yourself a thumbs up. You wrote so much in your journal today."

  "Everybody, pat yourself on the back, because you just read every word without even one mistake."

> ■ Mr. Mixay recognized that his class liked challenges and they especially liked "fooling" the teacher and surpassing his expectations. After the students had just learned something new and still needed to use all of their concentration for success, he would often set up a challenge. Thus when Mr. Mixay's class was supposed to spell the six irregular plural words he said, "This is very hard for students in your grade. Can you spell these very hard words? You will have to think very hard so I don't trick you, giving you these hard words." Naturally the students did their best work to hear Mr. Mixay shake his head and exclaim how amazed he was that they had learned to spell such hard words. During review sessions, Mr. Mixay told his students that he was going to try and trick them by giving them difficult words to read. He smiled as he said that he was sure that they could not remember all of those difficult words. Consequently, his students always rose to the challenge and read every word.

students are now reading in their stories. The more students read, formally spell, and use these words in their writing, the faster they will recognize them in text.

Fact or Fiction

A list of common questions about beginning instruction in word reading for students who are at risk is incorporated into the Fact or Fiction questions below. Determine how many reading myths you could identify as you read through the questions. Were you surprised at some of the answers? Compare your answers with those of a partner and discuss the questions that fooled you. Do effective teaching practices for students who are at risk mirror or differ from your philosophy about teaching reading? Select a question that involves a topic that you would like to research further.

1. **Beginning reading programs should stress using the context to figure out words because that is what skilled readers do.**

Fact   **Fiction**

Fiction. Research by Stanovich and Stanovich (1995) shows that the "skills of the good reader are so rapid, automatic, and efficient that the skilled reader need not rely on contextual information. In fact, it is the poor readers who guess from context out of necessity because their decoding skills are so weak" (p. 92). In addition, while context cues can be helpful in figuring out the meaning of words, they are less reliable as aids in word identification. For example, Gough and colleagues (1981) found that words can be predicted from surrounding text only 10 to 20% of the time. In our experience, reading approaches that stress the use of context too soon lead to students guessing at words, rather than strategically trying to figure them out. The approach taken in the text emphasizes sounding-out early in reading instruction. Sounding-out is helpful even when reading words that are not completely regular. Only later, when students have mastered the alphabetic principle and are encountering multisyllable words with irregular parts, is using the context suggested as a strategy—and then, only after known parts of words have been decoded first.

2. **An effective reading program for students who are at risk should include a high proportion of high-frequency sight words, since these are the kinds of words they are most likely to find in print.**

Fact   **Fiction**

Fiction. The problem with high-frequency sight words is that they have to be memorized to be learned. The presence of too many of these words before students attain the alphabetic principle can undermine the sounding-out strategy that you are trying to build, and encourage guessing. Reducing the number of words learned by sight makes initial reading easier for students by simply letting them concentrate on the mechanics of sounding out regular words (Carnine, Silbert, & Kame'enui, 1997). The approach taken in this text is that teaching some high-frequency sight words is unavoidable if students are to be able to read passages. It is recommended, however, to keep the proportion of sight words in beginning readers to less than 20% (Beck, 1981).

3. Drill on word reading skills does not reduce student motivation to read.

Fact   Fiction

Fact. When phonics instruction is systematic and explicit, students are made to apply their knowledge of phonics as they read words, sentences, and text (Armbruster et al., 2001). This means that students are provided with repeated practice of what they are learning. Repeated practice, or drill, is an indispensable part of teaching students who are at risk to read, particularly when learning material for the first time (Engelmann, 1995). Why, then, is such an important part of teaching often criticized and referred to as "drill and kill?" Although part of the answer to this question may be due to differences in philosophy, it is also true that drill can be abused as a teaching technique and that it needs to be conducted appropriately to be effective. Otherwise, drill and practice can cause students to become bored or frustrated. In our experience, drill can "kill" when students practice a skill that is too difficult for them, practice a skill in which they are already fluent, practice a meaningless skill, or when single drill sessions are carried out for long periods of time. On the other hand, drill can "thrill" when students have acquired a skill and need repeated practice to become more fluent, it is conducted for brief periods of time, it is used to strengthen an important skill, and the resulting fluency contributes to successful performance of higher-level skills. Despite the presence of much drill in our project, students exhibited an overwhelmingly positive attitude toward reading, largely because they were experiencing success (see the Preface and Chapter 3 for specific project PRIDE results related to student attitudes).

4. Decodable books are boring for children and reduce their motivation to read.

Fact   Fiction

Fiction. The purpose of decodable books is to give students an opportunity to apply the phonics skills they have learned to connected text. Because the words in decodable books are selected according to the sounds they contain, their prose can seem stilted and unnatural. For example, a book about "Nat the fat cat who sat on a rat" is definitely not award-winning literature. Nonetheless, for what they do, which is strengthening students' skill at sounding out words as they attain the alphabetic principle, decodable texts are an important part of an explicit, systematic reading program. When used appropriately, decodable books lead to high levels of student success and motivation to read, not boredom. Project PRIDE students were exposed to decodable books in all three instructional tiers, the books did not have a negative impact on their desire to read.

5. Since Letter Naming Fluency is such a good predictor of reading difficulties, we should spend a part of each day teaching students to identify letter names as quickly as possible.

Fact   Fiction

Fiction: DIBELS Letter Naming is a good indicator of how efficiently students can process written information. Knowing that a student is a slow processor is important, because it informs the teacher that the student requires more practice to become fluent in reading skills. However, there is no evidence to suggest that the act of identifying letters quickly itself is directly related to reading words. As Carnine, Silbert, & Kame'enui (1990) point out, knowledge of letter sounds is much more useful in pre-alphabetic reading. For example, letter names differ from the sounds said when beginning words are pronounced. Therefore, knowing the letters *m, a,* and *n* will not enable a beginning reader to read the word *man.* On the other hand, knowing the sounds for /m/, /a/, and /n/ will be of help to a reader attempting to decode the word *man.*

A P P L I E D   A C T I V I T I E S

1. A sample sequence of letter–sound introduction for a beginning reading program is shown below. Critique the sequence using guidelines proposed by Carnine and colleagues (2004) described in Table 3.4. Is the change systematic? Describe any changes you would make.

   h t b o a d p j x e q n s f k i c y m z w u l g r v

2. In the list of words below, circle the digraphs, underline the diphthongs, and cross out the consonant blends.

sand	chair	skin	boil	strap	she	round
church	brown	look	think	slam	boy	Grinch

3. Following is a list of CVC variants. Label each as to the type of CVC word it exemplifies. For example, *sat* would be labeled CVC; *trip* would be labeled CCVC.

pen ____	mask ____	brand ____	must ____
drag ____	scrap ____	pest ____	smell ____
spank ____	mist ____	tip ____	plan ____

4. Say the following consonant blends in unison as a group without adding schwas:

   gl   br   st   pr   str   cl   sn   fr

5. Mr. Hayes introduced the letter–sound /h/ yesterday. In the past few weeks he has taught his students to identify /m/, /a/, /s/, /f/, /t/, and /b/. Demonstrate how you would instruct Mr. Hayes' class today using the format in Table 3.4: Part B to teach the new and review sounds.

6. How would you provide differentiated instruction using the following lesson designed to introduce the /t/ sound?

   Show students a piece of poster board on which is displayed the letter *t* along with a picture of a tent. Explain that the letter *t* stands for the /t/ sound as in *tent.* Write the words *tiger* and *fast* on the board. Ask the students to read the two words.

   Distribute the *t* letter card. Have the children put the letter in their mini pocket charts and say the *t* sound.

7. Shown below are the results for three students on the DIBELS NWF measure given in January.

Identify the student who is performing at benchmark levels. How would you characterize the particular skill level for the two students not at benchmark levels? In a sentence or two, recommend a future instructional focus for all three students.

DIBELS Nonsense Word Fluency
Assessment and Score Sheet

Name: Shelby   **Date:** Dec. 5

w̲a̲b̲	pev	y̶i̶l̶	b̲u̲f	h̶u̶z	9 /15
l̲e̲n̲	y̲o̲c̲	z o v̶]	toc	ab	6 /14
leb	om	mis	ziv	huv	___ /14
maj	nep	iv	noc	kig	___ /14
				Total:	15 /57

DIBELS Nonsense Word Fluency
Assessment and Score Sheet

Name: Tyrone   **Date:** Dec. 5

W̲a̲b̲	pev	y̲i̲l̲	b̲u̲f	h̲u̲z	15/15
l̲e̲n̲	y̲o̲c̲	z̲o̲v̲	t̲o̲c̲	a̲b̲	14/14
l̲e̲b̲	o̲m̲]	mis	ziv	huv	5 /14
maj	nep	iv	noc	kig	___ /14
				Total:	34 /57

DIBELS Nonsense Word Fluency
Assessment and Score Sheet

Name: Shanique   **Date:** Dec. 5

w̲a̲b̲	pev	y̲i̲l̲	b̲u̲f	h̶u̲z̲	14 /15
l̲e̲n̲	y̲o̲c̲	z̲o̲v̲	t̲o̲c̲	a̲b̲	14/14
l̲e̲b̲	o̲m̲	m̲i̲s̲	z̲i̲v̲	h̶u̲v̲	13 /14
m̲a̲j̲	n̲e̲p̲	i̲v̲	n̲o̲c̲]	kig	11 /14
				Total:	52 /57

8. Shown below are the scores for Mrs. Green's first-grade class on the DIBELS NWF assessment in January. Identify which students are at benchmark, which students will need Tier 2 booster sessions, and which students, pending further testing, might be eligible for an alternative, intensive program in Tier 3.

Student	Nonsense Words: January Letter–Sounds Correct per Minute
Maria	28
Ladariu	42
Skylar	50
Tylar	17
Jatavia	45
Jaylin	38
Dezazh	66
Andrew	21
Delundre	72
Shanteria	40
Brant	56
Jarnecia	39
Christopher	48
Bryce	29
Erionah	66
Trae	78
Joshua	35
Marquez	29
Shaheed	77
Vantrell	47

9. Ms. Munoz wanted her students to practice reading the following words on the chalkboard. Demonstrate how she would teach these words using the format described in Table 3.5.

hop	shop	fish	dish
hot	shot	quick	that

10. The reading curriculum informs Ms. Foley that students need to learn the following sight words, which will be in the next story: *bough, buy,* and *month.* She plans to have students practice the following review words that came from last week's story: *ghost, steak.* Demonstrate how you would

instruct Ms. Foley's class using Table 3.8 for teaching sight words.

11. Karisha is a pre-alphabetic reader who has learned the following beginning reading skills:

Letter sounds: *a s m i t r b l w n f k h g*

Sight words: *a is his the*

Shown below are representative passages from three decodable books. Select the passage that would be most appropriate for Karisha. Indicate why.

Passage 1

Sam hit Kit in the hip. Sam is a big brat and will ram Matt.

Passage 2

Ed did run past his Dad. He ran fast and had fun.

Passage 3

Tom did help mom. Tom went to get milk and a big box of hot nuts.

12. Passages from two hypothetical reading programs are shown below. By the end of November, Ms. Tonnato's students, whose DIBELS NWF scores range between 18 and 25, have learned all of the short vowel sounds and the consonant sounds listed on the letter–sound chart at the end of Chapter 1. Ms. Tonnato wants to provide extra decodable reading for her students who do not have alphabetic principle. Which passage would be more likely to lead to student success? Justify your answer.

Passage #1

The girl looked out the window. The sun was shining in the sky. "I think I will go outside today," she said. She left the house. She walked past a food stand. There was a big pile of donuts at the stand. She walked past the apple tree. There was a big cow under the apple tree. So she went home to get some lunch. I will get a sandwich, some juice, and an orange to eat.

Passage #2

Fran is fast. She can jump and hop and run fast. She gets to the swing first. I am mad. I can not jump and hop and run fast. But then I stop and think. I can hum and sing and skip. I sing for gramps and hum for mom. I skip up and down the steps. I will be pals with Fran. I can help Fran hum and sing and skip. Fran can help me jump and hop and run fast.

REFERENCES

Archer, A. L., Gleason, M. M., & Vachon, V. L. (2003). Decoding and fluency: Foundation skills. *Learning Disability Quarterly: Journal of the Division for Children with Learning Disabilities, 26*(2), 89 (28 pp.).

Armbruster, B., Lehr, F., & Osborn, J. (2001). *Put reading first: The research building blocks for teaching children to read.* Washington, DC: Partnership for Reading.

Avery, P., & Ehrlich, S. (1992). *Teaching American English pronunciation.* New York: Oxford Press.

Beck, I. (1981). Reading problems and instructional practices. In G. E. MacKinnon & T. G. Waller (Eds.), *Reading research: Advances in theory and practice* (Vol. 2, pp. 53–95). New York: Academic Press.

Bursuck, B., Smith, T., Munk, D., Damer, M., Mehlig, L., & Perry, J. (2004). Evaluating the impact of a prevention-based model of reading on children who are at-risk. *Remedial and Special Education, 25,* 303–313.

Carnine, D. W., Silbert, J., & Kame'enui, E. J. (1990). *Direct instruction reading* (2nd ed.). Columbus, OH: Merrill.

Carnine, D. W., Silbert, J., Kame'enui, E. J., & Tarver, S. (2004). *Direct instruction reading* (4th ed.). New Jersey: Merrill Prentice Hall.

Cunningham, P. (2000). *Phonics they use: Words for reading and writing.* New York: Longman.

Bursuck B., & Damer, M. (2003). *Preventing reading problems in urban schools: Drilling and thrilling with Project PRIDE.* International Reading Association, Orlando, Florida, May 5, 2003.

Durgunoglu, A. (2002). Cross linguistic transfer in literacy development and implications for language learners. *Annals of Dyslexia* (52 pp.).

Elkonin, D. B. (1973). U.S.S.R.: Methods of teaching reading. In J. Downing (Ed.), *Comparative reading: Cross-national studies of behavior processes in reading and writing* (pp. 551–580). New York: MacMillan.

Engelmann, S., & Bruner, E. (1995). *Reading Mastery I: Teacher's guide.* Columbus, OH: SRA Macmillan/McGraw-Hill.

Foorman, B., Fletcher, J., & Francis, D. (2004). *Preventing Reading Failure* [Electronic version]. Retrieved from: http://teacher.scholastic.com/professional/teachstrat/preventing.htm#bio.

Fuchs, L. S., Fuchs, D., & Kazdan, S. (1999). Effects of peer-assisted learning strategies on high school students with serious reading problems. *Remedial and Special Education, 20,* 309–318.

Gersten R. G. (1996). The double demands of teaching English language learners. *Educational Leadership, 53*(5), 18–22.

Good, R. H., Simmons, D., Kame'enui, E. A., & Wallin, J. (2002). *Summary of decision rules for intensive, strategic, and benchmark instruction recommendations in kindergarten through third grade* (Technical Report No. 11). Eugene: University of Oregon.

Gough, P. (1983). Context, form, and interaction. In K. Rayner (Ed.), *Eye movements in reading* (pp. 331–358). Cambridge, MA: MIT Press.

Greene, J. F. (2004). *Language! A literacy intervention curriculum.* Longmont, CO: Sopris West.

Gunn, B., Biglan, A., Smolkowski, K., & Ary, D. (2000). The efficacy of supplemental instruction in decoding skills for Hispanic and non-Hispanic students in early elementary school. *Journal of Special Education, 34*(2), 90–103.

Kennedy-Manzo, K. (2003, December 17). Urban minority students performing on par with suburban counterparts. *Education Week* [Electronic version]. Retrieved from: www.edweek.org/ew/ewstory.cfm?slug=15naep_web.h23.

Kinder, D. (1990). *Sound and regular word spelling formats.* Unpublished manuscript, Northern Illinois University.

Lerner, J. (1989). Educational intervention in learning disabilities. *Journal of the American Academy of Child and Adolescent Psychiatry, 28,* 326–331.

Lindamood, P., & Lindamood, P. (1998). *The Lindamood® phoneme sequencing program for reading, spelling, and speech.* Austin, TX: Pro-Ed.

Lyon, G. (1998, April 28). *Overview of Reading and Literacy Initiatives.* Statement to Committee on Labor and Human Resources, Bethesda, MD [Electronic version]. Retrieved from: www.projectpro.com/ICR/Research/Releases/NICHD_Testimony1.htm.

Mathes, P., & Babyak, A. (2001). The effects of peer-assisted literacy strategies for first-grade readers with and without additional mini-skills lessons. *Learning Disabilities Research & Practice, 12*(1), 28–44.

McKenna, M. C., & Kear, D. J. (1990). Measuring attitude toward reading: A new tool for teachers. *The Reading Teacher, 54*(1), 10–23.

Moats, L. (2000). *Speech to print: Language essentials for teachers.* Baltimore, MD: Paul H. Brookes.

National Reading Panel. (2000). *Teaching children to read: An evidence-based assessment of the scientific research literature on reading and its implications for reading instruction.* Washington, DC: National Institute of Child Health and Human Development.

O'Connor, R., & Jenkins, J. (1999). Prediction of reading disabilities in kindergarten and first grade. *Scientific Studies of Reading, 3,* 159–197.

Share, D., & Stanovich, K. (1995). Cognitive processes in early reading development: Accommodating individual differences into a mode of acquisition. *Issues in Education: Contributions from Educational Psychology, 1,* 1–57.

Solman, R. T., Singh, N. N., & Kehoe, E. J. (1992). Pictures block the learning of sight words. *Educational Psychology, 12,* 143–154.

Speece, D., Mills, C., Ritchey, K., & Hillman, E. (2003). Initial evidence that letter fluency tasks are valid indicators of early reading skill. *The Journal of Special Education, 36,* 223–233.

Stanovich, K. E. (1993/1994). Romance and reality. *The Reading Teacher, 47,* 280–291.

Stuart, M. (1999). Getting ready for reading: Early phoneme awareness and phonics teaching improves reading and spelling in inner-city second language learners. *British Journal of Educational Psychology, 69,* 587–605.

Wanzek, J., & Haager, D. (2003). Teaching word recognition with blending and analogizing: Two strategies are better than one. *Teaching Exceptional Children, 36,* 32–38.

Wilson, B. (1996). *Wilson Reading System.* Millbury, MA: Wilson Language Training Corporation.

Wolf, M., Heidi, B., and Morris, R. (1986). Automaticity, retrieval processes, and reading: A longitudinal study in average and impaired readers. *Child Development, 57,* 988–1000.

4 Advanced Word-Reading

Key Terms

Affixes	Open syllable
Assistive technology	Prefix
Base word	*r*-controlled
Closed syllable	Root
Letter combinations	Suffix
Morphemes	VCe words

Objectives

After reading this chapter you will be able to:

1. Identify a sequence of essential advanced word-reading skills.

2. Use assessment data to diagnose student skills needed for advanced word-reading.

3. Implement strategies for teaching letter combinations and affixes as preskills for reading multisyllable words.

4. Implement strategies for teaching multisyllable regular words.

5. Adapt general education curriculum lessons in advanced word-reading.

In Chapters 2 and 3, you learned about teaching strategies that help students attain the alphabetic principle. By the end of first grade, students should be able to sound out CVC words in their heads, reading 50 or more letter sounds per minute on the DIBELS Test of Nonsense Word Fluency with at least 15 words read as whole words (Good, Gruba, & Kaminski, 2002). Students should also be able to read first-grade passages accurately and at a rate of at least 40–50 words correct per minute (Good, Kaminski, & Howe, 2005). Despite the significance of this accomplishment, if students are to become fluent enough decoders to tackle the reading comprehension demands of third grade and beyond, they still need to learn to apply their phonic skills to increasingly difficult words. Students need to learn to recognize and use larger letter patterns such as *igh, ing, dis,* and *sub* as they learn to decode multisyllable words. The purpose of this chapter is to provide you with explicit, systematic teaching strategies for advanced word-reading. Chapter 5 will extend this focus on accuracy by providing explicit strategies for developing reading fluency. Because accuracy and fluency are closely connected, once students have mastered the alphabetic principle, your teaching will emphasize these two areas of reading instruction.

Why Teach Advanced Word-Reading Skills When Students Have Already Attained the Alphabetic Principle?

In a perfect world, written English would be completely regular; there would be one written symbol or grapheme for each sound in spoken English. In such a world, students who could sound out words in their heads and meet benchmark levels on the DIBELS Nonsense Word Fluency assessment would be ready to work almost exclusively on reading fluency and comprehension. Unfortunately, spoken English has 41 to 44 sounds and written English only has 26 written letters. Readers rarely encounter letters that have one unique sound in all words. Sometimes the sound a letter makes depends on the adjacent letter. For example, *t* says /th/ as in *thing* or *that* when it comes before *h* in a word; *a* is sometimes silent when it comes after *e* in a word like *each*. Other times a letter's sound depends on letters appearing later in a word such as *made,* where the silent *e* at the end of the word makes the *a* say its name rather than its sound. An additional source of confusion occurs when letters in a word make sounds for no apparent reason, such as the *ai* in *said.*

Students who are ready to move beyond the beginning reading stage are likely to encounter other difficulties besides rule changes and irregularities. They must also be able to address the increasing prevalence of multisyllable words. Look at the following passage from an elementary school history textbook in which we have underlined all of the words containing three or more syllables.

> Militiamen were given little training. Occasionally regiments would meet at the town green where an officer would try to teach his men British battle formations. Training wasn't taken very seriously. Officers didn't demand discipline from their men because they were all friends (Egger-Bovet & Smith-Baranzin, 1994).

Ask yourself, "Would I be able to understand this passage if I were unable to read all or most of the multisyllable words?"

What Advanced Word-Reading Skills Do I Need to Teach?

Clearly, readers who are at risk need to learn strategies to decode words containing more complex combinations of letters as well as words that contain multiple syllables. As with other steps in the process of learning to read, students who are at risk require more explicit teaching of these strategies. Two approaches have proven effective in teaching advanced word-reading. The first approach emphasizes identifying known parts, and the second approach emphasizes decoding syllable types. In the first approach students are taught to identify one or more parts in the word, read the known parts first, and then read the whole word. For example, in order to read the word *production,* students first are taught the suffix *tion.* Then in another lesson they are taught the prefix *pro.* Finally, when learning this new word for the first time, they first read *pro* and *tion* before reading the whole word

TABLE 4.1 Six Syllable Types Used in Syllable-Type Instruction

Syllable Type	Examples	Description of Syllable Type
Closed	rabbit dependent rejection	A syllable having a short vowel and ending in a consonant (VC,CVC, CCVC,CVCC).
Open	table defame starvation	A syllable with a long vowel sound that is spelled with a single-vowel letter (CV,CCV).
Vowel Combinations	canteen proclaim unspeakable	A syllable with a vowel combination such as *ai, oa, ea,* or *oi* (CVVC, CCVVC, CVVCC).
R-controlled	vaporize surrender perfection	A syllable with a vowel combination such as *ar, or, er, ir,* or *ur.*
Vowel-consonant-e	escape obsolete windowpane	A syllable with a long vowel sound with a consonant and final *e* (VCe,CVCe,CCVCe).
Consonant-le	puddle rumble	A final syllable containing a consonant before *le.*

Source: Archer, A. L., Gleason, M. M., & Vachon, U. L. (2003). Decoding and fluency: Foundation skills for struggling older readers. *Learning Disability Quarterly, 26,* 89–101.

production. Similarly, for the more simple word *such,* students learn to read the letter combination *ch* first, and then the whole word (Engelmann et al., 1999).

In the syllable approach, students are taught six common syllable types that occur in written English (Archer et al., 2003; Greene, 2004; Wilson, 1996; Moats, 2001). These six syllable types, shown in Table 4.1, provide students with clues for figuring out the vowel sounds within the syllables. For example, a vowel within a syllable containing a consonant and final *e* would be long or say its name, as in *escape.* Once students are taught the syllable type, they learn to identify words by first identifying the syllable and then reading the whole word. For example, in *escape,* they would read /cape/, and then the entire word, *escape.*

The approach for advanced word-reading taken in this text is the part-by-part method, which is consistent with the synthetic phonics approach described in Chapter 3. While the syllable approach is also research-based (Green, 1996; Archer et al., 2003), its use of multiple rules may be too difficult for younger children who are at risk because they are likely to have oral language difficulties. On the other hand, the syllable approach may be adequate for older students or those who have reading disabilities with no problems in oral language. Examples of evidence-based syllable-based programs include *Language!* (Greene, 2004) and *Wilson Language* (Wilson, 1996).

Letter Combinations and Affixes

To read advanced words, students need the ability to decode clusters of letters. **Letter combinations** are one type of cluster formed when two or more adjacent letters make one distinct sound. The *ch* in *church,* *ar* in *mart,* *oi* in *boil,* and *ee* in *meet* are all examples of letter combinations. Adjacent letters in a cluster can be vowels, consonants, or a combination of both. A list of common letter combinations, along with key words guiding their pronunciation, is shown in Table 4.2. These letter combinations occur frequently in common

TABLE 4.2 Letter Combinations

Note: Letter combinations having more than one sound are in bold.

Letter Combination	Phonetic Pronunciation	Voiced or Unvoiced	Articulation	Stop or Continuous Sound ⚠ = Don't Add a Schwa	When Students Have Difficulty Saying the New Letter Sound:
ai	as in *tail*	voiced	More open smiling mouth position; tongue in middle of mouth; increased mouth tension	continuous	Same as /ā/
ar	as in *hard*	voiced	Tongue is curled back toward the /r/ position	continuous	Elongate this *r*-controlled vowel for 2 to 3 seconds so the student clearly hears both sounds pronounced and sees that the mouth begins in a smiley position. Prompt with a mirror if needed. In cued speech for individuals with a hearing loss, this sound is designated as a combination of the /ah/ vowel with a following /r/.
au	as in *fault*	voiced	Rounded lips; tongue moves back in mouth; increased mouth tension	continuous	English language learners often confuse this sound with /ŏ/. The /au/ sound is produced farther back and higher in the mouth. Ask students to pretend they are sadly saying, "/Au/, the poor kitty."
aw	as in *lawn*	voiced	Rounded lips; tongue moves back in mouth; increased mouth tension	continuous	Same as /au/
ay	as in *gray*	voiced	Same as the /ā/ sound in *trail*	continuous	Same as /ā/
ch	as in *chair, munching,* and *such*	voiceless	Tip of tongue briefly contacts roof of mouth: lips forward; burst of air expelled with sound	stop ⚠	Model how your lips come forward when you say the sound. Ask students to pretend they have a cold and make a /ch/ sneeze.

TABLE 4.2 Continued

Letter Combination	Phonetic Pronunciation	Voiced or Unvoiced	Articulation	Stop or Continuous Sound ⚠ = Don't Add a Schwa	When Students Have Difficulty Saying the New Letter Sound:
dge	as in *fudge*	voiced	Tip of tongue briefly contacts the roof of mouth; a burst of air is expelled with sound	stop ⚠	Same as /j/
ea	as in *meat** *ea* says /ē/ in 60% of words containing this combination.	voiced	Smiling mouth position with lips open wide; tongue high in mouth near front; increased mouth tension	continuous	Same as /ē/
ea	as in *bread*	voiced	Smiling mouth position; tongue centered in the mid front	continuous	Same as /ĕ/
ee	as in *keep*	voiced	Same as the /ea/ sound in *meat*.	continuous	Same as /ē/
er	as in *jerk*	voiced	Tongue is in center of mouth curled back towards the /r/ position	continuous	Mouth is slightly rounded for this r-controlled vowel sound. Have your students listen and then say the sound they hear for /er/ at www.thefreedictionary.com/er
ew	as in *stew*	voiced	Rounded lips; back of tongue in highest position; increased mouth tension	continuous	Same as /ōo/
igh	as in *night*	voiced	Smiley face; tongue and jaw raise to a high position	continuous	Same as /ī/
ing	as in *dusting*	voiced	Glide from the the /ĭ/ sound to /ng/	continuous	Same as /ĭ/ + /ng/
ir	as in *bird*	voiced	Same as /er/	continuous	Same as /er/

Continued

TABLE 4.2 Continued

Letter Combination	Phonetic Pronunciation	Voiced or Unvoiced	Articulation	Stop or Continuous Sound ⚠️ = Don't Add a Schwa	When Students Have Difficulty Saying the New Letter Sound:
kn	as in *knit*	voiced	Front of tongue behind upper teeth toward front of mouth: air expelled through nose	continuous	Same as /n/
le	as in *wiggle*	voiced	Tongue lifts behind upper teeth; air passes over sides of tongue	continuous	Same as /l/
ng	as in *sing, singer,* and *bring*	voiced	Back of tongue in contact with the soft palate toward the back of the mouth; air expelled through the nose	continuous, nasal	Point out that the back of the tongue makes the sound, while the front stays down. Have students make silly /ng/ singsongs varying intonation. For example, they could sing /ng/ to the tune to "BINGO."
oa	as in *soap*	voiced	Rounded mouth that shuts like a camera shutter; tongue in middle; increased mouth tension	continuous	Same as /ō/
oi	as in *join*	voiced	Tongue glides from low back to high front; jaw rises with the tongue; an oval-shaped mouth position to a smiling position; increased mouth tension	continuous	Begin with the /au/ sound (as in *awful*) and immediately slide into the /ee/ sound. Have students look at their mouths in the mirror as they form this sound.
o͝o	as in *book*	voiced	Slightly rounded parted lips; back of tongue high; relaxed facial muscles	continuous	Ask students to pretend that they are using all their energy while pushing a heavy elephant, saying this sound.
o͞o	as in *boot** *oo* says /o͞o/ in 59% of words containing this combination.	voiced	Rounded lips; back of tongue in highest position; increased mouth tension	continuous	Ask your students to pretend they just received their favorite toy as a birthday present as they say this sound of delight.

TABLE 4.2 Continued

Letter Combination	Phonetic Pronunciation	Voiced or Unvoiced	Articulation	Stop or Continuous Sound ⚠ = Don't Add a Schwa	When Students Have Difficulty Saying the New Letter Sound:
or	as in *corn*	voiced	The vowel glides toward the /r/ position	continuous	Elongate this *r*-controlled vowel for 2 to 3 seconds so the student clearly hears both sounds pronounced and sees that the mouth starts in a rounded position. Prompt with a mirror if needed.
ou	as in *cloud*	voiced	The mouth movement glides from one articulation position to another; jaw and tongue rise as the sound is said; lips move from open to a rounded position; increased mouth tension	continuous	Ask students to pretend they just bumped their foot into the table and because it hurts they say, "ow."
ow	as in *grow** *ow* says /ō/ in 50% of words containing this combination.	voiced	Rounded mouth that shuts like a camera shutter; tongue in middle; increased mouth tension	continuous	Same as /ō/
ow	as in *clown*	voiced	Same as /ou/ as in *cloud*	continuous	Same as /ou/
oy	as in *joy*	voiced	Same as for /oi/	continuous	Same as /oi/
ph	as in *phone*	unvoiced	Upper front teeth on lower lip: air gust expelled	continuous	Same as /f/
qu	as in *queen*	unvoiced	/qu/ sounds like /kw/. Refer to the description of those letter sounds and say this sound, quickly blending them together into one sound.	continuous	Ask students to make the sound of a cuckoo clock: "kwoo-kwoo."

Continued

TABLE 4.2 Continued

Letter Combination	Phonetic Pronunciation	Voiced or Unvoiced	Articulation	Stop or Continuous Sound ⚠ = Don't Add a Schwa	When Students Have Difficulty Saying the New Letter Sound:
sh	as in *show, ashes,* and *dish.*	unvoiced	Air passes between rounded lips; teeth close but not touching; tongue down	continuous	Ask students to put their fingers in front of their mouths to feel the air as they say the sound. Show students how /sh/ is the typical "be quiet" sound and ask them to make the sound with their pointer finger raised in front of their mouth.
tch	as in *catch*	unvoiced	Tip of tongue briefly contacts roof of mouth: burst of air expelled with sound	stop ⚠	Same as /ch/
th	as in *thimble, nothing,* and *path** *th* says this sound in 74% of words containing this combination.	unvoiced	Tip of tongue between the upper front teeth as air expelled	continuous	Ask students to stick out their tongues and silently blow.
th	as in *then, mother,* and *bathe*	voiced	Tip of tongue between the upper front teeth as air expelled	continuous	Ask students to stick out their tongues and blow. Emphasize that this sound tickles their tongues.
ur	*hurt*	voiced	Same as /er/	continuous	Same as /er/
wh	as in *when*	voiced	Same as /w/ since these days most native English speakers pronounce /w/ the same as /wh/**	continuous	Same as /w/

*Percentages for letter–sound combinations having two sounds come from Hanna, Hanna, Hodges, & Rudloff (1966) as cited in Carnine, D. W., Silbert, J., Kame'enui, E. J., & Tarver, S. (2004). *Direct instruction reading* (4th ed.). New Jersey: Merrill Prentice Hall; and Celce-Murcia, M., Brinton, D., Goodwin, J. M., & Goodwin, J. (1996). *Teaching pronunciation: A reference for teachers of English to speakers of other languages.* New York: Cambridge University Press.

**Celce-Murcia et al., 2002.

words. Note that the letter combinations include vowel and consonant digraphs as well as diphthongs, already defined in Chapter 3.

> Practice saying the sounds for letter combinations at the Tampa Reads website where you can listen to them: **www.tampareads.com/realaudio/vowelsnds/voweltest.htm.**

In contrast to letter combinations that have no distinct meaning, **affixes,** the second type of cluster, always have a distinctive meaning that modifies the word containing them. In Chapter 2, you learned that one way to divide and analyze words is by breaking them into syllables. You can easily clap out the four syllables in the word *unbeliever* as *un•be•liev•er.* If, instead of syllables, you decide to divide a word into its smallest units of meaning, you have three **morphemes** (the smallest parts of words that have a distinctive meaning):

un•believe•er

- *un* means *not*
- *believe* means to accept as real
- *er* means a person who does something

In this example word, *believe* is the foundational morpheme that establishes the basic meaning of the word. Because *believe* is a complete word that can stand by itself, it is called a **base word.** When the foundational morpheme is not a complete word, such as *struct* in the word *construction,* it is called a **root.** All multisyllable words have at least one base word or root. Morphemes that precede the root or base word are called **prefixes;** morphemes that are added to the end of the root or base word are called **suffixes.** In our example, *un* is the prefix and *er* is the suffix. Both suffixes and prefixes are categorized as affixes. For example:

reseat, seating, reseating

- The word *reseat* contains the morphemes *re + seat.* The prefix is *re; seat* is the base word. The prefix *re* is also categorized as an affix.
- The word *seating* contains the morphemes *seat + ing.* The suffix is *ing;* again, *seat* is the base word. The suffix *ing* is also categorized as an affix.
- The word *reseating* contains the morphemes *re + seat + ing.* Both the prefix *re* and the suffix *ing* are categorized as affixes; again the base word is *seat.*
- The base word *seat* contains the letter combination *ea.*

desirable, undesirable

- The word *desirable* contains the morphemes *desire + able.* The suffix is *able; desire* is the base word. The suffix *able* is also categorized as an affix.
- The word *undesirable* contains the morphemes *un +desire + able.* Both the prefix *un* and the suffix *able* are categorized as affixes; again the base word is *desire.*

pendant, dependent

- The word *pendant* contains the morphemes *pend + ant.* *Pend* is the root word meaning "to hang." The suffix *ant* is also categorized as an affix.
- The word *dependent* contains the morphemes *de + pend + ent.* Both the prefix *de* and the suffix *ent* are categorized as affixes; again the root word is *pend.*

> For a list of the most common prefixes, suffixes, and roots along with their meanings, visit: **http://ueno.cool.ne.jp/let/prefix.html, www.englishclub.com/vocabulary/prefixes.htm,** and **www.dummies.com/WileyCDA/DummiesArticle/id-1186.html.**

The careful teaching of these letter combinations and affixes as preskills to multisyllable word–reading is a key feature

TABLE 4.3   Affixes

Affix	Phonetic Pronunciation	Affix	Phonetic Pronunciation
a	afraid	less	restless
able	drinkable	ly	friendly
age	package	ment	shipment
al	animal	mid	midterm
be	behold	mono	monorail
bi	bicycle	ness	goodness
com	commit	ous	monstrous
con	confess	out	outlast
de	deport	post	postseason
dis	dismiss	pre	pretend
er	hotter	pro	provide
est	saddest	re	resell
ex	expand	semi	semicircle
ful	helpful	ship	friendship
im	imperfect	teen	fifteen
in	inside	un	unhappy
ing	dusting	uni	uniform
ion	action	ward	seaward
ish	punish	y	muddy
ive	captive		

Sources: Avery & Ehrlich (2002); Celce-Murcia et al. (1996); Edelen-Smith (1997); Ladefoged (1975); McCormick et al. (2002); Singh & Singh (1976).

of effective advanced word-reading programs (Archer et al., 2003). As with letter combinations, spend your limited class time teaching the affixes that most frequently are used in common words. A list of some of the more common beginning affixes is provided in Table 4.3; the meanings of the most common affixes are presented later, in Table 6.3. You will notice that two letter combinations, *er* and *ing,* are also affixes.

One-Syllable Words Containing a Letter Combination

After students have learned a particular letter combination, the teacher supports them as they decode words that contain the combination or affix. For example, Ms. Bland introduced the /ch/ sound to her students. They were able to read the new sound correctly for two days in a row when it was mixed in with the previously introduced combinations of *ai, ar, th,* and *sh.* Ms. Bland then began to teach the class how to read one-syllable words with *ch,* such as *much, champ,* and *rich.*

Words with the Vowel–Consonant–Vowel Pattern (VCV)

Once students can read all of the CVC variants as they attain the alphabetic principle, they are ready to read words that have long vowels, including words having the vowel–consonant–vowel pattern. While the approach to phonics instruction taken in this text has been to avoid teaching a lot of rules to children who are at risk, some rules are simple enough and work often enough to make their teaching worthwhile. The VCV rule fits into this category. Students are taught the rule that if there is a vowel–consonant–vowel pattern, the first vowel says its name. Examples of words having the VCV pattern are words that have the vowel–consonant–silent *e* pattern (**VCe words**) such as *make* and *like* and Vce words to which an ending has been added, such as *hoping, slides,* and *hated.* After students are taught to apply the rule to one-syllable VCe words, they learn to tell these words apart from CVC words, a difficult discrimination for many students who are at risk.

Regular Words with Two or More Syllables

Regular words with multiple syllables can be taught as long as students are able to decode each regular part. For example, Mr. Hunter could teach his students to read the word *export* because he had already taught them to decode the prefix *ex* and the letter combination *or.* When teaching the word, he first put a scallop under each of the parts, *ex* and *port,* before having students read each part separately and then blend the parts together into the word *export.* Other examples of regular, multisyllable words are *returning, inspection,* and *buttercup.*

Words with Two or More Syllables and One or More Irregular Parts

As students read increasingly difficult passages, they encounter multiple-syllable words that have one or more irregular parts. Usually these irregular parts involve vowels that do not say their most common sounds. For example, in the word *obeyed* students should be able to read the *ed* ending but are likely to have difficulty decoding the letters *ey.* Some students may also think that *o* says its sound rather than its name because it is followed by *b.* In the word *unusable,* students should be able to read the parts *un* and *able,* but the *u* in the middle of the word could be a problem because it says its name, despite the fact that it looks like it should say its sound, as in *us.* Words having a single consonant between two vowels in a word can also be problematic. For example, students may read the word *camel* as having a long *a* because of the seeming presence of a VCV pattern in the word. On the other hand, a student encountering the word *bacon* may think the *a* says its sound because of the apparent presence of a CVC pattern in the word. Fortunately, students can also apply their decoding skills to learn these new longer words.

One- and Two-Syllable Sight Words

Some words are so irregular that it makes sense to introduce them in the same way that sight words were introduced in beginning reading. Examples of these sight words include *chaos, stomach,* and *chief.* These words can be introduced by telling students the word, having them spell the word, and then having them say the word again (see Table 3.8: "Format for Reading Sight Words").

How Can I Assess Students' Advanced Word-Reading Skills?

Once students have attained the alphabetic principle, the primary way to assess their reading skills is through oral passage reading and comprehension. Strategies for using assessments in these areas are described more fully in Chapters 5, 6, and 7. However, there are students who, despite your best teaching efforts, may struggle learning their letter combinations and affixes. These are students who tend to read grade-level passages slowly and with more errors. They are likely to be your Tier 2 students. By assessing them directly on their advanced sounds, you can find out which sounds need more instruction. Additional instruction can then be provided during their booster sessions. To assess students on letter combinations and affixes, use the lists of the most common combinations and affixes that are shown in Tables 4.2 and 4.3. One way to assess student knowledge of combinations and affixes is to check your reading series and identify which letter combinations and affixes have been taught up to the time of the assessment. For example, by November, Ms. Mobley had taught the letter combinations *ch, sh, th, ea, ar, ur,* and *ow;* and the suffixes *a, ing, be, est,* and *ly.* When she decided to assess her Tier 2 students to see whether they had learned these sounds, Ms. Mobley selected a key word to assess each sound. She selected the word *chin* for *ch;* for *ar* she selected *part;* and for *ing* she selected the word *rusting.* She then developed a typed list of the keywords, asking her students individually to read each word as it looks in Figure 4.1. As her students read, Ms. Mobley marked her score sheet, shown in Figure 4.2, with a plus if a student read the word correctly and a 0 if not.

When scoring her students' answers, Ms. Mobley was careful to score a response as incorrect only if the student missed the targeted sound. For example, Deanna in Figure 4.2 read word number two as *bash,* rather than *dash.* However, although Ms. Mobley wrote the incorrect word that Deanna read as a note to herself, she still scored Deanna's answer as correct because she read the *sh* sound correctly. After giving this assessment to all of the students in her class, Ms. Mobley developed a group score sheet to help her make instructional decisions about which skills to identify for more group instruction. Table 4.4 depicts the group score sheet she used to summarize the class results.

Note that the sounds *sh, ea, a_e, ing, be,* and *est* have been learned by everyone. While these sounds will need to be periodically reviewed, they do not need to be targeted for reteaching. *Ch, th,* and *ur* have been learned by all of the students except Otis. Ms. Mobley can also review these periodically with the group, but give Otis individual help learning them.

chin	grow
dash	amaze
math	rusting
real	become
farm	funniest
turn	hardly

FIGURE 4.1 Informal Assessment of Letter Combinations and Affixes (Student Sheet)

Student: *Deanna*   **Date:** *Oct 23*
Teacher: *Ms. Mobley*

1. **ch**in +
2. da**sh** + *bash*
3. ma**th** +
4. r**ea**l +
5. f**ar**m 0 *firm*
6. t**ur**n +
7. gr**ow** 0 *grew*
8. **a**maze +
9. rust**ing** +
10. **be**come +
11. funni**est** +
12. hard**ly** +

FIGURE 4.2 Informal Assessment of Letter Combinations and Affixes (Teacher Score Sheet)

TABLE 4.4   Class Score Sheet for Assessment of Letter Combinations and Affixes

Date: _Oct 23_   Teacher: _Mrs. Mobley_

Sounds	Darrell	Gabriella	Deanna	Otis	Alexis
ch	+	+	+	o	+
sh	+	+	+	+	+
th	+	+	+	o	+
ea	+	+	+	+	+
ar	o	o	o	o	o
ur	+	+	+	o	+
ow	o	o	o	o	o
a_e	+	+	+	+	+
ing	+	+	+	+	+
be	+	+	+	+	+
est	+	+	+	+	+
ly	o	o	+	o	o

The sounds *ar, ow,* and *ly* need to be retaught to the entire Tier 2 group. Although the most common affixes, such as *re, ness,* or *full* (see Table 4.3), were not formally included in the assessment, Mrs. Mobley always asked the students to tell their meaning in order to determine whether she needed to teach both sound and meaning.

Sometimes older students have such extensive sight reading vocabularies that assessing letter combinations within words is not an accurate way to assess their skills. For example, Dontrell read the word *farm* correctly on his assessment, yet in a passage read the word *harbor* as "herber." He read *farm* correctly because he had memorized it, not because he could sound it out using the correct sound for *ar.* One way to prevent this problem is to try to select words that students are unlikely to have in their sight reading vocabularies. Another option is to assess the sounds in isolation (if possible) or within nonsense words (see TOWRE assessment in the sidebar on p. 82).

> Use the lists available at this website to generate word lists containing specific letter combinations or specific syllable patterns: **www.resourceroom.net/ readspell/wordlists/default.asp.**

How Can I Teach Students to Decode Advanced Words and Words with Multiple Syllables?

In Chapters 1, 2, and 3, a multi-tiered instructional approach was described that allows teachers to accommodate a range of learners who are at risk. The enhancements described in those chapters also apply to teaching the advanced word-reading skills just described. No matter what reading program you are using, your likelihood of success with students who are at risk will increase with the use of advance organizers, unison responding, perky pace, support for new learning using My Turn–Together–Your Turn, systematic error corrections, cumulative review, integrated motivational strategies, and by teaching to success.

The formats for teaching advanced word reading in this chapter can be used for large-group Tier 1 instruction as well as small-group Tier 2 booster sessions.

Identifying Letter Combinations and Affixes Introduced in the Curriculum

Teaching your students to identify common letter combinations and affixes in isolation before they read them in words greatly enhances their chance of success reading multisyllable words. The format for teaching combinations and affixes in isolation is shown in Table 4.5. This format is similar to the one used for teaching single-letter sounds (Table 3.4). Once students have attained the alphabetic principle, they learn letter combinations at a more rapid rate. Students who needed to practice new letter sounds like /b/ or /j/ for a week will now learn the sound for a new letter combination after only one or two days of practice. Because students now have more experience and knowledge with sounds, the teacher can introduce a new letter combination by telling students the sound and then asking them to say the sound by themselves. Togethers are only used as needed at this stage of skill development. The new sound is then practiced along with a number of previously introduced sounds using an alternating pattern. For example, when the new combination *ar* was first introduced, it was practiced using the following alternating pattern: *ar, ea, ar, th, ing, ar, ent, ea, sl, ar, br, ai, ea, ing,* and so on. Note that both letter combinations and affixes previously covered are included in a typical daily lesson.

Consonant blends such as *br* and *sl* can also be included in these practice sessions. Some programs teach blends as clusters, and students benefit from including them in their sound drill. Even in synthetic phonics programs where students are initially taught to read blends sound-by-sound, encouraging students to view blends as clusters ultimately helps build reading fluency. If the teacher notices that during story reading half of her class is incorrectly reading words that contain *dr* and *tr,* adding those two clusters to the daily practice will reduce confusion. Starting the lesson with a lively 2- to 5-minute letter-combination drill provides an effective transition to more difficult word- and story-reading.

The Suffix *ed*

Unlike the other affixes and letter combinations, the suffix *ed* can't be introduced cleanly in isolation because it has three different sounds. The sound that *ed* makes depends on the base word to which it is added. Therefore, teach *ed* separately by using your students' oral language to help them determine which sound of *ed* to use. Carnine and colleagues (2004) suggest writing the *ed* ending on the board before presenting a series of examples to demonstrate the three different *ed* sounds. For example, Mrs. Gibbs pointed to the information in Table 4.6 when she gave instructions to students to do the following activity: First she asked students to read the word *jump.* After pointing to the *ed* ending in the word *jumped,* she told students that *jump* plus *ed = jumped* (where *ed* takes on the sound of /t/). She then had the students read the word *land* before telling them that *land* plus *ed = landed* (where *ed* takes an extra syllable and the /d/ sound). Next, she had the students say the word *fill,* and told them that *fill* plus *ed = filled* (where *ed* takes on a /d/ sound with no extra syllable). Finally, Mrs. Gibbs tested the students' understanding by asking them to add *ed* to a series of orally presented words (What's *lift* plus *ed?* What's *kill* plus *ed?* What's *skip* plus *ed?*)

Many students who are at risk have difficulty doing this oral task. They may be influenced by their native language and routinely add a syllable to indicate past tense; they may use a dialect that does not routinely add past tense to verbs; or they may have articulation problems that make this task more difficult. These students need daily practice until they begin to hear and say these past tense endings.

TABLE 4.5 Format for New Letter Combinations and Affixes Introduced in the Curriculum

Outcome	After seeing a new letter combination or affix, students say its sound with 100% accuracy.
Materials Needed	Board, chart paper, or overhead transparency and writing implement. Write the letter combinations and affixes that will be reviewed with the new letter sound. Use an alternating pattern to teach the new letter combination or affix by writing it on the board followed by one review letter combination/affix, followed by the new letter combination/affix, followed by two review letter combinations/affixes. This pattern is continued until five letter combinations or affixes separate the last two new ones (examples: **ar** ea **ar** th ing **ar** ent ea re ou **ar** ai ea ing oo _le **ar**).
Signaling	*Loop signal for continuous sounds:* After looping to the end of the letter combination, hold your finger under it for two seconds as students say the sound before looping your finger back to the starting point. *Loop signal for stop sounds:* After looping to the end of the letter combination, bounce your finger out as students say the sound and return to the starting point.
Time	3–5 minutes

Instructions	**Teacher**	**Student**
	1. Advance Organizers	
	2. My Turn (Examples given for continuous and stop sounds.)	
	Point to the new letter combination or affix.	
	continuous sound: (finger to the left of letter) **"My turn. Here's our new sound for today."** (loop signal) **"/ar/."** (loop back to starting point)	/ar/
	stop sound: (finger to the left of letter) **"My turn. Here's our new sound for today."** (loop signal and bounce out) **"/ch/."** (back to starting point)	/ch/
	3. Your Turn	
	continuous sound: (finger to the left of letter) **"Your turn. What sound?"** (loop signal) (answer) (loop back to starting point) **"Yes, /ar/."**	/ar/
	stop sound: (finger to the left of letter) **"Your turn. What sound?"** (loop signal and bounce out) (answer) (back to starting point). **"Yes, /ch/."**	/ch/
	4. Individual Student Checkout	
	continuous sound: (finger to the left of letter) **"Individual turns. What sound? Inez."** (loop signal) (answer) (loop back to starting point) **"Yes, /ar/."**	/ar/
	stop sound: (finger to the left of letter) **"Individual turns. What sound? Shan."** (loop signal and bounce out) (answer) (back to starting point). **"Yes, /ch/."**	/ch/
	5. Your Turn to Read the Row (new plus previously learned letter combinations and affixes)	/ar/
	Starting at the first letter combination/affix move through the row of letters on the list, signaling for each letter combination/affix just as you did in Step 3. As you move through the list say, **"What sound?"** for each letter combination/affix.	/ea/ /ar/
	6. Individual Student Checkout	
	Point to random letters. Starting at the first letter combination/affix, move across the row of letters on the list, signaling for each letter combination/affix just as you did in Step 5. As you point to random letter combinations/affixes on the list say, **"Individual turns. What sound? Carmella."**	/ing/, /ar/, /ent/ . . .

Error Correction	If an error occurs at Step 3, immediately return to a My Turn–Your Turn pattern.
	If an error occurs at Step 5 or 6, immediately return to a My Turn–Your Turn pattern. Then alternate between the missed letter and familiar letters until students identify the missed letter correctly three times.

Continued

TABLE 4.5 Continued

Adaptations	
	■ If you are using a reading program that uses sound cards that have letter sounds accompanied by a rhyme or poem cue, you still need to do this straightforward, fast drill in addition to the sound cards so students develop fluency and don't rely on the rhyme.
	■ If your reading curriculum stresses two sounds for the same letter combination (e.g., /ē/ and /ĕ/ for *ea),* ask students to say two sounds for the combination, saying the most common sound first. If you introduce the letter combination in this way from the start, students will know which sound to say first. You can point to the letter combination and signal: **"Say the two sounds. First sound."** (student answer) **"Second sound."** (student answer)
	■ If your reading curriculum does not practice consonant blends in isolation but your students are consistently missing blends such as *tr* and *dr,* introduce the blends as letter combinations and provide extra practice each day.

Source: This script is based on one originally developed and field tested by Carnine, Silbert, Kame'enui, and Tarver (2004). *Direct Instruction Reading,* Fourth Edition. New Jersey, Merrill Prentice Hall.

Reading One-Syllable Words with Letter Combinations

Once students can read a letter combination in isolation, teach them to read it in words using the format shown in Table 4.7. In this approach, the teacher uses strategic underlining and a part–whole strategy to focus student attention on the new combination. The teacher begins by underlining the letter combination in the first three or four words. Students first read the underlined letter combination and then the entire word. After doing this procedure for the first three to four words, students then read the rest of the words in the list the fast way at least two times. The first time the teacher provides more think time, gradually reducing the amount each time thereafter to build fluency. At least one-third of the words in the list should have the new letter combination because newer skills require more practice. The remaining words contain review letter combinations to build student retention. A loop signal is used for reading the underlined combination; a side-slash signal is used for reading the whole word. These are the same signals shown in Figure 3.12.

Reading One-Syllable Words Ending in VCe

Reading VCe words is difficult for students because it is the first time they encounter long vowels that are not part of a vowel combination. There are two parts to the format for teaching students to read one-syllable words ending in VCe. These parts are shown in Table 4.8. In Part A, students are introduced to the vowel–consonant–vowel (VCV) rule: "When it's a vowel–consonant–vowel, the first vowel says its name." After saying the rule the teacher guides the students by applying it to four or five VCe words. After the rule has been successfully applied to each word, the students read each word the fast way. If the students make an error while reading words the fast way, the teacher guides them as they reapply the rule, reread the word, and then go back to the beginning of the list and read the words the fast way again. The goal for this activity is 100% accuracy.

TABLE 4.6 Action Words with *ed* Endings Tell Us What Happened in the Past

Base Word	Base Word: Past	Sound
jump	jumped	/t/
land	landed	/d/ + syllable
fill	filled	/d/

TABLE 4.7   Format for Reading One-Syllable Regular Words with Letter Combinations

Outcome	After seeing a one-syllable regular word that contains a letter combination, students orally read the word the fast way.
Materials Needed	Board, chart paper, or overhead transparency and writing implement. Write the regular words that students will read in rows on the board. For example, if students are reading eight words, write two rows of four words. On the first day, underline the new letter combinations before students read words containing them.
Signaling	Two-part signal: **"What sound?"** or **"What word?"** initiates the signal for unison answers.
	1. Loop signal. **"What sound?"** initiates the signal for unison answers.
	2. Side-slash-signal. **"What word?"** initiates the signal for unison answers.
Time	Depends on the number of words with new letter combinations introduced in the reading curriculum.

Instructions	**Teacher**	**Student**
	1. Advance Organizers	
	2. Your Turn with Sound Prompting	
	a. (finger just to the left of underlined sound) **"Your turn. What sound?"** (loop signal) (answer) (loop back to starting point). **"Yes,** (loop signal) **/sh/."** (loop back to the left of the word)	/sh/
	b. (pointing to the left of the word.) **"What word?"** (side-slash-answer) (loop back to starting point). **"Yes, *ship.*"**	ship
	3. Your Turn without Sound Prompting	
	After the first three or four words on the list, omit the sound prompting. Remember to use a longer think time the first or second time students read words on the list.	
	"What word?" (side-slash-signal under the entire word–answer) (loop back to starting point) **"Yes, *shall.*"**	shall
	"What word?" (side-slash-signal under the entire word–answer) (loop back to starting point) **"Yes, *wish.*"**	wish
	4. Individual Student Checkout	
	"What word? Bethany." (side-slash-signal under the entire word–answer) (loop back to starting point) **"Yes, *wish.*"**	wish
	Call on between one and three students to check for accuracy.	

Error Correction	If students make an error reading the new sound combination, ask them to tell you the sound and then read the word again. If students still make a mistake, move into a My Turn–Your Turn pattern. Then return to the beginning of the row and have students reread the words.
	If students make an error reading another sound they have previously learned, immediately have them sound out loud and then read the whole word. If they still make an error, return to a My Turn–Your Turn. Once the error is corrected, return to the beginning of the row and have students reread the words.
Perk up Your Drill	■ Some teachers send home a list of the words with their students for extra practice. On Friday afternoon, the class splits into assigned pairs. First one student reads to her partner who marks every correct word. Then the pair switches. The teacher monitors closely for any questions. Students keep track of their cumulative score from week to week by charting it on a thermometer.
Adaptations	■ The first two or three times through the word list, you will need to give longer "think time" as students sound out the words with the new combination.
	■ If the daily lesson in your reading curriculum introduces too many words, plan to spend two or three days on the lesson, dividing the words into smaller lists. You will want to avoid going longer than 15 or 20 minutes with this section of the lesson.

Source: This script is based on one originally developed and field tested by Carnine, Silbert, Kame'enui, and Tarver (2004). *Direct Instruction Reading,* Fourth Edition. New Jersey, Merrill Prentice Hall.

TABLE 4.8 Format for Reading One-Syllable Words That End with VCe: Part A

Outcome	After seeing one-syllable words that end with VCe, students orally read the words the fast way.
Materials Needed	Board, chart paper, or overhead transparency and writing implement. Write the regular words that students will read in rows on the board. In this beginning format, the word list should only contain VCe words. On the first day, underline the two vowels before students read words containing them.
Signaling	Two-part signal: 1. A finger snap 2. Side-slash-signal: **"What word?"** initiates the signal for unison answers. In Part B, a looping signal is used after the teachers asks **"What sound?"**

Instructions	Teacher	Student
	Note: The first few times you read VCe words, use a My Turn to show students how you apply the rule and read the words.	
	1. Teach students the rule for one-syllable words that end in VCVe. **"When it's vowel–consonant–vowel, the first vowel says its name."** Don't move on to Step 2 until students can say this rule.	When it's vowel–consonant–vowel . . .
	2. Point to the first word and ask, **"Does this word have a vowel–consonant–vowel?"** (pause) (finger snap) (answer) (point to VCV letters as you affirm) **"Yes, this word has a vowel–consonant–vowel."**	yes
	3. Point to the first vowel and ask, **"So does this letter say its name?"** (pause) (finger snap) (answer) **"Yes, this letter says its name."**	yes
	4. Point to the first vowel: **"Say the name of this letter."** (finger snap) (answer) (point to the first vowel) **"Yes, /ā/."**	/ā/
	5. Point your finger to the left of the first letter in the word, pause and ask, **"What word?"** (side-slash-signal under the entire word–answer) (loop back to starting point) **"Yes, name."**	name
	6. Repeat this pattern for all of the words.	
	7. After students read all of the words on the list, start at the beginning and read all of the words the fast way.	
	(point and pause) **"What word?"** (side-slash-signal under the entire word–answer) (loop back to starting point) **"Yes, name."**	name
	(point and pause) **"What word?"** (side-slash-signal under the entire word–answer) (loop back to starting point) **"Yes, gate."**	gate
	(point and pause) **"What word?"** (side-slash-signal under the entire word–answer) (loop back to starting point) **"Yes, sale."**	sale
	Gradually fade out your prompts. On day 2 or 3, you might begin omitting Step 4. If students are not successful, add that prompt for several more days. Once students can read the long vowel words when you omit Step 4, also omit Step 3 during the first time through the words.	
	8. Individual Student Checkout	
	(point and pause) **"Individual turns. What word? Austin."** (side-slash-signal under the entire word–answer) (loop back to starting point) **"Yes, gate."**	gate
	(point and pause) **"What word? Chan."** (side-slash-signal under the entire word–answer) (loop back to starting point) **"Yes, sale."**	sale
	Call on between one and three students to check for accuracy.	

Error Correction	If an error occurs at any step, immediately repeat steps 2–6. Repeat the rule as in step 1 if necessary.

TABLE 4.8   Continued

Format for Reading a Mixture of One-Syllable CVC Words and Words That End with VCe: Part B

Outcome	After seeing a combination of one-syllable CVC words and words that end with VCe students orally read the words the fast way.
Materials Needed	Board, chart paper, or overhead transparency and writing implement. Write the regular words that students will read in rows on the board. The word list should contain a mixture of words that end in VCe and CVC words in random order.
Signal	Three-part signal:

1. A finger snap.
2. Loop signal. **"What sound?"** initiates the signal for unison answers.
3. Side-slash-signal. **"What word?"** initiates the signal for unison answers.

Instructions	**Teacher**	**Student**
	1. Ask students to tell you the vowel–consonant–vowel rule (signal 1).	When it's vowel–consonant–vowel . . .
	2. Point to the first word and ask, **"Does this word have a vowel–consonant–vowel?"** (pause) (finger snap) (answer) (point to letters as you affirm) **"Yes, this word has a vowel–consonant–vowel."**	yes
	3. Point to the first vowel and ask, **"Do we say /ā/ or /ă/ for this letter?"** (pause) (finger snap) (answer) (point to letter as you affirm) **"Yes, /ā/ ."**	/ā/
	4. Point to the left of the word, pause, and ask, **"What word?"** (side-slash-signal under the entire word—answer) (loop back to starting point) **"Yes, *tame.*"**	tame
	5. Point to the second word and ask, **"Does this word have a vowel–consonant–vowel?"** (pause) (finger snap)	no
	6. Point to the first vowel and ask, **"Do we say /ā/ or /ă/ or for this letter?"** (pause) (finger snap) (answer) (point to letter as you affirm) **"Yes, /ăăă/."**	/ă/
	7. Point to the left of the word, pause and ask, **"What word?"** (side-slash-signal) (answer) **"Yes, *cat.*"**	cat
	8. Repeat Steps 1–4 for each of the words on the list.	
	9. After reading all of the words on the list, start at the beginning and read all of the words the fast way.	
	(point and pause) **"What word?"** (side-slash-signal under the entire word–answer) (loop back to starting point) **"Yes, *tame.*"**	tame
	(point and pause) **"What word?"** (side-slash-signal under the entire word–answer) (loop back to starting point) **"Yes, *cat.*"**	cat
	(point and pause) **"What word?"** (side-slash-signal under the entire word–answer) (loop back to starting point) **"Yes, *sap.*"**	sap
	(point and pause) **"What word?"** (side-slash-signal under the entire word–answer) (loop back to starting point) **"Yes, *gate.*"**	gate
	Gradually fade out your prompts. On day 2 or 3, you might begin omitting Step 3. If students are not successful, add that prompt for several more days. Once students can read the words when you omit Step 3, omit Steps 1 and 2 the first time through the words.	
	10. Individual Student Checkout	
	(point and pause) **"Individual turns. What word? Glynnis."** (side-slash-signal under the entire word–answer) (loop back to starting point) **"Yes, *sap.*"**	sap
	(point and pause) **"What word? Dyron."** (side-slash-signal under the entire word–answer) (loop back to starting point) **"Yes, *tame.*"**	tame
	Call on between one and three students to check for accuracy.	

Continued

TABLE 4.8   Continued

Error Correction	Repeat steps 1–4.
Perk up Your Drill	If students read interspersed VCe and CVC words on a first read with at least 90% accuracy, you can play the "I'll try to trick you" game. When students first see the new word list, tell them that each year you like to trick your students and have put up a challenging list of words to try to trick them. Using an animated tone of voice and gestures, tell the students that they will read the word list and try not to be tricked by any of the words. Students will use all of their effort to avoid mistakes so the teacher can't trick them. You will find that your students never tire of these challenges.
Adaptations	▪ Check to see whether students who have difficulty reading the words with long vowels are confusing the terms *name* and *sound.* In the beginning exercises, you may need to overemphasize the word *name* when you ask, **"Say the NAME of this letter."**
	▪ Students who are most at risk may need to learn the following preskills:
	▪ to identify letters as vowels or consonants
	▪ to tell the difference between a letter name and a letter sound.

Source: This script was adapted from *Strategic Engineering: Meeting the Needs of Diverse Learners: Trainer's Notes,* Valley Stream, NY: J/P Associates, Inc.; and from Carnine, Silbert, Kame'enui, and Tarver (2004), *Direct Instruction Reading,* Fourth Edition. New Jersey: Merrill Prentice Hall.

Once students are able to read lists of VCe words without error, they are presented with a mixture of VCe and CVC words in Part B to ensure that they only apply the VCV rule when appropriate. A common problem among children who are at risk is that once they learn to read long vowel words, they have a tendency to make all vowels long, whether they are or not. For example, after Mr. Gagliano taught his students the VCV rule, he noticed that during passage reading they were reading the words *hop* as *hope, tap* as *tape,* and *rip* as *ripe.*

In Part B of the VCV format, the teacher asks the questions that students will need to ask themselves in order to independently apply the rule to words and read them accurately: "Does this word have a vowel–consonant–vowel? So, do we say /ā/ or /ă/ for this letter? So what's the word?"

After the students have applied the rule to the list of words, they read the list of words the fast way until they are 100% accurate. As with Part A, errors are corrected by having students reapply the rule and then go back to the beginning of the list. Once again the goal is 100% accuracy for a given list of words. Since this reading skill is especially difficult for students who are at risk, teachers often spend several days practicing reading a mixture of CVC and VCe words until students are successful. Eventually, once students learn to apply the rule, they automatically learn to distinguish VCe and CVC words without any conscious thought.

With regard to signaling, a finger snap or hand clap is used for all rule application questions such as, "Is there a vowel–consonant–vowel?" The side-slash-signal is used when it is time for students to read the word. When the teacher asks, "So, do we say /ā/ or /ă/ for this letter?" a snap or clap is used.

Reading Regular Words with Two or More Syllables

The format for reading regular words with two or more syllables, which is shown in Table 4.9 (pp. 152–153), teaches students to see words as parts rather than as a collection of individual letters. Regular words with two or more syllables are words that can be broken into parts that can be readily decoded as long as students have the prerequisite decoding skills. For example, the word *returning* can be broken up into the parts *re + turn + ing.* As long as students are capable of decoding all three parts, they can be taught how to attack the word.

Providing Differentiated Instruction

In this four-part activity from a general education curriculum, students are introduced to reading VCe words involving the vowels *a, o,* and *i.* Read it carefully and consider whether you would use it without modification—and why or why not.

1. Hold up a Big Book, displaying the text as you read the rhyme. Ask the students to listen for words that have the /ă/ sound as in *Sam,* and the /ā/ sound as in *name.* Repeat the process for words with long and short *i* and *o.*
2. Frame words in the rhyme that have the /ă/ sound like in *bat.* Write these words on the board and ask students how the words are alike. Point out the CVC pattern and explain that words having the CVC pattern usually have a short vowel sound. Have students read the words. Repeat this process for long *a,* short i, long *i,* and short and long *o.*
3. Give letter cards to the students, read a series of words, and have students tape their letter cards to the board spelling out the words.

   at-ate; tap-tape; cap-cape; dim-dime; kit-kite; hid-hide; not-note; rod-rode; hop-hope.

4. Ask students to read the following words and phrases.

dive	bat	home	big
came	bit	rim	gave
stop	can	make	hand
bone	bike	got	gift

Rob's robe	Tim has time.
Smile and grin	Dave and Meg rode bikes.
Can of canes	Ken gave his mom a gift.
Jane and Jan	Hand me the rope.
The dog's bone	Is this note for Jake?
That is a fine pig.	

—End of Activity Set—

Analysis of Activity

The transition from long to short vowels is a difficult one for students who are at risk. First-grade teachers in Project PRIDE had to work extra hard each year helping students acquire this skill. Unfortunately, the instruction provided in Parts 1–3 is unlikely to prepare students to read the words, phrases, and sentences in Part 4. Part of the problem is that expecting students to complete Part 4 successfully is too big a goal, considering that this is the first day that the VCV rule is introduced. A more realistic goal would be to have the students apply the rule to word lists first. Only after they were successful on the word lists would the teacher move on to phrases and sentences. Students who are at risk may need several days of list practice before they are ready for the phrases and sentences.

A major problem with this lesson is that the instruction isn't explicit enough. Although the teacher points out VCe and CVC patterns, she never demonstrates with a "My Turn" to show how the silent *e* rule is applied to reading words. Nor are the students guided by the teacher as they apply the rule using a series of Togethers. This lesson could be easily adapted for your students who are at risk by using the format in Table 4.8. When reading each word, ask the students if there is a vowel–consonant–vowel. If there is, provide support so that they can tell you whether the vowel says its sound or name. If there is no vowel–consonant–vowel, guide the students to say that the vowel says its sound. When students are able to consistently apply the rule with teacher guidance, have them read lists of CVC and VCe words the fast way, using teacher guidance to apply the rule only as a correction procedure.

The four-part lesson also is inefficient. If the purpose of Part 1 is to help students discriminate between long and short vowels, this skill could be taught more directly using a few oral examples. For example, "In the word *cat,* the *a* says its sound; in the word *ate,* the *a* says its name. Listen as I say these words. Tell me if the vowel says its name or its sound." Part 2 of this activity could be eliminated altogether, because guiding students to apply the rule provides more direct practice on pattern recognition. Finally, in Part 3, the use of letter cards with individual students coming to the board to make words takes a lot of time and is difficult to manage. A more efficient approach would be to have students read word pairs on the board using a unison response format. In addition, the word list in Part 3 is too predictable; the short vowel word in the word pairs always comes first, allowing students to guess the correct vowel sound without having to apply the rule.

TABLE 4.9 Format for Reading Regular Words with Two or More Syllables

Outcome:	After seeing a regular word that contains two or more syllables, students orally read the word the fast way.
Materials Needed	Board, chart paper, or overhead transparency and writing implement. Write the regular words that students will read in rows on the board. For example, if students are reading eight words, write two rows of four words. On the first day, underline each part of the word before students read. *Reading* is written as <u>read</u> <u>ing</u>. *Slanted* is written as <u>slant</u> <u>ed</u>.
Signaling	Two-part signal: 1. Loop signal. **"Read this part"** initiates the signal for unison answers. Repeat for each part of the word, moving from left to right. 2. Side-slash-signal. **"What word?"** initiates the signal for unison answers.
Time	Depends on the number of words introduced in the reading curriculum.

Instructions	**Teacher**	**Student**
	1. Advance Organizers	
	2. Your Turn with prompting of word parts	
	"First you're going to read the parts of the word and then you'll read the whole word."	
	a. Place your finger to the left of the first underlined part of the first word written on the board (<u>read</u> <u>ing</u>). **"First part?"** (loop signal under the underlined part)	read
	b. Point to the left of the second underlined part of the word. **"Next?"** (loop signal under the underlined part)	ing
	c. Loop your finger to the left of the word. **"What word?"** (side-slash-signal under the entire word–answer) (loop back to starting point) **"Yes, *reading.*"**	reading
	Repeat this pattern for all of the multisyllable words on the list.	
	3. Your Turn without prompting of word parts	
	After reading all of the multisyllable words on the list, start again and read the words the fast way without prompting the parts.	
	(point and pause) **"What word?"** (side-slash-signal under the entire word–answer) (loop back to starting point) **"Yes, *reading.*"**	reading
	(point and pause) **"What word?"** (side-slash-signal under the entire word–answer) (loop back to starting point) **"Yes, *shelter.*"**	shelter
	4. Repeat 3, even faster.	
	5. Individual Student Checkout	
	(point and pause) **"Individual turns. What word? Johnny."** (side-slash-signal under the entire word–answer) (loop back to starting point) **"Yes, *candle.*"**	candle
	(point and pause) **"What word? Greta."** (side-slash-signal under the entire word–answer) (loop back to starting point) **"Yes, *tailor.*"**	tailor

Error Correction	If students make an error reading the individual parts, immediately have them first orally sound out that part of the word and then read the entire part as a whole. Ask students to read the whole word one more time. Finally return to the beginning of the row and have students reread all the words to that point.
	If students make an error reading the whole word the fast way, immediately tell students the word; then ask them to read the word parts again before reading the whole word. Once the error is corrected, return to the beginning of the row and have students reread all of the words.
Perk up Your Drill	■ If you write your words on the board, tell students that since these words are so big, you will now use magnets to mark rows that they have read correctly. You will need to add a new job to the weekly job board and each week one student will have the opportunity to stick the magnets

TABLE 4.9   Continued

Perk up Your Drill (continued)	to the board as correct rows are read. At the end of class, the assigned student collects the magnets and puts them in their box.
	■ Every time students read two rows of words correctly, have them raise their hands as if a fireworks display is rising into the sky. In unison, make the gentle sound of fireworks drifting back to the ground.
Adaptations	■ If students have had difficulty reading words with a new sound like /tion/, once they are reading the words accurately, find decodable books that emphasize that sound for more practice.
	■ If students have difficulty determining whether the vowel in an open syllable says its name or its sound, you can tell students that when you put circles above a letter, the letter says its name. Use this strategy when you anticipate that students will be unable to decode a new word such as *starvation* = star v̊a tion

Source: This script is based on one originally developed and field tested by Carnine, Silbert, Kame'enui, and Tarver (2004). *Direct Instruction Reading,* Fourth Edition. New Jersey: Merrill Prentice Hall.

In this format, the teacher uses a loop signal under each decodable part as students read the parts, then side-slashes as students read the whole word. Students read all of the words the fast way after they have first read them in parts.

When students misread the part or the whole word, the teacher must instantly analyze their mistake in order to select the appropriate error correction. If students misread a part of the word, the teacher immediately asks them to go back a step. The teacher then supports the students as they reread that part before reading the word again. Once students have read the missed part correctly, the teacher points slightly to the left of the word and has them once again begin reading the parts of the same word to give them some more immediate practice. When Mrs. Dettman came to the third word on Tuesday's list (*constrictor*), which she had underlined as con strict or, she asked everyone to read the first part, which they did with no problem. When she asked them to read the second part, they said, "*sicker,*" so she immediately put her finger slightly to the left of the *s* and asked them to sound out that part. As she looped from letter to letter, the students replied, "/s/ + /t/ + /r/ + /i/ +/c/ +/t/. Now when she asked them to read that part, they correctly answered *strict*. Mrs. Dettman enthusiastically told the group, "Yes, this part is *strict,*" before saying, "Let's read this word one more time. Read the first part." Her students then quickly read each part, *con + strict + or,* so she asked them to read the whole word, which they accurately did. Instead of having students move down the list and read the fourth word, Mrs. Dettman said, "Now let's start at the top of the list and see if this time we can get every word correct the first time." By giving the students this slightly delayed practice reading *constrictor* again, she ensured that they would be likely to read it correctly when they opened their books and read the boa constrictor snake story.

The second type of error correction is used when students read the parts correctly but blend them into a different word. If Mrs. Dettman's students had decoded the parts *con + strict + or* correctly, but then read the word as *contraction,* they would have made this second type of error. Recognizing the second type of error, Mrs. Dettman would switch to a "My Turn" strategy and tell students the word (*constrictor*). For immediate practice she would then ask her students to read the parts of the word (*con + strict + or*) before reading the whole word again (*constrictor*). Just as with the first error, Mrs. Dettman would return to the top of the list and ask her students to read all of the words again. Students should now move quickly through reading these words since they have had more practice decoding them. Of course, if students failed to blend *constrictor* correctly because they hadn't heard of that word before, Mrs. Dettman would teach the meaning of the word as well.

The Reflective Teacher

Teaching Multisyllable Words

Determining how to divide longer multisyllable words into parts is a challenging task for a teacher using systematic phonics instruction for the first time. Mr. Turner wanted his students to have a high level of success when reading Wednesday's words, so he carefully spent time before the lesson planning how to introduce the new words. He needed to determine how he should strategically divide each word so that students were most likely to read it correctly when they combined the parts. Following are all of Wednesday's new words introduced in the reading curriculum. Before school Mr. Turner wrote the words on the board and decided how he would teach them. Let's take a look at his thought process.

regular words: fleet   flock   glide   places   hoping   biking   making   probably   adventure   prescription   nervously   launched   horizon

sight words: papayas   chief

When Mr. Turner prepared his transparency, in the first row he wrote all words that he expected his students could accurately read as whole words without any extra help, even though this was the first time they were seeing them. Mr. Turner's students all had alphabetic principle, and they could decode words that contained letter combinations that they had already learned. Thus Mr. Turner started his list by writing *fleet, flock, glide,* and *places* at the top of the list. Even though *places* had an *s* ending, Mr. Turner's students had practiced *–s* and *–es* words and rarely made mistakes reading them the first time. He planned to use the format for reading words the fast way in Table 3.7 when his students read these words in unison.

In the next row Mr. Turner wrote the words containing a VCe pattern with an *ing* suffix (*hoping biking making*). Since he had previously taught the VCV rule but occasionally his students missed reading these words, he used Part B of the VCV Format (Table 4.8) when instructing these words. After his students said the rule and identified whether the vowel said its name or sound, Mr. Turner asked his students to read the whole word. When his students were able to read this type of word, he added words such as *hopping, mapping,* and *passing* to the list to give them additional practice in distinguishing between words that followed and didn't follow the VCV rule. Later he planned to photocopy a short, three-page decodable story with an emphasis on this type of word for more practice.

Since Mr. Turner's goal was to gradually increase the length of the word parts that students read, he decided to underline larger chunks in the next group of words. Although most of these chunks were also syllables, if Mr. Turner had divided the words into syllables, he would have divided *ably* into two parts instead of one. This is how he divided the words for instruction: prob ably, ad ven ture, pre scrip tion, nerv ous ly. When teaching these new words, Mr. Turner continued to use the format in Table 4.9.

Although Mr. Turner knew his students would have no problem adding the *ed* ending to *launched,* he had noticed that his students were still frequently missing the *au* letter combination in words. So he underlined that pattern in the word *launched,* because he planned first to point to the letter combination, then ask students the sound it made, and finally ask them to read the whole word (Table 4.7).

Mr. Turner had already taught his students *horizon* as a vocabulary word and believed that his students could easily apply their decoding strategies to read it if he used the format in Table 4.9. Even though the final *o* in this word is a schwa sound instead of a short *o* sound, because he had pretaught students the meaning of this word and used it in discussion, Mr. Turner anticipated that when students read the word the fast way they would probably say *horizon.* Mr. Turner divided the word this way: hor i zon. Although Mr. Turner had never taught his students the open-syllable rule, they had read enough word patterns that when they saw the *i* alone, they automatically read it as a long vowel, saying its name.

Finally, Mr. Turner taught *papayas* and *chief* as sight words using the format in Table 3.8. Since the word *papaya* was pivotal in the story, he planned to talk about the meaning when he introduced the word, providing vocabulary practice on the spot. During the Friday "listen to music" party that his students would most likely earn for the last 20 minutes of class, he planned to have some papayas cut so his students could taste them if they wanted to. Even if they were not brave enough to eat them, at least they would see what papayas look like, since the story had only a crude black-and-white line drawing of them.

When Mr. Turner was ready to teach these words, his overhead projection on the wall looked like this.

fleet	flock	glide	places	
swooping	flapping	pointing	battling	launched
prob ably	ad ven ture	pre scrip tion	nerv ous ly	hor i zon
papayas	chief			

Seize the Teachable Moment

Enhancers for Advanced Word Reading

1. Effective teaching of reading multisyllable words is enhanced by ongoing vocabulary instruction like Mrs. Gibbs' weekly "$100 words." Every Monday, Mrs. Gibbs selects a challenging multisyllable word related to positive character development. First she writes the word on the board and shows students how to decode it before giving them practice reading the new word. Mrs. Gibbs tells students what the word means before using it in sample sentences. Some students then have the opportunity to use the word in an original sentence they compose on the spot. At least once during the week, Mrs. Gibbs makes sure that students spell the word and use it in their writing. Each morning starts out with reading and discussing that week's $100 word. When Mrs. Gibbs has an extra 2 or 3 minutes during the day, she asks everyone to read in unison all of the $100 words taught from the beginning of the year and displayed on the black board.

    Students are eager to learn these words, because if they find an opportunity to use them in context during the day, Mrs. Gibbs gives them a fake $100 bill that can be used toward items in the treasure chest that she bought during summer garage sales. Latecia was delighted when her *Reading Mastery* teacher reminded the group that they needed to read the story one more time until they met their goal. This gave Latecia the opportunity to respond, "So, you want us to be *tenacious*." When her *Reading Mastery* teacher exclaimed about her use of such a big word, Latecia smiled and told her that it was one of their $100 words. When Latecia returned to the room, her *Reading Mastery* teacher told Mrs. Gibbs about Latecia's use of *tenacious* so she could get her bill. Throughout the year students learned to read and understand words like *cooperation, diligence,* and *compassion.*

2. In the afternoon, Mr. Szymck teaches a thematic unit, integrating science and social studies. He finds that during his unit, he has the opportunity to provide his students with extra review reading letter combinations that they have learned in reading. When he previews his lesson plans, he looks for any words that have patterns that his students have learned. At the start of the activity he has them read those new science words. During his unit on "Spring as a Time of Growth," he wrote the words *puddles* and *raindrops* on the board and asked students to read them. When the unit moved from the topic of water to trees, he selected the following words: *treetop, maple,* and *branches.*

3. Ms. Parker has three students in her class whose accuracy when reading stories is lower than it should be. She notices that they often stumble on words containing letter combinations that they have learned in class. Sometimes they seem to forget the sound made by the letter

Continued

Sound Sheet 12

Reading Curriculum 1st grade—Story 25:

Student Name: _____

Date: _____

Pretest

tr	ee	sh	ch	ay	br	kn	wh	igh	ai
er	th	gr	adge	or	st	est	udge	oa	qu

Practice

oa	adge	est	qu	udge	ai	or	ch	st	igh
udge	th	or	gr	oa	igh	th	ay	sh	tr
br	gr	er	ay	adge	ai	wh	est	ar	gr
st	kn	ch	ar	ai	qu	ee	br	adge	oa
ai	est	sh	gr	wh	st	er	udge	or	th
ar	ay	adge	qu	kn	ee	igh	tr	ch	wh
udge	or	th	ee	st	sh	ay	er	kn	est

Timed Test

udge	ai	oa	qu	igh	gr	kn	er	tr	ee
wh	or	est	br	sh	th	st	adge	ch	ai

FIGURE 4.3 Sound Sheet

Source: Idol, L. (1997). *Reading success: A Specialized Literacy Program for Learners with Challenging Reading Needs.* Austin, TX: Pro-Ed.

combination, although they have identified it during practice sessions. As these students read, Ms. Parker jots down notes on letter combinations that stump them. She plans to add these letter combinations to others that are routinely in stories that the class is reading in order to design sound sheets for extra practice. Figure 4.3 shows a sample sound sheet one teacher made (Idol, 1997).

When she develops the sound sheet, Ms. Parker keeps the number of sounds presented on the sheet to fewer than 30. If the students are more naïve learners, she reduces that number to 10. For letter combinations that have more than one sound, she expects the students to say both sounds as they go through the sheet, giving the most frequently used sound first. If students complete the first section (pretest) of the sound sheet quickly and with no errors, Mrs. Parker praises them for being 100% correct and stops the activity in order to provide more practice reading the story. If the students miss any of the letter combinations or are slow to identify them, she immediately tells students the sound (My Turn), says the sound with the students (Together) and asks them to repeat it (Your Turn). This sequence provides extra long-term memory practice.

In the second section of the sound sheets, the students read all of these same sounds arrayed in a different order. Whenever an error is made, Mrs. Parker uses the same error process as she did before. When students reach the final test section, she challenges them by relating that the goal is to say every sound correctly without making any mistakes. This time she does not correct errors, but saves her feedback until the end of the test section, "You told me the name of every sound," or "You only missed these two sounds so we will practice them again tomorrow." The whole process takes between 3 and 5 minutes. Mrs. Parker holds a copy of the student's sound sheet so she can mark any errors and keep track of the percentage of correct sounds. Students only move to a new sound sheet after 2 or 3 days of 100% accuracy. Because Mrs. Parker wants to connect these letter sounds to passage reading once the sound sheet practice is finished, she immediately asks these three students to reread the original story.

Putting the Pieces Together: Tiers 1–3

Students who are learning advanced word-reading also need fluency instruction to increase their reading speed. Chapter 5 will explain how a typical classroom day looks when advanced word-reading and fluency are the critical skills. Descriptions about how each tier can meet the needs of individual students as well as decision-making rules for any tier changes are detailed in that chapter. Table 4.10 (p. 158) depicts how advanced word-reading skills are taught in each of the five intensive, alternative programs described in previous chapters.

Research to Practice

Supporting Tier 3 Students In General Education Classrooms

From the time that Project PRIDE started, teachers wondered how they could integrate Tier 3 students into the general curriculum without causing frustration or backsliding. Would they be able to avoid the humiliation that can develop when students are expected to orally read frustration-level text during round-robin reading? How could the classroom teacher stay on top of what her students were learning when they might be going to three or four different groups? We knew that the school teams would need to plan ahead to avoid these common classroom dynamics.

At the beginning of the literacy project, we looked closely at the alternative *Reading Mastery* curriculum and wrote a summary sheet that Tier 3 teachers could give to classroom teachers. It listed all of the new sounds, words, and skills that were taught in Tier 3 for each set of ten lessons. A sample sheet is portrayed in Figure 4.4. At first the Tier 3 teachers sometimes forgot to distribute the summary sheets, or the classroom teacher just tossed them on a pile. But after a few months, teachers began to realize how helpful the information was. They could share it with parents during conferences, select appropriate decodable reading books or computer activities based on words the students had learned, and modify spelling lessons. Gradually, this new communication system became ingrained. Teachers recognized that *Reading Mastery* introduced ā before the general classroom curriculum did because of a different sequence of letter sounds taught, and they used the opportunity to have students in Tier 3 publicly read some ā words that no one else could read.

The following student(s) _____ have completed lessons 71–80 in the *Reading Mastery* curriculum. In these lessons they have learned:

Symbol	Sound	As In
l	lll	late
w	www	we
sh	shshsh	she

Regular Words: ant, āte, and, an, cāme, cut, dot, ēat, fēēt, fat, fig, fun, hot, hē, his, has, hat, hāte, hand, ill, in, lāte, lick, lock, land, lid, mud, mēat, mēan, māil, mill, nut, nāme, nāil, rock, rat, rug, rāin, rag, rut, sēē, sat, sit, sack, sock, sick, sand, sāil, sāme, sag, that, tan, us, wē, will

The more opportunities you provide for these students to practice their newly learned skills in class, the more adept they will become at using them.

If you have any questions or want some ideas regarding how to interject these skills into your classroom, please contact me.

FIGURE 4.4   **Summary Sheet for Intensive Reading Curriculum**

TABLE 4.10   Comparison of Five Common Tier 3 Approaches

	Direct Instruction: Reading Mastery	Lindamood® LiPS	Reading Recovery	Wilson Reading System	Language!
Does curriculum introduce advanced word-reading skills, explicitly, first presenting letter combinations, affixes, or syllables in isolation and then in words?	Yes	Yes	No	Yes	Yes
Does curriculum explicitly teach students to read multisyllable words by using prefixes, suffixes, and known word parts?	Yes	Emphasis is on syllables.	No	Emphasis is on syllables.	Emphasis is on syllables.
Does curriculum explicitly teach students to read multisyllable words by first teaching syllable rules and then providing practice applying them?	Emphasis is on morphemes/logical word parts.	Yes	No	Yes	Yes
Is connected text that contains advanced words students have learned part of the curriculum?	Yes	No, but it is encouraged.	No	Yes	Yes
Does curriculum incorporate spelling to reinforce word analysis? After students can read words, do they write the words?	Yes	Yes	Sometimes this occurs.	Yes, they are taught together, simultaneously.	Yes
Are decodable words that appear frequently in grade-appropriate reading text emphasized?	Yes	Both real and nonsense words/word parts are used.	No	Both real and nonsense words are used.	Yes
Are sight words pretaught before appearing in connected text?	Yes	Not a part of the LiPS program, but teachers are encouraged to do this.	No	Yes	Yes
Does daily instruction include a review of decodable and sight words recently learned?	Yes	This is up to teacher's discretion.	No	Yes	Word forms and phoneme/grapheme relationships taught are reviewed, but not the exact words previously taught.

During the first year, we were surprised to learn that there were no decodable books in any of the K–3 classrooms. Previously all book purchases had been for predictable books. Recognizing that students in Tiers 2 and 3 needed appropriate decodable books for outside reading, we scrambled to procure books. We went on hunting expeditions with teachers through dusty storerooms and attics to locate old decodables. We used project money to buy a starter supply of decodables. Whenever any discretionary money was available through Title 1 or Special Education funding, it immediately was earmarked for buying more. Gradually we built up classroom libraries that had a range of easy-to-difficult decodables so that students could select reading that was at their independent level. Teachers learned that when they set aside a small amount of time and routinely conducted small decodable reading groups with students in Tier 3, those students' progress increased. When volunteers were available to work with students in Tier 3, the classroom teachers used the summary sheets to select appropriate reading material.

Classrooms teachers learned to juggle reading activities when some students were out of the room for intensive instruction. During that time, students in the classroom did the activities that would be frustrating for a student in Tier 3. Other students practiced decoding multisyllable words, reading difficult sight words, and reading the lesson story. Tier 3 students never missed explicit vocabulary and conprehension instruction in the general education classroom. During spelling, some teachers assigned students in Tier 3 to a helping partner; sometimes the teacher gave them extra practice on their spelling words from *Reading Mastery.* Students in Tier 3 were never called on to orally read a text above their level.

Communication between the general education teacher and the Tier 3 teacher was encouraged in other ways. On parent night, parents were able to meet with both teachers; all testing results were given to every teacher; and team meetings included both sets of teachers. After all these changes, we monitored the results of our team communication and individual adaptations, charting student progress in each of the tiers and giving students the reading attitude interest survey displayed in the preface. Because students in Tier 3 enjoyed recreational reading and school-related reading as much as their peers, we knew that they were not frustrated with reading or demoralized by leaving the class for more intensive instruction. Even with the previously mentioned changes, we found that most of the students in Tier 3 were still not yet catching up to their peers. We wanted to see their reading achievement increase even more. Thus we looked for more ways to accelerate these students' learning. Depending on the school, the adaptations we made included longer time in the intensive curriculum class, coordination with the after-school program, extra tutoring, and additional training for Tier 3 teachers.

How Can I Teach Advanced Word-Reading Skills to English Language Learners?

With advanced word reading comes the expectation to read past-tense endings. Since the regular past-tense ending *ed* can be pronounced as a syllable (/ed/), as /t/, or as /d/, English language learners usually have difficulty determining what to say. If none of your strategies for teaching *ed* have worked, try helping students learn and apply the following rules (Avery & Ehrlich, 1992, p. 48). Your students will need a chart listing all of the unvoiced sounds.

A. If a verb ends with /t/ or /d/, the past tense is pronounced /ed/. An example is *wanted.*
B. If a verb ends with a voiced sound, the past tense is pronounce /d/. An example is *bagged.*
C. If a verb ends with an unvoiced sound, the past tense is pronounced /t/. An example is *baked.*

If you have a few minutes at the end of the day, the **Yesterday game** provides extra practice using past tense verbs. Write two sets of regular verbs on large cardboard cards: *ex, bake, bunt, hang, ski, arrive, ask, cross,* and *invent.* Once you have taught students irregular verbs, you can also add those words to the list. Divide your class in half and explain that everyone will be going back in time to yesterday. Assign a card holder for each team and ask that student to sit on a chair in front of their team and hold up one card for each person. You will need to monitor both teams and award points on a clipboard, so plan to stand in the middle. Since everyone is symbolically going back in time, when you say "Start," one person from each team walks backwards to the card holder. Once that person arrives at the card holder, she has to turn around and say a sentence that begins with "Yesterday, I . . .". If the card holder is displaying the word *bake*, the student might say, "Yesterday, I *baked* a cake." When you hear the correct past tense word used in a sentence, mark down a point for that team. The person then runs forward and taps another team member, and the game continues. The rules are that everyone gets a turn, and that running or walking backwards in a silly or dangerous manner forfeits one point for the team. Keep track of words that students miss, so you can review them later.

> Internet resources for teachers working with English language learners are listed at this website. Links are provided to journal articles and Internet resources. **www.iteachilearn.com/ uh/guadarrama/sociopsycho/paper. htm#research%20journals.**

Remember that games such as this one are too haphazard to teach skills, but they do provide students with an opportunity to practice what they have learned in class.

How Important Are Advanced Word-Reading Skills for Older Learners?

Most older learners who struggle with reading are challenged by multisyllable words, and only through explicit instruction will they acquire and learn to apply the word analysis skills of recognizing and understanding morphemes, prefixes, and suffixes. Without such knowledge, reading more difficult text becomes increasingly frustrating. The reading level of text becomes a critical issue for older learners who often have developed anxiety and avoidance toward all text because of a history of frustrating and embarrassing experiences. In addition to the difficulty of words, teachers should also consider simplicity of sentence structure and number of clauses, lengths of sentences and paragraphs, and whether the story or book includes subheadings that organize the information. Some teachers find that carefully selected newspaper and magazine articles are useful age-appropriate reading materials with an easier reading level. With such uncontrolled text, the burden is on the teacher to make sure that the text is not at a frustration level for the student. Other teachers select decodable chapter books that are written for older students. The older learner has expended hours of energy trying to cover up reading difficulties from peers and teachers and most likely will reject books that are perceived as "babyish." Although the text is at an easier level, none of the decodable books designed for older learners look like the picture books or books with large fonts that are written for younger students. Table 4.11 summarizes instructional needs for older learners depending on their reading level.

The REWARDS program, which is designed for older students, teaches "word relatives" for more advanced words in order to develop students' vocabulary and word recognition. Once a student learns to read *maintain*, the teacher also presents the words *maintainer*, *maintainable*, and *maintenance* (Archer et al., 2000). Both vocabulary and word-recognition skills are developed as students practice reading different forms of the same base word *maintain*, identifying how its meaning changes with various suffixes.

> Resources for older struggling readers are found at: **www.balancedreading. com/Feldman.pdf.**

TABLE 4.11   Instructional Needs of Older Struggling Readers

Lower than 2.0 Grade-Level Reading	Between 2.5 and 4.5 Grade-Level Reading	Between 4.0 and 7.0 Grade-Level Reading
Intensive word recognition ■ Sound/symbol ■ Decoding regular words ■ Common irregular words	Strategies for decoding longer multisyllable words ■ Affixes ■ Complex vowel patterns ■ Decodable chunks	Content-Reading Strategies ■ Text structure ■ Summarizing ■ Note taking ■ Mapping
Fluency building	Passage reading fluency	Passage reading fluency
Spelling/word study	Correlated spelling and word study	Expository writing
Independent reading at appropriate instructional level	Independent reading at appropriate instructional level	Independent reading at appropriate instructional level

Source: Feldman, K. (1999). The California Reading Initiative and Special Education in California developed by the Special Education Reading Task Force. Retrieved from www.calstat.org/leadershipinstitute/powerpoints/5. California Department of Education, Sacramento, CA.

What Games and Activities Will Reinforce Students' Advanced Word-Reading Skills?

Here are two games that can be adapted to a wide range of topics. The first game uses a science topic, but you can modify it to fit your curriculum.

Word Race

After students have learned to decode six difficult words from a reading selection describing ocean pollution and they accurately but slowly read them in the science story, use those words for a drill game so students get practice reading them at faster rates. Construct a table on your word processing program with five rows and six columns. Type each of the six words into a box in every row, placing each one in a different column. Divide your students into pairs and give each pair a word-table sheet and a cheap sand timer that can be flipped for a one-minute timing. When you say "Go," one student in each pair will flip the timer; the other student will begin reading all of the words starting in the upper left corner. If a student misses a word, his partner will ask him to sound out the word and then he'll try again until he reads all of the words in less than a minute.

Short or Long Sort

When you are working with a small group, the Short or Long Sort will provide extra practice for students who have learned a new long-vowel pattern. Make several sets of word cards with words containing short *a* and long *a* sounds and put each into an activity box. Select words similar to these:

rack	date	tank	play	grant
game	slap	pace	hail	safe
pant	hay	fame	mast	crash

Technology

Advanced Word-Reading Skills

Mr. Benvenuti had a student, Maia, in his fifth-grade classroom who was identified on an IEP as having learning disabilities. One of the recommendations on Maia's IEP indicated that the school team should use **assistive technology** to help Maia independently read textbooks above her reading level. Mr. Benvenuti knew that assistive technology includes a wide variety of technology applications designed to help students with disabilities to learn, communicate, enjoy recreation, and otherwise function more independently by bypassing their disabilities, but he was not aware of any technology other than taped readings that would help in this situation. Although Maia continued to receive daily systematic phonics instruction, she had not yet caught up to her peers. She could decode many multisyllable words, but words with more than three syllables presented problems.

When the special education teacher told Mr. Benvenuti that she was going to try having Maia use a Quicktionary Reading Pen II in class and at home, Mr. Benvenuti decided to use the Google search engine on the Internet to determine whether this pen would interfere with his classroom and whether it might help Maia. At a team meeting that was taking place next week, he wanted to bring credible information to the group. He knew that few scientifically based research studies have been done investigating whether technology devices and applications improve reading. Maia's special education teacher had explained that the Reading Pen wouldn't explicitly teach Maia to read more difficult words, but it should help her function more independently in content-area classes. As he read through the comments of people who had used the Reading Pen and those who had reviewed it, Mr. Benvenuti listed advantages and disadvantages noted by these individuals.

The description of the Reading Pen intrigued Mr. Benvenuti, who had never seen anything like this device. He found out that the pen, powered by two AAA batteries, is a portable assistive device that can scan a word or line of text and read it aloud. In addition, the pen can display the syllables of a scanned word and display the dictionary definitions of the word on its small screen. The newest version of the pen is able to read parts of the definition aloud. In order to use these functions, one operates seven small buttons via a menu structure. Mr. Benvenuti was relieved to hear that an earphone could be used so that only Maia would hear the speech. As he read the descriptions, Mr. Benvenuit decided to list all of the positive and negative aspects of the pen:

Positive Aspects to the Reading Pen
1. The pen scans hyphenated text, even when the hyphen comes at the end of a line.
2. The pen keeps a history of words that the student needs to read. Maia's special education teacher could use this list to determine which types of multisyllable words needed more practice.
3. The pen works for both right-handed and left-handed people.
4. The pen scans light text on a dark background as well as dark text on a light background.
5. The pen is compact, lightweight, and easy to transport.
6. The batteries last a long time.
7. The pen comes in a hard box that protects it in a school bag.
8. Using the pen is less embarrassing than having to interrupt the teacher or ask a peer about unknown words.

Negative Aspects to the Reading Pen
1. The quietest volume setting is very loud through the earphone. The loudest volume setting is clearly audible in a quiet room.
2. The definitions that come from the American Heritage College Dictionary are often wordy and complex for a younger student.
3. The pen requires excellent dexterity to scan the word, so the pen is not suitable for people with low vision or impaired fine motor control.
4. The process of scanning is time consuming. If Maia had to scan many words in the text, her comprehension would probably be significantly affected.

5. The pen would be an easy target for theft and, at a cost of more than $250, is expensive.
6. The pen has great difficulty reading handwritten words.
7. Although the pen can read different sized fonts, it has difficulty reading small fonts like those in a newspaper.

After looking at his list, Mr. Benvenuti decided that trying this assistive technology adaptation was a reasonable option when Maia was able to read material independently with 90% accuracy or better. He thought that given her current reading ability, the other IEP suggestion of tape recording the social studies and science books didn't give her the practice she could use reading that type of text. Looking at the possible negatives, he wanted to monitor closely how well the device worked. His biggest concern was whether operating the pen would be frustrating or slow her reading down so much that comprehension was negatively affected. Although he worried that dictionary definitions might be so complicated that they would be confusing, Maia had excellent verbal skills and would not need to use that function often. Mr. Benvenuti called the company to see if the school could use the pen for a carefully monitored trial period and was delighted when they agreed.

Motivating Your Students to Do Their Best

Extending the Teacher–Class Game

Depending on the age and maturity level of your students, you can use your creativity to spice up the Teacher–Class Game and further increase the motivation level of your students.

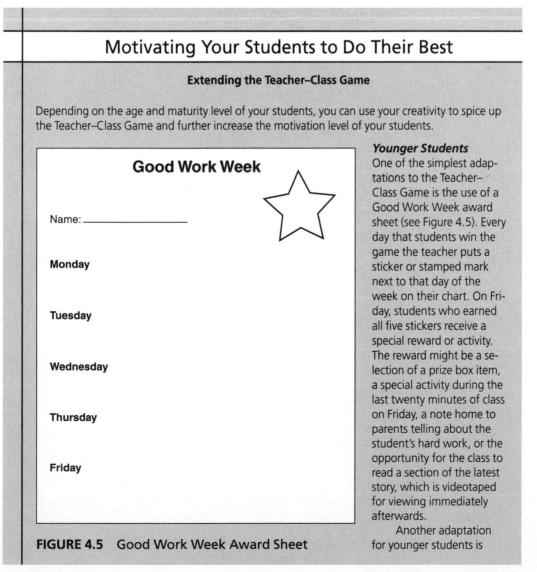

Good Work Week

Name: _____

Monday

Tuesday

Wednesday

Thursday

Friday

Younger Students
One of the simplest adaptations to the Teacher–Class Game is the use of a Good Work Week award sheet (see Figure 4.5). Every day that students win the game the teacher puts a sticker or stamped mark next to that day of the week on their chart. On Friday, students who earned all five stickers receive a special reward or activity. The reward might be a selection of a prize box item, a special activity during the last twenty minutes of class on Friday, a note home to parents telling about the student's hard work, or the opportunity for the class to read a section of the latest story, which is videotaped for viewing immediately afterwards.

Another adaptation for younger students is

FIGURE 4.5   Good Work Week Award Sheet

Continued

FIGURE 4.6 Climb the Mountain to the Castle Game

called the Climb the Mountain to the Castle game (Figure 4.6). Before starting the game, the teacher needs between 15 and 20 large cutouts that can be taped to the wall along with colorful construction-paper circles with large numbers printed on them (numbers 10–20–30, etc.). Getting pictures from the "images" section of Google is an easy and cheap way to get large printed pictures of the needed items. Cutouts that are needed for this motivation game include a castle, fairy tale characters (some menacing and some friendly), and an interesting animal character for each team or row of students. The castle is taped at the top of the classroom wall just below the ceiling. The numbered circles are taped up the side of the wall to create a path from the floor to the castle. The animal figures, which represent the student teams, all start on the beginning circle, 0. Fairy tale images are taped along the path to create interest: "Team 4 is about to go past the spooky forest. I hope they earn enough points to go right past it without stopping." As the teams earn points, their animals advance up the path toward the castle. When all of the teams reach the castle, the teacher will give everyone a reward or conduct a fun activity.

During the Castle game, the teacher divides the class into rows or teams. Each row or team earns teacher–class points during the reading period. At the end of each class, the teacher subtracts the number of points she earned from the points earned by each of the teams. That number is added to the cumulative total and the team animal advances the number of points earned that day. If Team 4 reached number 25 yesterday and earned 14 more points today, their animal would move to number 39 as it advances closer to the castle. The classroom wall should look like Figure 4.6. The teacher can use this game with any theme. Students can scuba dive past sharks and jelly fish to reach a treasure chest or they can be mountain climbers attempting to climb the path going to the top of Mt. Everest.

Older Students

Teachers can combine reading and math by having students earn fake money in a simulated banking experience. When students win the Teacher–Class Game they earn fake money that later can be exchanged for privileges or items. Students can earn play money or keep track of their totals in a bank book. Older students enjoy earning the privilege to omit one homework assignment, or earn a few minutes of extra chat time with friends. Other motivators include "work and eat" days, the opportunity to help younger students, and the opportunity to work to music.
A variation on the Climb the Mountain to the Castle game for older students is creating a simulated *Carmen Sandiego* game. Display a world map with an adventure trail across the continents. Students can earn points to travel past geographical barriers such as the raging Amazon River or Mt. Everest. For more of a political science focus, students can move past political hotspots around the world until they reach their destination. Clues to their secret mission are taped to different countries that they pass, and intermittently spaced *hot* cards tell them to move back a few spaces. The final destination spot card should inform students of the surprise they have been working for.

Take three pieces of yellow paper and make two header cards. Write "short *a* sound" on one card and "long *a* sound" on another. Add to the box a paper divided into two columns, each labeled with the two descriptions on the header cards. Ask students to first sort the word cards, putting them in the correct pile. Once students have sorted the cards, they should write each word in the correct column on the paper. Since you will not be able to monitor errors, select words that students can read with at least 95% accuracy. Your goal is to provide extra practice.

Fact or Fiction

1. **Phonics instruction is no longer necessary when students who are at risk have learned all of the single-letter sounds and can fluently decode one-syllable words.**

                  Fact   **Fiction**

Fiction. All students encounter a larger proportion of multisyllable words after second grade. Studies show that after fourth grade, students encounter approximately 10,000 new words each year (Nagy & Anderson, 1984). Many of these words are multisyllabic, and if students are unable to read them fluently, comprehension is significantly affected. Students who are at risk require explicit instruction to learn how to fluently read these more-difficult words. Instruction that stops with one-syllable words does not prepare these students for the challenging science and social studies texts they will need to read.

APPLIED ACTIVITIES

1. In the list of words below, underline all of the prefixes and circle the suffixes.

   boyish   watering   displeased
   prejudge   undesirable   writer
   mistreatment   government   gently

2. Divide the following words into their morphemes. Circle all affixes.

   government   deregulated   wonderful
   disagreement   rewritten   reshaped

3. You wonder if your students are ready for a story about a little boy who goes to Atlantic City. Although they have learned all of the single-letter sounds, they still do not know all of the letter combinations. Your first step in analyzing whether they are ready to read this story is identifying all of the letter combinations and affixes. Underline all of the letter combinations in the following sentences and circle the affixes.

   > Shawn looked up at the stars and wished he had fudge to eat. Whenever he went to the beach with his mom and dad, Shawn liked to get fudge. Shawn looked at his mom and said, "I am thinking about fudge now. You might think I want to play, but all I want is fudge. I do not want to go on the boat right now. A sailor needs fudge. Please go and bring me some fudge that will be chewy and hard to eat."

4. Two multisyllable words that your students will encounter in their next story are *carelessly* and *sodium*. Identify which of these words would be more difficult for students to learn. Explain your answer.

5. Map the phonemes in each of the following words. The first one is completed for you:

glade	g	l	ā	d					
bread									
grander									
bounty									
splashed									
gladden									
retake									
shoulder									
knight									
battle									
judged									
grassier									

6. Ms. Wilson gave her three Tier 2 students the test of affixes and letter combinations just described. Their results are as follows.

Sounds Known

ed, s, dge, er, ch, oo, oa, ou, ow, ay, or

Sounds Unknown

aw, ar, sh, wh, ea, th, ing, igh, ai, ee, y, ew

Using the passage in Applied Activity 3, identify which words Ms. Wilson's Tier 2 students will be able to decode and which words they will not be able to decode.

7. The purpose of the following lesson in the general education curriculum is to teach the affixes _ful, _ly, and _ness. Identify how this lesson may be problematic for students who are at risk. Describe how you would adapt the lesson to provide differentiated instruction and increase the likelihood of student success.

Lesson: Theme 5–Selection 4: Day 5

- Read a big book to the class. When you come to the word *beautiful,* show students the word and explain that when they come to a larger word that looks new, they can try looking for a base word they know and see if an ending has been added to it.

- Display a transparency that defines a suffix as "one kind of word ending that adds meaning to the base word." The transparency includes three examples broken into parts that are listed in columns. Read each example for the students.

Base Word +	Suffix =	New Word
joy	ful	joyful (full of joy)
neat	ly	neatly (in a way that is neat)
sad	ness	sadness (being sad)

- Introduce a four-sentence story about a boy who brings his pet mouse to school. In this story, three words are related to the examples above: *fearful, softly,* and *darkness*. When you come to these words, ask the students to identify the base word, suffix, the new word, and its meaning.

8. New words in Tuesday's reading lesson include:

   sighed   flights   brighter   frightened
   salesman   watchman   amazing   admiring
   topple   shoppers   mattress   button

   Demonstrate how you would teach these new words using the format in Table 4.9.

9. Ms. Carrier has just introduced to her students the *ou* letter combination in isolation. For the first day of word reading with *ou*, she selected the following words as examples: *sound, cloud, our, through, proud,* and *though*. Critique Ms. Carrier's choice of examples.

REFERENCES

Archer, A., Gleason, M., & Vachon, V. (2000). *Reading excellence: Word attack and rate development strategies. Teacher's guide.* Longmont, CO: Sopris West.

Archer, A. L., Gleason, M. M., & Vachon, V. L. (2003). Decoding and fluency: Foundation skills for struggling older readers. *Learning Disability Quarterly, 26,* pp. 89–101.

Avery, P., & Ehrlich, S. (1992). *Teaching American English pronunciation.* New York: Oxford Press. p. 48.

Canney, G., & Schreiner, R. (1977). A study of the effectiveness of selected syllabication rules and phonogram patterns for word attack. *Reading Research Quarterly, 12,* 102–104.

Carnine, D. W., Silbert, J., Kame'enui, E. J., & Tarver, S. (2004). *Direct instruction reading* (4th ed.). New Jersey: Merrill Prentice Hall.

Celce-Murcia, M., et al. (1996). *Teaching pronunciation: A reference for teachers of English to speakers of other languages.* New York: Cambridge University Press.

Edelen-Smith, P. (1997). How now brown cow: Phoneme awareness activities for collaborative classrooms. *Intervention in School and Clinic, 33*(2), 103–111.

Egger-Bovet, H., & Smith-Baranzini, M. (1994). *USKids history: Book of the American Revolution.* Little Brown & Company. p. 11.

Engelmann, S., Carnine, L., Johnson, G., Meyer, L., Becker, W., & Eisele, J. (1999). *Corrective reading: Decoding.* Columbus, OH: SRA/McGraw Hill.

Foorman, B., & Moats, L. (2004). Conditions for sustaining research based practice in early reading instruction. *Remedial and Special Education, 25*(1).

Friend, M., & Bursuck, B. (2006). *Including students with special needs: A practical guide for classroom teachers* (4th ed.). Boston: Allyn & Bacon.

Good, R. H., Gruba, J., & Kaminski, R. A. (2002). Best practices in using dynamic indicators of basic emerging literacy skills (DIBELS) in an outcomes-driven model. In A. Thomas & J. Grimes (Eds.), *Best practices in school psychology IV* (pp. 699–720).

Bethesda, MD: National Association of School Psychologists.

Good, R. H., Kaminski, R. A., & Howe, D. (2005, June). What data tell us about children and how to support their success. Presented at AZ Reading First Conference, Phoenix, AZ.

Good, R., Simmons, D., & Kame'enui, E. J. (2001). Utility of a continuum of fluency-based indicators of foundational reading skills for third-grade high-stakes outcome. *Scientific Studies of Reading, 5,* 257–288.

Greene, J. F. (1996). Language! Effects of an individualized structured language curriculum for middle and high school students. *Annals of Dyslexia, 46,* 97–121.

Greene, J. (1998, Spring/Summer). Another chance: Help for older students with limited literacy. *American Educator: American Federation of Teachers,* pp. 1–6.

Greene, J. F. (2004). *Language! A literacy intervention curriculum.* Longmont, CO: Sopris West.

Hanna, P., Hanna, J., Hodges, R., & Rodlof, E. (1966). *Phonemegrapheme correspondences as cues to spelling improvement.* Washington, DC: U.S. Government Printing Office.

Idol, L. (1997). *Reading success: A specialized literacy program for learners with challenging learning needs.* Austin, Texas: Pro-Ed.

Ladefoged, P. (1975). *A course in phonetics* (pp. 1–57). New York: Harcourt Brace Jovanovich.

McCormick, C., Throneburg, R., & Smitley, J. (2002). *A sound start: Phonemic awareness lessons for reading success.* New York: Guilford Press.

Moats, L. (2001). When older students can't read. *Educational Leadership, 58*(6).

Nagy, W., & Anderson, R. C. (1984). How many words are there in printed school English? *Reading Research Quarterly, 19,* 304–330.

Singh, S., & Singh, K. (1976). *Phonetics principles and practices.* Baltimore, MD: University Park Press. pp. 1–65.

Wilson, B. (1996). *Wilson reading system.* Millbury, MA: Wilson Language Training.

5 Reading Fluency

Key Terms

Aim line   PDA

Context   Prosody

Fluency   Round-robin reading

Graphophonemic strategies   Semantic strategies

Intonation   Syntactic strategies

Median score   WCPM

Norm

Objectives

After reading this chapter you will be able to:

1. Assess student oral reading fluency, including reading with expression.

2. Use oral reading fluency data to identify students at risk, diagnose their skill needs, place them into curriculum materials, and monitor their reading progress.

3. Implement the SAFER strategy for conducting group oral reading practice.

4. Implement strategies for building student reading fluency using repeated readings and other research-based methods.

As with phonemic awareness and the alphabetic principle, gains in reading fluency for students who are at risk are not likely to occur naturally. In order to meet grade-level benchmarks, students must increase their fluency levels from 40 to 50 words correct per minute in grade 1, to 90 wcpm by the end of grade 2, and 110 wcpm by the end of grade 3 (Good et al., 2002). Students who are at risk need systematic, explicit teaching if they are to make this progress and move beyond beginning reading accuracy to become fluent, accurate readers.

What Is Reading Fluency, and Why Do I Need to Teach It?

In May, Ms. Dornbush had two of her second-grade students, Darrell and Damon, read out loud from a grade 2 passage. When Ms. Dornbush recorded the percent accuracy for the two boys, she found that both of them read the passage with 94% accuracy. Ms. Dorn-bush was surprised at these results because she thought Darrell was a better reader than Damon. Darrell read more words and with good expression. He seemed to understand what he was reading. Damon, on the other hand, read haltingly, sounding out some of the words as he read. His reading lacked appropriate phrasing, he frequently failed to stop at periods, and read with little expression overall. Ms. Dornbush wondered, "How could two students who read so differently both score the same on a sample of their oral reading?"

The answer is that Ms. Dornbush's measures failed to take **fluency** into account. On a subsequent assessment, Ms. Dornbush recorded the number of words the boys read correctly per minute, a measure of their accuracy and fluency. This time the results revealed the differ-ences between their reading. Darrell read the grade 2 passage at a rate of 94 words correct per minute and made six errors. Damon read 68 wcpm and made four errors. Again, both read at 94% accuracy, but this time the results showed that there were major differences in flu-ency between the two boys. Darrell's rate exceeded the benchmark of 90 wcpm for the end of grade 2. This score indicates that Darrell is likely to have fewer problems reading fluently and comprehending grade 3 material. Damon's lower rate indicated he is likely to have problems in grade 3 unless he builds his reading fluency. By initially failing to take fluency into account, Ms. Dornbush left out a key piece of assessment information, without which program planning and progress monitoring would have been difficult.

Reading fluency is the ability to read text accurately, quickly, and with expression. All three of its elements—accuracy, speed, and expression—are essential if students are to understand what they read. In the example just described, Damon was reasonably accurate in his reading but read so slowly and with so little expression that comprehension prob-ably posed a problem for him. Darrell, on the other hand, read with accuracy, speed, and expression; when reading, he could focus most of his energy on making connections among the ideas in the text as well as between those ideas and his background knowledge. He was much more likely to understand what he was reading.

Fluency becomes increasingly important as students move through the grades. As stu-dents get older, they are expected to read greater amounts of more difficult material in less time. Students who read slowly, regardless of accuracy, have little chance of keeping up with their peers. They are also less likely to practice their reading, choosing other ways to spend their time such as watching television and being with friends (Archer et al., 2003). This lack of practice further widens the academic gulf between slow readers and their more fluent classmates in a rich-get-richer scenario (Stanovich, 1986). Figure 5.1 displays the progression of fluency skills from preschool to third grade.

Although fluency as discussed in this chapter involves reading connected text, the ability to read connected text fluently is dependent on foundational skills such as phonemic aware-ness, letter sounds, regular and sight word reading, vocabulary, and grammatical knowledge (Wolf & Katzir-Cohen, 2001). As described in previous chapters, before students who are at risk can apply these basic skills to connected text, they must first practice the skills in isolation until they are accurate and fluent. Not until they reach that level of success should those skills be applied to connected text.

> Read more about research-based fluency instruction: **www.prel.org/ products/re_/fluency-1.pdf.**

How Can I Assess Reading Fluency?

The ability to read passages accurately, fluently, and with expression requires that the reader engage in a number of complex processes all at the same time. The reader must translate letters into sounds, blend sounds into meaningful words, access words with-out thinking, make meaningful connections within and between sentences, relate text meaning to prior knowledge, and make inferences to supply missing information (Fuchs, Fuchs, Hosp, & Jenkins, 2001). The beauty of oral reading fluency assessments is that

---

Typical Achievements of Children in Reading Fluency

Preschool   Few children can read at this age, so reading fluency is nonexistent for most children.

Kindergarten–First Grade

- Few kindergarten children are reading text fluently, but most can name letters quickly, automatically, and accurately by the end of kindergarten.

- First graders are developing accuracy in decoding one-syllable words but may have some difficulty reading with expression or attending to punctuation (e.g., child may fail to pause at commas and periods).

- Children read at least 40 words correctly per minute in grade-appropriate texts by the end of first grade.

Second–Third Grade

- Prime time for the development of fluency—children are not only accurate but increasingly fast and automatic in reading grade-appropriate texts

- Read aloud with good expression and with attention to punctuation

- Recognize and use larger letter patterns (e.g., "-ight" and "-ear") in reading words

- Read at least 90 words correctly per minute in grade-appropriate texts by the end of second grade

- Read at least 110 words correctly per minute in grade-appropriate texts by the end of third grade

---

FIGURE 5.1   Fluency

Source: Good, Simmons, and Kame'enui, The importance and decision-making utility of a continuum of fluency-based indicators of foundational reading skills for third-grade high-stakes outcomes, *Scientific Studies of Reading,* 2001.

in minutes the teacher is given a quick snapshot of the extent to which all of these processes are working in concert. It is not surprising that students who are able to read accurately and fluently are also likely to understand what they read (Fuchs, Fuchs, & Maxwell, 1988). Since oral reading fluency develops gradually over the school years, student scores on oral reading fluency assessments over time provide teachers with a good indicator of student growth. The scores can also be used to determine which books are appropriate for instructional or independent reading. The measure of oral reading fluency described here is the DIBELS Oral Reading Fluency (DORF). This measure is based on measures of oral reading fluency originally developed by Deno and colleagues (Deno, 1985).

> Visit the official DIBELS website and view a teacher giving an oral reading fluency assessment to students. Directions to administer and score the test are available at the same website as are copies that can be downloaded at no charge. **http://reading. uoregon.edu/video/ORFEstablished Reader.mov.**

Scheduling the DORF

The DORF is first given in the winter of grade 1 and then at least three times per year thereafter. Forms and benchmarks are available through grade 6. The progress of students who score below established benchmarks should be monitored at least monthly.

Administering and Scoring the DORF

Directions for administering and scoring the DORF are shown in Figure 5.2. The teacher takes three 1-minute oral reading samples, using three passages at the student's grade

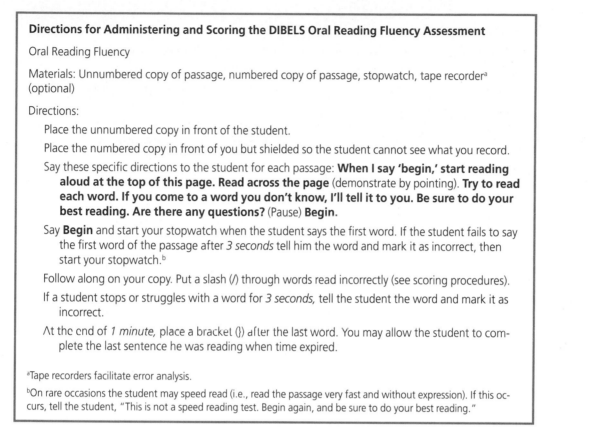

Directions for Administering and Scoring the DIBELS Oral Reading Fluency Assessment

Oral Reading Fluency

Materials: Unnumbered copy of passage, numbered copy of passage, stopwatch, tape recorder[a] (optional)

Directions:

Place the unnumbered copy in front of the student.

Place the numbered copy in front of you but shielded so the student cannot see what you record.

Say these specific directions to the student for each passage: **When I say 'begin,' start reading aloud at the top of this page. Read across the page** (demonstrate by pointing). **Try to read each word. If you come to a word you don't know, I'll tell it to you. Be sure to do your best reading. Are there any questions?** (Pause) **Begin.**

Say **Begin** and start your stopwatch when the student says the first word. If the student fails to say the first word of the passage after *3 seconds* tell him the word and mark it as incorrect, then start your stopwatch.[b]

Follow along on your copy. Put a slash (/) through words read incorrectly (see scoring procedures).

If a student stops or struggles with a word for *3 seconds,* tell the student the word and mark it as incorrect.

At the end of *1 minute,* place a bracket (]) after the last word. You may allow the student to complete the last sentence he was reading when time expired.

[a]Tape recorders facilitate error analysis.

[b]On rare occasions the student may speed read (i.e., read the passage very fast and without expression). If this occurs, tell the student, "This is not a speed reading test. Begin again, and be sure to do your best reading."

FIGURE 5.2   Directions for DIBELS Oral Reading Fluency Assessment
Source: Official DIBELS home page: http://dibels.uoregon.edu/ 2002–2004.

level. The teacher places the passage in front of the student and begins timing as soon as the student reads the first word. As the student reads, the teacher puts a slash through any words that are read incorrectly or left out. Self-corrections and the insertion of additional words are not counted as errors. The teacher stops the assessment at the end of 1 minute and puts a bracket after the last word read. The total number of words read, number of errors, and number of words read correctly per minute are then calculated. After the three passages are read, the student's median or middle score is noted. That **median score** of words read correctly per minute is the score used in instructional decision making.

Sample scoresheets for Cierra, a second-grade student, on the fall DORF assessments, are shown in Figures 5.3–5.5 (pp. 172–174).

Note that Cierra scored 28 words correct per minute on the first passage, 38 wcpm on the second passage, and 43 wcpm on passage three. Cierra's median score of 38 is the one that will be used in instructional decision making. Another important indicator provided by this assessment shows that Cierra's median errors per minute are 2. This score shows that Cierra is reading with a high degree of accuracy.

Interpreting DORF Scores

Benchmark levels for the DIBELS Oral Reading Fluency Assessment (DORF)—first grade through third grade—are shown in Table 5.1.

Students who score as *low risk* have met the benchmark and are on track for reading at grade level. For example, Rudy, who scored 62, met the first-grade benchmark at

Stars of the Sea

What fish looks like it belongs more in the sky than in the	12
sea? The answer is a starfish. Most starfish have five arms, but	25
some have many more. If a starfish loses an arm, it grows a new	39
one. A starfish can lose one or two arms and still be just fine.	53
A starfish can stretch its arms to as long as two feet. The	66
starfish uses its arms to move through water or along rocks. A	78
starfish has tiny tubes on the under sides of its arms. The tubes	91
are like sticky suction cups. The starfish can hold on to rocks	103
even in the waves. The tubes work like hundreds of tiny feet.	115
Starfish crawl along the ocean bottom, but they don't move very	126
fast.	127
A starfish eats tiny fish and plants. Its mouth is on the	139
bottom, in the center of the star. Their favorite food is shellfish,	151
and they can eat a lot. The starfish eats during high tide, when	164
the waves bring in lots of food. During low tide you might find	177
them holding onto the rocks and waiting for the tide to change.	189
Starfish come in many colors, including yellow, orange, red,	198
blue, purple, pink, and brown. They come in all sizes from tiny	210
to very large. When many different ones are in the same area	222
they look like a rainbow under water.	229

Total words: _29_

Total correct: _28_   Total incorrect: ___1___

FIGURE 5.3   DORF Assessment Passage 1: Cierra

TABLE 5.1   DIBELS Oral Reading Fluency Assessment Benchmarks for Grades 1–3

Grade	Beginning of Year		Middle of Year		End of Year	
	If score is . . .	Diagnosis	If score is . . .	Diagnosis	If score is . . .	Diagnosis
First			Less than 8	At Risk	Less than 20	At Risk
			8–19	Some Risk	20–39	Some Risk
			20 or more	Low Risk	40–50	Low Risk
Second	Less than 26	At Risk	Less than 52	At Risk	Less than 70	At Risk
	26–43	Some Risk	52–67	Some Risk	70–89	Some Risk
	44 or more	Low Risk	68 or more	Low Risk	90 or more	Low Risk
Third	Less than 53	At Risk	Less than 67	At Risk	Less than 80	At Risk
	53–76	Some Risk	67–91	Some Risk	80–109	Some Risk
	77 or more	Low Risk	92 or more	Low Risk	110 or more	Low Risk

Source: Good, R. H., Kaminski, R. A., & Howe, D. (2005, June). What data tell us about children and how to support their success. Presented at A2 Reading First Conference, Phoenix, AZ.

Twins

Six years ago my family grew from two people to four   11
people in one day. That was the day my sister and I were ~~born~~.   25
That was the day Mom and Dad had to start ~~buying~~ two of   38
everything. |My| mom and dad say we were much more than   49
twice the work of one baby. They also said we gave back more   62
than twice as much love and fun.   69

We look just alike because we are identical twins, but we   80
don't act just the same. My sister likes peas and beans and I hate 94
them. I like grape juice and she likes apple juice. She likes to   107
read. I would rather climb a tree than read a book.   118

Mom and Dad are the only ones who can tell us apart when   131
we dress the same. They know the secret. I have a mole on my   145
ear and my sister doesn't. We look so much alike that we can   158
even fool Grandma and Grandpa.   168

It's nice to be a twin sometimes. We always have someone   174
our own age who will share our secrets. Sometimes we don't   185
want to share everything. Sometimes it is nice to have my mom   197
or my toys all to myself. Dad says we aren't really that much   210
alike because no person is exactly like anyone else.   219

Total words: _40_

Total correct: _38_   Total incorrect: _2_

FIGURE 5.4   DORF Assessment Passage 2: Cierra

the end of the year and is at low risk for failing to read at grade level by the end of second grade. Cierra, the second-grade student shown in Figure 5.3–5.5, had a median score of 38 in the fall of the year. This means that Cierra is at *some risk* and we would predict she might not reach a benchmark score of 90 words correct per minute by the end of second grade unless she receives extra help in building her fluency. While the DORF benchmarks are generally comparable to other published oral fluency **norms** (Carnine et al., 2003; Hasbrouck & Tindal, 1992), the end-of-first-grade benchmark of 40 to 50 words correct per minute is considerably lower than the Carnine and colleagues' (2004) benchmark of 60.

In our estimation, a score of 40 should be viewed as a minimum, because our data show that the rate of growth needed to move from 40, and even 50, to the end-of-second-grade benchmark of 90 is challenging for many students who are at risk (Bursuck, et al., 2004). Crawford (personal communication, 2004) has proposed a more simplified system for identifying children who are at risk. He set ranges for each grade that represent normal growth over the course of the year. These are: Grade 1: 0–50 words correct per minute; Grade 2: 50–100 wcpm; Grade 3: 100–150 wcpm.

Oral reading fluency concerns do not end at third grade. Readers face increasingly higher fluency challenges as they mature. Table 5.2 lists older norms for oral reading fluency based on the DORF.

The Gray Oral Reading Test (GORT) is a standardized test of oral reading fluency whose norms may be useful, particularly for older students. For more information, see: **http://ags. pearsonassessments.com/group. asp?nGroupInfoID=a11445.**

I ride a big yellow bus to school. I stand on the corner of our | 15
street with my friends and we wait for the bus. My friend's | 27
grandma waits with us. When it's raining, she holds an umbrella | 38
to keep us dry. Sometimes when it's cold she brings us hot | 50
chocolate. | 51

I leave my house to walk to the bus stop after my parents go | 65
to work. I watch the clock so I know when to leave. Sometimes | 78
mom phones me from her office to remind me. Sometimes she | 89
can't call, so I have to be sure to watch the time. | 101

Our bus driver puts his flashing yellow lights on and then | 112
stops right next to us. When he has stopped he turns the red | 125
lights on so all the cars will stop. He makes sure we are all | 139
sitting down before he starts to go. He watches out for us very | 152
carefully. | 153

My friends and I are the first ones to be picked up by the bus. | 168
We like to sit right behind the bus driver and watch while he | 181
picks up all the other kids. We know where everyone lives. By | 193
the time we get to our school, the bus is almost full. Sometimes | 206
the kids get noisy and the driver has to remind us to keep it | 220
down. He says their noise makes it hard for him to concentrate | 232
and drive safely. I am glad that our bus driver is so careful. | 245

Total words: __45__

Total correct: __43__   Total incorrect: __2__

FIGURE 5.5   DORF Assessment Passage 3: Cierra

TABLE 5.2   DIBELS Oral Reading Fluency Assessment Benchmarks for Grades 4–6

Grade	Beginning of Year		Middle of Year		End of Year	
	If score is . . .	*Diagnosis*	*If score is . . .*	*Diagnosis*	*If score is . . .*	*Diagnosis*
Fourth	Less than 71	At Risk	Less than 83	At Risk	Less than 96	At Risk
	71–92	Some Risk	83–104	Some Risk	96–117	Some Risk
	93 or more	Low Risk	105 or more	Low Risk	118 or more	Low Risk
Fifth	Less than 81	At Risk	Less than 94	At Risk	Less than 103	At Risk
	81–103	Some Risk	94–114	Some Risk	103–123	Some Risk
	104 or more	Low Risk	115 or more	Low Risk	124 or more	Low Risk
Sixth	Less than 83	At Risk	Less than 99	At Risk	Less than 104	At Risk
	83–108	Some Risk	99–119	Some Risk	104–124	Some Risk
	109 or more	Low Risk	120 or more	Low Risk	125 or more	Low Risk

Source: http://dibels.uoregon.edu/benchmarkgoals.pdf. Dibels website says sources are from the following articles: Fuchs, L. S., Fuchs, D., Hamlett, C. L., Walz, L., & Germann, G. (1993). Formative evaluation of academic progress: How much growth can we expect? *School Psychology Review, 22,* 27–48. Hasbrouck, J. E., & Tindal, G. (1992, Spring). Curriculum-based oral reading fluency norms for students in grades 2 through 5. *Teaching Exceptional Children,* pp. 41–44.

Charting Progress on the DORF

By mid first grade, progress charts based on the DIBELS oral reading fluency assessment can be used to determine who needs the extra support of Tier 2. In addition to helping you monitor progress, progress charts help facilitate parent understanding and motivate students to improve. Figure 5.6 shows an example of a progress chart for a second-grade student. Misuou's chart shows that he started second grade at benchmark for reading, at 40 wcpm. His teacher drew an **aim line** from his first score in September to the final benchmark score of 90 wcpm needed in May. This sloping aim line enabled her to determine when he was on track for meeting the year-end benchmark. ORF scores that were above the aim line indicated that Misuou was on track. Likewise, the teacher could see when Misuou's progress stalled. The chart showed that beginning in January, Misuou was no longer on track to meet the May benchmark. As soon as his teacher saw that his January score was below the aim line, she switched Misuou into a Tier 2 booster group so he could get more support. Misuou's chart shows that the extra support was beneficial, and by May he was once again reading at grade level.

Making a progress chart for reading achievement using the Excel Chart Wizard is easy. The steps listed in Appendix A will show you how to make a chart like the one depicted for Misuou.

Students move into Tier 2 when their ORF scores are below the progress line, indicating that they are not on track for reading at grade level by the end of the year. If you are using 40 words correct per minute as the benchmark for first grade, January ORF Scores between 8 and 19 also qualify for Tier 2 support. Although students at benchmark might only take the ORF assessment three times a year, anyone who is in Tier 2 takes the test anywhere from once a week to once a month. In that way the teacher can monitor when scores are back on the growth line so Tier 2 can be discontinued. Once a Tier 2 student scores above the aim line for two months in a row, he is ready to move back to Tier 1 and continue without the support. More importantly, the teacher can also spot someone who has plateaued and analyze whether difficulties with advanced word reading or fluent reading of text are contributing to the lack of progress.

> Learn how to teach your students to self-graph their fluency growth on the computer: **http://journals.sped.org/ EC/Archive_Articles/VOL.35NO.2 NOVDEC2002_TEC_Article%204.pdf.**

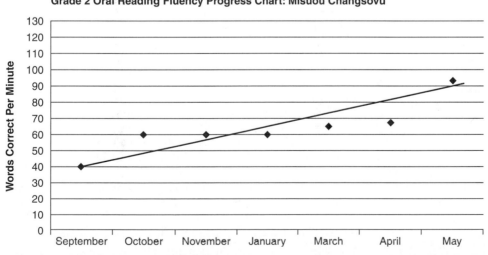

Grade 2 Oral Reading Fluency Progress Chart: Misuou Changsovu

FIGURE 5.6   DIBELS ORF Progress Chart

How Do I Measure the Growth of Students Who Are Significantly Behind Their Classmates?

The rate at which students make gains in reading follows a pattern (Shaywitz, 2003), with the greatest gains occurring in the early school years, then lessening with each subsequent grade. The rate of growth also differs within each school year, with maximum growth occurring at the beginning of the year and then tapering off toward spring (Shaywitz). Shown below are expected growth rates in oral reading fluency. Note that the *realistic* rates reflect the growth rates for typical children moving through the reading curriculum. The more *ambitious* rates apply to students who are behind in reading, as they need to make even greater gains in order to catch up.

Grade	Realistic	Ambitious
1	2	3.00
2	1.5	2.00
3	1	1.50
4	.85	1.10
5	.50	.80
6	.30	.65

Source: Fuchs, L. S., Fuchs, D., Hamlett, C. L., Walz, L., & Germann, G. (1993). Formative evaluation of academic progress: How much growth can we expect? *School Psychology Review, 22*(1), 27–48.

To demonstrate how these growth rates can help you measure the progress of your students who are behind, take the case of Daquan, a fourth grader whose DORF score at the beginning of the year was 75, making him at some risk and eligible for Tier 2 support. Daquan's rate of accuracy in grade 4 material was 93%, so his reading instruction was in grade 4 material, and his expected growth was based on his performance on grade 4 passages. (See section on placing students into the next reader on pp. 185–186.) Daquan's teacher set an ambitious growth rate of 1.10 for him. This meant that after 10 weeks she expected Daquan to be reading 11 more words correct per minute in grade 4 material (86 wcpm). At the end of the 10-week period she had Daquan read a grade 4 passage and he scored 83, a little below what was expected. As a result, the teacher added one more extra Tier 2 fluency building session per week for him.

Here is another example for a fifth-grade student named Carly. Carly is a Tier 3 student. In the fall, she read grade 5 material at a rate of 47 wcpm; her rate of accuracy was 79%. Her teacher, Mr. Braden, continued to assess her on easier passages and found that she could read third-grade passages with 91% accuracy, establishing grade 3 as her instructional level (see pp. 185–186). Her reading rate in grade 3 material was 68 wcpm. Mr Braden set Carly's growth at an ambitious 1.5 words per week in grade 3 material. After 4 weeks, he checked her fluency on grade 3 passages to see if she had made the expected growth of 6 wcpm (a score of 74 wcpm). When he found that she had, he felt comfortable keeping her current instructional supports in place.

For students such as Daquan and Carly who are behind their classmates in reading, short-term instructional progress can be evaluated using passages at their instructional level and the expected growth rates shown above. However, it is important to remember that only DORFs at students' chronological grade/age levels show whether they are at benchmark, some risk, or low risk. Thus, Mr. Braden also made sure that Carly was assessed three times per year using DIBELS benchmark assessments for grade 5.

Learn more about the three-cueing strategy at: **www.sedl.org/reading/topics/cueing.html.**

Bridging the Gap

How Should I Correct Errors During Oral Passage Reading?

An approach commonly recommended by teachers for correcting students' oral reading errors is called the three-cueing system. This strategy is based on the assumption that efficient readers use three different systems to attack words: graphophonemic, syntactic, and semantic. **Graphophonemic strategies** involve looking at the letters in words by breaking the word into parts or matching letters and letter combinations with the sounds they make. **Syntactic strategies** involve figuring out whether the word sounds right in the sentence, as if someone were talking. **Semantic strategies** focus on whether or not a word makes sense in a sentence. Advocates of the three-cueing system assume that poor readers miss more words because they are overly dependent on graphophonemic cues or the letters and sounds in words. As explained in the following example, this is not the case.

The purpose of error corrections in the three-cueing system is to focus student attention on syntactical and semantic cues and to de-emphasize looking at the letters in words. After a student error, teachers using the three-cueing system are likely to say, "Does that word make sense?" Then they direct students' attention to the meaning of the words surrounding the missed word or the order of the sentence. Students are told to look at the letters in the word only as a last resort. In the three-cueing system, only errors that change the meaning of the text are corrected. For example, consider these two student errors in reading the sentence:

The man rode his horse to town.

Student 1 read the word *horse* as /pony/. Student 2 read the word *horse* as /house/. In the three-cueing approach, the first error, identifying the word *horse* as /pony/ would not be corrected because the meaning of the sentence was unchanged. In contrast, the error made by student 2 indicated an overreliance on graphophonemic cues; student 2 would be corrected by being told to use semantic or syntactic cues to figure out the word (Hempenstall, 1999).

Adams (1998) has pointed out that the three-cueing system makes sense from the standpoint of reading comprehension; to get meaning from written text, readers need to use all three types of cues. However, as an approach to word identification, the three-cueing system is not consistent with the research (Adams, 1997). Research comparing the reading errors of good and poor readers has repeatedly demonstrated that proficient readers rely primarily on the letters in words when trying to identify them. The errors of proficient readers show that they most frequently attempt to decipher unknown words by using graphophonemic strategies in contrast to poor readers, who tend to guess by looking at pictures or using the context (Adams, 1990).

This research, when applied to classroom practice, indicates that when word identification is the objective, graphophonemic cues should be stressed. When students make an error during oral passage reading, regardless of type, the teacher should prompt them to look at the letters in the word and/or sound out the word. This correction discourages guessing by sending the message to learners that it is important to carefully read every word with high accuracy.

How Can I Measure How Well Students Read with Expression?

Although there is a strong relationship between students' oral reading fluency and reading comprehension, the extent to which students read with expression, using a level of **intonation** that reasonably approximates everyday speech, is also related to how well students comprehend what they are reading (Tindal & Marston, 1996). This ability to read text orally using appropriate phrasing, intonation, and attention to punctuation is termed **prosody.** Table 5.3 lists reading behaviors for students who read fluently and with expression compared to those who do not.

TABLE 5.3 Prosody Chart

	Expressive readers	Nonexpressive readers
Stress (loudness)	■ Use weak stresses thoughout reading.	■ Often stress every word.
	■ Stress increases at end of exclamatory sentences.	■ Sometimes use more than one stress per word.
Variations in pitch (intonation)	■ Have greater variations in pitch—rise and fall in voice pitch.	■ Have inappropriate pitch changes. Either sustain the same pitch for longer periods or use a rising pitch where a falling one is appropriate.
	■ Use a rising pitch at the end of a sentence that asks a question or that exclaims.	
	■ Use a downward pitch for a sentence making a statement.	
Duration (how long a word is pronounced)	■ Lengthen the word/vowel that precedes a comma. Lengthen the last word of a sentence.	■ Often lengthen other unexpected words in a sentence.
		■ Often do not lengthen word/vowels preceding commas or at the end of a sentence.
Chunk words into appropriate phrases	■ Use few pauses within sentences.	■ Pause between words and within words more frequently; pauses can last longer; often pause after every word; awkward word groups
	■ Use shorter pauses between sentences; shorter pauses after page turn.	
	■ Pause at commas.	■ Are vulnerable to disruptions in text such as page turns.
	■ Use punctuation to group words into natural units.	■ Chunk words with little attention to punctuation or clauses within the sentence.
	■ Often pause at end of clauses.	

Source: Based on information from Cowie et al., (2000) and Dowhower (1991).

Samuels (2005) has developed an assessment for expressive reading that is highly related to standardized tests of reading comprehension and that can be used along with the DORF measure just described. After students read a passage, the teacher scores their expression using the following 5-point scale:

1 = Reads single words. No "flow." Very choppy.
2 = Some phrasing is noted (2–3 words), but still choppy.
3 = Pauses for ending punctuation. Inflection changes may not be present.
4 = Appropriate "flow" and phrasing is noted as well as attention to punctuation with pauses and appropriate inflection most of the time.
5 = Reading generally "flows." Voice changes to reflect meaning changes. Appropriate ending inflections.

Although standard norms are not available for the scale, the student averages for fall in grades 1–8 are shown in Figure 5.7

It is recommended that you practice scoring with a colleague before you use the results to guide your instruction. During the practice session, you and a colleague should score a student's

Video clips of various students who score between 1 and 5 on this assessment are available at the following website: **www3.mpls.k12. mn.us/departments/speced/ resources/pdf/CBM/rubric.html.** Visit the site and see if your rating agrees with the examiners.

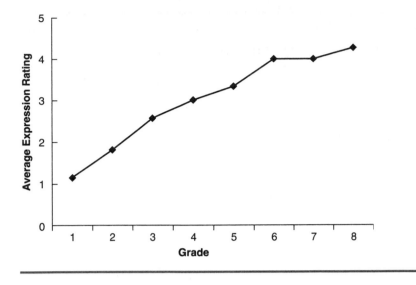

FIGURE 5.7 Average Reading Expression Ratings—Grades 1 to 8, Fall

Source: Samuels, J. (2005). Procedures for administration of reading measures. Retrieved from: pic.mpls.k12.mn.us/sites/97711090_59b5_4f98_964e_932ab29cf5be/uploads/procedures.pdf.

expressive reading together and compare your ratings, continuing this process until you have 90% agreement. Rating audio or video tapes of students reading may be more convenient and easier than practicing live.

How Can I Diagnose Student Error Patterns Using the DORF and Prosody Measures?

DORF information, along with the results from the expressive reading scale, helps teachers diagnose specific error patterns so that the appropriate support is provided. The various error patterns that can be gleaned from the results of these measures are described next.

Low Accuracy, Below Benchmark for Fluency, and Low Prosody Score

Often these students do not have phonemic awareness and the alphabetic principle, so instruction needs to focus on developing those skills. Students who have those foundational skills but still have low accuracy and fluency typically perform well on CVC words and high-frequency sight words, but tend to make errors on words containing letter combinations and multisyllable words. Shown in Figure 5.8 is the passage reading performance for Titus on a grade 1 passage in May. Titus scored 57 letter sounds correct per minute with 20 words read as whole words on DIBELS Nonsense Word Fluency, also in May.

For students such as Titus, assess knowledge of letter combinations and affixes using an assessment like the one described in Chapter 4, Figure 4.1. The results will let you know which letter combinations and affixes need to be taught. Titus can then be taught to decode single or multisyllable words having these sounds. Practice should include reading the words in both lists and passages. Because of Titus's low accuracy and fluency, one

---

Visiting Aunt Rose

My Aunt Rose invited me to spend the weekend. Aunt Rose   11
doesn't have kids. She said I could be her kid for two days. She's   25
like my big sister.   29

I like to go to visit my Aunt Rose's home. She likes to do the   44
same things I like. I like to go swimming. So does my Aunt   57
Rose. The pool where she goes also has a hot tub. I like to sit in   73
the hot tub. So does my Aunt Rose. I always bring my swimming   86
suit when I visit.   90

Our weekend was perfect. On Saturday we went out for   100
breakfast. I had strawberry pancakes with whipped cream. Then   109
we went shopping. She bought me a pink shirt. Then we went   121
swimming and sat in the hot tub.   128

On Sunday she helped me make oatmeal cookies. Then we   138
painted each other's nails. Our fingers and toes match. They are   149
bright pink. Then we went to the movies. We saw The Lion   161
King.   162

Aunt Rose drove me home. I handed my mother a plate of   174
the oatmeal cookies. I showed my brother my new shirt. Dad   185
admired my bright pink nails.   190

"Dad," I asked, "Could I live at Aunt Rose's?"   199

"No," he said. "If you went there all the time, it wouldn't be a   213
special treat."   215

Total words: _31_

Total correct: _25_   Total incorrect: _6_

FIGURE 5.8 DORF Progress Check: Titus

would expect that he would also have low prosody. Although the teacher can use some of the fluency practice sessions as an opportunity to increase Titus's awareness of punctuation and how it alters reading, at this stage of reading the focus should center on developing accuracy and fluency.

High Accuracy, Below Benchmark for Fluency, and Low Prosody Score

These students can read grade-level material accurately but slowly. Their oral reading usually lacks expression because they are so preoccupied with identifying each word, they are unable to think about the meaning of what they are reading. Typical ratings on the expression scale would likely be between 1 and 2. Damon, the student described at the beginning of this chapter, has this type of problem. Students such as Damon benefit from a combination of fluency building and practice developing expression.

At Fluency Benchmark but Low Prosody Score

This smallest group of students read at a rate that is at or above benchmark for their grade but their expression ratings are below average for their grade level. They show few indications that they are thinking about what they are reading. Problems with expression can include one or more of the following indicators: does not pay attention to punctuation, fails to group words together in meaningful chunks, and intonation shows little resemblance to live speech.

Although Kassandra met the ORF benchmark and decoded all of the words, she read the passage in a choppy, monotone voice:

> "Six . . . . . . year . . . . s ago my . . . . . . fam . . . ily . . . . grew from two . . . . . . people to four . . . . . people in . . . . one day. That . . . . . . was the day my sister . . . . . . and I were . . . . . born. That was the . . . . . . day Mom . . . . and Dad had . . . . . to start . . . ."

As she read, Kassandra did not use appropriate inflection at the end of sentences and did not adapt her reading to account for punctuation. Although she used some phrasing, she frequently paused in the middle of prepositional phrases or verbs.

Kassandra would benefit from some of the expression-building activities described in the next section of this chapter.

Lacking Specific Skills

As you are scoring a student's oral reading performance, you may detect patterns of student errors that show difficulty with a particular letter combination, affix, or sight word. For example, when Dominique was reading, he missed the words *coat* and *throat,* pronouncing them as *cot* and *that* respectively. His teacher Ms. Sanchez detected a skill pattern; Dominique could not decode the letter combination *oa.* Ms. Sanchez noticed that several other students in class were having difficulty with this letter combination as well. Therefore, Ms. Sanchez decided to reteach the *oa* combination, first reintroducing it in isolation using the format in Table 4.5 and then integrating *oa* into the daily word lists using the format in Table 4.7. Another teacher, Mr. Utomwen, noticed that many of his students were repeatedly missing the word *chaos* in a new story they were reading. Mr. Utomwen retaught the sight word *chaos* using the format for teaching sight words in Table 3.8.

Over- or Under-Dependence on Context

Sometimes students reading orally make errors that point to no obvious skill deficit. For example, Trais missed 6 words out of 100, but all of the words contained different sound patterns. His teacher, Mr. Nguyen, noticed that for all of the errors except one, the word Trais substituted made sense in the context of the sentence, but was still incorrect. For example, he read the sentence, "Leon *laid* the book on the table as "Leon *left* the book on the table." This pattern of errors revealed that Trais was overly dependent on context. The word *left* made sense but was incorrect, and didn't convey the same meaning as well. Students who are overly dependent on context benefit from being rewarded for accuracy in order to break this habit. For example, Mr. Nguyen was able to reduce Trais's context errors by rewarding him for accurate reading. He first told Trais, "Your goal is to read these three pages making no more than one error. You'll earn two points for meeting your goal." When Trais was working toward earning points for extra time on the class computer, he was motivated to read more carefully and look at the sounds in the words, not leaping to conclusions based on what made sense.

Another student, Evan, read the sentence, "Simone ran to the *waterfall,*" as "Simone ran to the *warning.*" Unlike the previous example, the word Evan substituted did not make sense. Evan's teacher, Ms. Williams, had noticed that Evan made this type of error at least three times for every hundred words he read. To help Evan and two other students who had a similar problem, Ms. Williams formed a small group and for 5 minutes daily read pairs of sentences to Evan and his classmates in the group. One sentence made sense and one didn't as in the following examples: "The dog licked his master's hand," and "the dog licked his master's here." The students were required to identify and repeat the sentence that made sense. This simple exercise, originally suggested by Carnine et al. (2004), helped Evan and his classmates begin to think about what sentences mean, rather than thinking about them only as a string of words.

How Can I Teach My Students to Read Passages Accurately and Fluently?

Reading fluency readily can be viewed within the classic *good news–bad news* framework. The bad news is that reading fluency does not develop naturally. If left alone, it is **not** likely to increase. The good news is that fluency increases with practice, provided that practice is guided by someone, be it a teacher, classmate, parent, or classroom aide. In fact, some researchers include practice within their definitions of reading fluency. For example, Samuels (1979) referred to reading fluency as a behavior that shows gradual improvement over time through practice.

The two most common techniques used to provide students with reading practice are oral passage reading and strategies that encourage students to read silently, such as Sustained Silent Reading (SSR). In their report, the National Reading Panel (2000) concluded that despite its broad intuitive appeal, at the present time no evidence supports the use of approaches that encourage students to silently read material of interest, either in or out of class. Although future studies may show otherwise, this finding seems to make sense when it comes to students who are at risk. These students may be reluctant to put much effort into their silent reading because reading is such a struggle for them. The fact they are likely to select books that are too difficult or easy for them can further undermine their motivation to read. Finally, students who are learning to read need feedback on their performance and teachers cannot closely monitor silent student reading. For all of these reasons, the teaching strategies for building passage-reading accuracy and fluency covered in this text stress oral passage reading, a method of building fluency for which there is considerable research support. The passage-reading strategies described here include what is referred to in this text as Successful, Anxiety-Free, Engaged Reading (SAFER) and repeated readings.

SAFER

Traditionally, oral passage reading in general education classes has been conducted using what is commonly called a **round-robin** approach. In this method, all students in the class read aloud from the same book, regardless of their reading levels. The teacher calls on individuals to read, following a predetermined order. Round-robin reading has been correctly criticized in a number of areas. First, when students of varying reading levels all read from the same book, it will be too difficult for some and too easy for others. The students for whom the reading is too easy are likely to become bored. Students called on to read material that is too difficult are likely to become embarrassed and frustrated. Second, when students are called on in a predetermined order, they tend to pay attention to the part they are scheduled to read and ignore the other parts of the passages. Thus, the level of practice the students actually engage in is minimal. If the goal of oral reading is to provide students with a successful experience while building their reading fluency, it is unlikely this goal will be met using round-robin reading.

This text recommends the SAFER procedure as an effective, high-success, low-stress approach to providing students with needed reading practice. SAFER is based on procedures for instructing group oral reading originally developed by Carnine and colleagues (2004). The SAFER group oral reading procedure incorporates many of the Tier 1 enhancements described in previous chapters and is done with small groups of students having similar reading levels. The text read is carefully matched to students' reading levels. Thus, every student in the group is capable of reading the passages successfully. (See the following section for tips on placing students in appropriate reading books in order to form homogeneous groups.) Using SAFER, students are called on in random order and asked to read amounts of text that vary from one to three sentences, following along with their fingers as other students read. These SAFER components maximize student practice by encouraging students to be attentive even when it is not their turn. They also allow the teacher to monitor student performance. SAFER is also carried out at a perky pace. Teacher talk is kept simple, students are called on quickly and efficiently, comprehension questions focus on key main ideas and supporting details, and errors are corrected quickly yet systematically. Finally, increased practice is provided on an as-needed basis by requiring that students reread stories when their accuracy as a group falls below criterion levels. The teaching procedures for SAFER are shown in Table 5.4.

In Part 1, students read the story orally using the procedures just described. Students are expected to follow along with their fingers when other students in the group are reading, because that ensures that they are paying attention. Finger pointing also allows you to monitor whether they are following along as directed. Next, announce the oral reading goal, which is to read the story as a group with at least 97% accuracy. This goal means that for every 100 words read, students are allowed to make three errors. If the accuracy of the group is below 97%, have students reread the story using the procedures shown in Part 2. This feature is important because you want students to be solid on skills they have learned thus far before moving to a new story with a new set of skills. Sometimes the group scores below 97%, but the errors are due to the performance of only one or two students. In that case, schedule extra passage reading for them instead of requiring the entire group to reread the story.

When an error occurs, first let the student read several more words to allow for self-correction. If the student fails to self-correct, you have two options. You can tell the student the word or have the student use the sounding-out strategy. For irregular words that are missed, tell the student the word. If the word is regular, encourage the student to sound out. If using the sounding-out strategy, particularly when teaching in groups larger than three students, be careful that the sounding-out correction does not take too much time. Lengthy corrections can cause the other students in the group to go off task. If the student struggles in sounding out the word, immediately tell the student the word and write it down so that later you can review the same word. Once the student has read the word correctly, have her go to the beginning of the sentence and reread. Making the student reread the sentence allows for more practice reading the word and also enables the student to reestablish the word-reading flow necessary for comprehension. Encouraging accurate reading during SAFER reading sessions will help students who are at risk develop the habit of careful attention to text. In a study with third-grade children who had learning disabilities, Pany and McCoy (1988) found that students who previously made many oral reading errors significantly improved both on accurate word reading and comprehension when immediate corrective feedback was given after every oral reading error. In contrast, feedback that was given only on errors related to the meaning of the text had no impact.

Once students are reading longer stories, determining a 97% accuracy level becomes more challenging. A general rule of thumb is that two or fewer errors on a longer page of

TABLE 5.4 Format for SAFER (Successful, Anxiety- Free, Engaged Reading): Post Alphabetic Principle

Outcome	Students who have scored 50 phonemes per minute or more on the DIBELS Nonsense Words Assessment with at least 15 read as whole words or who are reading second grade or higher leveled text will read a book at their instructional level with at least 97% accuracy.
Materials Needed	Use text that is at the students' instructional level.
Signaling	None
Time	Between 15 and 30 minutes

Instructions	**Teacher**
	Advance Organizers: When you tell students your behavior expectations, remind them that they must use a pointer finger to follow along with the reading.
	Steps to reading stories in the curriculum and decodable books:
	1. Call on individual students randomly and have them read between 1–3 sentences of the story.
	2. Expect the other students to follow along with their fingers.
	3. Call on students quickly and avoid unnecessary tangential teacher talk by focusing comprehension questions to key ideas, vocabulary, and supporting details. (Refer to comprehension and vocabulary strategies in Chapters 6 and 7.)
	4. Write missed words on the board. At the end of the story have students sound out each missed regular word and read it. If the word is a sight word, use the initial sight-word teaching format to review the word, having students orally spell it.
	5. Move on to the next story when students read the story with between 97–100% accuracy. The error limit is based on the number of words in the story. Before reading tell students what the error limit is. When children exceed the error limit, discontinue reading and have students practice the words they missed and reread the story.
Error Correction	a. When a student makes an error, let the student read several more words, then say, **"Stop."** Do not use an abrupt or loud voice. By waiting you are giving the student a chance to self-correct.
	b. Point out to the student what error was made, indicating whether he misidentified a word, skipped a line, or omitted a word.
	c. Model the correct pronunciation of the word, or have the student sound it out. Then, ask the student to read from the beginning of the sentence. Treat omitted words as errors.
	d. Remember to write the missed word on the board for later practice, as described in Step 4 above. Use the list of story errors as an opportunity for extra word reading practice.
Perk up Your Drill	■ When students finish a story, talk briefly about the next story they will read in order to heighten their curiosity and enthusiasm.
	■ Most students want the attention they get through answering a question. Instead of looking for students with hands raised to answer your questions, tell your class that you are looking for students who followed along during the story reading.
Adaptations	■ Whenever possible, coordinate other activities during the day with the current story. If the story is about growing bean seeds, integrate related activities into your science period. If the story is about a historical character, try and expand on the students' knowledge by developing a related social studies lesson.
	■ During story reading, if a student consistently does not follow with her finger, try having her sit next to you so you can redirect more often with a touch on the shoulder or a point to the page. If that tactic still does not work, look at her Oral Reading Fluency Scores. Students who are reading text at a frustration level are usually unable to follow along after the first few sentences.

Source: This script is based on one originally developed and field tested by Carnine, Silbert, Kame'enui, & Tarver (2004). *Direct Instruction Reading* (4th ed.). New Jersey, Merrill Prentice Hall.

text is acceptable. Once the students make between 5 and 10 word-reading errors, stop the oral reading and immediately teach those missed words using the procedures in Table 5.4:

- Students sound out each missed regular word and read it.
- Teacher uses the initial sight word teaching format to review sight words, having students spell them.

After students have practiced reading the missed words, resume reading from the beginning of the difficult section. This time students should read with a higher level of success.

As individual students in the group read and you record their errors, you are able to detect error patterns that may require new teaching. For example, Mr. Sax's students missed the following words during passage reading: *around, sound,* and *loud.* They struggled with the /ou/ sound in each of these words. Before the students reread the story, Mr. Sax conducted a mini review, first reteaching /ou/ in isolation (see Table 4.5) and then in a word list (see Table 4.7). Just before reading the story, Mr. Sax directed the students' attention to each of the three words in context and had them read each word before starting the story.

If no obvious error patterns are present, it is still helpful to practice words missed in a list before the story is reread. Do not put missed articles or connecting words such as *a, and,* or *the,* in lists, but point out to the student that one of them was missed and ask her to reread the sentence. Remind students about the importance of reading each word in the passage carefully.

How Do I Place my Students in the Right Reader?

Over the course of a typical school day, students are required to read a variety of books for a number of different purposes. The classroom basal reader provides a context for teacher-directed instruction of reading skills. Typically students are provided with instructional support as they read their basals, which comes in the form of instruction in word reading, vocabulary, and comprehension. Classrooms having literature-based programs may use trade books as the context for instruction rather than basals. Theoretically, in literature-based programs, students receive similar teacher supports but on an individual basis. Teachers may also use these instructional readers with their students to develop fluency, or they may select books specifically for that purpose. Independent reading includes all books students select for pleasure or to complete assignments. As these activities are done independently, students are expected to carry them out with minimal teacher support.

It is important to select reading material that is of a level of difficulty appropriate to the activity. For example, text that students read with teacher support can be somewhat more difficult than material that students are expected to read independently. In either case, the material cannot be so difficult that students become frustrated.

Armbruster and colleagues (2001) ascribe three levels of difficulty to classroom books or passages: independent-level text, instructional-level text, and frustration-level text. Independent-level texts can be read with at least 95% accuracy on a first or cold read with no more than one in 20 words being difficult for the student. Material at the independent level is appropriate for fluency training as well as any reading task receiving little teacher support. Instructional-level text is unrehearsed material the student can read with at least 90% accuracy with no more than one in 10 words being difficult for the student. Material at the instructional level

> Lexile measures can help teachers match students to the appropriate reading material. For more information go to: **www.Lexile.com.**

> Ms. Luden wanted to see whether a book was appropriate for her student Akayla. Here is what she did.
>
> 1. Ms. Luden selected a representative passage of about 200 words from the book and had Akayla read orally for 1 minute. She scored Akayla's performance the same way she did when giving DIBELS Oral Reading Fluency (DORF).
> 2. Ms. Luden calculated the number of words Akayla read, the number of errors she made, and the number of words she read correctly. The results were as follows:
>
>   Total Words Read = 93
>   Errors = 3
>   Words Correct = 90
>
> 3. Ms. Luden calculated Akayla's percentage correct by dividing the number of words read correctly (90) by the total number of words read (93). Akayla's percentage was 97%, two percentage points above the independent level. The book is appropriate for Akalya to read independently or to build Akayla's fluency.

FIGURE 5.9 Placing Students in the Right Reader

is appropriate for basal texts or literature-based tasks as long as the student is getting full instructional support as he or she navigates through the reading. Frustration-level text is text that students read with less than 90% accuracy. Text at this level is too difficult under any circumstance unless there is a provision for having the material read to the student. Because of their frustration, students who are reading text at this level are likely either to fidget excessively by squirming in their seats or to tune out, looking away from their reading. An example of how to determine whether a book is appropriate for a student is shown in Figure 5.9.

If time permits, you will improve the accuracy of your findings by taking three reading samples from the text and using the middle score in deciding on the appropriateness of the book. Table 5.5 shows that Mr. Haas assessed Abdul on three passages from a book and found that his percentages correct were 91, 93, and 95. The middle score was 93%, indicating that the book was at Abdul's instructional level. Mr. Haas knew that he would need to provide Abdul with some help if he were to successfully read and comprehend this book.

How Can I Increase My Students' Oral Reading Fluency and Develop More Expression?

The following activities will help increase your students' oral reading fluency rates. When the oral reading fluency scores of Tier 2 and Tier 3 students don't increase, fluency training

TABLE 5.5 Calculations for Abdul's Reading Samples

	Words	Errors	Words Correct	% Words Correct
Reading Sample 1	93	8	85	$93\sqrt{85} = 91\%$
Reading Sample 2	89	6	83	$89\sqrt{83} = 93\%$
Reading Sample 3	91	5	86	$91\sqrt{86} = 95\%$

is usually the missing ingredient. Although accuracy in reading is important, often it is not sufficient for fluency. Many students who are at risk require additional practice sessions to develop their automatic reading with increasingly more difficult text. As you work to improve your students' reading fluency, remember that activities designed to increase fluency always involve reading aloud. Ideally these fluency sessions involve passage rereading, are brief and scheduled frequently, and enhance the general curriculum. You have learned that fluent reading is also dependent on student performance on key phonological, phonic, vocabulary, and syntactical skills (Wolf & Katzir-Cohen, 2001). Teachers also must take great care to teach these foundational skills to automaticity using the teaching strategies described throughout this text.

Repeated Readings

This method of building student fluency can be done individually or in small groups. It only works if the students have previously read the material at an accuracy rate of 95% or higher.

1. Select a 100–300 word passage from the story just read or from other material.
2. Set a goal for each student that is 40% above the student's most recent fluency figure. For example: Ramone scored 54 words correct per minute on his most recent DORF assessment. 40% higher than that would be 54 + (54 X .40) = 54 plus 22 = 76. So the fluency goal for Ramone would be 76 words correct per minute.
3. Time the student's reading of the selected passage for 1 minute. Tell the student that the goal is to read the passage until he is able to read it at 76 words correct per minute. If the student meets the goal on the first reading, move to another passage or another student. If the student does not meet the goal, have him continue reading until he meets the goal. Usually it takes between three and five tries to meet the goal.
4. Let the student chart his score to provide extra motivation through a visual record of his progress. See Figure 5.10 for an example of a speed chart.
5. Use one or more of the following strategies along with the re-readings when the goal you set is not reached on the first reading:

   - Model reading the passage for the student before he rereads the passage. The model can be provided by the teacher, another student, or even a taped reading.
   - Allow the student to silently read the passage prior to rereading it.
   - Provide drill on missed words or phrases after each reading.

Taped Readings

Ask the student to read silently a short passage that she can read with at least 95% accuracy before allowing her to read the passage into a tape recorder. Have her replay the tape so she can follow along with the text in order to listen to how her reading sounds. Encourage her to record the passage again and listen to the improvement.

Partner Reading

Since you are only one person, you cannot schedule enough one-on-one fluency sessions to meet the needs of a classroom where many students are at risk. You can overcome this problem by carefully organizing partner readings.

   - Pair students whose reading levels are in the top half of your class with students whose levels are in the bottom half and adjust according to personality issues.

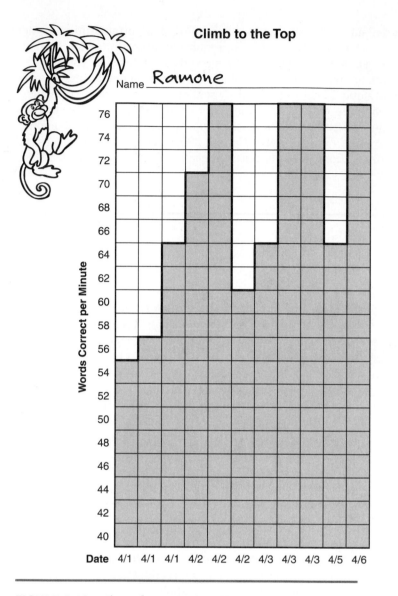

FIGURE 5.10 Chart for Speed Drills

- Select reading material for this activity that the lower performing student can read with at least 95% accuracy.
- Tell your students that they will be reading partners for the next three weeks.
- Designate the more advanced reader as first-read partner and always have him read first to model how the text should be read.
- Give both students the opportunity to read as well as to be tutors.
- Use partner reading to conduct student speed drills or other fluency activities.

Page Races

This variation of student speed drills works well with partners. Give each pair of students a timer which you have taught them how to use, a grid for marking times, and a page of independent-level reading. The timer starts when the student begins reading and stops when she reaches the end of the page. The student who is timing tells the reader how

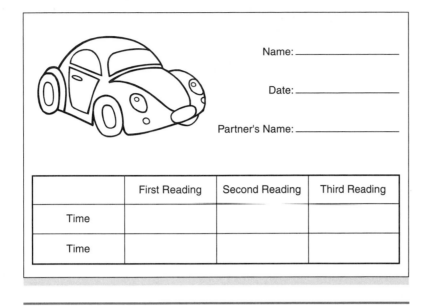

	First Reading	Second Reading	Third Reading
Time			
Time			

FIGURE 5.11 Page Races Worksheet

fast she read the page before recording the time in the chart depicted in Figure 5.11. The reader's goal is to beat that time on the second reading. If any words are skipped or missed, the reader starts again.

Echo Reading

Read one sentence of text aloud with appropriate intonation and phrasing. Ask the student to imitate this oral reading model. Continue this pattern of reading until the student can imitate more than one sentence at a time.

Neurological Impress Method

Select a short passage that the student can read with high accuracy, since you will not correct him during the reading. Sit slightly behind the student, holding the book in front of him so that you speak toward his dominant ear. Read together as in "one voice," moving your finger along the line of print as a focus for his eyes. Later the student may assume the finger-following functioning or you may guide his finger as an intermediate step. Special focus should be on moving the finger smoothly and without pause from the end of one line to the beginning of the next. The finger and voice should be synchronized throughout the passage reading. Read the passage slightly beyond his normal rate, so attention is paid to longer phrases. By speeding up the reading, you are encouraging the student to read at a faster pace.

Choral Reading

Give your students a short poem or song which they can read with at least 95% accuracy. Practice reading the text in unison until everyone is reading it together as a chorus. Later you can divide the students into groups and assign various parts of the passage to each. Invite the principal to your room and give a short performance.

TABLE 5.6   Reading Fluency Chart

My Partner _____ :

After the 2nd reading:

Yes	No	Read every word correctly
Yes	No	Read without skipping any words
Yes	No	Read faster
Yes	No	Read with more expression

Source: Adapted from Murray, B. (1999). *Developing Reading Fluency. The Reading Genie,* http://www.auburn.edu/%7Emurraba/fluency.html

Different but the Same

Show your students how the same sentence is read differently depending on the final punctuation. First write a sentence three times, ending each with with a different punctuation mark:

Lynne runs fast.

Lynne runs fast?

Lynne runs fast!

After modeling each sentence by overexaggerating your intonation, ask your students to read and mirror your inflection. Do this type of activity until your students no longer need your modeling to phrase new sentences.

Think about Your Reading

Buy some cheap clipboards at a dollar store and put one copy of the Reading Fluency Chart in Table 5.6 on each clipboard. After giving everyone a copy of the last book they read accurately, a clipboard, and a pencil, demonstrate how a good reader uses expression and phrasing. Then demonstrate how a choppy reader reads the same pages. Tell students that everyone will have a turn to be a listener and a reader and explain what they will be looking for when their partners read. After students are divided into pairs, explain that the first reader begins reading. During the first read-through, the listener identifies any words that have been omitted or misread. The second time the story is read, the listener checks off each quality on the checklist. Before switching roles, the listener shows the checklist to the reader and explains the markings.

Reading in Chunks

Write a sentence on the board or on student worksheets in chunks of text that match how one would read it aloud. Poems and song lyrics work well for this kind of activity. Model how you read the sentence, pausing at the end of lines, before having everyone read it in unison with you. Practice reading text like this one with the students, until you are all reading with one voice:

"Help! Help!"
cried the Page
when the sun got hot.
"King Bidgood's in the bathtub,
and he won't get out!
Oh,
who knows what to do? (Wood & Wood, 1985)

Scallop the Text

Take a page of text that students can accurately read and draw scallops connecting phrases that logically are read as a unit. If doing this activity with one student, give him a copy of the page so he can follow the scallop pattern with his fingers as he reads. If doing with the class, put the page on an overhead transparency so students can follow your finger scoops. Reread the text until the sound, the speed, and rhythm are acceptable. Then ask the student to read the same text without the scallop marks to see if the smooth reading transfers.

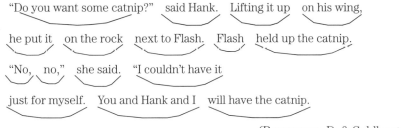

(Rasmussen, D. & Goldberg, L. 2000, p. 73)

Readers' Theatre

As long as students can read them accurately, plays work well for repeated readings with an emphasis on expression. If you are working with a large class, you can divide the students into small choral reading groups to minimize waiting time. The first one or two times through the play, whenever a group reads without expression, model how the group can make the reading sound more lively.

Duet or Shared Reading

Have pairs of students reread stories that they have previously read accurately using an every-other-word pattern. The first student reads the first word, the second reads the next word, the first student reads the third word and so on until the story is completed. Students enjoy this activity which increases fluency and develops a higher level of attention to text. Teachers can also take a turn doing this activity with a student.

> Learn about three fluency building programs: *Read Naturally*, *Great Leaps*, and *Headsprout*. Their websites contain useful information and tips on developing fluency. **www.readnaturally.com**, **www.greatleaps.com**, and **www.headsprout.com.**

How Important Is Fluency for Older Learners?

Because significant numbers of older students do not read at grade level, many teachers in schools with large numbers of students who are at risk confront the same dilemma as this eighth-grade teacher faced each day:

Effective Teacher at Work

Support Independent Reading of Longer Words

One Project PRIDE teacher recognized that successful readers need a certain degree of boldness in approaching new multisyllable words in text. If readers are fearful that they cannot read a new word, they may pause too long or risk skipping a key word that is pivotal to the meaning of the text. Sometimes students who are not confident about their ability to decode freeze when they come to longer words. This PRIDE teacher recognized that her students needed to develop a confident inner voice that would immediately move them into reading such words. She also recognized that since the students were good at reading nonsense words on the DIBELS Nonsense Words Assessment, they should be successful reading longer words by starting to read the first part of the word. After all, syllables are often similar to nonsense words.

Thus, during oral reading, every time students stopped at a multisyllable word and looked helplessly at her or at the book, this teacher reminded them, "Start sounding out the first three letters and you'll probably know the rest of the word." Sometimes she felt like a nag repeating this strategy. Every once in a while when a student would pause at a longer word, the teacher would ask the class to give advice to the reader. By then students could easily describe what they should do. Gradually, she observed her increasingly emboldened readers tackling tough words. They would ask her about the meaning or use a dictionary only after trying to decode a long word by themselves. By the end of the year, the students in this class read with the highest accuracy and fluency of all of our PRIDE schools, and we suggested that all of the teachers use this tip for more difficult words in text.

> This year our district is emphasizing literacy. They gave me a two-hour reading/language arts block. I got a set of eighth-grade literature books and a set of eighth-grade grammar books. There are thirty-four kids in the block. Only one or two can actually read the eighth-grade literature book . . . . you know, Edgar Allen Poe short stories. It's ridiculous. These kids can't read this stuff. Lots of these kids can't read more than about third-grade level, if that. I've brought in a lot of books my own kids had when they were little, just to try to get them reading. (Greene, 1998)

One of the greatest challenges for subject area teachers of older students with reading problems is obtaining reading material that is at students' instructional or independent level. Frustration-level text will only result in higher anxiety levels or tuning out. To solve this problem, some teachers scour the Internet and school libraries to find subject area text that they can photocopy for their students' and use for fluency practice.

If previous teachers have not expected older learners to orally read passages accurately, students will initially complain that your high expectations are "picky." In response to the complaining, stop a student after a word-reading error that affects the meaning of the text and point out exactly how the wrong word or omission of the word changes the meaning of the text. Teachers help their students strategically think about the importance of careful reading by periodically explaining that accurate reading is essential for success on the job, for success on quizzes in classes, and for following directions. Because fluent, accurate reading requires so much concentration for the older learner who is not reading at grade level, charting progress on a graph can inject much needed motivation. Charting progress on a pre-drawn graph or an Excel program helps students concretely see their upward progress. Information on how to construct your own progress graphs is covered in Appendix A.

When content-area text in subjects such as social studies and science is routinely at a frustration level for older students, teachers cannot use the text to improve their reading skills. Only oral reading of instructional-level text benefits struggling older readers. How-

Seize the Teachable Moment

Making Time for Fluency Building

Fluency will only improve if students have the opportunity to read out loud and receive feedback on their reading. You cannot afford to skip oral reading time. Squeeze more oral reading time into any time during the day when you have a few minutes to fill before moving to a new activity.

- When students go to the computer lab, work individually with those students at risk whose fluency has plateaued.
- If you have a morning field trip, fit reading into the afternoon. Because everyone will be tired, you will need to be especially energetic as you motivate students to do their best work. Reading should never be skipped during a scheduled school day.
- When gym class is cancelled for the day, do more oral reading.
- If your students need more oral reading time, make those activities a priority rather than art projects or video watching.
- If you play a video for your class, pull out one or two students for more oral reading practice. Most of your students would prefer having concentrated time and attention with a teacher rather than watching a video.
- If you have a sustained silent reading time for your class, use the time to work with one to three students for oral reading. If you have the students use their quiet voices and work in a corner of the room, you will not disturb the other students.

ever, there are times when students are unable to read their textbooks but need them to gain access to class content. These same students also experience problems communicating what they have learned because they can't read classroom tests. One promising software program to help with these problems is Read & Write Gold Scanning. This program allows teachers to scan any paper-based document and convert it into an audio file. Students can then listen to their textbooks and tests. Although this method does not provide systematic instruction to increase the reading skills of older learners, the adaptive technology allows students full access to the general education curriculum and a fair and equitable way to demonstrate what they have learned.

Putting the Pieces Together: What Does a Tier 1 Classroom Look Like?

First and Second Grade

After Christmas, most of Ms. Erdmann's first-grade students in Tiers 1 and 2 met the DIBELS Nonsense Word Fluency benchmarks. Although she encouraged them to sound out longer words, they could easily read three- and four-letter words with short vowels. Still, adapting the general education reading curriculum for a class of students who are at risk takes preplanning. If Ms. Erdmann was going to maintain a perky pace throughout her lessons, she needed to know exactly what sounds and words to teach and review. Our teachers have found that summary daily lesson guides help them teach the essential skills each day. The guides make planning easier, ensure teachers do not omit key words, and help the flow of instruction. One of Ms. Erdmann's daily lesson plans is displayed in Figure 5.12.

Although this lesson was developed for Houghton Mifflin (2004), other phonics-based series stress the same essential reading skills.

About 5 minutes after the lesson started, Ms. Erdmann was ready to begin teaching the new words for the day. Before she went through the list, she taught one of the two new vocabulary words (*hatch*) that was in the lesson's story. In addition to teaching students how to decode the targeted vocabulary word, she also taught its meaning.

On this day, and every day, Ms. Erdmann started with a brief practice of the new letter combination or affix introduced in the curriculum and review of recently learned ones. These are shown in the letter–sound correspondence section of the lesson outline. Although not shown here, Ms. Erdmann also wrote a list of CVC, Vce, and long vowel letter combinations so that students had extra practice differentiating *make* from *mash*, *play* from *plan*, and *can* from *cane*.

Then Ms. Erdmann walked to the dry erase board where she had written the targeted words earlier in the morning. By this time of the year the new words always included words with new letter combinations and affixes, increasingly more multisyllable words, and a few sight words. On this day, the *ou* and *ow* combinations were practiced in words. All of the day's sight words were review words. Ms. Erdmann used word reading formats from Chapters 3 and 4 to teach these words.

Word reading was followed by reading the decodable story, *The Stout Hound,* which provided more practice on the new letter combinations. Ms. Erdmann was glad when second semester came because she preferred the easier SAFER reading format to the earlier unison format. Although she focused on accuracy the first time through the story, Ms. Erdmann also integrated comprehension questions. From past years she knew that decodable stories sometimes needed a little livening up so she hammed up the dialogue when modeling how a sentence could be read for expression. Ms. Erdmann believed that she could make any story interesting, but sometimes she had to be more theatrical and discuss more background knowledge.

Although she preferred to do more than one reading of the story, Ms. Erdmann still had to include spelling and writing in the literacy schedule. The shopkeeper story was not difficult, so she planned to have her students do partner reading right after lunch. Since her students in Tier 3 were reading different stories, she paired them up to read a story from their reading series. As she began to emphasize fluency more, she had to devise ways to fit in short rereadings. Although she could not count on all of her parents, several would listen to their children read if the stories were sent home. Ms. Erdmann encouraged the other students to read to a younger sibling or grandparent so that they could get more practice.

Beyond Second Grade

By the middle of second grade, students in Tier 1 have learned to decode a large percentage of the most common affixes and letter combinations. Word-reading increasingly focuses on teaching students to decode more difficult multisyllable words. Although the classroom routine will be structured like that for first grade, the emphasis on specific activities shifts. Students know their basic phonics skills but still need to apply them to more difficult words. By the middle of second grade, teachers begin to spend a larger percentage of time on vocabulary instruction and comprehension in addition to fluency building activities.

What Can I Do for Students Who Still Aren't Learning to Read More Fluently?

By mid first grade, progress charts based on the DIBELS oral reading fluency assessment can be used to determine who needs the extra support of Tier 2 (see earlier assessment

Phonemic Awareness: (already mastered: now embedded in word reading tasks)

Letter–Sound Correspondences (Table 4.5)

Intro: ou   ow (2)

Review: oo (2) sh ew tch ing ue o_e o igh ing ang ung

Regular Words (Tables 4.7 and 4.9)

Intro: br<u>ow</u>n, f<u>ou</u>nd, h<u>ow</u>, cr<u>ow</u>n, sc<u>ou</u>t, <u>ou</u>t, c<u>ow</u>, sh<u>ou</u>t, l<u>ou</u>d,
round, d<u>ow</u>n, cr<u>ow</u>d, n<u>ow</u>, st<u>ou</u>t, gr<u>ou</u>nd, t<u>ow</u>n, h<u>ou</u>nd

<u>pic</u> nic, <u>rab</u> bit, <u>up</u> set, <u>nap</u> kin, <u>prin</u> cess, <u>bas</u> ket,
<u>hap</u> pen, <u>in</u> vent, <u>ten</u> nis, <u>traf</u> fic, <u>down</u> town

Review: playing, splash, moaned

Sight Words (either not decodable or students have not learned to decode letter–sound combinations in these words; Table 3.8)

Intro: no new words

Review: about, because, teacher, could, under, water, through, there

Passage Reading (Table 5.4)

Phonics Library: *The Stout Hound*

Error Limit: 2

Vocabulary (Figure 6.2)

hatch: Hatch means to come out of an egg. What does hatch mean?

- The egg started to move around because a baby dinosaur was going to come out of it. Was the baby dinosaur going to hatch or not hatch? Why?
- The green stem of a daisy plant grew out of the ground. Was the plant hatching or not hatching? Why?
- The baby alligator has a special egg tooth to cut through the egg it has been living in. Does the baby alligator have an egg tooth so he can hatch or not hatch? Why?
- Desiree slipped on a banana peel when she was running through the cafeteria and landed on the ground. Did Desiree hatch or not hatch? Why?
- Fish often come out of their eggs in open water. Do the fish hatch or not hatch in the open water. Why?
- I forgot to water my cactus plant and it died. Did the cactus plant hatch or not hatch? Why?
- What does hatch mean?

Spelling:

Regular Words (Figure 3.14)

Intro: grab grim trap trip

Review: (none)

Irregular Words (Table 3.8 adapted)

Intro: cow, down, now

Review: (none)

Challenge Words: crowded

Comprehension: Complete all of the comprehension and vocabulary activities listed in the book that *will extend students' understanding of the passage and mastery of comprehension strategies and vocabulary.* Many of the grammar and spelling activities contain related comprehension skills.

FIGURE 5.12 First Grade, Daily Lesson Guide 8, Theme 8: Selection 2: Day 1

section). In Chapter 3 we described a typical first-grade Tier 2 booster group that meets for 30 minutes as a small group outside of the classroom. In the winter semester when daily words begin to include more long vowels and multisyllable words, first-grade students continue to practice decoding those more difficult words in their booster sessions. In addition, teachers use extra moments during the day to develop fluency by providing extra decodable reading to students in Tier 2. Any extra volunteers are assigned to provide even more oral reading time. By January, any first-grade student who scores between 30–49 wcpm on the Nonsense Words Fluency assessment and/or in the "some risk" category on the Oral Reading Fluency Assessment should receive Tier 2 support. Lower scores indicate that Tier 3 intensive support is needed.

Beginning in second grade when students know the majority of letter combinations, Tier 2 booster sessions shift their focus almost exclusively to developing fluency by providing an opportunity for rereading stories in the curriculum. Classroom teachers now conduct the booster sessions by scheduling a daily Tier 2 reading group into a time of day when other students are independently working or silently reading. If accuracy is high, the teacher might schedule student speed drills one day, closely monitored partner reading the next day, and chunk reading the third day.

What Can I Do for Students Who Struggle with Advanced Word-Reading Skills and Fluency, Despite Daily Tier 2 Booster Sessions?

A small group of first-grade students will stay on track for grade-level reading with Tier 2 support as they learn phonemic awareness skills and begin developing alphabetic principle. However, the progress of some students stalls when their DIBELS Nonsense Words Score is in the 20s or low 30s. These students plateau at that level and even with additional time reading decodables, they are unable to automatically read simple CVC words. Unless these students are moved into a more intensive reading program, they will continue to laboriously sound out each word before reading it.

Students who have been in a differentiated instructional program since kindergarten and have not needed intensive support will rarely if ever move to Tier 3 once their decoding skills are established. With explicit teaching they should learn to apply these skills to increasingly longer words.

First-Grade Tier 3 Placement Rules.   The recommended decision rules for placement into Tier 3 in grade 1 are as follows:

> In January of grade 1, student scores below 30 on Nonsense Words Fluency Assessment and/or below 8 on first-grade oral reading fluency.

> Note: This cutoff of 8 wcpm will be higher if you set the benchmark for the year-end first-grade ORF at 60 wcpm rather than 40.)

Second-Grade Tier 3 Placement Rules,   The recommended decision rules for placement into Tier 3 in grade 2 are as follows:

> In September of grade 2, student scores below 26 on second-grade oral reading fluency.

Third-Grade Tier 3 Placement Rules.   The recommended decision rules for placement into Tier 3 in grade 3 are as follows:

In September of grade 3, student scores below 53 on third-grade oral reading fluency.

Table 5.7 describes how fluency is taught in several of the alternative programs described in previous chapters. The REWARDS program, designed to increase the fluency of struggling older readers who can read at a fourth-grade or higher level, is included in this section for the first time.

TABLE 5.7   Comparison of Four Common Tier 3 Approaches

	Direct Instruction: Reading Mastery	Wilson Reading System	Language!	REWARDS
Does curriculum incorporate fluency practice into lessons after students read stories with high accuracy?	Yes, assessments are timed. In order to move to the next lesson, students must meet the specified accuracy and rate criteria set for the passage.	Emphasis is on prosody rather than on time. Students orally read text while scooping meaningful chunks.	Three "fluency builders" consisting of phonetically predictable words based on skills taught are included in each unit.	Teachers are instructed to have students read carefully selected passages from content-area text. Students record the number of correctly read words on the last timing and transfer the information to a fluency chart.
Are fluency practice sessions scheduled at least several times a week?	Yes, fluency is integrated throughout the curriculum. Performance on timed assessments is graphed.	A minimum of 2–3 lessons per sub-step is recommended with the first lesson introducing the concept, the second lesson building accuracy, and the third lesson building fluency.	Yes, 1-minute timings on selected skill drills are done daily until a goal is reached. Performance on timed assessments is graphed.	Fluency practice is included in each of the 20, 40- to 50-minute lessons.
Do fluency practice sessions gradually become more challenging?	Yes, passages include more difficult words in longer sentences as students progress through the curriculum.	Fluency is not considered to be the number of wcpm, but rather the effortless and accurate decoding of more challenging words.	Words become more challenging, but the basic format of the drill—isolated words—remains the same.	As students learn to read more multisyllable words, teachers are able to select increasingly more difficult content-area text for fluency practice.
Are specific word-per-minute goals established?	Word-per-minute goals are set for reading assessment passages. Recommendations are that first-graders finish Reading Mastery 11 by the end of first grade to have grade-level fluency.	No.	Separate fluency goals are set for phonetic words and sight words. Students are expected to reach goal for 2 out of 3 days for each drill page.	Yes the wcpm goals are: grades 4–5: 120–150 grades 6–8 150–180 grades 9–12: 180–200
Is fluency assessed regularly?	Yes, assessments every few lessons on passage reading.	No.	Yes, daily through 1-minute timed drills on isolated words.	Yes, daily.
Is fluency practiced with passages and stories that students have previously read with high accuracy?	Yes.	Each sentence and story/passage is read silently, then orally while scooping with finger or pencil.	No.	Accuracy is always stressed before fluency. Students decode difficult words before reading them in passages.

Effective Teacher at Work

A Team Uses Data-Based Decision Making

In January, the first- and second-grade teaching teams looked at the latest DORF scores to plan for Tier changes based on the assessment. Ms. Shackmann served as the recorder so she could compile a master list of changes and photocopy them for everyone. After Christmas, the team realized that a student whose assessment results indicated he should move to Tier 2 for more support had never been moved. The team recognized that improved communication was necessary to avoid such slip-ups. In order to prevent any other student from slipping through the cracks, the team members each had a form like the one shown in Table 5.8. They used the DIBELS Second Grade Benchmarks posted at http://dibels.uoregon.edu/benchmark.php to determine who was in Tier 1, Tier 2, or Tier 3. During their team meeting, they filled out the last two columns once they made individual student decisions.

TABLE 5.8   Second-Grade Data

Student Name	Teacher	Sept. DIBELS ORF	Nov. DIBELS ORF	Jan. DIBELS ORF	Tier for Dec.	Tier for Jan.	Changes for Jan.
Tony	Jones	50	54	59	1	2	move to 2
Greg	Jones	65	92	106	1	1	—
Jalisha	Jones	9	12	15	3	3	move to a smaller Tier 3 group
Serabia	Jones	50	50	52	2	3	move to 3
Sonya	Jones	55	87	89	1	1	—
Taylor	Jones	43	69	79	2	1	move to 1
Justin	Jones	23	31	47	3	3	—
Simone	Jones	32	43	55	2	2	
Lanecea	Jones	24	53	73	3	2	move to 2
John	Entwistle	60	66	91	1	1	—
Carrie	Entwistle	38	64	78	2	1	move to 1
Shantrel	Entwistle	46	48	56	1	2	move to 2
Mike	Entwistle	46	53	69	1	1	—
Tan	Entwistle	37	47	61	2	2	—

Based on the tests scores and confirmation by the teachers that further testing was not needed, the following changes were made:

Lanecea (2nd grade) moved from Tier 3 to Tier 2. Test results showed that her progress had dramatically increased these past few months, and she was now reading second-grade text at 73 wcpm, a level of performance warranting a move back into the general education curriculum. However, Lanecea's *Reading Mastery* teacher was anxious about her moving into Tier 1, afraid that because Lanecea was shy, Tier 1 instruction within the larger class might not provide her with enough support to maintain her success. Although Lanecea's DORF score indicated that she could be placed into Tier 1, the team moved her into Tier 2 to provide her with extra support for the first few months. The team decided that if, following the next progress monitoring period, Lanecea maintained her current progress in the general education curriculum, they would move her into Tier 1. The general education teacher said she thought Lanecea was ready for the move to Tier 1 because she had noticed Lanecea had begun to read the science and social studies materials used in class. The teacher suggested assigning a volunteer tutor to Lanecea for some extra support. Meanwhile, the *Reading Mastery* teacher would contact Lanecea once a week and ask her about stories she was reading in the new class.

Serabia (2nd grade), a student diagnosed with ADHD, needed to make a move in the opposite direction from Lanecea. After summer school, Serabia, who had been in Tier 3, was reading at grade level and after much discussion was moved into Tier 2. In the early fall, she continued to make progress, so the decision seemed appropriate. However, Serabia's DORF scores were unchanged since November, and she was rapidly falling behind. The team hypothesized that because she was so distractible, the small group helped her pay more attention to the lessons. Whatever, the reason, Serabia needed that extra support and so was moved back to the fastest moving Tier 3 group.

The team wanted to discuss Jalisha, who was not progressing in her intensive Tier 3 group and whose DORF scores were virtually unchanged. The teaching coach agreed to watch her during reading group to determine if the teaching strategies needed fine-tuning. Following the observation, the coach felt that Jalisha would benefit from working in a smaller group, so a back-up plan was worked out. One of the trained paraprofessionals who was an experienced Tier 3 teacher would begin taking Jalisha and another student in a group of two. The team agreed to check back on Jalisha in a month to see if the smaller group had triggered more progress.

Tony and Shantrel needed to move from Tier 1 to Tier 2 because they were still scoring in the 50s on the DORF, below the January cutoff for Tier 1 of 68.

Taylor and Carrie no longer needed Tier 2 support. For two assessments in a row, their DORF scores were above the aim line. It was agreed that their general education teacher would monitor them closely, giving another DORF next month to be sure that they continued making progress without Tier 2 support.

At the end of the team meeting, Ms. Shackmann summarized the changes to make sure her notes were accurate. Because it was Thursday, the team agreed that all of the group changes would begin the following Monday.

How Can I Help Develop the Expressive Reading Skills of My English Language Learners?

Many English language learners first need to recognize prosodic features in spoken English. In some other languages, changed word order indicates emphasis, in contrast to English, which often relies on intonation and stressed words (Celce-Murcia et al., 1996). Students can easily miss keys to comprehension when listening to a conversation, such as when a sarcastic sentence is interpreted as a statement of fact. Shades of meaning are lost when word emphasis is not interpreted. For example, the meaning of the word, *okay,* is affected by the way it is said. A reluctant worker who does not want to do a job will say, *okay,* in a resentful tone of voice drawing out each syllable. Another person hearing about plans for a much-awaited vacation is likely to enthusiastically respond "*okay!*" in a thumbs-up tone of voice, signaling approval. A disgruntled teenager who knows she has no other choice but to babysit her brother on a Friday night might roll her eyes and say *okay,* in a somewhat sarcastic tone of voice. Interpreting intention of the speaker and the meaning behind what he is actually saying is a challenge for English language learners. This first step of interpretation is necessary before English language learners can reproduce these expressions in their own speech or in reading dialogue.

You can use dialogue in stories to help develop your English language learners' attention to the meaning of what they are reading. Bring the characters to life and point out expressive changes in their speech, changes that you want your students to hear in their heads as they read the text. For example in the book, *Where the Wild Things Are,* when you come to the passage:

> his mother called him "WILD THING!"
> and Max said "I'll EAT YOU UP!"
> so he was sent to bed without eating anything.

You should model the rude, defiant tone that Max used when he talked back to his mother and then go an extra step by explaining that his mother sent him to bed for talking so rudely to her. Model how you overemphasize the word "anything," using hand gestures and facial expressions to convey the concept of *nothing.* Ask everyone to read the sentence using the tone of voice you did. You might want to take the lesson a step further and ask, "Did Max eat bread?" "Did Max eat dessert?" Expecting your students to reply in full sentences provides even more directly-related language practice.

In *Teaching American English Pronunciation* (1992), Avery and Ehrlich suggest some additional activities for helping students develop more expression.

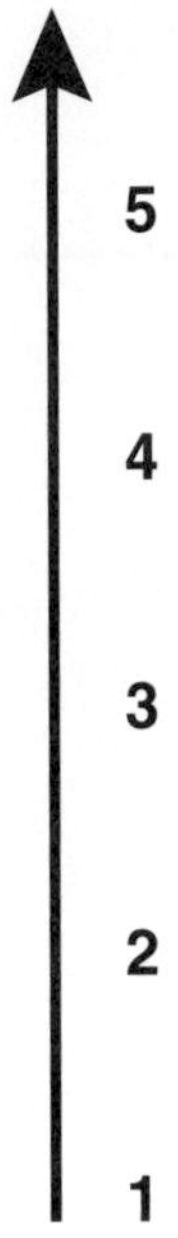

Up and Down the Scale

Students whose first language is not English may need practice saying words with different pitches. When your class is reviewing vocabulary (see Chapter 6), you can use this 1-minute activity portrayed in Figure 5.13. On the board draw an upward facing arrow alongside the numbers one through five written in a vertical column. Point to the bottom number (1) and model saying a word in a low pitch before having the student repeat. Point to number 2 and repeat at a slightly higher pitch. Go all the way up the scale until you reach number 5. Then reverse and move down pitch levels. Emphasis is on producing and hearing different levels of pitch and developing vocal muscles necessary to use in speech.

5

4

3

2

1

FIGURE 5.13
Up–Down
Scale

Turn Up the Volume

Show students how to say a letter sound or word, take a breath and say it louder, take a breath and say it louder, and finally take a breath and yell it out. This activity works well for everyone when the class needs a 1-minute break to release energy.

Variety Is the Spice of Life

Have your students memorize a sentence or short poem before changing how they recite it. First ask them to change one thing about their oral presentation. For example:

a. First read the poem *slowly* before reading it *quickly.*
b. First read the poem *quietly* before reading it *loudly.*
c. First read the poem in a *high pitch* before reading it in a *low pitch.*

Once students can change one dynamic, have them change two. For example, ask them to read *slowly* and *quietly* before reading it *quickly* and *loudly.* Try some other combinations. Finally, ask students to change three dynamics. Ask them to read the poem *quickly, quietly* and with a *low pitch.* Ask them to read it *quickly, loudly,* and with a *high pitch.*

The Reflective Teacher

Always Learning

Mr. Rundall taught third grade for 10 years. Every summer when the state returned test score results, he was disappointed that more students in his class did not meet the state standards. After attending a summer inservice on teaching fluency, he realized that he had not taught this skill explicitly. Perhaps if he used some of the suggestions and increased fluency, his students' comprehension would improve enough to pass those state tests.

Thus, Mr. Rundall was determined to begin the new school year and try the new ideas he had learned. Several times a week, he scheduled fluency practice sessions into the schedule. Because this was his first time teaching fluency, Mr. Rundall spent several minutes at the end of each day analyzing how the lessons went. He wanted to pinpoint how he could improve his lessons and what things were working. As he thought about the lesson, he listed things that he would do differently next time. These are some of the questions that Mr. Rundall asked himself after each fluency lesson:

1. Did I remember to tell the students the purpose of the fluency training and how it relates to improved reading? Was my explanation motivating and clear?
2. Did the organization of my materials minimize transition times and any potential behavior problems?
3. Were the materials effective or could they be improved? Could students use the timers without needing extra assistance?
4. Did I pre-teach the fluency activity adequately, so that the pairs of students were able to get to work, following the activity instructions?
5. Were the charts for graphing progress motivating to the students; were students able to record easily their results on them? Can I improve the charts?
6. Are there any materials I need to review before I do this activity again?

How Can I Use Games and Activities to Reinforce Students' Fluency Skills?

Once students are fluent with a poem, story, or play, search out opportunities for your students to read the text aloud. Kindergarten teachers may appreciate if you volunteer a pair of readers each day. Obtain a plastic microphone that plugs into a radio and let students pretend that they are recording on TV. The microphone can also serve as a motivator when students are reading a story for the third time. Poems read by your students can enliven morning announcements. Some schools allow students to read to other students in the lunchroom. Videotape your class reading and let them watch the tape to see themselves. Invite the principal or custodian into class in order to watch a choral reading. Parents always enjoy seeing their children perform. Take your students' fluent reading to the next step and encourage them to read proudly for an audience.

If younger students routinely read past final punctuation as if it is not there, spend a few days conducting punctuation walks. The first time you do this activity, you will need to show your students how you walk your fingers, starting at the beginning of the text and stopping at final punctuation. Ask students to put their two walking fingers on the first word in the sentence. When you say, "sentence," tell them to walk their fingers to the end of the sentence, stopping at the punctuation mark. When you repeat the word, "sentence," they should walk their fingers to the end of the next sentence. Continue in this pattern until the end of the story. Once students can easily do a basic punctuation walk, you may want to

Technology

Fluency Tracking

PDAs, or Personal Development Assistants, can help teachers record, compute, and organize students' fluency scores. PDAs are small handheld digital devices that store information, provide data, and chart progress. They can be adapted for wireless use and synchronized with the web. Software programs for oral reading fluency assessments allow the teacher to mark student errors as you are giving the test. The software alerts the tester to the end of the test so there is no need for a stopwatch. Since the new data are automatically added to previous month's scores, the teacher can easily check to make sure that the student has made continuous progress. One click of the PDA software produces an aimline for each student based on testing results. Some software programs even list suggested activities for individual students, based on their scores. Teachers can see the results of their entire class on one page and by clicking on a student's name can see the actual test as scored.

Create your own reading fluency scoresheets by going to **www. interventioncentral.org** and clicking on the OKAPI *Reading Probe Generator.*

ask them to name the punctuation mark when they reach it. For added emphasis, you can have them say, "period," in a matter-of-fact voice tone; "question mark" with the rising inflection one uses at the end of a questioning sentence, and "exclamation mark," in a dramatic exclamatory tone.

Motivating Students to Do Their Best

Working Independently

When a teacher works with one group of students on fluency practice, the other students need to be engaged in productive work that will not disrupt the reading group. One key to conducting smaller reading groups is to recognize that some students have never learned to work independently. Independent work skills require specific instruction and practice, just as other classroom skills and knowledge do. Six steps used to teach independent work skills are listed, followed by more detailed descriptions for each step:

1. Identify and explain the skills and rules necessary to work independently.
2. Show students what working independently looks like.
3. Give students practice working independently in small groups with well-defined activities while you monitor closely. Use a timer to establish a clear concrete beginning and end to the independent work time practice.
4. When working with a small reading group, sit facing students who are working independently in order to maximize monitoring. Use the timer until students no longer need it as a reminder.
5. Provide feedback and reward students for working independently.
6. Make adaptations for individual students when necessary.

Prepare for Teaching Students to Work Independently

Before you begin teaching students to work independently, determine several activities students can complete independently with at least 90% success. Students will not quietly work if they are frustrated. If Ms. Legolis introduced describing words on Monday and on Tuesday asked her students to work independently on a worksheet that required them to find describing words in sentences, many of the students would still not have the skills to do that work. The ensuing frustration could lead to a number of off-task behaviors. In contrast, if Mr. Dane gave his students a review sheet requiring them to circle the nouns and verbs, a skill that they learned well but still needed to review, the students would have the skills to do that work. Giving students a task to complete when they do not have the skills to complete it independently sets them up for failure.

Step 1: Identify and explain the skills and rules necessary to work independently.
Establish and enforce rules for independent work times. You might want to use the following rules:

- Respect others by keeping hands, feet, and objects to yourself.
- Once the timer is set, no talking is allowed until the timer rings. Don't interrupt the teacher when she is working with a group. For 15 minutes no one can talk.
- Work on your assigned activity at your assigned spot until the timer rings. If you are working at the tables and finish your work, then select one of the books in the middle of the table to silently read/look at.
- If you follow the rules after I set the timer, you'll earn 5 points when the timer rings.

Some classes require very tight rules and don't allow talking or laughing during this independent work time. Teachers who decide to set such stringent rules know that in their class a quiet giggle predictably turns into raucous laughter disturbing everyone's work; that a quiet request for help from one's neighbor can easily turn into elbow shoving. In other classes, students can sharpen pencils when needed or quietly ask a neighbor for help. The teacher has to determine the maturity level of the class before establishing rules. Students typically will fit into one of the three categories described in Figure 5.14.

The Project PRIDE teachers found that students willingly worked quietly in order to earn a point for their team or table. A display chart on the wall was used for the cumulative point totals. Some teachers used a more concrete award after teams earned 20 or 30 points. Other teachers found that students were motivated by the rising point totals on the displayed chart.

Step 2: Show students what working independently looks like.
Your students who have the greatest need to learn independent work skills are those who will profit least from your verbal descriptions. Show these students what working independently looks like. Tell your students that you want to show them what quiet working looks like and sit at a desk with a pencil and paper. After quietly working for several seconds, tell students what you are doing and refer to the rules, **"This is quiet working. Mrs. Bara is quietly working until the timer rings."** Move to a computer and work quietly for a few seconds, once again telling students, **"This is quiet working. Mrs. Bara is working without interrupting the teacher."** Return to a table and read a book before telling students, **"This is quiet working. Mrs. Bara finished her work and took a book on the pile next to the table."** Your lesson will make more of an impression on students if you also include nonexamples. At this point

---

☺ Those students whom you encourage to **neatly complete** all work.

☺ Those students whom you encourage to complete **all** work.

☺ Those students who are still working on **following the quiet rules** while sitting with their work. You know that it is a challenge for these students to sit quietly and hope to increase the quality of their independent work gradually.

FIGURE 5.14   Expectations for Independent Work

Continued

you can add a bit of humor and theatrics for motivation. Sit next to one of the students at a table and start chatting to him. Tell your students, **"This is not quiet working. Mrs. Bara forgot and is talking."** If students are not supposed to go to the pencil sharpener during quiet work time, pretend you are a student who has left her seat to do that and once again say, **"This is not quiet working. Mrs. Bara forgot that she isn't supposed to sharpen pencils during quiet work time."**

After showing the students examples and nonexamples, ask them more abstract questions and tell them to put their thumbs up or down depending on the answer:

- **"Should I talk to my neighbor and ask for her pencil?"** Dramatically shake your head no and expect that the students have their thumbs down.
- **"Should I work like this?"** As you quietly work, look to see all thumbs up.
- **"Should I get up and go to the sink?"** Another emphatic head shaking **"no."**

Step 3: Give students practice working independently in small groups with well-defined activitites while you monitor closely.

If simply talking about and watching the teacher model good behavior were enough, schools would have far fewer discipline problems. However, as with any skill, learning how to work independently takes practice. First, ask three or four students to come up and show everyone else how they can quietly work on a paper while everyone else watches. After two or three minutes, praise their quiet working and ask the rest of the class to clap for them.

After the small group has modeled quiet, independent working, tell the class that it is now their turn to practice. Set the timer for a predetermined number of minutes. Give the students a worksheet or project they can easily do. Before you set the timer, remind the students of the rules. For kindergarten set the timer for only 1 minute; for second grade and above, set it for 3 or 4 minutes. You need everyone to be successful this first time. As students work, closely monitor, walking around the room so you can redirect anyone who is not following the rules. Any time students break a rule, remind them that they are not working and must get back to work. When the timer rings, praise the students who have followed the rules and give team points to rows of students that worked diligently. In a matter-of-fact voice tone tell teams that haven't earned points why they didn't earn them, **"Two students at table four were talking. That team doesn't earn a point."** If students were not successful, tell the class that they need to practice again until they are successful, and repeat the process.

Practice quiet independent work using the timer at least twice a day. Gradually increase the time until students can work independently for longer periods of time.

Step 4: When working with a small reading group, sit facing students who are working independently in order to maximize monitoring. Use the timer until students no longer need it as a reminder.

Once students can independently work for 10 minutes, you can begin holding reading groups during that time. Sit facing the class with your all-seeing eye focused to catch any rule infractions. If you are successful in teaching your students to work independently, you should rarely need to say anything.

Step 5: Provide feedback and reward students for working independently

Always provide verbal feedback at the end of the independent work time and award points. When students reach second grade, a 20-minute stretch of independent work is realistic.

Step 6: Make adaptations for individual students if necessary

Even when you have followed all of these steps in teaching students to work independently, some students may still need a little extra structure. For example, if you have an extremely impulsive student who needs more monitoring, pull up a desk near you and have that student work in closer physical proximity to your booster group. The student can still earn the point for working, as long as he can follow the rules during the period that the timer is set.

Fact or Fiction

Fluency is the most neglected reading skill, especially as students get older. Perhaps because of this neglect, misconceptions about fluency appear frequently in the educational literature. This section lists Fact or Fiction questions regarding instruction in reading fluency for students at risk.

1. **Student ability to read passages correctly and fluently is highly related to scores on high stakes state tests of reading comprehension.**

   Fact   **Fiction**

   Fact. Given the current emphasis on accountability, schools are rightfully concerned about how their students perform on high stakes state reading tests. The assessments that teachers use to identify students who are at risk in reading and monitor their progress should be related to these high stakes tests. Only then can teachers be reasonably assured that they are identifying the right children for extra help and that the students receiving extra support are progressing along a path that leads to meeting state standards. Some educators claim that many students who perform well on assessments of oral reading fluency are "word callers," or students who read words accurately and fluently, but without understanding what they are reading. Thus, the question of how students who perform well on tests of oral reading fluency perform on state tests of reading comprehension is important and legitimate.

   Good (2002) studied the reading performance of a group of third-grade students from the state of Oregon and found that of 91 students who attained benchmark levels of 110 words correct per minute in oral reading fluency in May of grade 3, 90 students, or 99%, met standards on the Oregon Statewide Assessment Test (OSAT). Of the 23 students scoring below 70 words correct per minute, only 4 students, or 17% of the students, met state standards. Like all state tests, students had to answer comprehension questions and respond to reading material in order to pass the Oregon test. Thus, almost every student who could read fluently also had high levels of comprehension. This study, along with other comparable studies, demonstrates that the vast majority of students who can fluently read are also comprehending what they are reading and that the "word caller" phenomenon is not as prevalent as commonly thought.

   That said, students who are at risk still need explicit systematic instruction in vocabulary and comprehension. Specific strategies for teaching vocabulary and reading comprehension are described in Chapters 6 and 7.

2. **In beginning reading, it is not necessary to correct student errors in oral passage reading when those errors retain the meaning of the passage.**

   Fact   **Fiction**

   Fiction. Research cited by Adams (1991) indicates that when word identification is the objective, graphophonemic cues should be stressed. When students make an error during oral passage reading, regardless of whether it makes sense, the teacher should prompt them to look at the letters in the word and/or sound out the word. This correction discourages guessing by sending the message to learners that it is important to carefully read every word with high accuracy.

APPLIED ACTIVITIES

1. Use Tables 5.1 and 5.2 to identify which of the following students' May oral reading fluency scores are at benchmark:

Marissa	2nd Grade ORF	=	65 wcpm
Phil	3rd Grade ORF	=	111 wcpm
Zion	1st Grade ORF	=	36 wcpm
Sean	4th Grade ORF	=	112 wcpm
Grayson	1st Grade ORF	=	61 wcpm
Mario	2nd Grade ORF	=	93 wcpm
Glenn	4th Grade ORF	=	122 wcpm
Jaquesia	3rd Grade ORF	=	101 wcpm
Jolynn	5th Grade ORF	=	129 wcpm
Christopher	4th Grade ORF	=	131 wcpm
Leroy	3rd Grade ORF	=	98 wcpm
Won Chui	2nd Grade ORF	=	82 wcpm
Tameka	1st Grade ORF	=	33 wcpm

2. Follow the directions in Appendix A and replicate Misou's ORF progress chart.

3. A third-grade student, Juan, read 62 wcpm on the DORF he took during the first week of September. When he was retested 6 weeks later, his teacher, Mr. Staley, used the rate of *expected weekly growth* chart to determine whether Juan's score of 75 wcpm showed progress similar to a typically successful child in third grade. What did Mr. Staley find?

4. Because Ruben, a first grader, is behind his peers in oral reading fluency, Mrs. Wasmullen wants to make sure that his weekly gain in words read correctly per minute is at least at the "ambitious" level noted on the rate of expected weekly growth chart. If Ruben is reading 15 wcpm in January, how many words per minute should he be reading 10 weeks later to show a rate of progress at the ambitious level?

5. Latisha is a second-grade student in Ms. Carter's class. Latisha scored 45 words correct per minute on the January administration of the DIBELS Measure of Oral Reading Fluency. This score was well below the January benchmark of 68 words correct per minute. Describe the steps Ms. Carter needs to take as she uses *repeated readings* to build Latisha's fluency.

6. In December, Sara's third-grade teacher gave her three passages to read aloud, in order to assess her fluency. On the first passage, Sara made nine errors, reading a total of 83 words; on the second passage, Sara made 10 errors, reading a total of 67 words; on the third passage, Sara made eight errors, reading a total of 94 words. What was Sara's median oral reading fluency score? Based on these results, what areas of concern would you have? What other assessment that you have learned about in this book would you also give to Sara and why?

7. Form a group with three other students from your class, select a page from this book, and take turns conducting a SAFER reading group using the format from Table 5.4. One person in the group should be designated to miss three words. After each person has a turn teaching the group, give feedback on how closely he followed the format. Was the error correction procedure followed? Was the pace perky? Were turns between 1 and 3 sentences? Did you write missed words so you could practice them after the reading?

8. Select three sequential reading lessons from a first-grade regular education reading curriculum and develop a guide sheet for each lesson to accompany that day's lesson. Use the adapted lesson guide in Figure 5.12 as your model to identify critical reading skills.

9. Mr. Orcutt is a second-grade teacher. In December he noticed that many of his students were below the aim line for reading at grade level by the end of the year. He decided to set aside 15 to 20 minutes every day for fluency activities. As of Friday, his students read the 26-page story *Brave as a Mountain Lion* with 97% accuracy. Develop a week's worth of lesson plans for the fluency portion of his reading period based on his teaching 26 pages about mountain lions. How many pages will students read for fluency development? Will they practice fluency activities with the same or different pages every day? Adjust your plans so you are prepared to account for student success or failure.

10. *First Step:* Make a progress chart for Janelle who is a fourth grader. Include a benchmark line and an aim line based on her September assessment. Use the following information to get her started:

    You plan to give Janelle an ORF assessment in September, November, January, and May. Her first score in September is 80 wcpm. She is a relatively accurate reader, missing only two words.

    Second Step: Once you have developed the Progress Chart, fill in the following information:

    Janelle's November score was 89 wcpm; her January score was 88 wcpm; and her May score was 102 wcpm. All of her readings continue to show a high rate of accuracy.

Third Step: Determine whether Janelle met the fourth-grade benchmark. Was there any point during the year when you would have recommended more support for Janelle? If so, describe in detail what type of support you would have provided. What Tier placement provides appropriate support based on the ORF scores?

11. Break up into groups of three and discuss your experiences learning a foreign language. When you read aloud in the foreign language, how did your prosody and speed compare with that in English? When you spoke the language you were learning, how did your fluency compare to your everyday language? Did any teaching techniques that the foreign language teacher used help you become more fluent? What were some strategies that the foreign language teacher could have used to help your prosody?

12. Identify which error pattern each of the following students display. Also describe what teaching format from the text that you would use to remediate.

a. Dasia was reading grade 2 passages and missed the following words (What Dasia said is in parentheses)

couch (cook)	round (ruined)
sound (send)	ground (grinned)

b. Esmerelda is a third grade student who is unable to read even grade 1 level material accurately and fluently. Her most recent score on DIBELS NWF was 37. Esmerelda still confuses long and short vowels.

c. Ramona scored at the benchmark level of 110 on grade 3 material. However, when she reads she fails to address punctuation, and reads with little intonation.

REFERENCES

Adams, H. (1990). *Beginning to read: Thinking and learning about print.* Cambridge, MA: MIT Press.

Adams, M. J. (1998). The three-cueing system. In F. Lehr and J. Osborn (Eds.), *Literacy for all issues in teaching and learning* (pp. 73–99). New York: Guilford Press.

Archer, A. L., Gleason, M. M., & Vachon, V. L. (2003). Decoding and fluency: Foundation skills. *Learning Disability Quarterly: Journal of the Division for Children with Learning Disabilities, 26*(2), 89.

Armbruster, B., Lehr, F., & Osborn, J. (2001). *Put reading first: The research building blocks for teaching children to read.* Washington, DC: Partnership for Reading.

Avery, P., & Ehrlich, S. (1992). *Teaching American English pronunciation.* New York: Oxford Press. p. 48.

Bursuck, B., Smith, T., Munk, D., Damer, M., Mehlig, L., & Perry, J. (in press). Evaluating the impact of a prevention-based model of reading on children who are "at-risk." *Remedial and Special Education,* December 2004.

Carnine, D. W., Silbert, J., Kame'enui, E. J., & Tarver, S. (2004). *Direct instruction reading* (4th ed.). New Jersey: Merrill Prentice Hall.

Celce-Murcia, M., et al. (1996). *Teaching pronunciation: A reference for teachers of English to speakers of other languages.* New York: Cambridge University Press.

Cowie, R., Douglas-Cowie, E., & Wichmann, A. (2002). Prosodic characteristics of skilled reading: Fluency and expressiveness in 8–10-year-old readers. *Language and Speech, 45*(1), 47–82.

Crawford, D. (May, 2004). (personal communication).

Deno, S. L. (1985). Curriculum-based measurement: The emerging alternative. *Exceptional Children, 52*(3), 219–232.

Dowhower, S. (1991). Speaking of prosody: Fluency's unattended bedfellow. *Theory Into Practice, 30*(3), 165–175.

Feldman, K. (1999). The California Reading Initiative and Special Education in California developed by the Special Education Reading Task Force. Retrieved from: www.calstat.org/leadershipinstitute/powerpoints/5. California Department of Education, Sacramento, CA.

Fuchs, L. S., Fuchs, D., Hosp, M. K., & Jenkins, J. R. (2001). Oral reading fluency as an indicator of reading competence: A theoretical, empirical, and historical analysis. *Scientific Studies of Reading, 5*(3), 239–256.

Fuchs, L. S., Fuchs, D., & Maxwell, L. (1988). The validity of informal reading comprehension measures. *Remedial and Special Education,* 20–29.

Greene, J. (1998). Another Chance: Help for older students with limited literacy. *American Educator,* Spring/Summer, 1.

Good, R. (April 12, 2002). *Catching kids before they fall: What schools can do.* Presentation at the Illinois Branch of The International Dyslexia Association, Lincolnwood, Illinois.

Good, R. H., Simmons, D., & Kame'enui, E. (2001). The importance and decision-making utility of a continuum of fluency-based indicators of foundational reading skills for third-grade high-stakes outcomes, *Scientific Studies of Reading, 5*(3), 257–288.

Good, R. H., Simmons, D., Kame'enui, E. A., & Wallin, J. (2002). *Summary of decision rules for intensive, strategic, and benchmark instruction recommendations in kindergarten through third grade* (Technical Report No. 11). Eugene, OR: University of Oregon.

Hasbrouck, J. E., & Tindal, G. (1992). Curriculum-based oral reading fluency norms for students in grades 2 through 5. *Teaching Exceptional Children, 24*(3), 41–44.

Hempenstall, K. (1999). Miscue analysis: A critique. *Effective School Practices, 17*(3), 85–93.

Murray, B. (1999). *Developing Reading Fluency. The Reading Genie.* Auburn University. Retrieved from: www.auburn.edu/~murraba/.

National Reading Panel (2000). *Teaching children to read: An evidence-based assessment of the scientific research literature on reading and its implications for reading instruction.* Washington, DC: National Institute of Child Health and Human Development.

Pany, D., & McCoy, K. M. (1988). Effects of corrective feedback on word accuracy and reading comprehension of readers with learning disabilities. *Journal of Learning Disabilities, 21,* 546–550.

Rasmussen, D., & Goldberg, L. (2000). *A King on a Swing.* SRA, Columbus, Ohio, 73.

Samuels, S. (1997). The method of repeated readings. *The Reading Teacher, 50,* 376–381.

Shaywitz, S. (2003). *Overcoming dyslexia: A new and complete science-based program for reading problems at any level.* New York: Alfred A. Knopf.

Sibley, D., Biwer, D., & Hesch, A. (2001). *Unpublished Data.* Arlington Heights, IL: Arlington Heights School District 25. [On-line.] Available: www.aimsweb.com/_lib/pdfs/ORF_Benchmarks.pdf

Stanovich, K. E. (1986). Matthew Effects in reading: Some consequences of individual differences in the acquisition of literacy. *Reading Research Quarterly, 21,* 360–407.

Tindal, G., & Marston, D. (1996). Technical adequacy of alternative reading measures as performance assessments. *Exceptionality, 6,* 201–230.

Wolf, M., & Katzir-Cohen, T. (2001). Reading fluency and its intervention [Special Issue on Fluency]. *Scientific Studies of Reading, 5,* 211–238.

Wood, A., & Wood, D. (1985). *King Bidgood's in the Bathtub.* New York: Harcourt Brace Jovanovich.

6 Vocabulary Instruction

Key Terms

Diagnostic assessments

Figurative meaning

Hypertext

Idiom

Keyword method

Literal meaning

Matthew Effect

Modeling

Narrow reading

Nonexample

Outcome assessments

Overgeneralize

Screening assessments

Semantic mapping

Objectives

After reading this chapter, you will be able to:

1. Provide a rationale for teaching vocabulary to children who are at risk.

2. Identify the key components of an effective vocabulary curriculum.

3. Use assessments to diagnose student vocabulary needs.

4. State guidelines for deciding which vocabulary words to teach.

5. Implement strategies for teaching new vocabulary directly using examples, synonyms, definitions, keywords, and semantic maps.

6. Implement strategies to teach students to decipher the meaning of words independently by using contextual analysis, morphemic analysis, and the dictionary.

7. Describe strategies for teaching vocabulary to English language learners.

8. Describe strategies for teaching vocabulary to older students.

9. Describe ways to facilitate student practice of newly learned vocabulary words.

In Chapters 2 through 5 you learned how to teach students to read accurately and fluently. While accurate, fluent reading is necessary for reading with understanding, it is not sufficient. Students also need to know the meanings of the words they are reading. As students move into reading third- and fourth-grade level text, a larger percentage of your instruction will shift toward teaching students to comprehend increasingly difficult text. Their success in understanding text hinges on knowing the meanings of the words they now can decode. In Chapter 6 you will learn about the key role that vocabulary instruction plays in reading.

Both decoding and comprehension are easier when students have an extensive vocabulary. If students already know the meaning of a word they can blend words more readily after reading the individual parts, particularly for multisyllable words. For example, Alex was trying to read the word *hilarious.* He was able to read the regular parts /hil/ and /ous/. He then began to try different sounds for the irregular vowels in the middle of the word. After trying several sounds, he was able to make the connection between his oral knowledge of the word *hilarious* and the written word *hilarious* because the word was part of his oral vocabulary. Of course Alex's previous knowledge of the word *hilarious* could have also helped him decode the word using context clues. At this level of reading, decoding, vocabulary knowledge, and context clues enable the reader to quickly and accurately read the new word.

Knowledge of vocabulary is also important for reading comprehension. As students learn to decode text of increasing difficulty, they are more likely to encounter words that are not part of their oral language, especially when reading expository text. As a result, students often need instruction in key vocabulary to make sense of what they are reading.

Often a significant gap in vocabulary knowledge separates students who are at risk from their classmates. A large percentage of students who are at risk start school with considerably smaller vocabularies. Some of these differences are attributed to poverty. Before entering school, young students whose parents have jobs categorized as "professional" can be exposed to twice as many words as students whose parents are on welfare; 50% more words than students whose parents are considered "blue collar"(Hart & Risley, 1995). Children from poverty are more likely to have less time and fewer opportunities for speaking, listening to conversation, and listening to stories read aloud. Students who come from households where English is not the first language may be just beginning to develop skills in learning and understanding English. For other students, speech and communication problems may increase the difficulty in learning more abstract words. Louisa Moats described this gap in vocabulary knowledge as "word poverty," estimating that students who enter grade 1 with linguistic advantages, know approximately 20,000 words while those who are linguistically disadvantaged only know about 5,000 words (Moats, 2001).

During the school day, students learn vocabulary in two ways: directly and indirectly. Because the majority of words are acquired indirectly through independent reading, when students lack the reading accuracy and fluency necessary to engage in high levels of independent reading, this source of vocabulary enrichment is closed off to them. Stanovich (1986) described the rapidly widening gap between students who read independently and those who don't as the **Matthew Effect,** loosely translated as "the rich get richer and the poor get poorer." Students who read more learn more vocabulary words and acquire more background knowledge. In contrast, students who have reading problems often find reading so frustrating that they develop attitudinal problems and rarely or never choose to read independently. One research study showed that students who read independently for just ten minutes per day experienced higher rates of vocabulary growth than students who did very little independent reading (Jitendra et al., 2004). Reading problems may in turn spawn attitudinal problems, so that many students who are at risk rarely or never choose to read independently because the experience of reading is so frustrating. In addition to independent reading, listening to books and participating in daily conversation are two main sources for indirect vocabulary acquisition during the school day.

Students who are at risk are also unlikely to strategically use context clues to learn the meaning of vocabulary words on their own (Pany, Jenkins, & Schreck, 1982). In order to use context clues to figure out unknown words when reading or listening, students must understand the meaning of at least 95% of the words in the communication. When students with limited vocabularies do not understand basic story words such as *pal, branches, barn,* or *choose,* they are unlikely to figure out the meanings of more challenging words introduced in a new story or an explanation of a story related by the teacher.

While this lack of vocabulary knowledge accounts for many of the increased challenges behind teaching students who are at risk, it does not present an insurmountable obstacle. Vocabulary, like fluency, is too often ignored as part of ongoing reading instruction, despite the fact that it can be taught directly. Research shows that students who are at risk learn new words at the same rate as other students if they are directly taught vocabulary in school. The challenge lies in catching them up to their peers by increasing that rate of learning. Only a teacher-directed curriculum emphasizing vocabulary has a chance at bridging the gap (Biemiller, 2001). Students need to be taught the meanings of some words directly, and they must be taught how to figure out words on their own using context, morphemic analysis, and the dictionary. In this chapter, strategies for assessing vocabulary knowledge and selecting and teaching essential vocabulary words are described.

> Learn more about the research support behind effective vocabulary instruction at this website: **http://idea.uoregon. edu/~ncite/documents/techrep/ tech13.html.**

What Vocabulary Words Do I Choose for Instruction?

Teaching vocabulary explicitly and systematically takes time and effort, both in planning and teaching. Because of the time and effort involved in teaching vocabulary, the number of words that can be taught directly is limited. It is estimated that teachers can realistically teach 300 words per year, which translates to about 8 to 10 per week (Armbruster, Lehr, & Cohen, 2001).

Armbruster and colleagues (2001) suggest that you should teach your students three kinds of words: important words, useful words, and difficult words. Important words are words that students need to know to understand the particular text they are reading. Useful words are high frequency words that the students are likely to see repeatedly in their reading. Difficult words are words that are hard for students to understand such as words that have multiple meanings; these are words that are either spelled the same but pronounced differently, such as *invalid* (not true), or *invalid* (weak or ill); or are spelled and pronounced the same, but have different meanings, such as *catch,* as in *catch* a ball, *catch* a cold, *catch* someone's attention, and so on.

Consider Mr. Halpern, who was selecting words to prepare his students to read the story "The Golden Goose" (Open Court, *Collections for Young Scholars,* 1995). The following words were underlined by the publisher as being possible vocabulary words: *Simpleton, cider, jug, feasted, inn, innkeeper, sexton, hayfields, pastor, cellar, disappeared,* and *court.* Mr. Halpern decided to spend two days preparing his students to read the story. He knew that realistically he could present no more than two words per day, so he had to decide which four words he would teach his Grade 2 students directly. He eliminated *cider* and *jug* because he felt that these were common words that his students would already know. He decided not to teach *inn* and *innkeeper* because he felt these words could be easily figured out from their context. Mr. Halpern made a mental note to make sure and include these terms in his questions after the story reading. He eliminated *pastor* and *sexton* because these words were not common and were not important for the meaning of the story. He wasn't sure whether his students, who were from the city, would know *hayfields,* but he decided not to teach it anyway because it was not important for the meaning of the story. Mr. Halpern settled on *Simpleton,* because *Simpleton* was the main character and the personal qualities that led him to be called *Simpleton* were important for the meaning of the story. Mr. Halpern also decided to teach *disappeared* and *feasted* because these were high frequency words. *Court* was the fourth word he opted to teach because it was high frequency and with its multiple meanings would be difficult.

In the process of deciding how to teach specific vocabulary, you need to recognize that an individual's reading vocabulary, speaking vocabulary, and listening vocabulary are not the same and that principles that apply to one do not necessarily apply to the other. Naturally, in this book, our main focus is reading vocabulary, although effective teaching of vocabulary also involves speaking vocabulary, listening vocabulary, and writing vocabulary. A teacher reading a book about volcanoes to students is enriching their listening vocabularies when emphasizing *lava* and *cinders*. Later when students use those terms to describe the papier-mâché volcanoes they made, they are engaging their speaking vocabularies. When those same students read a story about a child whose eyes are tearing from a *cinder* as she runs down the mountain attempting to escape the *lava* flow, the words are becoming part of their reading vocabulary. If the teacher makes *lava* one of the week's spelling words and assigns students to write a paragraph about how they would escape a lava flow in their town, that word is used in their writing vocabulary. Because research indicates that for increased comprehension, students need at least 12 encounters with a new word, teachers cannot afford to miss opportunities to teach vocabulary in a variety of contexts throughout the school day (McKeowon, Beck, Omanson, & Pople, 1985).

How Do I Assess My Students' Vocabulary Knowledge?

Vocabulary assessment presents more challenges than other assessments previously discussed in this book. The assumption behind vocabulary testing is that the more words on a test that students identify, the larger their vocabulary. Because only a small sample of words represent the thousands of possible vocabulary words for an assessment, the words selected have to represent a wide body of knowledge. The first question teachers should ask when assessing vocabulary is whether the test provides information on the intended vocabulary they want to test. A vocabulary assessment where students name pictures or provide definitions for words is assessing their speaking vocabulary, whereas a multiple choice assessment where students circle the correct definition of words is assessing their reading vocabulary. Next, teachers should ask if the test is testing vocabulary or some other skill. On a multiple choice assessment, students who know the meaning of the words but cannot decode many of them will be penalized for reading mistakes. Their low score may reflect a decoding deficit rather than limited vocabulary.

Teachers also need to determine whether the vocabulary assessment is testing expressive vocabulary by requiring the students to actively write or say the word or definition. Because students' receptive vocabulary is usually higher than their expressive vocabulary, they will often get higher scores on assessments where they only have to select an answer from ones that are provided. A final concern related to vocabulary assessment is the time that it can take in contrast to the other brief assessments discussed thus far in this book. Some of the tests have to be given individually to each student for between 10 to 20 minutes. If the teacher has no support to help assess students, classroom instructional time can be compromised.

In 2002, the Institute for the Development of Educational Achievement (IDEA) analyzed reading assessments for kindergarten through third grade. The Institute's final report identified only the most rigorous tests which had research support indicating that they had high validity (meaningful) and reliability (accuracy and consistency). Assessments for screening, diagnostic testing, progress monitoring, and outcome assessment were included for each of the main areas identified by the National Panel Reading Report. Figure 6.1 describes these assessments for vocabulary including test recommendations for each type.

Screening assessments are brief tests conducted at the start of the school year and designed as a first step in identifying students who may be at a high risk for delayed development or academic failure in the tested skill area. Further diagnostic evaluation is needed for students who have difficulty with a screening assessment in order to determine whether they need extra or alternative instruction.

1. **Peabody Picture Vocabulary Test–3rd Edition (PPVT-3)** This assessment is designed as a measure of receptive language and is individually administered.

2. **Texas Primary Reading Inventory (TPRI): Listening Comprehension** During this individually administered assessment, the child answers questions about a story that has just been read aloud.

Diagnostic Assessments are longer and more in-depth assessments that provide detailed information about a student's skills and instructional needs. They help the teacher plan effective instructional support if needed.

1. **Iowa Test of Basic Skills (ITBS)** ITBS includes language, listening, and vocabulary subtests. This test can be administered to a group or individually. On the vocabulary portion of the test, picture-word matching is used for K and 1 and word definitions for grades 1 and 2. In grades K and 1, the words are presented orally; in grades 1 and 2, the words are presented in writing.

2. **Test of Word Knowledge (TOWK)** This assessment is individually administered to students.

   Level 1 Subtests

   > **Expressive Vocabulary**–students name pictures that represent nouns and verbs
   > **Receptive Vocabulary**–students select pictures that represent specific words
   > **Word Definitions**–students describe definitions of words
   > **Word Opposites**–students match words with their antonyms
   > **Synonyms Subtests**–students match words with their synonyms

   Level 2 Subtests Figurative Usage, Multiple Contexts, Synonyms, Word Definitions, Conjunctions and Transition Words, and Word Opposites

3. **Texas Primary Reading Inventory (TPRI)** Listening Comprehension (see screening assessments)

4. **Wechsler Individual Achievement Test–II (WIAT-II)** This assessment is individually administered to students.

   Listening Comprehension–includes multiple-choice matching of pictures to spoken words or sentences and replying with one word to a picture and a dictated clue

   Oral Expression–includes repeating sentences, generating lists of specific kinds of words, describing pictured scenes, and describing pictured activities

---

Outcome Assessments: Year-end assessments that identify whether students achieved grade-level performance in the area tested.

1. **Iowa Test of Basic Skills (ITBS)** Language, listening, and vocabulary subtests (see diagnostic tests)

2. **Stanford Achievement Test–9th Editions (SAT-9)** This is a group or individually administered assessment

   Listening Comprehension–assessed with selections and questions that reflect the kinds of real-life listening material that students are confronted with, including stories, poems, instructional material, directions, advertisements, and announcements.

   Reading Vocabulary–This subtest assesses three kinds of vocabulary. Students select synonyms, differentiate between multiple meanings of a word, and use context clues to determine the meaning of words.

3. **Test of Word Knowledge (TOWK)** (see diagnostic tests)

4. **Wechsler Individual Achievement Test–II (WIAT-II)** (see diagnostic assessments)

5. **Woodcock Reading Mastery Test–Revised (WRMT-R)**

   Word comprehension–On this individually administered subtest the child provides synonyms, antonyms, and analogies.

FIGURE 6.1 Vocabulary Assessments

Source: Adapted from: Kame'enui, E., Francis, D., Fuchs, L., Good, R., O'Connor, R., Simmons, D., Tindal, G., & Torgesen, J. (2002). *An analysis of reading assessment instruments for K–3*. Institute for the Development of Educational Achievement, University of Oregon, http://idea.uoregon.edu/assessment/

What Methods Do I Use to Teach Key Vocabulary Words?

Once you have selected the key words in a story, the next step is to decide whether to teach the word directly or indirectly. Direct teaching of vocabulary involves teaching students the meaning of vocabulary using examples, synonyms, definitions, and graphic organizers. Indirect methods include teaching students to use strategies such as context clues, morphemic analysis, or dictionary usage so that they can figure out the meaning of a word on their own. Strategies for teaching students vocabulary both directly and indirectly are described in this section.

Selecting Examples for Direct Instruction of Vocabulary

Ms. Vetrano was a kindergarten teacher in an at-risk school who was teaching her students the color *red.* She showed her students the following examples of red: red play dough, red car, a doll with a red dress on, and a red ball. Ms. Vetrano then pointed to her red dress and asked the children if it was an example of *red.* Most of the children answered, "No." Ms. Vetrano then pointed to a blue ball and asked whether it was *red,* and this time many students replied, "Yes." Frustrated by her students' lack of basic knowledge, Ms. Vetrano might shrug, and blame the parents or preschool for not getting her students ready for kindergarten. She might also attribute the lack of learning to the students having a bad day or the moon being full. However, a close look at Ms. Vetrano's examples shows that her students were simply responding based on the examples they were given. First, Ms. Vetrano taught the concept of red using only examples that were toys. Selecting play dough, a toy car, a doll and a ball for examples probably gave her students the false impression that only toys could be red. When she pointed to her red dress and asked the students whether it was red, the students didn't think so because her dress wasn't a toy. Logically, the students now believed that if something wasn't a toy, it couldn't be red. Ms. Vetrano could have improved her teaching of *red* by using a greater range of red things as examples: red clothes, red books, red crayons, etc.

Another problem with Ms. Vetrano's examples surfaced when students answered her second question. After her instruction, students thought that all toys were red because all of the examples used were red toys. Because children tend to **overgeneralize** or draw too general a conclusion, Ms. Vetrano needed to prevent this error by showing the students **nonexamples** that were also toys. For example, after showing the students a red ball, she could have shown them a blue ball and said that it was *not* red. Similarly, she could have shown other toys of a different color and explained that they weren't red either. Ms. Vetrano's lesson on teaching red demonstrates the importance of example selection when directly teaching the meaning of vocabulary. Unless teaching examples and nonexamples are selected carefully, students may reach the wrong conclusions about the vocabulary you are teaching. To avoid these errors, always use a range of positive examples to broaden the concept being taught, as well as at least two nonexamples to rule out overgeneralizations.

Teaching Vocabulary by Modeling

When teaching vocabulary to younger students whose limited language makes it unlikely that they will understand verbal explanations, **model** examples and nonexamples as you directly teach the word. For example, if you were teaching the meaning of *next to,* you could not verbally explain this vocabulary term without showing the position of one object next to another as you said the phrase. For one of your examples you might put a book *next to* the wall. You might choose to move a chair *next to* the desk. You might stand *next to* a student. Each time you said the new vocabulary term, you would demonstrate, so that students could physically see the placement of the object. Modeling also helps you teach concepts that are difficult to define such as *plaid,* a concept that can only be explained by presenting visual examples.

When using this technique to directly teach vocabulary, the teacher first models a series of positive examples and nonexamples of the new vocabulary word or concept. When Ms. Robertson was teaching the adverb *slowly* to her kindergarten students, she modeled the following examples and nonexamples. During her demonstration she said the key word with extra emphasis, to be certain that students' attention was on that word.

1. Mrs. Robertson walked very slowly in the front of the room and said, "I am walking *slowly.*"
2. She then wrote the name of a student in the class very slowly on the board and said, "I am writing *slowly.*"
3. She also waved goodbye very slowly and said, "I am waving goodbye *slowly.*"
4. Next, she ran quickly in place and said, "I am *not* walking *slowly.*"
5. Finally, she quickly wrote a student's name on the board using exaggerated speed and said, "I am *not* writing *slowly.*"

After presenting examples and nonexamples, Mrs. Robertson then tested how well students knew the examples just presented. For this phase of the teaching process, Mrs. Robertson walked slowly in front of the room and asked, "Am I walking *slowly* or *not slowly*?" After students answered correctly, she wrote a name slowly on the board and asked, "Am I writing *slowly* or *not slowly*?"

Once students can accurately answer the structured testing questions, the teacher asks the students to decide whether to say the new word or other review vocabulary words in response to open-ended questions.

When Mrs. Robertson reached this part of the lesson, she wrote a name slowly on the board and asked, "How am I writing?" The students who knew to use the key vocabulary term in their responses, answered, "slowly." Mrs. Robertson then ran fast in place and asked the students, "How am I running?" The students responded with the word *quickly,* a review word covered the previous week. If they had not already learned that term, they probably would have answered, "not slowly." Each time students answered the question, they had the opportunity to practice saying the new vocabulary term.

Some teachers who want to emphasize oral language in their classroom expect their students to answer vocabulary questions in complete sentences. In these cases, students would answer, "No you are not walking slowly," or "Yes, you are walking slowly." The more opportunities students have to say the word, the greater the likelihood that it will become a permanent part of their vocabulary. A general teaching format for vocabulary that can be used for modeling is shown in Table 6.1.

When you use this format to directly teach vocabulary asking students to answer in unison, you have substantially increased the active practice opportunities for saying the new word at least five times in one quick session. Follow these guidelines when developing your questions for modeling as well as for the synonym and definition formats that follow.

Guidelines for Developing Vocabulary Questions

Use the Names of Your Students in Your Examples Whenever Possible   Using the names of real students can be very motivating. Also, integrating students' names into examples that are specifically tied to their lives in some way is a good way of tapping into your students' background knowledge.

TABLE 6.1   Teaching Vocabulary Through Modeling

Outcome	Given 3 examples and 3 nonexamples of the new word, the students will say whether each is an example or nonexample, telling how they knew the answer, with 100% accuracy.
Materials Needed	Preparation for this activity includes selection of words. If objects are used for modeling, they should be readily available so instruction does not lag. Either pre-write the questions you will ask or jot notes about the questions on a sheet you can use for reference.
Signaling	Depending on the word, you will use one of these signals: Signal 1: Use fingersnaps/handclaps to signal a unison response for your questions. Signal 2: Use a loop signal if asking a question about a picture.
Time	Between 2 and 5 minutes per word.
Rationale	Knowledge of vocabulary is important for reading comprehension.
Tips	■ Although you will ask for unison answers during this activity, often you will want to ask individual students to answer *why* and *how do you know* questions, which have longer answers. ■ Animate your questions with gestures and emotion related to the scenario. ■ Always phrase questions so students have the opportunity to say the vocabulary word. Rather than answering with a simple "no," expect students to answer, "not (*vocabulary word*)."

Instructions	**Teacher**	**Student**
	1. Advance Organizers	
	2. My Turn	
	■ If modeling a word, show students three positive examples and three nonexamples of the word. If teaching the word *eyebrow,* point to your eyebrow and say, "This is an eyebrow." For a nonexample, you might point to Jason's foot and say, "This is not an eyebrow."	
	3. Your Turn Ask students direct questions about the vocabulary word related to positive and negative examples. Intermix your type of questions. Students should answer 6 questions correctly before moving on to the next step.	
	■ If modeling the word *eyebrow,* you might point to Shondra's chin and ask this nonexample question, **"Is this an eyebrow or not an eyebrow?"** You might point to Kendra's eyebrow and ask this example question, **"Is this an eyebrow or not an eyebrow?"**	not an eyebrow an eyebrow
	4. Review of previously learned words (example- and nonexample-based questions) interspersed with questions about the new word.	
	5. Individual Student Checkout Ask two or three students to answer questions about the new word and/or review words.	

Error Correction	If students make an error, immediately return to a My Turn–Your Turn pattern. Later in the lesson ask students about the word they missed to provide more practice. Only use a "Together" if students have difficulty pronouncing the vocabulary word and could use the practice saying it with you.
Perk up Your Drill	■ The use of students' names and the names of other staff in the building is motivating to students. ■ Students are motivated by humorous questions and examples. They especially like absurd questions. ■ Relate questions to events that have occurred in school life.

TABLE 6.1 Continued

Adaptations	■ If you expect students to answer in complete sentences, get them into the habit of consistently answering in this way. In the beginning, some classes will answer in a complete sentence if after they answer in one or two words, you simply ask them, "Tell me in a complete sentence." In other classes where students have fewer language skills, in the beginning you will need to model the complete sentence before they repeat it. If you are consistent in expecting a complete sentence, the students will soon learn the patterns so they can do that.
	■ You will want to use more "Togethers" with ESL students who could use practice articulating words.
	■ Make sure when you use your students' names that your questions do not reflect discriminatory stereotypes. For example, when asking questions about words related to feats of strength, use girls' names as well as boys' names.

Source: This script is based on one originally developed and field tested by Carnine, Silbert, Kame'enui, & Tarver (2004). *Direct instruction reading* (4th ed.). New Jersey, Merrill Prentice Hall.

> When she taught the vocabulary word *sniffing*, Ms. Carlstrom used the name of Titus, a student in her class who liked apple pie. "Titus loves apple pie. When he walked in the door of his house the other day, he did this (teacher makes a sniffing noise) thinking that his grandmother had made an apple pie. Was Titus sniffing or not sniffing?"
>
> "Tell me again what *sniffing* means."

End by Providing a Practice Opportunity

Even if the answer is "Not (vocabulary word)," give your student the opportunities to respond. Ms. Carlstrom used the following nonexample when she presented the word *sniffing*.

> "If a lion sounds like this (teacher makes a lion's roar) while he's chasing an elephant, is the lion *sniffing* or **not** *sniffing?*" Her students laughed as they answered, "not sniffing."

Reflect the Students' Lives with Relevant Questions

Construct your questions so they reflect experiences in the students' lives, material they are learning at school, or popular media they have seen or heard. One question Ms. Carlstrom asked connected her example of sniffing to a unit she was doing about sources of energy.

> "When Renauld went into his house, he did this (teacher makes a sniffing sound), because he thought he smelled natural gas, which has a smell when it is leaking. Was Renauld sniffing, or not sniffing?"

Use the Exact Vocabulary from the Story in Your Questions and as the "Correct" Responses

Always write your questions so students listen to and use the exact vocabulary word used in the story. If the past tense word is used in the text, ask your questions so that the students have to answer in the past tense. Many students who are at risk routinely do not use the past tense form of words in their conversations. Because the meaning of text is often affected by the tense of a verb, providing extra practice using past tense verbs should also improve students' accuracy comprehending text and writing about events that happened in the past. Sometimes the phrase "Tell me. . . ." can help with the phrasing of these questions.

> In all of the examples for the word *sniffing* just described, the students were required to answer with the word *sniffing*, as opposed to sniff or sniffed. If the word had instead been *sniffed*, Ms. Carlstrom would have stated her question like this: "Tell me whether I *sniffed*, or whether I did not *sniff.*"

Mix in *Why* Questions After Example and Nonexample Questions   Students' answers to *why* questions give you a good idea about whether they understand the meaning of the word. After Ms. Carlstrom was sure that her students knew the definition of *sniffing*, she asked a *why* question to gauge her students' understanding of the word:

> "This word is *sniffing*. What's the word?"
>
> "*Sniffing* means smelling with short breaths. What does *sniffing* mean?"
>
> "Watch me. (Make a sniffing noise.) Was I *sniffing* or *not sniffing?*"
>
> "Why do you say that?"

Using Synonyms to Teach New Vocabulary Directly

In this teaching strategy, teachers use a known word to teach students an unknown word having the same meaning. For example, if students don't know the meaning of the word *residence,* but know the meaning of *home, home* can be used to teach *residence.* Let's look at how a teacher uses synonyms to teach the meaning of a new word:

> Mr. Gilman first told his students, "A residence is a home." He then proceeded to present a series of examples and nonexamples of residence. For example, he held up a photo of a house and asked, "This is a picture of Condy's home. Is it her residence or not her residence?" After his students answered, he asked, "Aquanetta went to the mall. Is the mall her residence, or not her residence? How do you know?" After six or seven examples and nonexamples, he moved into the next phases of his teaching and reviewed the new word *residence,* with other vocabulary words that students had learned the past few weeks. Mr. Gillman pointed to a picture of a hotel and asked, "Is this a *residence*? How do you know?"

A sample series of teaching examples for the word *timid* is shown in Figure 6.2.

Using Definitions to Teach New Vocabulary Directly

The first step in teaching vocabulary using definitions is to have a clear, understandable definition. In most cases you cannot select definitions straight from the dictionary without adapting them. Beck, McKeown, and Kukan (2002) point out that dictionary definitions are constructed primarily to meet space limitations. Because of this constraint, dictionary definitions can be vague and misleading. Consider the problems with these dictionary definitions as described by these authors.

> *Conspicuous:* easily seen
>
> *Typical:* being a type
>
> *Exotic:* foreign; strange; not native
>
> *Devious:* straying from the right course; not straightforward
>
> The definition for *conspicuous* fails to communicate that something can be easily seen, yet not be conspicuous. *Conspicuous* is something that pops out at you and that is not conveyed by the definition presented here. The definition for *typical* is so vague it sheds little light on what the word means. The definition for *exotic* includes three possible meanings but it is unclear whether all, some, or one have to be present for something to be exotic. The definition for *devious* could be easily misinterpreted. A young learner may conclude that *devious* has to do with crooked walking or getting lost. (Beck et al., 2002, p. 34)

Dictionary definitions may also contain difficult words that students may be unable to decode or may not know the meaning. Take, for example, the definition of *illusion:* a mistaken perception of reality. This definition includes a number of words that may be un-

---

Synonyms: Examples and nonexamples for teaching the word *timid*:

1. Before presenting examples and nonexamples, have students look at the word and repeat the synonym after you until they can easily say it:

   timid "*Timid* means easily frightened or shy. What does *timid* mean?"

2. Ask students questions based on examples and nonexamples of *timid*.

   ■ The new student was shy on the first day of school. Was the new student timid or not timid? How do you know?

   ■ Gabriel enjoys making everyone laugh. Is Gabriel timid or not timid? Why?

   ■ Sara is not afraid to talk in front of the class. Is Sara timid or not timid?

   ■ Marissa became easily frightened during the play and forgot her lines when she saw all the people in the audience. Did Marissa become timid or not timid? Why?

   ■ William is very friendly and outgoing. He can make friends with anyone. Is William timid or not timid?

   ■ A deer is a shy animal. Is a deer timid or not timid?

   ■ (Teacher makes a scared face with matching body posture.) Do I look timid or not timid?

   ■ On the first day of camp, Jorie was so afraid that she could hardly talk. Was Jorie timid or not timid? How do you know?

   ■ Lionel always raises his hand in class because he likes to explain the answer. Is Lionel timid or not timid? Why?

   ■ (Teacher swaggers around the room with an "I am cool look" on his face.) Do I look timid or not timid?

   ■ A robin will fly away as soon as a person comes close to it. Is a robin timid or not timid? Why?

   ■ A grizzly bear will growl and run after a human who is trying to escape from him. Is a grizzly bear timid or not timid? Why?

3. Ask students to tell you the definition for the word *timid* one more time. Ask review questions about previously learned words.

   ■ What does *timid* mean? What does *nonsense* mean? Kendra moved from Swan Hillman School to Lewis Lemon School when she was in first grade. Would you say that Kendra *transferred* or *did not transfer* schools?

FIGURE 6.2   Direct Teaching: Synonyms

Source: Adapted from Carnine, D. W., Silbert, J., Kame'enui, E. J., & Tarver, S. (2004). *Direct instruction reading* (4th ed.). New Jersey, Merrill Prentice Hall.

familiar to students, including *perception* and *reality*. The definition "to believe something is true when it is not" would be much easier to understand.

Sometimes the definitions provided in students' reading series are clearer than dictionary definitions, but there are no guarantees. Therefore, when using definitions to teach words, it is recommended that you write your own definitions or modify dictionary or basal definitions to make them more clear. Carnine and colleagues (2004) suggest a helpful strategy for writing a clear, comprehensive definition. They describe definitions as having two key elements: a small class to which the word belongs, and a statement of how the word differs from other members of the class. For example, take the word *sniffing*. Its class is *smelling,* and it differs from other ways of smelling because it is smelling using short breaths. Another example would be the word *south*. South is a direction (class) and it differs from

---

Teaching Definitions: Examples and nonexamples for teaching the word *permanent*

1. Before presenting examples and nonexamples, have students look at the word and repeat the definition after you. Say the definition slowly and with emphasis so students can easily repeat it. With more difficult definitions, you may need to inject some "Togethers" when teaching the definition. You and the students will repeat the definition together until they are able to say it by themselves.

   "Permanent means 'meant to last for a long time.' What does *permanent* mean?"

2. Ask students questions based on examples and nonexamples of *permanent*.

   - Molly bought an ice cream cone on a hot day. Is an ice cream cone permanent or not permanent? Why?

   - The Mayor of Chicago paid the artist, Pablo Picasso, to build a large concrete sculpture that sits in the plaza. Is the sculpture permanent or not permanent? Why?

   - Patrick put his old plastic action figures into a box when he left for college. The action figures are made out of strong plastic and will probably last until his grandchildren are old enough to play with them. Are these action figure toys permanent or not permanent? Why?

   - Stuart wrote a secret spy note to his friend on paper and told his friend to destroy it after reading the message. Is the note permanent or not permanent? Why?

   - After Maria's baby teeth fell out, new, larger teeth grew in her mouth. Maria's mother told her that if she brushed these new teeth every day, she would have them for the rest of her life. Were the new teeth permanent or not permanent? Why?

3. Ask students to tell you the definitions for the word one more time. Ask review questions.

   "Tell me one more time what *permanent* means?"

FIGURE 6.3   Direct Teaching: Definitions

Source: Adapted from Carnine, D. W., Silbert, J., Kame'enui, E. J., & Tarver, S. (2004). *Direct instruction reading* (4th ed.). New Jersey, Merrill Prentice Hall.

other directions in that it is the direction opposite north. Beck and colleagues (2002) suggest using student-friendly definitions that define words using everyday language. For example, taking the word *sniffing* that was just defined, a student-friendly definition might read: when someone is smelling something using short breaths. Another example of a student-friendly definition is this definition for the word *chores:* small jobs that have to be done every day or every week. Finally, consider this student-friendly definition for the word *recipe:* a set of directions for how to cook something.

Once your definition is developed, you can begin teaching your students the new vocabulary word. As you point to the word on the board, assess its readability and determine whether to ask students to read the word or tell them what it says. Next say the definition, having them repeat it after you. Then, present a series of examples and nonexamples in the form of questions. As suggested earlier, use at least two positive examples of the word, making sure these examples have enough range to prevent misconceptions, as well as two nonexamples to help students rule out inappropriate generalizations. Figure 6.3 lists examples and nonexamples for the word *permanent.* Your examples should be presented in an unpredictable order.

Using Semantic Maps to Teach New Vocabulary Directly

Semantic maps are visual representations of vocabulary that help students organize subject matter by having students categorize, label the categories, and discuss concepts related to a target word. The parts of the map are used to teach the class of words to which it belongs (What is it?), its characteristics (What is it like?), and some examples. A sample semantic map for *spider* is shown in Figure 6.4. When teaching the word *spider,* the teacher first presents the word to the students and places the word spiders into the center of the map. The teacher then presents some information about *spiders* by describing them to students, having students read from their texts, or view a video or DVD on spiders. If *spider* is a review word, the teacher skips the presentation of information and proceeds directly to constructing the map, asking students to supply the information, and providing support when they have forgotten details. Under the "What is it" category, the teacher writes the larger class of living things to which spiders belong as *arachnid.* When she asks students to describe "What it is like," the teacher helps students identify the characteristics of spiders: that they have eight legs, are up to 3 inches long, and eat insects or small vertebrae. Examples of spiders are then written. If the prior discussion went into more detail she might lead the students to list the individual spiders as being either *ground spiders* or *web spiders.* An effective followup activity is having students complete blank semantic maps of spiders as independent work in class or as homework.

Semantic maps can also be used to show the relationships between words. Note the "emotional map" developed by Barton (1996) for the word shown in Figure 6.5, and the horizontal map developed by Foil and Alber (2002) for the word *music* shown in Figure 6.6.

Using Keywords to Teach New Vocabulary Directly

The **keyword method** (Jitendra, Edwards, Sacks, & Jacobson, 2004) uses mnemonics to make vocabulary more meaningful to students and hence easier to understand and

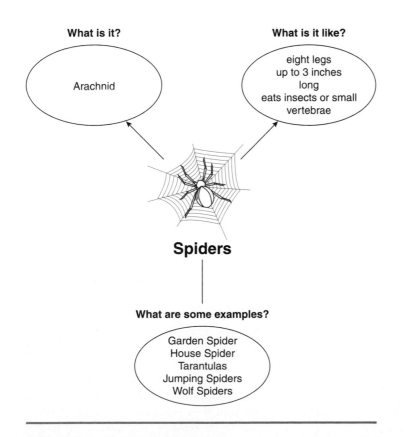

FIGURE 6.4 Semantic Map

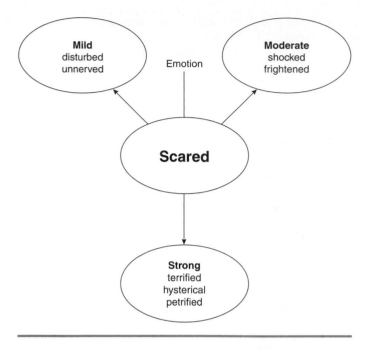

FIGURE 6.5 Emotional Word Web

Source: From Barton, J. (1996). Cited in H. W. Catts & A. G. Kamhi (2005), *Language and reading disabilities* (2nd ed.). Boston: Allyn & Bacon, p. 191.

FIGURE 6.6 Vertical and Horizontal Semantic Maps

Source: Foil, C. R. & Alber, S. R. (2002). Fun and effective ways to build your students' vocabulary. *Intervention in School and Clinic, 37*(3), p. 134.

remember. This method involves two key components, the keyword and a visual depiction of the vocabulary word. First the teacher selects a keyword that sounds similar to some part of the vocabulary word. The keyword should be familiar to the students, concrete, and easily pictured. For example, Mastropieri, Scruggs, and Fulk (1990) taught the word *apex,* meaning the highest point, by first associating it with the keyword *ape.* For the visual that ties together the keyword, *ape,* with the definition *apex,* Mastropieri and colleagues showed students a picture of an ape sitting on the highest point of a rock. Students were more apt to readily recall the definition of *apex* by thinking of the keyword (*ape*) and picturing that ape sitting on the highest point of a rock. An example of the keyword image for *apex* is shown below in Figure 6.7. The keyword method is most effective for students at risk when the keywords and corresponding visual image are generated by the teacher rather than the students (Bos & Vaughn, 1998).

FIGURE 6.7 Keyword for Apex

Using Context to Teach Independent Word-Learning Strategies

While the direct instruction of vocabulary is an essential part of reading instruction, students learn most new vocabulary on their own, through independent reading. Students who are at risk may be cut off from this rich source of vocabulary for a number of reasons. Certainly, problems with reading accuracy and fluency are the most serious impediments to independent

Seize the Teachable Moment

Teaching Vocabulary in Context

Chapter 3 presented the use of decodable books as a valuable practice activity for students who have yet to attain the alphabetic principle. Decodable books are an excellent vehicle for reading practice because the text is limited to words containing sounds the students know. Yet teachers often worry that the narrow word selection evident in decodable text limits student access to needed instruction in vocabulary. Beck and colleagues (2002) argue that this doesn't have to be the case; that even though the words themselves may be of little use in enriching students' vocabularies, the *ideas* in the stories can be characterized using words that are quite sophisticated.

For example, Ms. Falth's Tier 3 students were reading *Lad and The Fat Cat,* one of the Bob books (Scholastic, 1976), which are among the most basic decodable books. One of the pages shows a cat sitting in a box with the words, *The cat is Kit. Kit sat in a box.* After students read this page, Ms. Falth engaged them in a discussion about the word *independent.* She explained that cats were very *independent* and asked the students to say that word after her. Ms. Falth then explained that the word *independent* means doing things on your own—without any help. She said that cats are very independent and described ways that her cat at home was independent. She then asked her students to give examples from their own lives about independent cats. Ms. Falth then showed students the picture of the cat in the box and asked how they believed the cat felt about being in the box given their independent nature. Ms. Falth concluded the discussion by talking about things the students can or like to do independently.

Even when words are introduced prior to reading, students who are at risk may not remember them by the time they get to the word in context. While the meanings of new vocabulary are often taught before text is read, it sometimes helps comprehension to introduce the meaning of a word at the moment the word is encountered in the text. The word can then be integrated more readily into the context and provide strong support for comprehension. Beck and colleagues (2002) suggest several teaching strategies for introducing the meanings of words in context. One option is to give a simple explanation of the word or what it means in context.

For example, while reading the story *Coyote Places the Stars* (Taylor, 1997), Ms. Reed's students read this sentence:

Bears bounded out of their dens.

Ms. Reed told her students that bounded meant "jumped lightly along." When bears *bounded* out of their den, they jumped lightly along. She emphasized the past tense ending to the verb as she described the action. She further explained that the bears were bounding along because they were curious to see what the Coyote had done with the stars.

Another option for teaching new words when encountered in context is to provide support or a scaffold for helping the students figure out the word on their own from the words around it. Beck and colleagues (2002) describe this exchange between a teacher and students when they come upon the word *glimpse* while reading Roald Dahl's *Charlie and the Great Glass Elevator* (1972, p. 88).

Through the glass floor of the elevator, Charlie caught a quick glimpse *of the huge red roof and the tall chimneys of the giant factory. They were plunging straight down into it.*

Ms. T.: What do you think *glimpse* means?

Jen: Like a piece of something.

Ms. T.: A piece of something?

Jen: Yeah. I think a piece of the roof or the chimney came in and hit him.

Ms. T.: Oh, I see how you could get that idea. But glimpse means "a quick look at something, kind of a peek." So he was getting a quick look at the roof and chimney as the elevator fell. (Beck, 2002, p. 43)

Notice how Ms. T. stepped in to give the meaning of *glimpse,* allowing her to maintain a perky pace and not lose the attention of the rest of the students. Still, Ms. T. took the time to query Jen as to how she arrived at her answer. This simple questioning allowed Ms. T. to express understanding as to how Jen arrived at her answer, and, in so doing, was able to preserve Jen's dignity as a learner.

reading. Also, the meaning of vocabulary words is not always made accessible by authors whose primary intention is to tell a story or explain a phenomenon (Beck et al., 2002). Thus, reading to learn requires strategies that students who are at risk may lack. You need to systematically and explicitly teach these strategies just as you taught word-reading skills.

Using context clues to figure out the meaning of new words is one important independent vocabulary strategy students need to know. Ruddell (1999) has identified five types of context clues that can help students learn the meaning of new vocabulary within natural contexts. These are defined in Table 6.2 and include synonyms, definitions, antonyms, examples, and general clues. Learning to identify all of the various types of context clues is likely to be overwhelming for younger students so it may be more appropriate for older students (Baumann et al., 2003).

Teaching students to use context clues, especially when the context clues are definitions, examples, or more general clues is a difficult skill for beginning teachers who will need to preplan how to indirectly teach vocabulary this way. Later, when they have more experience, teachers learn how to more naturally teach these clues on-the-spot during the first reading of a story. Figure 6.8 provides an example format a teacher can use when teaching vocabulary words this way.

In this format, the teacher presents a small section of the passage that contains the new word as well as words before and after that word to help students figure out its meaning. In the example shown here, students are led to figure out the meaning of the word *logical.* They first read the passage, and then the targeted word, which is underlined. The teacher

TABLE 6.2   Types of Context Clues

Context Clue	Example
1. Definition	The author gives you a definition for the word *zenith* in the sentence.
	When the sun hits its **zenith,** which means *right overhead,* I could tell it was noon by the tremendous heat.
2. Synonym	The author uses another word that means about the same as the word you are trying to understand.
	Captain Jackson's uniform was **impeccable.** In fact, it was so *perfect* that she always had the highest score during inspection.
3. Antonym	The author uses another word that means the opposite or nearly the opposite of the word you are trying to understand.
	The soldier was very **intrepid** in battle, in contrast to the person next to him who was quite *cowardly.*
4. Example	The author gives you several words or ideas that are examples of the word you are trying to understand.
	Tigers, lions, panthers, and leopards are some of the most beautiful members of the **feline** family.
5. General	The author gives you some general clues to the meaning of a word, often spread over several sentences.
	Patriotism was a *very strong force* in the South. People *loved their part of the country* and were *very proud to be a Southerner.*

Note: In Context Clue Section, italicized words provide context clues for bold words.

Source: Baumann, J. F., Boland, E. M., Olejnik, S., & Kame'enui, E. J. (2003). Vocabulary tricks: Effects of instruction in morphology and context on fifth-grade students' ability to derive and infer word meanings. *American Educational Research Journal, 40(2),* 447–494.

1. Give students a short reading passage of several sentences that contain a vocabulary word you have decided to teach. Select a passage where context clues are provided in the text.

   Example: It was while he was serving in the Illinois legislature that Lincoln decided he'd like to study to become a lawyer. He had a lawyer's <u>logical</u> mind, and he had a special knack for proving his side of an argument. Step by step, he could lay out the facts in a clear and uncomplicated way until soon enough he'd have everyone convinced.

2. Ask one student to read the passage before identifying the underlined word.

   Teacher: **"Kyle, read this passage about Lincoln."**

3. Ask another student(s) to find either the synonym or the definition of the underlined word in the passage.

   Teacher: **"How did Lincon prove his side of an argument, Cyndie?"**

   Cyndie: "Step-by-step he laid out the facts in a clear and uncomplicated way."

   Teacher: **"Yes, Lincoln explained all of the facts of a case *step-by-step in a clear and uncomplicated way.* That is how his mind worked. Everybody, let's read that last sentence together."**

   Class: "Step by step, he laid out the facts in a clear and uncomplicated way until soon enough he'd have everyone convinced."

   Teacher: **"Greg, what is a logical mind?"**

   Greg: "A mind that lays out the facts step-by-step in a clear and uncomplicated way."

4. Ask students to reread the sentence and substitute the synonym or definition for the vocabulary word.

   Teacher: **"So I could read, 'He had a lawyer's *mind that laid out the facts step-by-step in a clear and uncomplicated way.*' That's how a logical mind thinks. Everyone, let's read the entire second sentence together, but instead of reading *logical,* use the definition."**

   Class and
   Teacher: "He had a lawyer's mind that lays out the facts step-by-step in a clear and uncomplicated way and he had a special knack for proving his side of an argument."

   Teacher: **"Kwame, it's your turn to read the second sentence with the definition for *logical.*"**

   Kwame: "He had a lawyer's mind that lays out the facts step-by-step in a clear and uncomplicated way and he had a special knack for proving his side of an argument."

Notes:

■ Synonym context clues are easier to teach than definition context clues. You will need to provide more support through questions and Togethers for longer definitions.

■ Use regular error correction strategies when students make an error. Often students who are at risk will have difficulty with verb tense and pronouns when substituting a definition for the vocabulary word. In these cases, use more Togethers, and model the way to say the revised sentence before asking students to do the same.

FIGURE 6.8   Indirect Teaching: Context Clues

Adapted from: Carnine, D. W., Silbert, J., Kame'enui, E. J., & Tarver, S. (2004). *Direct instruction reading* (4th ed.). New Jersey, Merrill Prentice Hall.

then asks questions that lead the students to figure out the word. In the example, the teacher asks, "How did Lincoln prove his side of an argument?" In the final step the students read the passage with the same word *logical,* and then read it again substituting a synonym or definition that means the same thing.

Although the strategy of using context clues to learn new vocabulary is helpful, it also has its limitations. First, some context clues may be easier to uncover than others. As Carnine and colleagues (2004) point out, when the defining words are separated from the target word by other words not related to its meaning, or when the definition of the word is stated negatively, using the context is made more difficult. Notice how *imprint* is defined in context below.

> Sometimes a fossil is only an *imprint* of a plant or animal. Millions of years ago, a leaf fell off a fernlike plant. It dropped onto the swampy forest soil, which is called peat. The leaf rotted away. But it left the mark of its shape in the peat. The peat, with the *imprint* of the leaf, hardened.

The words that explain *imprint,* "mark of its shape," come well after the first reference to it, and before the second reference, thus rendering the context clues less accessible than if they had come right after *imprint.* This means that the teacher may need to provide more support if students are to learn this new word. One suggestion would be to use the following think-aloud technique.

> "Let's see. The word imprint is *underlined.* That means it's important and probably a word I'll need to figure out. What does it mean when a word is underlined in the story? Now I need to look at the words around imprint to see if I can figure it out. Hmm, sometimes the meaning of the word isn't right next to it in the story." (Reads next part starting with Millions.) "This sentence tells how a fossil is made. I don't see the meaning yet. Wait—now it says the leaf left the mark of its shape in the peat. That's what an imprint is—a mark of something's shape."

In this next example, deriving the meaning of the word *swamp* is complicated by the presence of the word *not* included in a negative definition.

> Back when the dinosaurs lived here, my town was a big swamp. The land was not dry like it is now.

In this example the teacher might ask the following questions to guide students to the meaning of *swamp.*

> "Read the passage. What's the underlined word? (swamp). It says the land was *not* dry like it is now. If land is not dry, then what is it? (wet) Yes, wet. So, what kind of land do you think a swamp is? (wet land). Don't forget, when you see a word explained using the word not, you have to think extra carefully about what it means. You can get tricked."

When teaching your students to use context clues, be sure to use examples of varying difficulty to better prepare them for the realities of reading real texts. For example, when Mr. Chaney taught his third-grade students how to use context clues to figure out the meaning of new words, he first used examples where the clarifying words immediately followed the target word. When his students were able to decipher word meaning for these examples, Mr. Chaney moved to more difficult examples where the clarifying words were separated from the word which was stated as a negative. This answer required a higher degree of inference.

Using Morphemic Analysis to Teach Independent Word-Learning Strategies

Unfortunately, not all words are explained by the words around them so students need other strategies to figure out new words. Another strategy teaches students to figure out new words using morphemes. Morphemes can be whole words such as the word *spell,* or they may be word parts such as the prefix *re,* or the suffix *less.* To demonstrate how morphemes can be used to figure out the meaning of new vocabulary words, let's look at the word *care-less,* which consists of two morphemes: *care* and *less.* If students know that *less* means *with-*

out, they know that *careless* means doing something without care or without being careful. Similarly, the word *misspell* can be broken into the parts of *mis* and *spell.* If they know that *mis* means *not,* then they know that *misspell* means to *not spell* or *spell incorrectly.*

For morphemes to be helpful to students in figuring out vocabulary, they must be clearly recognizable in a word, and be readily translatable into a meaningful definition. Both *misspell* and *careless* fit that criteria. Unfortunately, not all words with morphemes are so clear-cut. The meanings of many words are difficult to determine using morphemes alone. Take these examples:

> The word *epidermis* is composed of two morphemes: *epi,* which means *beside or upon,* and *dermis,* which means *skin.* The literal definition of *epidermis,* based on its morphemes is, *upon the skin.*

> The word *evolution* is composed of three morphemes: *e,* which means *out; volut,* which means *turns; and tion,* which means *the act of.* The literal definition of evolution, based on it's morphemes, *is the act of turning out.*

> The word *irreducible* is composed of four morphemes: *ir,* which means *not; re,* which means back or *gain; ducere,* which means *to lead;* and *ible,* which means *capable of being.* The literal definition of *irreducible,* based on its morphemes, *is not capable of being led back (to the original).*

Ducere is difficult to translate into a meaningful definition. Other morphemes have multiple meanings or are not readily recognizable. Because the utility of using morphemes varies, it is suggested that you teach your students the morphemes that are most useful. A table of useful morphemes identified by Ruddell (1999) is shown in Table 6.3. Note that the morphemes are organized according to families having common meanings. Additional common morphemes are shown in Table 6.4.

TABLE 6.3   Useful Morphemes in Vocabulary Development

Prefix and Suffix family or type	Meaning	Instructional Vocabulary Example words
1. "Not" prefix family	*un, dis, in, im* = not	*disloyal, unaware, invisible, imperfect*
2. "Before," "during," and "after" prefix family	*pre* = before *mid* = during or middle *post* = after	*prejudge, midtown, postgame*
3. Excess prefix family	*out* = better or more than *over* = too much or many *super* = more, better, or higher	*outlive, overflow, superhuman*
4. Number prefix family	*uni, mono* = one *bi* = two *semi* = part, half, or occurring twice	*uniform, monofilament, bicolor, semiarid*
5. Prefix *re*	*re* = again or back	*recharge, rehire*
6. "State or quality of" suffix family	*ship, ness, ment* = state or quality of	*friendship, loneliness, excitement*
7. Suffix *ward*	*ward* = in the direction of	*skyward, northward*
8. Suffix *ful*	*ful* = full of or characterized by	*merciful, helpful*

Source: Baumann, J. F., Boland, E. M., Olejnik, S., & Kame'enui, E. J. (2003). Vocabulary tricks: Effects of instruction in morphology and context on fifth-grade students' ability to derive and infer word meanings. *American Educational Research Journal, 40(2),* 447–494.

TABLE 6.4 Additional Common Morphemes

Morpheme	Approximate Meaning	Sample Word
circum	around	circumnavigate
er	teacher	one that does
ex	out	export
est	the most	happiest
hyper	hyperactive	beyond, more than
il	not	illegible
inter	between	intertwine
less	without	helpless
ous	perilous	full of
sub	below	submarine
tri	three	tripod

Using Word Parts to Teach Vocabulary

There are several steps in teaching students to use word parts to learn new vocabulary. (Carnine et al., 2004)

The Students Read the Morpheme and Learn Its Meaning   The first part is to make sure the students can decode the morpheme. Next, the meaning of the morpheme is taught by itself, and in words. For example, Mr. Francisco taught his students to decode the morpheme *ful,* which means "full of." Then he taught them the meaning of *ful.*

> **"This word part says *full,* what does it say?"** (full).

> **"*Ful* means full of. What does *ful* mean?"** (full of).

> **"So what does this part say?"** (full). **"What does it mean?"** (full of).

Model Applying the New Morpheme to Different Words   Once students knew the definition of the new morpheme, Mr. Fransisco modeled how to figure out the meanings of several words containing ful:

> **"The word parts in *careful* are *care* and *ful*. What are the word parts in *careful*?"** (*care* and *ful*). **"So, careful means *full of care*. What does *careful* mean?"** (Full of care). **"Listen to this sentence. Allisandra was *careful* with her nails. When it came to taking care of her nails, Allisandra was full of care. So, what are the word parts in *careful*?"** (*care* and *ful*). **"What does *careful* mean?"** (full of care).

Ask Students to Tell a Sentence That Contains the Word   Mr. Francisco called on two students to verbally construct sentences.

> **"Chyron, tell me a sentence that has *careful* in it."**

Repeat the Process with a Second Word That Contains the Same Morpheme

> **"Let's do another word, *peaceful*. The word parts of *peaceful* are *peace* and *ful*. What are the word parts of *peaceful*?"** (*peace* and *ful*). **"*Peaceful* means *full of peace*. What does *peaceful* mean?"** (Full of peace). **"The neighborhood was very**

peaceful **last weekend. The neighborhood was full of peace, or very quiet. So what does peaceful mean?"** (full of peace). **"Greta, tell me a sentence that has** *peaceful* **in it."** (The fighting stopped and the day became very peaceful.)

Review Previously Introduced Word Parts   Mr. Francisco asked students to tell the meaning of two morphographs they learned last week.

"What does *re* **mean? What does** *dis* **mean?"**

Ask Students to Identify the Parts of Words Containing Previously Introduced Morphemes   For review, Mr. Francisco asked:

"What are the parts in *restart*?**"** (*re* and *start*). **"What does** *restart* **mean?"** (to start again) **"Tell me a sentence with** *restart*.**"** (The car stalled and Rob had to restart it.) **"What are the parts in** *afternoon*?**"** (*after* and *noon*). **"What does** *afternoon* **mean?"** (A time of day that is after noon or after 12:00.) **"Tell me a sentence with the word** *afternoon* **in it."** (Meet me after school in the afternoon.)

> The Lexile Power Vocabulary Website at **www.lexile.com/DesktopDefault.aspx?view=ed&tabindex=2&tabid=16&tabpageid=183** assists teachers in grades 2 through 12 develop their students' vocabulary skills.

Individual vocabulary word lists for books frequently used as literature in classrooms contain target vocabulary words along with each word's definition, pronunciation, part of speech, sentences where the word is used in context, and a vocabulary assessment when the book is finished.

Using the Dictionary to Teach Independent Word-Learning Strategies   Because the definitions listed in a dictionary may be vague or contain words that students can neither decode nor understand, Beck and colleagues (2002) recommend using learner's dictionaries with students. These dictionaries, which were originally developed for English language learners, use language that is accessible for any students who struggles with language. The *Collins COBUILD English Language Dictionary* (1987) is an effective example. Dictionaries that contain clear sentences about each key word also help students apply that meaning to their reading.

Besides abstract, unclear definitions, dictionaries often present multiple word meanings. Multiple meanings are difficult to comprehend for students who are at risk. An example of teaching students multiple meanings using the dictionary is shown in Table 6.5 (page 231).

Before students can look up words in the dictionary, they need to learn several preskills. These preskills include:

1. Identifying letters.
2. Saying letters in an a–z sequence.
3. Knowing the concepts of *before* and *after.*
4. Knowing alphabetic order for the first letter.
5. Determining the relative position of letters from each other: When you call out a letter, students should be able tell you which letter comes after and which letter comes before the named one. When a student opens the dictionary to the *o* page, looking for the word *dirigible,* he needs to know that *d* comes before *o,* indicating that he needs to jump ahead to the front quarter of the dictionary.
6. Knowing alphabetic order to the second letter.
7. Knowing alphabetic order to the third letter.
8. Scanning a dictionary page to locate a given word.
9. Knowing what guide words are, and how to locate words using them.
10. Knowing how to interpret the most common abbreviations used in dictionary entries.
11. Knowing how to interpret the most common pronunciation tips.

Research to Practice

Vocabulary Instruction

In its summary of the research on vocabulary instruction, the report of the National Reading Panel (2000) stated that "Dependence on a single vocabulary instruction method will not result in optimal learning" (p. 427). Students need to learn some words directly; others indirectly. In the classroom, they should be taught between 5 and 10 words a week through modeling, synonyms, definitions, keywords, and semantic maps. They need to learn to use the dictionary, to use context clues, and to learn common morphemes. Baumann and colleagues (2003) combined two of the methods of independent word learning described in this text, context clues, and morphemic analysis, to teach vocabulary words to fifth-grade students. They taught students the following three-part strategy called the vocabulary rule (Figure 6.9).

When you come to a word, and you don't know what it means, use:

1. **Context Clues:** Read the sentences around the word to see if there are clues to its meaning.
2. **Word-Part Clues:** See if you can break the word into a root word, prefix, or suffix to help figure out its meaning.
3. **Context Clues:** Read the sentences around the word again to see if you have figured out its meaning.

FIGURE 6.9   Vocabulary Rule

Source: Baumann, J. F., Boland, E. M., Olejnik, S., & Kame'enui, E. J. (2003).Vocabulary tricks: Effects of instruction in morphology and context on fifth-grade students' ability to derive and infer word meanings. *American Educational Research Journal, 40*(2), 447–494.

In order to carry out Step 2 of the vocabulary rule, Baumann and colleagues (2003) taught their fifth graders the following strategy for identifying word parts and using them to figure out the meaning of a new word. Figure 6.10 lists the steps to finding word-part clues.

1. Look for the **Root Word,** which is a single word that cannot be broken into smaller words or word parts. See if you know what the root word means.
2. Look for a **Prefix,** which is a word part added to the beginning of a word that changes its meaning. See if you know what the prefix means.
3. Look for a **Suffix,** which is a word part added to the end of a word that changes its meaning. See if you know what the suffix means.
4. Put the meaning of the **Root Word** and any **Prefix** or **Suffix** together and see if you can build the meaning of the word.

FIGURE 6.10   Word-Part Clues

Source: Baumann, J. F., Boland, E. M., Olejnik, S., & Kame'enui, E. J. (2003).Vocabulary tricks: Effects of instruction in morphology and context on fifth-grade students' ability to derive and infer word meanings. *American Educational Research Journal, 40*(2), 447–494.

Before learning this strategy, students were taught essential preskills that they needed to apply for this combined strategy. They learned to identify common affixes and state their meanings, as well as identify and describe the five types of context clues: definitions, synonyms, antonyms, examples, and general context clues.

Baumann (2003) compared a group of students who received this combined context–morphemic analysis strategy with a group receiving teacher direct instruction on words from their social studies text. The results showed that the group receiving the independent word-learning strategy was better able to read previously unknown words that could be figured out using morphemic and contextual analysis. The other group, however, was more successful in learning the vocabulary that both groups studied from the same textbook. These findings are consistent with those of the National Reading Panel, which explains that when it comes to teaching vocabulary, multiple methods should be used, including direct instruction as well as strategies for figuring out words independently.

TABLE 6.5 Teaching Multiple Meanings Using the Dictionary

Teacher	Students
1. The teacher reads the word in context. **"The doctor gave the sick boy a *shot* of very strong medicine."**	
2. The teacher asks students to find word in their dictionaries. **"Let's see if we can figure out the meaning of the word *shot* using the dictionary. Everyone, find the word *shot* in your dictionaries and raise your hand when you have found it."**	Students raise hands

3. The teacher helps students think through selecting the correct definition.
 	
"There are three definitions in the dictionary. We know that dictionaries often have more than one definition for a word. Let's see if we can figure out which one fits our sentence from the story.
 	
I'm going to read each definition and we'll try to figure out which one fits our sentence about the sick boy.
 	
  1. The sound of firing a gun.
  2. A kick, throw, or hit in some games to score points.
  3. Medicine placed under the skin by a needle.	

Let's talk about the first one. The sound of firing a gun. Does that fit what the doctor is doing to the boy?"	Everyone: No
"Why doesn't it fit, Simone?"	Simone: The doctor isn't shooting a gun or something at the boy.
"Let's look at the next one. A kick, throw, or hit in some games to score points. Everyone, does that fit what the doctor is doing?"	Everyone: No
"How do you know, Latrese?"	Latrese: The doctor isn't playing a game with the boy, he's trying to make him feel better.
"Let's look at the last definition. Medicine placed under the skin by a needle. Everyone, does that fit what the doctor is doing?"	Everyone: Yes
"Manny, how do you know?"	Manny: He's putting medicine in him to make him feel better.
"So, everyone, what definition fits our sentence?"	Everyone: Medicine placed under the skin by a needle.
"Yes. Now, when we talk about the old west in social studies today, we'll talk about a different definition for shot. Which one do you think will fit into that story, Garth?"	Garth: The sound of firing a gun.

How Can I Teach My Students to Answer Vocabulary Questions on High Stakes Tests?

Given increased accountability, your students will take high stakes tests in the early primary grades. As mentioned in an earlier chapter, students who read accurately and fluently on grade-level material are likely to perform at or above standard on high stakes tests. Nonetheless, being test wise can have a favorable impact on performance. Being test wise means that students are familiar with the test formats and are able to apply strategies that increase their chances of getting correct answers, even when they are unsure of the correct answer. Vocabulary questions are an important part of the reading portion of most high stakes tests. This section identifies question types your students are likely to encounter on their high stakes tests, and describes strategies to help them answer vocabulary correctly.

Three of the most common types of vocabulary items on high stakes tests include using the context, synonyms, and multiple-meaning formats (Educational Resources Inc., 2004). Examples of each of these types of items follows.

Using the Context

Alonzo thinks the stars are beautiful. He likes to *gaze* at them for hours. When he is in the country, the sky is very black so he can see the stars well.

A person who *gazes* at the stars—

A. dislikes them
B. draws them
C. looks at them
D. talks to them

Synonyms

An *incredible* story is:

A. boring
B. unbelievable
C. unhappy
D. long

Multiple Meanings

When Dashika finished the 10-mile race, she was *dead.*

In which sentence does the word *dead* mean the same thing as in the sentence above?

A. The roses in my garden are *dead.*
B. The beach is *dead* in the winter time.
C. The soldier was a *dead* shot with the rifle.
D. The camper was *dead* after climbing uphill for 2 miles.

Strategies for teaching students to answer each of these types of vocabulary questions are described in Table 6.6. Note that first the steps involved in answering the questions are clearly specified. The examples described employ think-alouds to make it clear to students not only what they have to do to answer a question, but what they need to be thinking about as they do so. Think alouds have been shown to be an effective strategy for teaching comprehension to students who are at risk (Gersten et al., 2001).

TABLE 6.6 Strategies for Answering Vocabulary Questions on High Stakes Tests

---

Question Type 1: Using Context Clues to Determine Meaning

Example	Alonzo thinks the stars are beautiful. He likes to *gaze* at them for hours. When he is in the country, the sky is very black so he can see the stars well.
	A person who *gazes* at the stars—
	A. dislikes them
	B. draws them
	C. looks at them
	D. talks to them
Strategy	Read only the underlined vocabulary word and try to pick out the correct definition based on what you already know.
	If you can't figure out the correct definition, go back and read the sentence. Underline the clue words that can help you find the definition and try again.
	If you still can't find the definition, substitute each of the choices into the sentence and pick the one that makes sense.
	If you still can't answer the question, guess one of the answers you think might be right.
Applied Strategy	**"Let's see. The underlined vocabulary word is *gaze*. Let's see if any of the choices means *gaze*. Hmm . . . Dislikes them? Draws them? Looks at them? Talks to them? I'm not sure what the answer is."**
	"I'm going to read the sentence and see if I can find words that might give me a clue about the meaning of gaze. I think the words *see the stars well* are important, so I will underline them in the sentence. But I'm still not quite sure of what the answer is."
	"OK. Now I'm going to substitute each choice word in the sentence and see which makes sense.
	He likes to dislike them for hours? That doesn't make sense at all. He likes to draw them for hours? I don't think he would be able to draw the stars at night. It couldn't be that one. He likes to look at them for hours? That one seems to make sense since it talks about being able to see the stars in the dark. I'll check the last one out just to be sure, but I think the answer is *look*. He likes to talk to them for hours? That doesn't make sense. So, I think the answer is C, *looks at*."

Question Type 2: Multiple Meaning Formats

Example	When Dashika finished the 10-mile race, she was *dead*.
	In which sentence does the word *dead* mean the same thing as in the sentence above?
	A. The roses in my garden are *dead*.
	B. The beach is *dead* in the winter time.
	C. The soldier was a *dead* shot with the rifle.
	D. The camper was *dead* after climbing uphill for 2 miles.
Strategy	Read the underlined vocabulary word.
	Read the bolded sentence containing the word and think of a simple definition or words that mean the same thing.
	Read each of the four possible answer sentences substituting your definition instead of the word.
	After each sentence, ask yourself, "Does this make sense?" If not, cross out that choice and repeat for the other choices.
	If you still can't come up with the answer, take a guess by picking one of the choices you think might be right.
Applied Strategy	**"The underlined word is *dead*. Dead has many meanings. I need to figure out what it means in the bolded sentence. First I'll read that sentence. When Dashika finished the 10-mile race, she was *dead*. Well, even though a 10-mile race is very long, I don't think Dashika is likely to die from it. I think she would be *very tired*. So I think *dead* here means very tired. Let me put *very tired* in each sentence and see which one makes sense."**

Continued

TABLE 6.6   Continued

Applied Strategy (Continued)	"The roses in my garden are very tired. That doesn't make sense. Roses don't get tired. I'm going to move to the next one. The beach is very tired in the winter time. That doesn't make any sense either. Then how about next one? The soldier was a very tired shot with the rifle. That doesn't make sense either. Let's try the last one. The camper was very tired after climbing uphill for 2 miles. That makes sense. The camper would be tired after that climb. So the answer is D."

Question Type 3: Synonyms

Example	An *incredible* story is: A. boring B. unbelievable C. unhappy D. long
Strategy	Ask yourself what the word means without looking at the definitions given below. See if your definition is one of the four choices. If your definition is not one of the four choices, try to put each choice in a sentence and ask yourself, "Is that **incredible**?" If you still can't come up with an answer that makes sense, make a guess on one of the choices you think might be right.
Applied Strategy	"What does *incredible* mean? I think it means *funny.* Let's see if that is a choice. Hmm . . . It isn't. Now I'm going to try to put each of the choices into a sentence and see if I can figure out the meaning of *incredible* that way." "An incredible story. A boring story? Incredible and boring don't mean the same thing." "An incredible story. An unbelievable story? That seems right. I remember my brother talking about an incredible band. He said they were so good, he couldn't believe it. I'll look quickly at the other two choices, but I think B is the right answer. Let's see—*unhappy*? No—*long*? No, that isn't right either. I'm going to answer B for this question."

How Can I Provide Extra Vocabulary Practice for My Students?

Thus far, a number of effective strategies for the initial teaching of vocabulary to students at risk have been described. While these strategies are effective in introducing vocabulary to students, by themselves, they are not enough. Reading research is quite clear that "multiple encounters are required before a word is really known, that is, if it is to affect comprehension and become a useful and permanent part of the student's vocabulary repertoire" (Beck et al., 2002, p. 73; National Reading Panel, 2002; Stahl & Fairbanks, 1986). Beck and colleagues presented 10 new words each week. Students then practiced these words during that week as many as eight to ten times. These researchers provided much review on words presented in previous weeks as well. Beck stresses that these repeated exposures must be rich, meaning that students are actively involved in "using and thinking about word meanings and creating lots of associations among words" (p. 73). This extra practice must extend beyond the classroom into community environments as well.

Practice Activities for New Words

This section describes strategies for providing students with multiple exposures to new words. Remember that you need to provide more support and return to explicit teaching if students cannot complete these activities with at least 80% success. Student errors on these assignments provide you with an opportunity to give feedback and use an error correction strategy. If students are old enough or you can quickly scan the worksheets, correct them on the spot, so students will profit from the immediate feedback.

Preprinted Response Cards and Write-On Response Boards   These two practice activities recommended by Foil and Alber (2002) can be carried out with large groups, because both involve the use of unison response. As stated elsewhere in this text, because everyone is participating, unison response formats help students pay attention and increase the opportunities for practice. The teacher distributes cards that have the vocabulary word printed in large letters on the front side and the definition and an example sentence printed on the back.

After every student has several cards, the teacher tells everyone a definition and students hold up the correct vocabulary word. In another adaptation of this same activity, the teacher distributes dry-erase boards to each student along with dry-erase markers. The teacher then establishes the word bank by writing a list of vocabulary words on the board. As with the preprinted word cards, the teacher tells a definition, and students answer by writing the appropriate word from the word bank on their slates. To maintain momentum, the teacher must maintain a perky pace and use a clear signal throughout the lesson (e.g., "Boards up; card up"). Foil and Alber (2002) point out that the whiteboards don't allow for as many student answers because writing on the slates takes more time than just holding up a preprinted card. However, they state that the activity may be just as worthwhile because writing the words reinforces spelling skills.

Classwide Peer Tutoring   Another way to provide extra vocabulary practice is through structured peer tutoring. In this approach, used by Miller, Barbetta, and Heron (1994), the teacher provides each student with a folder that has two pockets attached on the inside. The teacher prints "go" on one pocket, and "stop" on the other pocket. The teacher also provides students with index cards on which a vocabulary word is written on one side, and its definition on the other. The students work in pairs in which they take turns being the tutor. The tutor shows each vocabulary word to his partner and asks the partner to restate the definition. Praise is given for correct answers, and corrective feedback in the form of a My Turn–Your Turn is provided for incorrect answers. Words mastered (three consecutive days correct) are put in the "stop" pocket. Words that have yet to be mastered are placed in the "go" pocket. After a predetermined time, usually around 5 minutes, the students switch roles. After both students have had their turn, they chart the number of words they have mastered on a graph taped to the inside of the folder. Words in the "stop" pile are reviewed periodically in subsequent days. As with any peer tutoring procedure, tutors need to be carefully trained, and their teaching tactics closely monitored.

Never Too Many Questions   After teaching a vocabulary word, teachers need to find every opportunity to ask questions about the new word. They can ask questions immediately after students know the definition, they can ask questions before lunch, they can ask questions when the word surfaces in the story. *Who, what, where, why, when,* and *which* questions like the following provide extra opportunities for students to use the new words they have learned:

- What would you do if your best friend let you use a *delicate* glass to drink out of and you broke it? Have you ever broken anything that was *delicate* and what was it?
- What are some things that make you *anxious?* Why?
- When have you seen a *procession* and what kind of procession was it?

Making Choices   This activity recommended by Beck and colleagues (2002, p. 56) forces students to think about the precise definition of the word as applied to authentic descriptions. Even better, students answer in unison, so everyone is engaged in responding to the questions:

> If any of the things I mention is a *competition,* say "competition." If not, don't say anything at all.

- a relay race
- The Olympics
- lunch with a friend
- the school spelling bee
- watching a movie

> If any of the things I mention is something that might make you *chuckle,* say "chuckle." If any of the things I mention might make you *sob,* say "sob."

- your mom tickling your toes
- burning your hand on a hot plate
- watching a cartoon show where a mouse fools a cat
- seeing a clown pull a quarter out of someone's ear
- losing your money for lunch

Word Associations   In another activity, Beck and colleagues (2002, p. 44) have students make a connection between a new vocabulary word and a word that they already know and then describe why they made it. If a teacher had directly taught the words *glitter, pessimist, rubbish, arid,* and *antonyms,* he would write the five words on the board and ask the class to answer the following questions in unison:

- Tell me the word that goes with gold? (answer: glitter)
- Tell me the word that goes with opposites? (answer: antonyms)
- Tell me the word that goes with parched? (answer: arid)
- Tell me the word that goes with negative? (answer: pessimist)
- Tell me the word that goes with garbage? (answer: rubbish)

Thumbs Up–Thumbs Down   This adaptation of a self-reflection activity in *Bringing Words to Life* (Beck et al., 2002; p. 45) provides review for descriptive words previously taught in class. The teacher asks students to hold their thumbs up if a trait she calls out describes them and to hold their thumbs down if the trait does not describe them. Individual students are asked to tell why they selected their answer.

- Are you independent? Why?
- Are you mischievous? Why?
- Are you gullible? Why?
- Are you assertive? Why?
- Are you loyal? Why

Narrow Reading   An adjunct to directly teaching a "big concept" vocabulary word is **narrow reading,** where the teacher can assign different texts on the same topic so that the learner encounters the word in different contexts. Schmitt and Carter (2000) recommended narrow reading as one strategy so students read the new vocabulary in a variety of texts. If students have just learned the meaning of *circuit* and *electrical current,* the teacher might have everyone read the book *The Magic School Bus and the Electric Field Trip* by Joanna Cole; photocopied pages 41–44 of *Electricity and Magnetism Fundamentals,* by Robert Wood; and a choice of either the section on circuits in *All About Electricity,* by Melvin Berger; or the section on circuits in *The First Book of Electricity,* by Sam and Beryl Epstein.

Practice Activities for Review Words: Coordinate Vocabulary with Writing Activities

When students have the opportunity to write vocabulary words they have learned, they are more apt to remember the word when they read it in text. If the word is a spelling word, design the activity so that students practice independently spelling the word. If the word is not a spelling word, provide a written model on the board, overhead projection, or paper so students write it correctly. These are some activities you can use for vocabulary review practice:

Fill-In-the-Blank Stories   Vocabulary words are listed at the top of the page unless they are also spelling words, and students fill in the blanks of a story with appropriate words.

Dictionary Race-and-Rite   Each student needs a dictionary, pencil, and paper for this activity. Students are divided into three teams. If students are expected to know the spelling of the word, the teacher says the word; if students do not know the spelling, the teacher points to the word and asks students to read it. When the teacher says, "look it up," the students race to look up the word in the dictionary. As soon as they have found the word, they write it along with the dictionary page number. Then they immediately write a complete sentence using the word. When a student has completed the task, she holds up her thumb. At a set time, the teacher says "stop" and quickly scans the papers of whichever team has the most thumbs raised. That team gets one point for every person who wrote the correct page number as well as a complete sentence.

The Goodbye List   The teacher keeps a list of vocabulary words that have been taught on a chart which is titled, "The Goodbye List." Each morning he writes between five and 10 vocabulary words on the board. When students enter the room, they know that they are supposed to write the word, a definition of the word, and a sentence showing correct usage of the word. They can earn three points per vocabulary word toward their language arts grade for doing this activity correctly. If 90% of students get all three points for a word two days in a row, the word is taken off the Goodbye List. Students are encouraged to shrink the list so that the teacher is "forced" to teach even more words because he cannot keep up with his hardworking class.

Vocabulary Words as Themes   When students are asked to write a paragraph, story, or descriptive paper, the assignment should be structured so that they use targeted vocabulary words. If students have just read *Cloudy with a Chance of Meatballs,* ask them to write several sentences about what would happen if they were walking outside in the *hail.* If students have been studying about the early American *colonists,* ask them to write a page about what hardships they would face as a *colonist* on the moon.

Grids   The teacher prepares a worksheet using the table function of a word processing program. Vocabulary words are listed in the first column and students are asked to write synonyms and/or antonyms in the next column(s). The teacher needs to determine whether a dictionary or textbook is necessary for student success.

Word Journals   Once your students know basic word processing, they can use their computer lab time to make personal dictionaries using the vocabulary words you have taught. Complete instructions for teaching this activity and making a dictionary page template are detailed at www.microsoft.com/Education/aardvark.mspx.

Activities for teaching vocabulary are found at: **www.readingfirst.virginia.edu/index.php/elibrary/C11/.**

How Do I Teach the Language of Learning?

Teachers of younger students who are at risk are often frustrated when teaching vocabulary, because many of their students come to school unable to speak using more than three- and four-word utterances, use prepositions, or answer *where, what,* and *why* questions. Given that oral language deficits are a risk factor for later reading problems (Catts, 1993; Wilson & Risucci, 1988; Sticht & James, 1984), these teachers' concerns are well placed. Students' oral language skills, along with listening comprehension skills, affect their ability to comprehend text. Although teaching vocabulary is essential, it is often not sufficient. Louisa Moats describes what is needed to overcome the language gap that presents additional challenges for so many students from poverty:

> From the time they enter preschool, students must experience language stimulation all day long if they are to compensate for their incoming linguistic differences. Teachers must immerse them in the rich language of books. Children need to rehearse the rules of discourse, such as staying on topic, taking turns, and giving enough information so the listener understands. Children must learn how to speak in discussions, to question, paraphrase, retell and summarize, as the recently developed standards for listening and speaking now specify. Teachers must teach directly the form, meaning, and use of words, phrases, sentences, and texts. Everything from the articulatory features of /k/ and /g/ to the construction of an organized essay is grist for the instructional mill. (Moats, 2001)

Because teachers do not have the training of speech pathologists, they often feel at a loss in developing their students' oral language skills, a loss which is substantiated by research. Close examination of typical school curriculum and methods reveals that classroom exposure to literature, use of an informal language experience approach, infrequent opportunities to talk, and infrequent feedback and correction of oral language have little impact on developing students' language skills (Beimiller, 2003). By the second year of Project PRIDE, we realized that all of the kindergarten students needed a more structured language curriculum providing extensive practice. An account of the program, *Language for Learning,* is given in the Research to Practice section beginning on page 240. If students who are at risk are going to comprehend written text at grade level, their classroom curriculum must ensure that the following language skills essential for learning are developed at as early an age as possible. Language curricula used in preschool and kindergarten should teach these skills.

- Answers simple "Wh-" questions (who, what, where, and why) in a full sentence.
- Understands and answers questions for sentences that include a subject + action + object (e.g., "The girl makes cookies.") and a subject + action + location (e.g., "The camel walks on the hill.")
- Uses prepositions (on, on top of, over, in front of, in between, into, inside, beside, under, beneath, behind, in back of, through, out of).
- Understands quality (alike, same, different), amount (all, more, few), size (big, little, short), opposites and categories (containers, vehicles, months, food, numbers).
- Uses articles (the, a, an) in conversation.
- Answers yes/no questions in a complete sentence.
- Knows colors, shapes, and numbers.
- Uses possessives (his, hers) and personal pronouns (we, she).
- Answers more complex "Wh-" questions (e.g., "What can you do with a shovel?" "Why do you go to school?").
- Follows three-part sequence of directions (e.g., "Put your crayons in your desk, put your papers in your cubbies, and get your coats.").
- Uses *and* to chain together two concepts or actions.

- Relates information in more than one complete sentence about an experience that happened in the past.
- Uses irregular tense verbs in conversation (hit, caught, sat).
- Speaks in complex sentences of more than four words.
- Tells what happens *first, middle,* and *last* in a sequence of events.
- Tells a story about an event or experience.
- Understands and describes the difference between things that are the same and things that are different, such as the difference between children and grown-ups.
- Uses all parts of speech in conversation.
- Uses plurals, past tense verbs, and present progressive (ing) in speech.

> Learn more about *Language for Learning* at: **www.sraonline.com/ index.php/home/curriculum solutions/di/languageforlearning/ 106.**

How Important Is Vocabulary for Older Learners?

When an older student does not derive meaning from what she is reading, the teacher needs to assess the student's benchmark skills in order to determine whether she has developed alphabetic principle, can decode multisyllabic words, can read fluently, and has acquired an adequate vocabulary to read grade-level text. Whether assessment shows that reading deficits include earlier reading skills or just vocabulary deficits, instruction always should include the direct teaching of vocabulary. An older student has not had access to the indirect learning of new words through extensive reading, and thus a key reading skill problem expands into a larger word knowledge problem.

Vocabulary instruction will incorporate many of the same direct and indirect teaching strategies as used with younger students, but can be "more rooted to text" (Beck et al., 2002, p. 85), with the teacher discussing the author's selection of words and how the choice of a word affects the author's communication with the reader. Word study should rely less on synonyms and more on teaching similarities and differences between words. Beck and colleagues (2002) recommend that word study at this level incorporate the following three design elements.

Frequency   Because of the content area demands for older students, the teacher should plan on teaching 10 words per week. Words taught during previous weeks should be repeatedly reviewed.

Richness   A variety of activities should actively involve students in writing, speaking, and associating the word with other words. Activities should be designed so that students use critical skills in applying what they have learned about the meaning of the word. The authors recommend that rather than have students memorize the definition of a word, the teacher should introduce three related definitions of the word during the week. Answering timed true/false questions also helps students clarify and refine the meaning of new words as well as developing fluency.

Extension of Words Beyond the Classroom   The use of a *Word Wizard* helps students use active listening to hear new vocabulary words outside of the classroom. Students earn points on the *Word Wizard* chart by bringing in evidence that they heard, saw, or used one of their assigned vocabulary words outside of the classroom—in other classes, at home, in the mall, watching TV, in a book, or any other source.

Research to Practice

Language Development

The year before Project PRIDE started, we observed the kindergarten classes in our three schools and took data on students so we could make the best decisions for fall when we started working in the classrooms. During the observations, we saw that although teachers read to students every day and engaged in language experience activities such as cooking, growing plants, and constructing objects related to thematic units, the language poverty of students persisted. Many students' discourse when answering teachers' questions, conversing on the playground, or describing what happened the night before was more typical of a three-year-old than an end-of-year kindergartner. Simply teaching phonemic awareness, letter sounds, and beginning decoding would be inadequate unless we could also develop the students' language skills, so necessary for comprehension.

We decided to supplement the already established classroom language experience with the *Language for Learning* direct instruction curriculum (Engelmann & Osborn, 1999). The *Language for Learning* curriculum was selected because it incorporates explicit and systematic instruction of listening comprehension and oral language, provides many opportunities for each child to answer questions throughout the lessons, and introduces a careful sequence of skills. Because we did not have the resources to provide the curriculum to everyone, we were not sure it was necessary for all students, and the teachers were resistant to teaching a scripted language curriculum, we decided to teach it to students with the lowest language skills. When we tested the kindergartners before the project started using the curriculum pretest, our observations about low language skills were confirmed; approximately 40% of the students had such low language skills that they tested into the beginning lessons of the program. These children were not yet using prepositions, they could not repeat a six-word sentence, they did not use articles in conversation, or use the word *not* in a complete sentence such as "He is not driving a car." Some still did not know the difference between their *chin* or *cheek* and could not differentiate between their first and last name. How could we hope to get them to fully develop reading comprehension when their language was so impoverished?

Thus we decided to test all of the kindergartners at the start of the year and weed out those with the lowest language skills. These children would receive *Language for Learning* for a half-hour in groups ranging between two and eight children. In order to do this, special education teachers, student teachers, paraprofessionals, and Title 1 teachers were trained to teach the language groups. Getting a large group of students to answer questions in unison is difficult teaching and requires that the teacher be extremely observant of how the students answer in order to know what to do or say next. At one school, the kindergarten teacher believed that all of her students needed the program and decided that she would teach the larger group of students who had received higher scores on the pretest.

What a relief it was to see the capable teachers blossom as they rolled up their sleeves and learned how to teach this curriculum! The teachers expressed their surprise at discovering what difficulty so many of the children had with "first" and "next" and how much practice they needed to learn those concepts. Talking about "*an* elephant" in contrast to "*a* book," and selecting the right article doesn't come easy when a child hasn't picked up that convention from the environment. After Christmas, the kindergarten teachers noticed that many of the children in *Language for Learning* were beginning to surpass their peers. Teachers mentioned that a number of parents talked at parents' night about how their children said that language time was the favorite part of their school day. After the end-of-the-year district tests, one of the teachers approached us describing all of the questions that only the children in *Language for Learning* knew. Because these were the children who arrived at school with the least language, she was surprised to see these results. The children were sequentially naming the days of the week, the seasons of the year, identifying more body parts, and using plurals. It looked as if the intensive half-hour of talking and more talking while sustaining attention to wait for the teacher's signal was helping these children learn language concepts more efficiently.

That year we gave the *Slingerland Listening Skills Comprehension* test to all of our kindergarten students at the beginning and end of the school year. We were interested in seeing whether the children who received *Language for Learning* made progress in listening comprehension and whether they were able to catch up to their classmates who entered kindergarten with higher language skills. The results showed that the *Language for Learning* group made significant gains in listening comprehension and that the gap between them and their peers was virtually erased.

The data were unequivocal. Because of the success of *Language for Learning,* and because so many of our students were at risk, we decided to teach *Language for Learning* to all of our kindergarten students. The students who had the least language would continue to meet in smaller groups, but the kindergarten teachers would begin teaching the language curriculum to the rest of the class for between 20 and 30 minutes every day. Because teaching a larger language group was more of a challenge, all of the teachers used the "Climb the Mountain to the Castle" game (p. 165) as they taught their language groups. When we met during the year, the teachers related that they felt as if they were learning to teach language for the first time. Until they taught the program, teachers had not been aware of many critical sequential language skills needed for more expressive conversation. They found themselves integrating the *Language for Learning* skills into activities throughout the day.

How Can I Teach Vocabulary to English Language Learners?

Many vocabulary words that readers encounter have **literal,** or actual, **meanings** such as the word *creek* in a story where Laurel, a main character, says, "I'm getting my pole and going fishing in the *creek.*" The reader can picture Laurel casting for fish in a shallow creek at the bottom of the hill where she is going fly-fishing. Other words or phrases, such as **idioms,** have **figurative meanings** where the meaning is not literal, implying more than what is said on the surface. When Stephano says, "I crashed my car and am *up a creek,*" the idiom *up a creek* means *in trouble.*

Idioms that have figurative meanings present additional challenges for English language learners. Phrases such as "to smell a rat," or "hot under the collar" must be learned as a whole, because they cannot be understood from the meanings of the separate words within them. While some idioms are regarded as slang and typically heard in oral language, other idioms are regarded as formal or informal. They are liberally sprinkled through much fiction and narrative reading and comprehension of the text depends on the reader perceiving them as a whole and knowing their meaning.

The same recommendations given for teaching vocabulary also apply to teaching idioms. Teachers should ignore the more obscure idioms and focus their teaching on ones that students are more likely to encounter in their reading. Idioms with clear meanings should be taught first. When first teaching an idiom, teachers should consider whether learning the literal meaning of the idiom will help the student remember it. For example, the idiom, "roll with the punches," means to make it through times of hardship. This phrase came to be used because rolling with the punches is a technique used in boxing where the objective is to avoid receiving a direct hit. The boxer tries to move away from the punch in an attempt to avoid the blow or at least ward off an easier, less painful glancing blow. Because this example helps the reader make sense of the idiom, the teacher could explain it when she introduces the word.

Whether the teacher refers to the literal background of the phrase or not, each idiom has a figurative meaning that the student can apply to text. Irugo (1986) recommends that teachers portray the meaning of the idiom as concretely as possible. Pictures that depict the meaning of the idiom can help the student remember the phrase, as can stories in which the phrase is used in a humorous context. Unless an idiom is supported by context in the beginning, English language learners are less likely to remember it, so having students role play the idiom or act out sentences containing the idiom are effective teaching techniques. If the students' first language has a similar idiom, connecting the English idiom to that one will help the students' retention of the new phrase. Mr. Swiggums displayed the picture in Figure 6.11 on the SMART Board in front of his classroom and explained that "a drop in the bucket" is something that is not very important because it is small. He asked his students to look at the picture and see how small the water drop looked in the much larger bucket. A drop in a large bucket isn't important because you would need so many drops to fill the bucket. Next Mr. Swiggums asked his students to read in unison "A drop in the bucket" which was written next to the picture. He wanted to be sure that everyone clearly heard the new idiom and could read it. Mr. Swiggums explained that when Charlotte broke her pencil she said, "It's just a drop in the bucket," because Charlotte's dog was sick, her mom had yelled at her that morning for ripping her dress, and her best friend wasn't talking to her. Compared to the bigger problems of her dog's illness, her mom's anger, and losing her best friend, breaking a pencil was not important. Breaking the pencil was a very little problem. Breaking the pencil was just "a drop in the bucket." As Mr. Swiggums said "Just a drop in the bucket," he shrugged his shoulders, threw out his hands, and made a facial expression reflecting that breaking the pencil was not important. He then asked his students to mimic his body language as they said, "just a drop in the bucket," together.

FIGURE 6.11   A Drop in the Bucket

Source: www.goenglish.com/adropinthe bucket.asp.

In order to help develop students' ear for hearing English idioms, Celce-Murcia and colleagues (2002) recommend that teachers use idioms for controlled practice activities when students are learning to use correct rhythm patterns and word-stress in connected speech phrases. The following idioms, all containing the word *talk,* are recommended for an oral speech practice session:

> all talk and no action
> talk is cheap
> talk a blue streak
> talk shop
> talk through your hat
> talk someone's head off (Celce-Murcia et al., 2000, p. 170)

For English as a Second Language resources and activities related to teaching vocabulary visit: **http:// depts.gallaudet.edu/englishworks/ reading/main/vocabulary.htm.**

To learn the origins of some of the most common idioms used in the United States visit **www.pride-unlimited. com/probono/idioms3.html#q** and **www.goenglish.com/Idioms.asp.**

A teacher using this strategy would go through the list, first saying each phrase before students repeated it imitating the teacher as closely as possible. Although students would not yet know the meaning of many of these idioms, they would be gaining familiarity with hearing the key words used within the larger idioms.

A number of Internet websites have defined idioms and illustrate them with descriptive or humorous pictures. Downloading the pictures from these sites gives the teacher easy access to instant demonstration materials. In the general reference section of larger bookstores teachers can also find worksheets and explanations about how common idioms originated.

Technology

Vocabulary

The National Reading Panel Report indicates that computer technology can benefit the development of reading vocabulary. Several research studies investigating computer-aided vocabulary instruction for students at risk report increased scores on vocabulary assessments given after the conclusion of the computer intervention (Johnson, et al., 1987; Horton et al., 1988; Segers & Verhoeven, 2003). However, too few rigorous studies have been conducted to determine what type of computer instruction is most effective in teaching reading vocabulary. Because software programmers have used a number of different strategies in their reading vocabulary teaching programs, teachers can be confused by all of the options. We have identified some of the current instructional design features available in software programs for teaching vocabulary so you can be a more informed consumer when selecting a program.

The buyer must beware of spending money for a program that is little more than a standard vocabulary worksheet. In these programs the student either matches a definition to each vocabulary term or writes the word of a definition. If the answer is correct, a pleasant chime sounds or text on the screen indicates that the answer is correct. If the answer is not correct, an unpleasant beep sounds or text pops up indicating an error. Student errors do not affect the sequence of instruction and the student is expected to begin answering the next question whether he was right or wrong. A score is displayed at the end of the activity.

Vocabulary computer programs with more sophisticated designs may include some of the following features:

■ **Immediate feedback for answers**—When students answer incorrectly, the program will either reteach the word or display the correct answer.

■ **Effective error correction**—When students answer incorrectly, after leading the student to answer correctly, the program will re-ask the same question so that the student has the opportunity to answer correctly one more time.

■ **Digitized or synthesized speech**—A study by Hebert and Murdock (1994) showed that students learned more vocabulary when a computer program integrates speech with the computer instruction.

■ **Pictures or animation for teaching**—Some programs teach initial vocabulary displaying pictures or animations to illustrate new words. For example, the word *locomotive* might be illustrated by a train chugging down a track. Programs for younger students who are not yet reading often require students to select pictures that match a word spoken by a story character.

■ **A variety of student responses appropriate for students' age and developmental level**—Students may click a mouse or touch their finger to the screen to select a vocabulary word or picture, move an object to a picture of a vocabulary word, paint pictures of vocabulary words, type in letters of a vocabulary word, select multiple choice options related to the vocabulary word (i.e., antonym, synonym, correct sentence with blank, definition) or select key vocabulary terms written in hypertext (see below). Students' hands are not large enough to learn word processing until third grade, so programs for younger students should utilize a mouse or point-touch screen.

■ **Easy record keeping**—Some programs allow students to save their scores or the programs automatically save their scores so the teacher can monitor progress.

■ **Number of new vocabulary words learned**—Some programs introduce large sets of vocabulary words; others limit the number of vocabulary words introduced and do not introduce more until students have success with the first set. In one study Johnson and colleagues (1987) studied two groups of students in grades 9 through 12. One group learned vocabulary from a computer program that only introduced small sets of seven words; the other group's program introduced a larger set of 25 words. At the end of the intervention, the researchers concluded that the students who learned from the program that introduced small sets of words learned the specified 50 vocabulary words more quickly.

Continued

- **Teacher selection of vocabulary words**—Some flexible programs allow the teacher to input up to 20 vocabulary words, definitions, and sentences. Other programs teach predetermined vocabulary words.
- **Motivation**—Sotware programs teaching vocabulary have a wide variety of motivational strategies. Some programs teach vocabulary words in the context of playing games including 'Indiana-Jones-type' adventures or Save the Planet mysteries; some teach vocabulary within the context of interesting stories; some attach success with the ability to earn clues to solve a mystery; some use percentage correct scores as a motivator. Always check to see that the motivator does not consume too much instructional time
- **Hypertext**—During the past fifteen years, **hypertext** has increasingly been used as one computer software strategy to teach vocabulary. With hypertext, the software designers link designated words (which are usually indicated by a different text color) to a database. Depending on their preferences, readers can select the designated words and bring on screen the information in the data base. Pressing a word might link the reader to a definition of the word, to a picture of the word, to a clue for figuring out the word, or to a video of someone describing the word. Students reading electronic books on screen can select a word and immediately obtain information on it. More research is still needed to determine whether hypertext is an effective vocabulary teaching strategy and, if so, which kinds of hypertext work best with what types of students. Note the visual aspects of the hypertext. Programmers indicate that hypertext of dark letters on a light background is less tiring for the reader.

What Games and Activities Will Reinforce the Students' New Vocabulary and Language Skills?

If students who are at risk are going to learn the vocabulary they need for success in reading harder text, vocabulary and language instruction must be ongoing throughout the school day, during transition periods between classes, and in science, math, art, social studies, and music classes.

> Link to a free talking picture dictionary at **www.languageguide.org/ english.** Pictures are arranged into categories such as insects or colors. Running the mouse over the picture triggers a hypertext box containing the spelling of the word while a voice simultaneously says the word.

In Ms. DeMarco's class, vocabulary development is integrated into almost every daily activity. During morning announcements, the principal talks about the inspirational word of the week. After introducing the definition for the word *honorable,* the principal briefly uses the word in context to describe an individual who accomplished great things because he or she had honorable traits. The principal talks about an honorable action the person did. By the end of the week, everyone in the school knows the word *honorable.* After announcements, Ms. DeMarco, the teacher, tells students to think of someone who could be described by the mystery word. As students wait in line to go to the bathroom, she holds an impromptu discussion talking about individuals whom the children believe have honorable characteristics.

When the literacy block of time begins, Ms. DeMarco directly pre-teaches three words that are in the story. A vocabulary word from last week is reviewed. As students practice reading new words that will be in the story, she selects one or two that are more difficult for the students to decode, because they don't know the meaning. Ms. DeMarco quickly gives the definition of the word and tells the meaning before asking everyone to say the meaning. She then asks several questions that force the students to use the new word in their answer. During the second reading of the story, she asks several questions requiring students to use their new vocabulary words. Students are expected to answer in complete sentences, so they get practice developing their language skills. Spelling instruction provides an opportunity to talk again about one of the words on the list, *straddle*. Because everyone needs a stretch, Ms. DeMarco asks everyone to straddle their desk chairs, to touch the floor, to stand up, and to straddle their chair again before going back to work.

The time allotted for writing brings more opportunities to use new words. Ms. DeMarco asks the students to write about what the fox saw on his morning route to work. Besides asking students to use the vocabulary word, *route,* in their written paragraphs, Ms. DeMarco also informs the students that she wants them to use two other vocabulary words, *creatures* and *enchanted.* Ms. DeMarco always has students work on grammar at the end of the literacy time block, and today's practice exercises using irregular past tense forms of verbs is so difficult, she decides to have the students practice in unison as a group so she can provide modeling and error corrections until they have more success with using these words in sentences. When students line up for lunch, they have to say the name of a friend and an adjective starting with the same letter as that name. Everyone had enjoyed this grammar activity so much earlier in the week that Ms. DeMarco used variations of it during free times.

The rest of the day is as vocabulary–language intensive as the morning. Ms. DeMarco misses no opportunities in math, science or social studies to teach related vocabulary terms. She is always informed about what students are learning in art or music class, so she can reinforce new vocabulary learned in those classes. Ms. DeMarco anchors her direct teaching of vocabulary by having students read, spell, and write new vocabulary words as well as use them in oral communication. If there are a few moments as students are waiting to go home at the end of the day, she will throw in a quick vocabulary or language game. Some of the game activities she interjects at those times follow.

Absurdity Is Fun   What would happen if a cougar startled everyone at recess? Why aren't our shoes made of concrete? What would happen if our shoes were made of concrete? What would happen if a mouse made a thundering noise? Ms. DeMarco likes to ask absurd questions because they are excellent for getting children to think and express their ideas.

Thumbs Up–Thumbs Down   Ms. DeMarco's students needed more practice identifying complete sentences. After teaching students to identify complete sentences and having them select complete sentences when incomplete sentences were given as choices, she started doing the following activity. She put up a large picture on the board and asked students to describe in a complete short sentence what they saw (e.g., There is a train. There is a bridge.). Next, she had her students create more complex sentences using connectors (e.g., "There is a train, and there is a bridge," or better still, "There is a train crossing over a covered bridge."). In order to get everyone to participate, she had the other students in the class indicate if their classmate used a complete sentence or not by giving a soundless "thumbs up or down." When students gave incomplete sentences, she immediately moved into a My Turn correction and had everyone say the complete sentence after her. During this activity, she tried to use pictures that enabled students to use some of their new vocabulary words.

Plurals, Plurals, and More   Either because of dialect or because English is a second language, many students in Ms. DeMarco's class did not correctly use plurals, especially irregular ones, in formal syntax when answering questions or writing stories. She tried to include a plural-singular discrimination activity into her classroom schedule several times a week, even if for only a short time to, provide practice. When students made errors, she used an effective error correction.

Ms. DeMarco divided the class into two teams to play the plural game. Everyone on Team #1 was given a card with *yes* written on one side and *no* written on the other. Once the card was up, it couldn't be switched or the team didn't get a point. The members of

Team #2 sat in a line ready to walk up to the front and answer questions. Ms. DeMarco used a new vocabulary word the students had been learning or a word whose plural form needed practice. The first student on Team #2 walked up to the front and Ms. DeMarco said, "I see one *canyon.*" Ms. DeMarco then asked, "Say it for *six,*" The same student had to answer, "I see six canyons." After the student said the sentence, the Team #1 members held up their card to indicate whether the correct answer was given. Students on Team #1 got a point if the correct plural was used. Students on Team #2 got a point if every card (or 9 out of 10 cards) had the correct answer. Some questions that Ms. DeMarco asked included:

I see a *deer.* Say it for *eight.*

A *chime* rang today. Say it for *three.*

Kwame fought a *lion.* Say it for *two.*

Motivating Your Students to Do Their Best

Structuring for Positive Behavior

When you are conducting a challenging reading class, you cannot afford to waste a minute of instructional time dealing with disruptive behaviors. Before the school year begins, be proactive and plan the physical classroom environment to reflect environmental strategies supported by research as effective ways to help students stay on task, focused on their work. One of your first decisions should be determining where students will sit during large and small reading groups. Studies investigating the behavior of high-risk students showed that students have more on-task behavior and decreased disruptive behavior when they have more personal space. In classrooms where students have more space between each other, teachers are even rated by their students as more sensitive and friendly (Paine et al., 1983). If students sit at desks, teachers often can reduce behaviors that are disruptive to the class by simply moving the desks farther apart.

In younger classrooms, students often sit on the rug during group reading time. In classrooms that are not physically large enough to have a large rug area, the wigglier children will often begin jostling each other with their elbows while invading each other's personal space. In these circumstances, teachers find themselves frequently correcting students to keep their hands and feet to themselves. In these smaller classrooms, chairs might present a better alternative for getting students to do their best work. Sometimes only one or two students in the class have a difficult time when the group is reading on the rug. For those students, a carpet square, a taped off area, or a chair often provides the structure needed to listen and participate in the group. If older students sit around tables, reducing the number of students at one table provides more space between them.

Use of frequent activity shifts and periodic physical movement to provide students with the opportunity to stretch will also help students' concentration. The younger the student, the more activity shifts are needed. For example, after students who are sitting on the rug practice the sound for the letter *n,* one teacher inserted a 2-minute activity where everytime she said the *n* sound, the students jumped up like frogs. Then after a short practice session blending words, the teacher asked everyone to walk to their tables to write the letter *n.* The writing practice was followed by a game where everyone stood up and in unison answered *yes* or *no* to vocabulary questions the teacher asked. Although a teacher in an older classroom can stretch teaching activities out over longer periods of time, periodic 1- or 2-minute stretch breaks can still release energy before students begin the next activity.

Teachers should also be sensitive to students' need for water. If students are actively answering in unison, their throats become parched after a while, causing them to become uncomfortable. In order to avoid this distraction, some teachers allow their students to carry water bottles; others always stop for a moment at the water fountain when the class is in the hall en route to special activities.

Fact or Fiction

1. **Children learn more words directly, from instruction in school, than they do indirectly, from listening or conversing.**

Fact	Fiction

    Fiction. Research shows that children learn most words indirectly through everyday experiences with oral and written language (Armbruster et al., 2002). Proficiency in reading is the single most effective independent word learning strategy (Jittendra et al., 2004). While there is an important place for teaching vocabulary directly using the strategies described in this chapter, teaching your students to be accurate, fluent readers may be the single most important contribution you can make to improve their vocabulary.

2. **The meaning of most words can be discerned from using the words around them ("in context").**

Fact	Fiction

    Fiction. Unlike oral language, written language lacks features that support word learning such as intonation, body language, and shared physical surroundings (Beck et al., 2002). Also, the actual words surrounding a given word in written context often provide few clues to its meaning; in fact, they can even be misleading (Beck et al., 2002). Using context effectively depends on accurate and fluent decoding, skills often lacking in students who are at risk. Nonetheless, sometimes context clues are helpful, and the ability to use the context can empower students to learn words while they are reading independently. It is recommended that the strategies used to teach students to use the context described in this chapter be one part of your total vocabulary program. Before deciding whether to use this strategy, make sure that the particular context of the target word can be realistically used to decipher its meaning.

3. **It is important to make sure that students know the meaning of all potentially unknown words before they read a story.**

Fact	Fiction

    Fiction. Armbruster and colleagues (2002) point out several reasons why teachers should not teach all potentially unknown words in a story directly. The text may have so many words that are unknown to students that there is not enough class time to teach them all directly. Also, students can comprehend text without knowing the meaning of all the words. Finally, students need to be able to figure out words on their own if they are to benefit from the greatest potential source of new vocabulary learning; independent reading. Criteria for selecting words for direct instruction described in this chapter included teaching words that are important, useful, and difficult.

APPLIED ACTIVITIES

1. The following vocabulary words have been identified in your reading series for the upcoming story about a farmer who planted a seed that grew into a large turnip: *granddaughter, planted, grew, strong, enormous,* and *turnip.* Assuming you only have time to teach your second grade students the meaning of two of these words, which words would you choose to teach? Justify your selections.

2. For the next 48 hours, make a list of words that you don't know the meaning of and note where you encountered each word. For example, you may not know the meaning of a word used by a TV broadcaster, a word mentioned in a lecture, a word you read in the newspaper, or a word in directions for your new software program.

3. Develop either a student-friendly definition or synonym for each of the following vocabulary words: *survive, frontier, nearby, tame,* and *orchard.*

4. For two of the words above, one using a synonym, and the other a definition, develop a series of student questions to teach the meaning of the word using examples and nonexamples. Model your questions after ones shown in Figures 6.2 and 6.3. For each word, include at least three positive and three negative examples.

5. Develop a keyword for one of the following words: *burly, cram, epic, enzyme,* or *pow-wow.* In developing the keyword, use a similar process to the one used for the word apex in Figure 6.7.

6. Develop a semantic map to teach students the range of words that can be used to represent the word *soft.* Your semantic map should help students better understand the concept of soft by categorizing its different qualities.

7. Shown below is a passage from a Grade 2 basal. Tell how you would teach students to use context clues to figure out the meaning of the word *lack.*

   The thick cloud of dust, rock, and smoke would swirl around the world, blocking the sunlight for months or even years. Without sunlight, the earth would grow very cold. Their idea is that the <u>lack</u> of sunshine caused dinosaurs and other life forms to die.

8. Identify the words below that you would teach using morphemic analysis. For one of these words, develop a mini-script telling what you would say to your students when teaching them to use morphemic analysis to figure out its meaning.

careless	bicolor	winless
confusing	demented	unspeakable
discouraged	useful	substandard
discipline	uncomfortable	revocable

9. Your students came across the following sentence in their readers: The boys and girls made a *dash* for the playground. You had them look up the word *dash* in their dictionaries and they found the following three meanings:

   a. a rush: We made a *dash* for the bus.
   b. a small amount: Put in just a *dash* of pepper.
   c. a short race: He won the fifty-yard *dash.*

   Develop a mini script that you could use to teach students to figure out which meaning of *dash* is used in the story.

10. After lunch you can squeeze in 10 more minutes of vocabulary instruction. This week you have directly taught the following vocabulary words: *slight, hull, reflected, curve, eclipse,* and *prairie.* Plan activities you could do during that time this week to provide more practice for your class.

11. Select two idioms that contain the same word and describe at least two concrete activities you could use to teach the idioms to English language learners.

12. Analyze the strengths and weaknesses of a vocabulary software program.

REFERENCES

Armbruster, B., Lehr, F., & Osborn, J. (2001). *Put reading first: The research building blocks for teaching children to read.* Washington, DC: Partnership for Reading.

Barton, J. (1996). Interpreting character emotions for literature comprehension. *Journal of Adolescent & Adult Literacy, 40*(1), 22–28. Cited in H. W. Catts & A. G. Kamhi, (2005), *Language and reading disabilities* (2nd ed.). Boston: Allyn & Bacon, p. 191.

Baumann, J., Edwards, E., Boland, E., Olejnik, S., & Kame'enui, E. (2003). Vocabulary tricks: Effects of instruction in morphology and context on fifth-grade students' ability to derive and infer word meanings. *American Educational Research Journal, 40*(2), 447–494.

Beck, I., McKeown, M., & Kucan, L. (2002). *Bringing words to life: Robust vocabulary instruction.* New York: The Guilford Press.

Beimiller, A. (2001). Teaching vocabulary: Early, direct, and sequential. *American Educator, 25,* 24–28.

Beimiller, A. (2003). Oral comprehension sets the ceiling on reading comprehension. *American Educator, 27*(1), 23–25.

Berger, Melvin (1995). *All About Electricity.* New York: Scholastic.

Bos, C. S., & Vaughn, S. (1998). *Strategies for teaching students with learning and behavior problems* (4th ed.). Boston: Allyn & Bacon.

Carnine D. W., Silbert, J., Kame'enui, E. J., & Tarver, S. (2004). *Direct instruction reading* (4th ed.). New Jersey: Merrill Prentice Hall.

Catts, H. (1991). The relationship between speech-language impairments and reading disabilities. *Journal of Speech and Hearing Research, 36,* 948–958.

Celce-Murcia, M., et al. (1996). *Teaching pronunciation: A reference for teachers of English to speakers of other languages.* New York: Cambridge University Press.

Cole, Joanna. *The magic school bus and the electric field trip.* New York: Scholastic, 1997.

Collections for Young Scholars. (1995). Chicago: Open Court Publishing.

Dahl, R. (1972). *Charlie and the great glass elevator: The further adventures of Charlie Bucket and Willy Wonka, chocolate-maker extraordinary.* New York: Knopf.

Davidson, J., Elcock, J., & Noyes, P. (1996). A preliminary study of the effect of computer-assisted practice on reading attainment. *Journal of Research in Reading, 19*(2), 102–110.

Drucker, M. J. (2003). What reading teachers should know about ESL learners. *The Reading Teacher, 57*(1), 22–29.

Educational Resources Inc. (2004). *Strategies for high-stakes tests.* Unpublished manuscript.

Engelmann, S. & Osborn, J. (1999). *Language for learning.* Columbus, OH: SRA/McGraw Hill.

Epstein, S., & Epstein, B. (1977). *The first book of electricity.* New York: Franklin Watts.

Foil, C. R., & Alber, S. R. (2002). Fun and effective ways to build your students' vocabulary. *Intervention in School and Clinic, 37*(3), 131–139.

Gersten, R., Fuchs, L. S., Williams, J. P., & Baker, S. (2001). Teaching reading comprehension strategies to students with learning disabilities: A review of research. *Review of Educational Research,* 279–320.

Hart, B., & Risley, T. R. (1995). *Meaningful differences in the everyday experiences of young American children: The everyday experience of one and two year old American children.* Baltimore, MD: Paul H. Brookes.

Hebert, B. M., & Murdock, J. Y. (1994). Comparing three computer-aided instruction output modes to teach vocabulary words to students with learning disabilities. *Learning Disabilities & Practice, 9*(3), 136–141.

Horton, S., Lovitt, T., & Givens, A. (1988). A computer-based vocabulary program for three categories of student. *British Journal of Educational Technology, 19*(2), 131–143.

Irugo, S. (1986). A piece of cake: Learning and teaching idioms. *ELT Journal, 40*(3), 236–242.

Jitendra, A., Edwards, L., Sacks, G., & Jacobson, L. (2004). What research says about vocabulary instruction for students with learning disabilities. *Exceptional Children, 70*(3), 299–322.

Johnson, G., Gersten, R., & Carnine, D. (1987). Effects of instructional design variables on vocabulary acquisition of LD students: A study of computer-assisted instruction. *Journal of Learning Disabilities, 20*(4), 206–213.

Kame'enui, E., Francis, D., Fuchs, L., Good, R., O'Connor, R., Simmons, D., Tindal, G., & Torgesen, J. (2002). *An analysis of reading assessment instruments for K–3.* Institute for the Development of Educational Achievement, University of Oregon. [online]. Available: http://idea.uoregon.edu/assessment/

McKeown, M., Beck, I., Omanson, R., and Pople, M. (1985). Some effects of the nature and frequency of vocabulary instruction on the knowledge and use of words. *Reading Research Quarterly, 20,* 522–535.

Mastropieri, M. A., Scruggs, T. E., Fulk, B. J. M. (1990). Teaching abstract vocabulary with the keyword method: Effects on recall and comprehension. *Journal of Learning Disabilities, 23,* 92–96.

Miller, A.D., Barbetta, P. M., & Heron, T. E. (1994). START tutoring: Designing, training, implementing, adapting, and evaluating tutoring programs for school and home settings. In R. Gardner, D. M. Sainato, J. O. Cooper, T. E. Heron, W. L. Heward, J. Eshleman, & T. A. Grossi (Eds.), *Behavior analysis in education: Focus on measurably superior instruction* (pp. 265–282). Monterey, CA: Brooks/Cole.

Moats, L. (Summer 2001). Overcoming the language gap. *American Educator, 25*(2), 5, 8–9. www.aft.org/american_educator/summer2001/lang_gap_moats.html

Paine, S., Darch, C., Deutchman, L., Radicchi, J., & Rosellinni, L. (1983). *Structuring your classroom for academic success.* Champaign, IL: Research Press.

Pany, D., Jenkins, J. R., & Schreck, J. (1982). Vocabulary instruction: Effects on word knowledge and reading comprehension. *Learning Disability Quarterly, 5,* 202–215.

National Reading Panel. (2000). *Teaching children to read: An evidence-based assessment of the scientific research literature on reading and its implications for reading instruction.* Washington, DC: National Institute of Child Health and Human Development.

Ruddell, R. B. (1999). *Teaching children to read and write: Becoming an influential teacher* (2nd ed.). Boston: Allyn & Bacon.

Schmitt, N., & Carter, R. (2000). The lexical advantage of narrow reading for second language learners. *TESOL Journal, 9*(1), 4–9.

Segers, E., & Verhoeven, L. (2003). Effect of vocabulary training by computer in kindergarten. *Journal of Computer-Assisted Learning, 19,* 557–566.

Sinclair, J. (Ed.). (2003). Learner's dictionary: Concise edition. Glasgow, UK: Collin's Cobuild.

Stahl, S. A., & Fairbanks, M. M. (1986). The effects of vocabulary instruction: A model-based meta-analysis. *Review of Educational Research, 56*(1), 72–110.

Stanovich, K. E. (1986). Matthew effects in reading: Some consequences of individual differences in the acquisition of literacy. *Reading Research Quarterly, 21,* 360–407.

Sticht, T., & James, J. (1984). Listening and reading. In P. Pearson (Ed.), *Handbook of research on reading* (pp. 293–318). New York: Longmans.

Taylor, H. (1993). *Coyote places the stars.* New York: Simon & Schuster.

Wilson, B., & Risucci, D. (1998). The early identification of developmental language disorders and the prediction of the acquisition of reading skills. In R. Masland & M. Masland (Eds.), *Preschool prevention of reading failure* (pp. 187–203). Parkton, MD: York Press.

Wood, R. (1997). *Electricity and magnetism fundamentals.* New York: McGraw-Hill.

Comprehension

Key Terms

Comprehension
Comprehension strategies
Expository text
Fix-up strategies
Inference
Main idea
Metacognitive skills
Monitoring text
Narrative text
Plot

Prior knowledge
Pronoun referents
Retelling
Setting
Signal words
Story grammar
Story map
Summarization
Theme
Think-alouds

Objectives

After reading this chapter you will be able to:

1. Define reading comprehension including four key factors that influence it.
2. Describe the knowledge and skills students need to comprehend narrative and expository text.
3. Assess student reading comprehension skills.
4. Implement teaching strategies to effectively teach reading comprehension skills.

What Is Reading Comprehension, and Why Teach It?

Ms. Linder was examining the performance of her students on the most recent state high stakes reading test. She noted that about 60% of her students met or exceeded standards on the test. Almost all of these students had also met benchmark on the most recent DIBELS assessment in oral reading fluency. Not content with having 40% of her students score below grade level on the state test, Ms. Linder reminded herself that most of these students had problems using and understanding oral language as well. Ms. Linder noticed that she had a smaller number of other types of readers in her class, also. Ricardo, a student whose primary language was Spanish, scored above benchmark on the DIBELS Oral Reading Fluency assessment but still failed to meet standards on the state test. Benjamin, a student who was diagnosed with dyslexia, struggled with reading fluency but had strong oral language and reasoning skills. Although Benjamin scored below benchmark on the DIBELS, he was still able to score above standard on the state test.

Reading comprehension is the active process of getting meaning from written text. Reading comprehension problems such as those evidenced in Ms. Linder's class occur all too often. Results from the most recent National Assessment of Educational Progress (NAEP) in reading, a national test that focuses primarily on comprehension, show that about 38% of fourth graders and 29% of eighth grade students failed to attain even basic levels (NAEP, 2005) of reading performance. As in Ms. Linder's class, students have comprehension problems as a result of a variety of factors. Shankweiler and colleagues (1999) studied a group of poor comprehenders and found that while most of the students who could not comprehend had decoding problems of comparable magnitude, about 10% had comprehension problems even though they were good decoders. Often these poor comprehenders are English language learners such as Ricardo, who moved to this country two years ago. Another 20% of the students in the class could comprehend what they read despite having some decoding problems. These students resemble Benjamin. Just as with phonemic awareness, alphabetic principle, fluency, advanced word reading, and vocabulary, "one size does not fit all" when it comes to reading comprehension.

In its simplest form, reading is the ability to decode and understand the meaning of written words. However the process of deciphering the meaning of written words is exceedingly complex because it is influenced by a number of important factors including the person who is reading, the text being read, the task the reader is trying to accomplish, and the context in which the reading is being done (Rand Reading Study Group, 2002). A visual display of these four factors is shown in Figure 7.1, followed by a more in-depth description. Effective comprehension instruction takes into account all four factors.

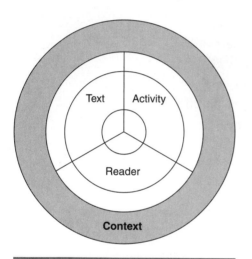

FIGURE 7.1 Factors That Affect Reading Comprehension

Text

Several characteristics of the text itself influence whether a reader comprehends text; these include text readability, text structure, and text organization. Traditionally, educators have looked to text readability as one gauge of text difficulty. Text readability formulae take into account factors such as sentence and word length as well as syntactic structure. For example, to calculate the projected grade level of a text, a teacher can use the Dale-Chall readability formula, which are based on an average sentence length and the number of unfamiliar words (Chall & Dale, 1995). The authors of this readability formula determined that readers typically find it easier to read, process, and recall a passage if the words are familiar and the sentences shorter. During the past two decades, the emphasis has shifted from classic readability formulae to other text features that also affect comprehension. The clarity of writing contributes to the ease of comprehending a text, including the presence of clear pronoun references, explicit or obvious connectives such as *because, since, therefore,* and transition elements between ideas.

Text structure refers to the way certain types of text are organized to form a framework or pattern (Bos & Vaughn, 2006; Englert & Thomas, 1987). Students who can recognize these patterns have an easier time understanding what they read. The two broadest categories of text, **narrative text** (fiction) and **expository text** (nonfiction) are then broken down into subcategories. Science fiction, tall tales, and mystery stories are subgenres of narrative text. Examples of expository text include biographies, letters, and textbooks. Narrative text is generally much easier to comprehend than expository text, which is characterized by a greater density of technical vocabulary as well as concepts requiring considerable student background knowledge. Keep in mind that comprehension in one kind of reading matter does not automatically transfer to comprehension in others. Jahil's ease in understanding and remembering expository science text does not ensure that he will have the same facility with narrative text. If Jahil does not understand irony, he will have difficulty comprehending a narrative text that is satirical. Table 7.1 lists some differences between narrative and expository text.

It is important to teach your students what these text structures are, how to recognize them in text, and how to use them to understand what they are reading. Narrative text, which has a **plot,** can be organized into meaningful parts called **story grammars** including **theme, setting,** character, problem, attempts at resolution, resolution, and reactions. Later in this chapter, visual organizers called story maps, which are used to help organize student's thinking about narrative text, will be discussed in more detail.

Expository text is also organized in specific ways, but unlike narrative text, each piece of expository text does not have the same structure. Expository text usually includes more than one text structure. Fortunately, there are key structures that occur with enough frequency to make manageable the assessing of common expository text structures and the teaching of their identification as a comprehension tool. Table 7.2 shows a list of the five common expository text structures, the ideas they communicate to the reader, and the key words that signal their presence.

Each of these expository text structures has a related graphic organizer or organizers that teachers can use to assist comprehension during or after reading. A sample of some of those organizers and how to teach them will be discussed later in this chapter.

TABLE 7.1 Comparison of Narrative and Exposition

Narrative	Expository
Purpose to entertain.	Purpose to inform.
Consistent text structure; all narratives have same basic organization.	Variable text structures; different genres have different structure.
Focus on character motivations, intentions, goals.	Focus on factual information and abstract ideas.
Often require multiple perspectives taking understanding points of view of different characters.	Expected to take the perspective of the writer of the text.
Can use pragmatic inferences, i.e., inference from similar experiences.	Must use logical-deductive inferences based on information in texts.
Connective words not critical—primarily *and, then, go.*	Connective words critical—wide variety of connectives, e.g., *because, before, after, when, if-then, therefore.*
Each text can stand alone.	Expected to integrate information across texts.
Comprehension is generally assessed informally in discussion.	Comprehension often assessed in formal, structured tests.

Source: Catts, H. W., & Kamhi, A. G. (1999). *Language and reading disabilities* (2ne ed.). Boston: Pearson Education; p. 159. Copyright © 1999 by Pearson Education. Reprinted by permission of the publisher.

TABLE 7.2   Expository Text Types and Characteristics

Text Type	Function	Signal Words
Descriptive	The text describes something or where something is.	**Description Signals** let the reader know where: *above, over, under, outside, between, down, of, in front of, on top of, beside, to the right/left, behind, across, along, outside, inside, near, appears to be, nearby*
Sequence/ procedural	The text tells how to do or make something. The text relates a sequence of events.	**Sequence** or **Time Signals** let the reader know information about *when* something is happening: *first . . . next . . . then, second . . . third, following this step, finally, initially, afterward, preceding, while, as, then, at last, now, ever since, in quick succession, eventually*
Cause/ effect	The text gives reasons why something happens. The text tells what might happen next.	**Cause/Effect Signals** let the reader know when one thing is the result of something else: *because, since, reasons, then, therefore, for this reason, results, effects, consequently, so, in order, thus, as a result, thus, hence*
Problem/ Solution	The text states a problem and offers solutions to the problem.	**Problems/Solution Signals:** *a problem is, a solution is*
Comparison/ Contrast	The text shows how two things are the same or different.	**Compare/Contrast Signals** let the reader know about how things are alike or different: *different, same, alike, similar, although, however, on the other hand, but yet, still, rather than, instead of, as opposed to*
Enumerative	The text gives a list of things that are related to the topic.	**Example Signals** let the reader know that this is what something means: *an example is, for instance, another, next, finally, for example, in other words, such as, in the same way as, specifically, much like, similar to*

A third text characteristic that affects comprehension is text organization. Text that is clearly organized around one or two "big ideas," explicitly communicating their presence to the reader is easier to understand than text emphasizing smaller details. Big ideas are the major concepts in a text that give meaning to all of the smaller details. For example if in the title or an introductory list of objectives, the author of a science article highlights the big idea that the flow of energy can be controlled by conductors and insulators, and then makes explicit connections in the text between these big ideas and smaller details, the reader will be more likely to understand the text and generate insightful questions about the content.

Comprehension involves understanding various types and levels of information. The ease with which children access information from text depends on how explicitly it is written. For example, information directly stated in the text is easier to understand than information that needs to be inferred. Because texts vary in explicitness, comprehension instruction should reflect that variability by using both explicit and implicit text (Dale, 1966; Bos & Vaughn, 2006). In explicit text, information is stated directly in the text and can be learned using a minimum of background knowledge. This type of text is the easiest to comprehend. In text that is implicit, students need to use their background knowledge and reasoning skills to make sense of it. For example, Ms. Chao had her students read the following paragraph:

> Susan got a pretty doll for her birthday. The doll cost her parents a lot of money. She also got a new tennis racket and two new CD's. But Susan still didn't feel happy.

First Ms. Chao asked her students, "What did Susan get for her birthday?" This question required explicit information because the answer was directly stated in the text. Next, Ms. Chao asked her students, "Why was Susan unhappy?" This question asked for implicit information since the answer was not directly contained in the text; the students needed to use their background knowledge and reasoning skills to answer it (Bos & Vaughn, 2006).

This website explains how you can improve students' understanding of textbook content: **www.ldonline. org/ld_indepth/teaching_ techniques/understanding_ textbooks.html.**

Reader

Prior knowledge, or the knowledge and skills that readers bring to the reading process also strongly influence comprehension. First and foremost is a reader's ability to decode text accurately and fluently enough to allow him to think about what he is reading. It is often claimed that large numbers of students, called "word callers," can fluently read text but do not comprehend what they are reading. In reality, research shows that only about 2.5% of students fall into this category, thus emphasizing the strong relationship between fluency and comprehension (Shankweiler, 1999). Students who effortlessly read the words in a text almost always have the resources needed to comprehend the information in comparison to students whose energy and attention is consumed by laborious decoding. Strategies for producing fluent, accurate readers were covered in Chapters 1–5.

A student's background, language, and vocabulary knowledge also affect comprehension. If Carla has visited the Southwest, she is more apt to understand a mystery that takes place in the Arizona desert. If Connor's grandmother talks about her homeland of Vietnam, he is likely to understand clearly a well-written expository text about the Vietnam War. Strategies for building student vocabulary and other oral language skills were described in Chapter 6. Because comprehension is "an active process that requires an intentional and thoughtful interaction between the reader and the text" (National Reading Panel Report, 2000, p. 13), readers must actively employ various comprehension strategies as they read. Good readers make predictions based on background knowledge, focus on looking forward and backward in the text to find important information, paraphrase, explain, summarize and construct conclusions about what they read (Pressley et al., 1995; Smith, 1999). They employ fix-up strategies such as underlining or using a dictionary when they recognize they are not fully understanding the text (Keene, 2002).

Activity

The nature and purpose of the reading task also affect comprehension (Moats, 2005). Motivation to continue reading can depend on whether an individual is reading for pleasure or to acquire new information. Is the text voluntary reading or part of a job or school requirement? Before the reader starts, does she have prior interest or background knowledge about the reading? All of these factors can affect students' motivation to persist and continue reading until they achieve understanding. Finally, reading may be tied to extrinsic consequences that include grades or test scores or intrinsic consequences that involve feelings of amusement, satisfaction, or enlightenment (Moats, 2005). Consequences can affect all aspects of comprehension including whether students stick with a task and the desire to select the correct strategies, monitor understanding, and employ fix-up strategies if needed. Gato might not have had any interest in Antarctica before reading a book on that topic that his teacher selected, but halfway through his reading, he is so interested in learning more about the emperor penguins and how the ice is beginning to melt that he starts rereading the book again so he understands all of the information.

Context

Finally, the context in which reading occurs can have a significant effect on comprehension, especially the amount of support provided for reading by peers and teachers. McEwan (2001) explains,

Students must experience success if they are to progress in reading proficiency. Therefore, teachers must structure learning situations that ensure success. Success increases the willingness of students to work harder and to endure some frustration. Teachers can control a student's success in three ways: (a) selection and sequencing of instructional objectives (b) grouping of students for instruction and (c) instructional procedures and activities. (p. 84)

Specific strategies for carrying out each of these are described throughout this chapter and text. Feelings of inadequacy for the task can consume the reader's attention and diminish effort. The extent to which reading is valued at home or within a student's peer group also can affect the effort that goes into reading challenging material for understanding. If several third grade girls are reading *The Babysitter's Club* or Harry Potter books and then at recess discussing the hair-raising stories, other third graders are likely to pick up the same books. Many schools have strengthened their reading culture by providing incentives to students who read a certain number of books by holding book fairs and by routinely encouraging parents to read to their children. Teachers and building principals who are readers themselves and have a personal passion for reading are more likely to convey that enthusiasm to students.

What Underlying Skills Do Students Need to Comprehend Text?

Oral Reading Fluency

We have often explained that students who can read text accurately and fluently are much more likely to be able to understand what they read. Therefore, systematic, explicit instruction in phonics and oral reading fluency is at the heart of any good instructional program in reading comprehension (Pressley, 2002).

Oral Language

Chapter 6 emphasized the importance of oral language skills, including knowledge of vocabulary and figurative language. Students who come to school deficient in oral language need direct instruction in those oral language skills essential for adequate listening, speaking, and, ultimately, reading Most instruction in reading comprehension consists of students discerning the meaning of groups of paragraphs, or passages. Yet, students' ability to understand passages depends largely on their ability to understand sentences. Moats (2005) points out that because the structure of written language is different from oral language, many children may struggle in understanding written sentences even if they are able to understand oral ones. In addition, the ability to process sentence structure efficiently aids overall reading comprehension as well as written composition (Moats, 2005). For these reasons, effective comprehension instruction often needs to include some explicit instruction at the sentence level.

Sentence Repetition

Sentence repetition, or the ability to repeat verbatim a simple sentence pronounced by the teacher is an important yet difficult skill for many young children who are at risk for reading difficulties. Both listening and reading comprehension depend on children being able to hold information in working memory as they simultaneously process new information.

Carnine and colleagues (2004) recommend providing 3 to 5 minutes of daily practice for students who cannot perform this skill. Practice can start with a simple My Turn where the teacher says the sentence, followed by a Your Turn. If students are unable to exactly repeat the sentence the teacher can provide more support by saying the sentence emphasizing the deleted or mispronounced part with a "pause and punch." In a pause and punch, the teacher increases her voice volume as she says the words which were difficult for the students as in, "The BIG rabbit hopped UNDER the fence." If a pause and punch doesn't provide enough support, the teacher should move into a Together turn, saying the sentence together with students until they can say it independently (Kozloff, 2005). If students continue to struggle, the teacher should start with short 3- to 4-word sentences and gradually increase the length as students progress. When students are able to repeat longer sentences exactly and with normal intonation, they are ready to move to the next oral language skill.

Many students also need to be taught to comprehend what Carnine and colleagues (2004) refer to as the question words: *who, what, when, where,* and *why.* The authors recommend teaching *who* and *what* questions first, as these are the easiest. Instruction should follow a developmental sequence next focusing on *when* and *where* questions before the more difficult *why* questions. To teach the question words, start instruction at the My Turn–Your Turn level as in this example of teaching *who* and *what.* As with sentence repetition, if students make errors while answering the questions, add the support of Together practice. In the beginning use a pause and punch when saying the critical question words.

My Turn

Teacher: **"Sarah picked up the rabbit. WHO picked up the rabbit? Sarah. (pause) WHAT did Sarah do? Picked up the rabbit."**

Your Turn

Teacher: **"Tabitha ate a peach. Say that."**
Students: "Tabitha ate a peach."
Teacher: **"WHO ate a peach?"**
Students: "Tabitha."
Teacher: **"WHAT did Tabitha do?"**
Students: "Ate a peach."

Teachers should set high expectations for their students during oral language activities, requiring their students to use the correct past tense verb form of *ate* when they answer. Once students have learned to answer all five types of questions, teachers can provide cumulative review using one sentence as the basis for student answers and eliminating the pause and punch in their questions.

Your Turn

Teacher: **"Elston swam in the pool yesterday because it was hot. Say that."** (students answer)
Teacher: **"Who swam in the pool?"** (students answer)
Teacher: **"What did Elston do in the pool?"** (students answer)
Teacher: **"Where did Elston swim?"** (students answer)
Teacher: **"When did Elston swim?"** (students answer)
Teacher: **"Why did Elston go swimming?"** (students answer)

Question words can be taught orally or using written text. As with any comprehension activity, be sure that the reading material can be read with at least 90% accuracy before using it for comprehension activities.

Another aspect of written language that can make comprehension at the sentence level more difficult is the use of **pronoun referents**, which are the nouns to which pronouns refer. A general rule of thumb is that the closer the pronoun is to its referent, the easier it is to understand. Consider this section of text:

> Now life began to change. The Eskimo hunters could see that these tools were useful. So they became traders, too. They trapped more furs than their families needed.
>
> Then they brought the furs to the trading posts. There they could trade the furs for supplies they had never had before. Because the new tools helped Eskimo hunters get along better, they became part of the Eskimo environment. (Brandwein & Bauer, 1980; cited in Friend & Bursuck, 2006)

Many readers may have trouble figuring out who *they* refers to in this passage because the author did not clearly indicate the referent. Although the placement of most pronouns is not this problematic, they must be explicitly taught because even basic pronoun referents can be difficult for students who are at risk (Carnine et al., 2004; Friend & Bursuck, 2006). As with other skills in this section, the teacher first must analyze the text students will be using, anticipate problems, and, through explicit instruction, prevent these problems from occurring, thus enhancing comprehension. Before students read, the teacher identifies unclear pronouns. Next students underline those pronouns in a passage. Finally, a series of questions asked by the teacher shows students how to find the pronoun referents, as in the following example, from Friend and Bursuck (2006). During the question session the teacher should pause and punch the pronouns as he says them.

Passage

Curtis and Dorva skipped school. They were grounded for a week. He was sorry. She got mad.

Student Questioning

Teacher: **"Curtis and Dorva skipped school." WHO skipped school?**
Students: "Curtis and Dorva."
Teacher: **"THEY were grounded for a week." Was Curtis grounded?**
Students: "Yes."
Teacher: **"Was Dorva grounded?"**
Students: "Yes."
Teacher: **"HE was sorry." Was Curtis sorry?"**
Students: "Yes."
Teacher: **"Was Dorva sorry?"**
Students: "No."
Teacher: **"SHE got mad." Did Dorva get mad?**
Students: "Yes." (Friend & Bursuck, 2006, pp. 336–337)

Students who are at risk are more likely to have difficulty comprehending text with problematic sentence structure. Moats (2005) has identified five types of sentence structure that may impede student comprehension. These structures are shown in Figure 7.2.

To help students with these problematic constructions, Moats (2005) suggests identifying problematic constructions in advance of reading a story and then monitoring student understanding of them. Moats (2005) also suggests paraphrasing difficult sentences for students as well as engaging the students in *sentence coloring*. In sentence coloring, after several My Turns, students read the same sentence several times with different phrasing or intonation to "color" the meaning of the words (Moats, p. 23). For example, Ms. Battaglia's class came across the sentence, *They will understand only this?* while reading a newspaper editorial

a. **Passive Voice**
Summer clothes *are to be replaced* by winter clothes.
New ideas *are often misunderstood* by those with firmly held biases.
The white minivan *was hit* head-on by the motorcycle.

b. **Double Negative**
We had *no* reason to think she was *un*stable.
There was *no* evidence that the suspect was *not* at home as he had claimed on the night of the robbery.
It was *not* true that he *dis*liked the gift.
I did *not* advise him *never* to reveal his intentions to her.

c. **Verb Tenses and Auxiliaries**
Under orders, *we were to be patient* for hours.
Would it not have been easier to say "yes"?
What would he be doing if he were here?

d. **Prepositions and Articles**
He put the paper *aside* to read the book.
He put the paper *beside* the book.
He put the paper *inside* the book.
This is *the* major problem.
This is *a* major problem.

e. **Ambiguous Phrases, Word Order, and Placement of Phrases**
Folding diapers would be expensive.
Hanging plants would require light.
They will understand only this.
Only they will understand this.
The drunken driver with the VW struck the woman.
The drunken driver struck the woman with the VW.

FIGURE 7.2   Problematic Sentence Structures

Source: From Moats, L. C. (2005). *Language essentials for teachers of reading and spelling. Module 6: Digging for meaning: Teaching text comprehension.* Boston: Sopris West (p. 22).

on the street riots in France. Ms. Battaglia wanted to be sure her students understood the impact of the question mark on the meaning of the sentence. She read the sentence to her students, coloring it to emphasize the *question* by emphasizing the word *this* at the end and using intonation denoting a question: *They will understand only* ***this?*** To provide contrast, she colored the sentence in a different way, as it would be spoken without the question mark, emphasizing the word *they* this time: ***They*** *will understand only this.* Ms. Battaglia then had her students say the sentence each way, commenting on the different meaning of each, including what the original sentence meant within the context of the editorial.

Carnine and colleagues (2004) suggest another effective strategy for teaching students to comprehend sentences written in the passive voice. The teaching format involves constructing a short sentence in the active voice and then rewriting or saying it in the passive voice. Initially the teacher begins with a My Turn, using a think-aloud, before asking questions to check for understanding. For example, in teaching passive voice, Mrs. Eckstein used the following minimally different sentences: *Allonzo screamed at Clarissa* and *Clarissa was screamed at by Allonzo.* First, the teacher thinks aloud and says, "Clarissa was screamed at by Allonzo; that means Allonzo did the screaming and Clarissa was screamed at." The teacher then repeats each sentence and moves into a Your Turn, asking, "Who was screamed at?" and, "Who did the screaming?" Students have mastered this skill when they can accurately answer questions about novel sentences without a My Turn.

Background Knowledge

Jeanne Chall (2001) coined the term "fourth-grade slump" to describe a pattern of declining test scores that begins once many students reach fourth grade. Students in the slump do not regress in fourth grade, but rather they are expected to read increasingly difficult text that contains more specialized vocabulary and abstract ideas. Often they have no frame of reference to the topics or issues in the higher-level text. Even more alarmingly, the gap between students unable to read increasingly difficult text and their peers only continues to widen until it becomes what has been described as the "eighth-grade cliff." In a downward spiral, these students are now cut off from the steadily increasing background knowledge or knowledge of the world that they could be learning through assigned and recreational reading.

Ironically, researchers have concluded that the "fourth-grade slump" results from a lack of background knowledge in the first place. Cognitive psychologists explain that adept readers connect their background knowledge to new knowledge that they read in a text. Constructing meaning from text is an active dynamic process requiring the reader to use knowledge brought to the text. E. D. Hirsch (2000) described this process when he wrote, "It takes knowledge to gain knowledge" (p. 2). Remember a time when you read a text for which you had no background knowledge. For example, if you have little or no background in higher-level European cultural history, reading the following paragraph makes little sense. If your background knowledge does not include the book mentioned in this text, you have few clues about the meaning of unknown vocabulary words. Hours later you will probably not remember this information you read:

> Since his death, Musil criticism has suffered from a polemical opposition between those who want to salvage Musil for a left-wing, Enlightenment tradition and those who are fundamentally apolitical and attracted primarily to his mysticism. The most basic level of this controversy concerns the philological problems of Musil's massive *Nachlass* and his intentions for the completion of *The Man without Qualities*. The difficulty of resolving this debate lies not only in the open-endedness of Musil's work but also in his attempt to dissolve the polar style of thought which assumes the firm oppositions between romanticism and positivism, idealism and materialism. (Luft, 1980, p. 3)

Did you feel a rising tension as you tried to extract the meaning from this text? In a discussion of the relationship of prior knowledge to comprehension, the *National Reading Panel Report* authors explain the relationship of background knowledge to reading comprehension:

> A reader must activate what he or she knows to use it during reading to comprehend a text. Without activation of what is known that is pertinent to the text, relevant knowledge may not be available during reading, and comprehension may fail; this is analogous to listening to someone speak an unknown foreign language.

If students at risk for reading difficulties are to move past the fourth-grade slump, they need an *information-rich* curriculum from the time they enter school. The information that students learn, whether it be the names of continents, information about the pyramids of Egypt, the origins of the early American civilization, or the properties of an alloy are stored in long-term memory, available for use when reading books on related subjects.

The following strategies prepare students who are at risk to build their background knowledge and avoid the fourth-grade slump.

- Develop classroom libraries that have at least 50% nonfiction books. Although adults often assume that students prefer reading fiction, a study by Kletzien and Szabo indicated that when elementary students of both genders are given quality fiction and nonfiction books, they choose nonfiction at least 50% of the time (Kletzien & Szabo 1998).

- Use strategies described in Chapter 6 to teach vocabulary.
- Integrate gradual and cumulative teaching of information about the world we live in starting in kindergarten. Young children enjoy learning important information about things they know nothing about, as long as it is taught well.
- Plan lessons so that students are reading as much expository text as narrative text during reading classes.
- Use *narrow reading* to develop students' depth of knowledge on a specific subject area. Planning an in-depth unit in science or social studies using multiple reading sources about the same subject is more effective than a less intensive approach. Lionel will know more about the Civil War if the teacher includes as part of the lesson plans a short story about Robert E. Lee, a book about Harriet Tubman and the Underground Railroad, a movie and discussion about President Lincoln, and a writing assignment about an article discussing a Yankee soldier's life.
- Weave background information into every subject area. If your third-grade students are drawing a picture of their school, teach them the meaning of *architecture* and *three-dimensional.* Everyone should be encouraged to use these same terms when they draw another building they have chosen.
- Use strategies to activate prior knowledge and use them as a check to indicate when you need to supply missing background knowledge.

> Investigate Core Knowledge lesson plans written by teachers who are developing an information-rich curriculum: **www.coreknowledge.org/ CK/resrcs/lessons/index.htm.**

What Are the Essential, Scientifically-Based Reading Comprehension Strategies of the National Reading Panel?

Skilled readers construct meaning before, during, and after reading by using a set of comprehension strategies to integrate information from the text with their background knowledge (National Reading Panel, 2000). These reading **comprehension strategies** are conscious plans under the control of the reader who makes decisions about which strategies to use and when to use them. Metacognition, the awareness of one's thought processes while reading along with the ability to plan, monitor, and select effective strategies when there is a problem with comprehension, enables a reader to effectively apply comprehension strategies to create meaning (Pressley, 2002).

While every reader benefits from learning and refining comprehension strategies, many students who are at risk will never move past the fourth-grade slump unless they receive explicit instruction in using them. Up until about 20 years ago, the prevailing practice for teaching reading comprehension was to provide students with practice activities consisting largely of passages followed by written comprehension questions. Very little time was spent directly teaching reading comprehension skills until pathbreaking research in the field of cognitive psychology provided evidence that, as with decoding skills, comprehension skills also need to be taught explicitly and systematically.

> Learn more about how to apply reading comprehension strategy instruction at **http://teacher. scholastic.com/reading/best practices/comprehension/prompts thatguide.pdf.**

Research supports the position that students can be taught to monitor their strategic behavior and performance and that this training can improve their reading. The National Panel Report analysis concluded that the seven strategies in Table 7.3 have a firm scientific basis for improving text comprehension (Armbruster et al., 2001; National Reading Panel, 2000; Texas Education Agency, 2000).

TABLE 7.3   Comprehension Strategies

Comprehension Monitoring	This metacognitive process is a general competence in which readers are aware of what they do understand and do not understand. They recognize when "fix-up' strategies are necessary and which ones will resolve comprehension problems.
Cooperative Learning	This "student-centered instructional approach in which students work in small, mixed-ability groups with a shared learning goal" is sometimes called collaborative learning (Friend & Bursuck, p. 508).
Graphic and Semantic Organizers	These are visual representations of narrative or expository text that help the reader recognize its structure and comprehend it.
Self-Questioning	Throughout the reading process, the reader generates and asks questions.
Story Structure Analysis	Students learn to identify the framework of a story by analyzing the grammar of narrative text, including the story elements of setting, characters, motivation, problems, plot, and theme. The reader often completes a graphic organizer called a story map that more concretely displays these story elements.
Summarizing	This strategy involves pulling together or synthesizing information in one's own words.
Answering Questions	Text-explicit and text-implicit questions guide the students' understanding about what they have read.

Comprehension Monitoring

For students to learn how to monitor their comprehension, teachers must not only teach them to use specific comprehension strategies, but also when to use them. If you ever read and comprehended a nineteenth-century Russian novel by Tolstoy, you will remember that whenever you became confused about the character referred to in the text, you stopped your reading to check the character list and determine exactly who was speaking and what the relationship was to the main characters, then asked yourself whether the dialogue now made sense given the character clarification. When two characters had almost identical names, you stopped and double-checked the spelling to make sure you knew who was speaking. Proficient readers are aware when they do not know a word or when the text does not make sense and they know how to apply the **fix-up strategies** described in Table 7.4, deciding which ones will help them with specific problems. **Monitoring text** is not a natural process, but research demonstrates that it can be taught.

Armbruster and colleagues (2001, p. 50) have described several comprehension monitoring strategies that students may use.

Identify Where the Difficulty Occurs   "I don't understand the second paragraph on page 76."

Identify What the Difficulty Is   "I don't get what the author means when she says 'Arriving in America was a milestone in my grandmother's life.'"

Restate the Difficult Sentence or Passage in Their Own Words   "Oh, so the author means that coming to America was a very important event in her grandmother's life."

Look Back through the Text   "The author talked about Mr. McBride in Chapter 2, but I don't remember much about him. Maybe if I reread that chapter, I can figure out why he's acting this way now."

TABLE 7.4 Fix-Up Strategies

Sounding out unknown words	Slowing down and rereading
Looking up a word or name (e.g., dictionary, encyclopedia, glossary, Google, Wikipedia)	Making a prediction and periodically checking whether the text corresponds to that prediction; adjusting the prediction if necessary
Reading the preface, the chapter summary, the back cover or looking for a review of the book	Taking notes during reading, making a graphic organizer, outlining the text
Reflecting on what the author is trying to say in the book	Talking to another person about a difficult section of the book
Thinking about how the book relates to background knowledge; to the reader's experiences	Creating a visual image about what the book is about
Checking the Internet for information related to a difficult section	Determining whether the information is necessary for understanding the text and ignoring it if not

Look Forward in the Text for Information That Might Help Them Resolve the Difficulty   "The text says, 'The groundwater may form a stream or pond or create a wetland. People can also bring groundwater to the surface.' Hmmm, I don't understand how people can do that . . . Oh, the next section is called 'Wells.' I'll read this section to see if it tells how they do it" (p. 50).

Cooperative Learning

To conduct instruction in a cooperative learning group, the teacher divides the class into small groups comprised of diverse students who are at different levels and have different perspectives. The group works on a clearly defined, well-structured learning activity, and expectations are that all students will participate to increase active learning time. One way to use cooperative learning is through literature circles. These can be structured as cooperative learning experiences if the teacher carefully preplans. In a literature circle, students have the opportunity to practice comprehension strategies and receive feedback from the teacher and their peers. Four or five students who have read the same book form a group to explore it in depth, assuming roles assigned by the teacher. These roles, shown in Figure 7.3, can include:

Discussion director—leads the discussion and develops questions for the group.
Summarizer—summarizes the reading selection.
Literacy reporter—finds memorable passages that are out of the ordinary.
Illustrator—develops a drawing or graphic organizer for key concepts or situations in the reading selection.
Vocabulary enricher—identifies difficult words, finds out their meaning from resources, and writes down their definitions.
Connector—finds links between this book and other books or information from the world outside.
Investigator—unearths background information related to the book.

To structure the activity, the teacher gives each student a job sheet to fill out. The individual jobs are explicitly taught by the teacher who first models how the job looks (My Turn). Next students practice the jobs as a class so that the teacher can give feedback (Together) before everyone begins to work independently in the literature circle (Your

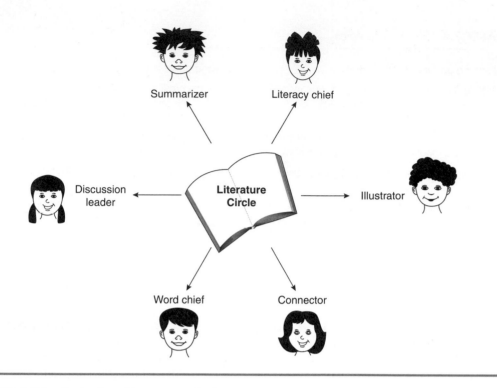

FIGURE 7.3   Roles in a Literature Circle

Turn). Each student is responsible for completing an information sheet related to her job description. A typical sheet given to a Summarizer is shown in Figure 7.4.

At the end of each session, students evaluate their own participation in the group as well as the effectiveness of the group as a whole when they complete a scoring sheet rating those factors. On a scale of 1–3, students rate their own performance on dynamics such as whether they encouraged others to participate, how well they stayed on topic, and whether they gave reasons for their opinions.

Despite its demonstrated effectiveness, cooperative learning must be conducted with great care. Dunston (2002) relates that "the double edge of the peer discussion sword lies in the challenges teachers face in successfully implementing it in their classrooms" (p. 142). She explains that teachers are challenged by behavior management issues when they are facilitating literature circle groups. In order to use cooperative learning time effectively, teachers must ensure that students stay on task, that group members who are less socially adept are allowed to have an equal opportunity to discuss, and that students refrain from devaluing others' opinions. In addition, the teacher must carefully structure all instructional activities for struggling readers, allowing them to listen to the text before any group activities take place. Another adaptation is to periodically assign the literature group a text that is at the struggling students' instructional level, thus reducing the risk of embarrassment in front of their peers. The key to providing effective comprehension instruction in a cooperative group is to preplan, closely monitor, and provide well-structured tasks.

Graphic and Semantic Organizers

Students with attention or listening problems may benefit from the additional accommodations of having a completed graphic explained to them prior to instruction for use as an advance organizer, and then completing a blank organizer after instruction with the teacher for extra practice and review.

Blackline Master
Literature Circle Role Sheet
Summarizer

Name _____   Circle _____

Book _____

Meeting Date _____   Assignment: Pages ____ to ____

Summarizer: Your job is to prepare a brief summary of today's reading. Your group discussion will start with your 1–2 minute statement that covers the key points, main highlights, and general idea of today's reading assignment.

Summary:

_____
_____
_____
_____
_____
_____

Key Points:
1. _____
2. _____
3. _____
4. _____

Connections: What did today's reading remind you of?

_____
_____
_____
_____
_____
_____

FIGURE 7.4 Literature Circle Role Sheet

Source: www.allamericareads.org/lessonplan/strategies/during/litcirc3.htm. Reprinted with permission.

Archer and Gleason (2004; cited in Friend & Bursuck, 2006) suggest the following guidelines for constructing graphic organizers when using them to help students comprehend expository text (pp. 327–328).

a. **Determine the critical content (e.g., vocabulary, concepts, ideas, generalizations, events, details, facts) that you wish to teach your students.** Helping students focus on the most critical information is important for several reasons. First, struggling readers may have trouble identifying the most important information in an oral lesson or textbook chapter. In most cases this information will be content stressed in your state's standards. Second, it is easier for students to remember several main ideas than many isolated details. Third, putting too much information on a graphic organizer can make it so visually complex that students may have trouble interpreting it.

b. **Organize the concepts in a visual representation.** Because the purpose of a graphic organizer is to clarify interrelationships among ideas and information, you should keep the visual display as simple as possible. Figure 7.5 shows a completed comparison–contrast graphic organizer.

Attribute	Native Americans	Colonists
Land	Shared	Owned
	Lived close to it without changing it	Cleared it
	Respected it	Used it

Summary

Native Americans and colonists had different ideas about the land. Native Americans shared the land whereas the colonists owned individual pieces of it. Native Americans lived close to the land; they respected and did not change it. Colonists used the land for their own gain.

FIGURE 7.5   Comparison–Contrast Concept Map

Source: Friend and Bursuck (2006). *Including students with special needs* (4th ed). Boston: Allyn & Bacon, p. 327.

c. **Design a completed concept map.** Completing the map before you teach with it ensures that the information is clear and accurate and can be presented to your students in a timely manner.

d. **Create a partially completed concept map (to be completed by students during instruction).** Requiring students to fill out the map as you present your lesson is an excellent way to keep them on task. Also, many students with special needs benefit from a multisensory approach; seeing the information on the graphic, hearing it from the teacher, and writing it on the map helps them retain the information presented.

e. **Create a blank concept map for students to use as a postreading or review exercise.** This structure for review is easy for students who are then more likely to put the information in long-term memory.

Once you have constructed graphic organizers, you can use them as follows:

a. Distribute partially completed concept maps to your students.

b. Place a transparency of the completed map on an overhead projector. Place a piece of paper under the transparency so that you expose only those portions you wish students to attend to. Limiting the amount of information you present at one time helps students with attention problems who have trouble focusing on more than one piece of information at a time.

c. Introduce the information on the concept map, proceeding in a logical order; stress the relationships between the vocabulary, concepts, events, details, facts, and so on.

d. At natural junctures, review concepts you have introduced by placing the blank map on the overhead and asking students questions about the content. This review is essential for students who have difficulty learning large amounts of information at one time.

> Download free graphic organizers from these two websites: **www.region15. org/curriculum/graphicorg.html** and **www.eduplace.com/graphic organizer/index.html.**

e. At the end of the lesson, review the critical content again using the blank concept map. You can also have students complete the blank maps for homework. These maps help students organize their studying and also help you find out what they have learned (pp. 326–327).

Self-Questioning

One way that readers become actively engaged with text is by asking themselves questions as they read. Through questions, students can reflect on what they are reading, asking why the author chose the words he did or let the character come to such a devastating end, why the main story character would fall in love with that rude person whose personality is so different, or whether the spurned lover has a chance of making a comeback. Kyle might notice while reading a social studies book that the authors didn't include enough information about the foxholes during World War I. That observation might lead him to ask himself whether it's worth looking for another book that describes what daily life in the foxholes was like. Later when Kyle begins reading about the Battle of Verdun, he might ask himself who it seems will be the victor of that battle. Once the information is provided in the text he'll ask himself whether his prediction was correct. Kyle, like other competent readers, is not aware that he monitors his comprehension routinely by asking himself whether he has understood a section just read until he comes to a section where he has to answer, "no." As soon as Kyle realizes he read the page or pages without complete understanding, he immediately goes back to the beginning of the section. Just as with other comprehension strategies, self-questioning can be explicitly taught and included into multiple-strategy instruction. Teachers can prompt students to ask questions at different points in the text by starting with the main question words: who, what, where, when, why, how.

Questioning the Author (QtA) is a strategy developed by Isabel Beck and colleagues that gets students started by providing them with strategy questions that they can eventually ask themselves when they read. The teacher gives the students one or more paragraphs to read and then asks them to answer these questions.

1. What is the author trying to tell you?
2. Why is the author telling you that?
3. Does the author say it clearly?
4. How could the author have said things more clearly?
5. What would you say instead? (Beck, McKeown, Hamilton, & Kucan, 1997)

Finally, strategic readers need to routinely ask additional questions as a part of self-monitoring. Questions such as "Does this make sense?" "What parts of this story are different from my reading predictions," and "Do I need to take notes to understand?" help students know when to apply fix-up strategies to increase their comprehension.

Story Structure Analysis: Teaching with Story Maps

Story maps are graphic organizers that provide students with a visual guide to understanding and retelling stories. They have been shown to help students with special needs read with better comprehension (Carnine et al., 2004; Pearson & Fielding, 1991.) Figure 7.6 (Friend & Bursuck, 2006) shows a story map that a second grade teacher, Ms. Barrows, used to teach her students the story *The Funny Farola* (Miranda & Guerrero, 1986). As the students read the story, Ms. Barrows guided their comprehension by asking the students questions about the various story elements and then recording the correct answers on the story map. An example of how Ms. Barrows helped her students identify the story setting and problems is shown here.

Ms. Barrows: Where do you think the story takes place? It's hard to tell, because the writers don't come right out and say it.
Lovell: I think it takes place in a city.
Ms. Barrows: Why do you think so, Lovell?
Lovell: Because it sounds like it's a big parade, and cities have big parades.
Ms. Barrows: Good thinking, Lovell. When stories don't come out and say things, we have to figure it out by thinking hard, and that's what you did. Let's all fill in the setting on our maps. [They do.] Remember, we said last week that all stories have a problem that needs to be solved. Read the next four pages and find out what the problem is here. [The students read the passage.] What's the problem?
Justin: Well, Dora's little brother and sister got lost at the parade.
Ms. Barrows: Right. That's one problem. Write it on your maps. Now, does anyone see another problem?

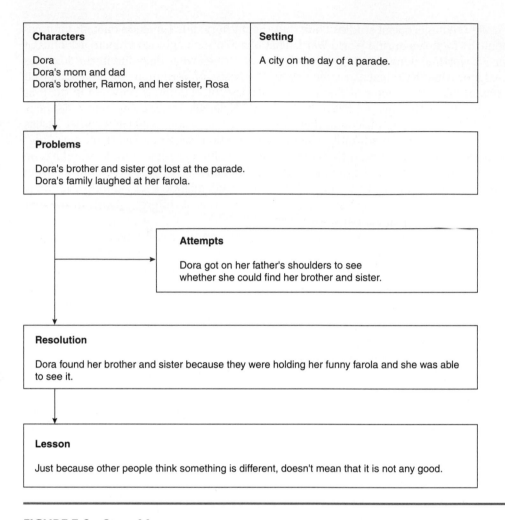

Characters	Setting
Dora Dora's mom and dad Dora's brother, Ramon, and her sister, Rosa	A city on the day of a parade.

Problems

Dora's brother and sister got lost at the parade.
Dora's family laughed at her farola.

Attempts

Dora got on her father's shoulders to see
whether she could find her brother and sister.

Resolution

Dora found her brother and sister because they were holding her funny farola and she was able
to see it.

Lesson

Just because other people think something is different, doesn't mean that it is not any good.

FIGURE 7.6   Story Map

Eliseo: I know. Dora made a farola that looked like a frog and everybody laughed at her.
Ms. Barrows: Eliseo, what's wrong with a farola that looks like a frog? I thought it looked cute.
Eliseo: I think it was because Dora's was different from everyone else's. In the pictures in the story, there were no farolas that looked like animals.
Ms. Barrows: That's right, Eliseo. Let's all put this problem on our maps. [They do.] Let's read the next page and find out what Dora and her mom and dad attempted to do to try to find her brother and sister. (pp. 330–331)

Summarizing

A **summary** is a synthesis of the important ideas in a text (Armbruster et al., 2001, p. 53). Summarizing helps students identify the main ideas in expository text and recognize important story elements in narrative text. Summarizing can also help students evaluate their understanding of what they have read, tell important and unimportant information apart, and better remember what they have read. Summarizing can be done periodically after each paragraph or section or at the end of the reading. For narrative text, students can use a story map to summarize the story such as the one shown in the previous section for *The Funny Farola*. For expository text, students state in their own words the main idea and supporting details of several related paragraphs. For example, Ms. Tara's students came up with the following summary based on several paragraphs from their social studies textbook about the United States economy after World War II: "A combination of the housing boom and baby boom had a positive effect on the economy. Jobs were plentiful, and wages were high. Still, not everyone shared in the good economic times of the 1950s."

Answering Questions

The National Reading Panel Report (2000) indicates that answering questions is probably best used as part of a multiple strategy teaching package. The Question–Answer Relationship (QAR) is one strategy that helps students who have difficulty answering **inference** questions, or questions that do not have a concrete answer spelled out in the text. These students need explicit instruction to learn how to answer questions where they must infer the answer connecting their background information, textual content, and clues presented in the reading. Teachers introduce the QAR strategy by explaining to students that there are two types of questions they answer about what they have read. Answers to the first type of question are in the reading, usually in one sentence. Answers to the second type of question come from thinking about what they already know. Students are then introduced to the four specific kinds of questions, depicted in Figure 7.7, that they answer during or after their reading.

In the Book QARs

Right There
The answer is in the text, usually easy to find. The words used to make up the question and words used to answer the question are **Right There** in the same sentence.

**Think and Search
(Putting It Together)**
The answer is in the story, but you need to put together different story parts to find it. Words for the question and words for the answer are not found in the same sentence. They come from different parts of the text.

In My Head QARs

Author and You
The answer is *not* in the story. You need to think about what you already know, what the author tells you in the text, and how it fits together.

On My Own
The answer is *not* in the story. You can even answer the question without reading the story. You need to use your own experience.

FIGURE 7.7 Four Types of Questions

Source: T. E. Raphael. Teaching question–answer relationships revisited. *The Reading Teacher, 391*(6), p. 519. Reprinted with permission of International Reading Association.

TABLE 7.5 Answers to Questions

Type of Question	Question	What Mrs. Garcia Said
Right There	What type of winter was it in Boston?	The first sentence tells me that it was a cold winter in Boston. The information is **right there** in that sentence.
Think and Search	Why did Peter and Thomas look like roly poly cubs?	The second sentence tells me that the boys looked like roly poly cubs because they wore so much clothing, and I remember that the first sentence told me that it was cold in Boston. If they were going outside in the cold, they needed to put on all those clothes, which made them look like little cubs. By **searching** through the first two sentences and using my brain **to think,** I found the answer.
On My Own	Do you think that the boys will deliver all the wood?	The story doesn't tell me anything about this, but I can figure something out **on my own.** I know that wood is heavy. If it's cold outside maybe it is snowing and the roads are slippery. The boys might fall in the snow and not be able to deliver those heavy logs to everyone.
Author and Me	What kind of transportation do you think the boys used when they went to deliver the soap and candles?	The **author** doesn't tell me anything about the kind of transportation they used. But the author does write that the story happened a long time ago back in 1774. **I** know that cars weren't invented then and that people either rode horses, rode in carriages pulled by horses, or walked. Since these were young boys, I imagine that they walked.

After introducing the four types of questions, the teacher then asks students to read three or four sentences displayed on an overhead and uses a My Turn to show how and why she would answer each of the questions. For example, Mrs. Garcia completed the example grid in Table 7.5 and explained to the class how she arrived at the answer to the four questions that were based on this passage.

> It was a cold winter in Boston back in 1774, but the cut wood had to be delivered. Ethan who was 9 years old and Jeb who was 10 looked like roly poly cubs when they went out, they wore so much clothing. Mom, who was sick from the fever, stayed at home close to the fire.

Another question answering strategy called the Survey-Question-Read-Recite-Review method (SQ3R) (Robinson, 1961, 1970) helps students understand and remember expository text. When reading a new text, students are taught to survey or scan the main parts of the text including the title, headings of paragraphs, introduction and conclusion. After a quick preview, students are encouraged to read questions provided by the text or by the teacher in order to focus on the main ideas in the text from the start. Answering the questions becomes a main purpose of reading the text. On their first read through the text, students start closely reading the text, taking notes, and jotting down unclear words. Students then reread the text, this time answering the questions. Because students remember more of what they learn if they repeat the information verbally, students next say the answers they have developed out loud. They are encouraged to explain their answers to a friend or classmate, focusing on the main points of the reading. Finally, cumulative review is provided when students review their notes a few days later.

Effective Teacher at Work

Demonstrating the KWL Plus Textbook Reading Strategy

An important component of teaching a reading comprehension strategy is to demonstrate its appropriate use. The following script shows how one teacher uses modeling to present a textbook-reading strategy to her eighth-grade class.

Teacher: Let's review the textbook-reading strategy we talked about yesterday. Please take out the cue cards you made in class yesterday.

The teacher has students read each step individually and asks them what each step involves. Questions such as, "What are the steps? What might you do with the information you think of when brainstorming? What do you do after you read the passage?

Teacher: Now that we've reviewed each step, we need to learn how to use the whole strategy effectively. Before we move on, though, let's read aloud all of the steps together as a group. When I point to the letter, say the letter, and when I point to the meaning, you read its meaning.

The students read the steps aloud: "*K* means 'what you already know,' *W* means 'what you want to know,' and *L* is 'what you learned.'"

Teacher: Good. Now I'm going to demonstrate how to use the strategy with an article I found about crayons. I'll put the passage on the overhead, as well as give each of you a copy so you can follow along at your desks. I'll work through each step of the strategy orally and write the information obtained at each step on the board. Use your cue cards to help you see what step of the strategy I'm on.

The teacher then goes through the text, demonstrating correct usage of the steps and asking for feedback. The teacher also goes back over each step, asking the students to verify that all of the steps to the strategy were followed and to explain how they were followed.

Teacher: What do I do now that I have a passage assigned to read? First, I brainstorm, which means I try to think of anything I already know about the topic and write it down.

The teacher writes on the board or overhead known qualities of crayons, such as "made of wax," "can be sharpened," and "several different brands."

Teacher: I then take this information I already know and put it into categories, like "What crayons are made of" and "Crayon colors." Next, I write down any question I would like to have answered during my reading, such as "Who invented crayons? When were they invented? How are crayons made? Where are they made?" At this point, I'm ready to read, so I read the passage on crayons. Now I must write down what I learned from the passage. I must include any information that answers the questions I wrote down before I read any additional information. For example, I learned that colored crayons were first made in the United States in 1903 by Edwin Binney and F. Harold Smith. I also learned that the Crayola Company owns the company that made the original Magic Markers. Finally, I must organize this information into a map so I can see the different main points and any supporting points.

At this point the teacher draws a map on the chalkboard or overhead.

Teacher: Let's talk about the steps I used and what I did before and after I read the passage.

A class discussion follows.

Teacher: Now I'm going to read the passage again and I want you to read the passage again. I want you to evaluate my textbook-reading skills based on the KWL Plus strategy we've learned.

The teacher than proceeds to demonstrate the strategy incorrectly.

Teacher: The passage is about crayons. Well, how much can there really be to know about crayons besides that there are hundreds of colors and they always seem to break in the middle? Crayons are for little kids, and I'm in junior high so I don't need to know that much

Continued

about them. I'll just skim the passage and go ahead and answer the question. Okay, how well did I use the strategy steps?

The class discusses the teacher's inappropriate use of the strategy.

Teacher: We've looked at the correct use of the strategy and we've seen how mistakes can be made. Are there any questions about what we did today? Tomorrow we will begin to memorize the strategy steps so that you won't have to rely on your cue cards.

Source: From *A Script for How to Teach the KWL Strategy,* by S. Butson, K. Shea, K. Pankratz, and M. Lamb, 1992. Unpublished manuscript, DeKalb: Northern Illinois University. Used with permission in Friend and Bursuck, p. 363, *Including Students with Special Needs: A Practical Guide for Classroom Teachers* (4th Edition).

How Can I Use Multiple Strategies to Maximize Student Gains in Reading Comprehension?

You have just learned about seven reading comprehension strategies that are research-based. These strategies can be even more effective when used together. The National Reading Panel determined that readers benefit when multiple comprehension strategies are taught during the process of reading narrative or expository text (NPR, 2000.) Multiple Strategy instruction should include teaching students when specific comprehension strategies are most effective—before, during, or after the reading, as depicted in Figure 7.8.

One way to teach students to use multiple strategies at once is called reciprocal teaching (Palincsar & Brown, 1988). Friend and Bursuck (2006) describe reciprocal teaching as:

> [A] way to teach students to comprehend reading material by providing them with teacher and peer models of thinking behavior and then allowing them to practice these thinking behaviors with their peers. At first, the teacher leads the dialogue, demonstrating how the strategies can be used during reading. As instruction goes on, the teacher gives the students more and more responsibility for maintaining the dialogue. Eventually students are largely responsible for the dialogue, though the teacher still provides help as necessary. (p. 371)

In reciprocal teaching students are taught the skills of summarizing, self-questioning, predicting, and clarifying. In the example that follows this passage from a U.S. history text, Mr. Buerhle used reciprocal teaching with his students (Kinder, 1990).

Economic Benefits of the Colonies

The English government had many economic reasons for wanting to build colonies in the New World. One of these had to do with England's balance of trade. The balance of trade compares what a nation buys from other nations with what other nations buy from it. If other nations buy more from it than the nation buys from others the balance of trade is good.

England did not have a good balance of trade. It needed many goods that it did not make or grow. The English weather was too cold to grow sugar cane, and England did not have enough trees to supply the wood needed to build ships. As a result, England had to buy goods such as sugar and wood from other nations. In turn, other nations bought wool and other products from England. If England had colonies in the New World, they could supply raw materials to England. These products from nature, such as wood, were necessary if England were to improve its balance of trade.

The colonies could also become a new market, or place to sell products for English goods. The colonists would need many supplies, such as tools and cloth, and English merchants would provide them. This would create more business and more jobs in England.

Before reading a text, students who are strategic often do the following:

- Activate background knowledge related to the text.

- Preview the text in order to make predictions and/or visualize the upcoming content.

- Ask questions about the text.

During their reading, students who are strategic often do the following:

- Predict future events/content in the text.

- Monitor their own understanding.

- Use fix-up strategies when they come to content they don't understand or remember (reread, use resources, decode, change speed, etc.).

- Generate questions about the reading.

- Make inferences.

- Make connections between ideas, concepts, and characters in the text.

- Synthesize by combining information from different sources, combining it with their background information.

- Visualize what is happening.

- Take notes.

- Evaluate the text: Is it believable? Is it interesting? Is it well written?

- Construct responses to the text.

After they have read text, students who are strategic often do the following:

- Generate questions about the text.

- Summarize and identify the main idea of the text.

- Recall content.

- Extend the knowledge gained from text to other reading, writing, speaking, or art activities.

- Evaluate the content and ideas in the text.

- Outline the text.

- Use text as a stepping stone for further reading.

FIGURE 7.8   Multiple Comprehension Strategies

In time, many English merchants grew rich from this trade with the colonies. The English government also grew rich by taxing the people who shipped the goods to the colonies. (Reich & Beiler, 1988)

After reading the passage, Mr. Buerhle then demonstrated (My Turn) the skills of summarizing, self-questioning, predicting, and clarifying. He looked at his students and said, "I have a question. How could the colonies make England rich? (self-questioning) As I think about it, the British could sell their products to the colonies. They could also get raw materials from the colonies so they could manufacture goods to see and improve their balance of trade (clarifying). To summarize, the British want to be rich and powerful by having the colonists buy only from them, and by using the colonies' raw materials to manufacture goods for export (summarizing). I wonder what the Colonists will think about England's trade policy? I also wonder what England will do to make the colonies only trade with them?

The *ReadingQuest.org: Making Sense in Social Studies* website has hyperlinks to twenty-seven reading strategies that can be integrated into social studies instruction: **http://curry.edschool. virginia.edu/go/readquest/strat.**

(self-questioning) I think that England will use its military to force the colonies to trade just with them (predicting)."

In the Research to Practice feature on page 275, the teacher uses reciprocal teaching to teach students to describe the main idea. Note how the teacher also emphasizes important metacognitive skills such as clarifying the meaning of difficult vocabulary words. Remember that research shows that the most important part of the technique is the teacher's releasing control and turning the dialogue over to the students (Englert & Mariage, 1991).

How Can I Assess and Monitor My Students' Progress in Reading Comprehension?

As with any skills, you need to assess your students' comprehension skills to learn who is experiencing difficulty (screening), what specific problems they are having (diagnosis), and whether they are acquiring the reading skills you are teaching them (progress monitoring). Reading comprehension assessment should occur in the following areas: oral reading fluency, oral language, listening comprehension, basic literal and inferential comprehension, narrative comprehension, expository comprehension, and metacognitive skills.

Screening

To identify which students are having comprehension problems, give the DIBELS Oral Retell Fluency assessment to your students as part of giving DIBELS Oral Reading Fluency. In this measure, after reading each passage orally for one minute, students describe what they have just read—trying to tell everything they can remember. Circle the total number of words in the students' responses. While there are no benchmarks for oral retell fluency, Good says that students' retell scores should be typically about 50% of their oral reading fluency score. He further states that it is unusual for a child reading over 60 words correct per minute to have a total retell score that is 25% or less than their fluency score. For these students with low recall scores, their oral reading fluency score alone may not be an accurate indicator of their overall reading proficiency. For example, a child reading 60 words correct per minute would be expected to use about 30 words in his retell of the passage (50%). If his retell is about 30 words, then his oral reading fluency of 60 wcpm provides a good indication of his reading comprehension skills. If his retell is 15 words (25%) or less, there may be a comprehension concern, and you will need to give more specific comprehension measures.

For example, shown in Table 7.6 (p. 276) are the May benchmark scores in oral reading fluency and oral retell fluency for Mr. Edwards' third-grade class.

Note that 14 students all scored at benchmark in oral reading fluency, which at this time of year is 110 words correct per minute. Unless other evidence—such as a standardized, curriculum-based, or state high stakes measures showing comprehension problems—indicates low reading scores, Mr. Edwards can reasonably assume that these students are making adequate progress overall in reading comprehension. However, note that Brittany and Bridget scored at benchmark levels in oral reading fluency, but their oral retell scores of 20 and 25 respectively are less than 25% of their fluency scores. These students may be having trouble with comprehension and Mr. Edwards will need to gather other information on their reading comprehension skills. Note also the scores of Keshauna, Lynn, Akaria,

---

Research to Practice

Reciprocal Teaching

The students in this class have just read a section of text that focuses on Loch Ness. They are now applying the search, summarize, and evaluate steps of POSSE.

Teacher: What is the main topic the text is talking about?

Peg: The Loch Ness monster.

Teacher: What was this section about? What was the main idea?

Peg: Oh, the lake. I have two questions: "What is a lake?" and "What lives in it?"

Teacher: Do you mean this particular lake or any lake?

Peg: This lake. Joe?

Joe: It's foggy, it's deep, and it's long and narrow.

Peg: Don?

Don: The land beside the lake. You don't know if it is real soft and could fall through it.

Teacher: So it could be soft and swampy.

Ann: I think the Loch Ness monster lives there.

Teacher: Is Ann answering your question, Peg?

Peg: No.

Teacher: What was your question?

Peg: I had two: "What is a lake?" and "What lives in the lake?"

Joe: But the book never answered that. I have a question about the main idea. Aren't we supposed to ask a question about the main idea?

Teacher: Just about what we read.

Joe: Yes, but Peg asked us, "What lives in the lake?" but it doesn't really mention that in the book.

Teacher: That's true. The major idea has to do with Loch Ness and what it looks like. A minor idea that we inferred rather than directly read in the article was that the Loch Ness monster lives in the lake.

Peg: Are there any clarifications?

Students: No response.

Teacher: I have a clarification. You had trouble reading some of these words and I wondered if you know what some of them mean. What does *ancestors* mean?

The teacher continues discussing vocabulary.

Source: From Making Students Partners in the Comprehension Process: Organizing the Reading "POSSE" by C. S. Englert and T. V. Mariage, 1991, *Learning Disabilities Quarterly, 14,* pp. 133–134. Used by permission of Council for Learning Disabilities.

Apryl, Alexis, and Nandi. All of these students scored below benchmark in oral reading fluency, which, given the strong relationship between oral reading fluency and comprehension, would by itself be good reason to suspect they may be having comprehension problems.

TABLE 7.6 DIBELS Oral Reading Fluency and Oral Retell Fluency Scores—May, Mr. Edwards: Grade 3

Name	DIBELS Oral Reading Fluency Score	DIBELS Retell Fluency Score	Name	DIBELS Oral Reading Fluency Score	DIBELS Retell Fluency Score
Demel	127	60	David	152	75
Samantha	112	49	Dendall	144	65
Keshauna	89	25	Edgar	111	56
Bridget	133	25	Taylor	136	65
Jordan	118	62	Alexis	105	47
Lynn	64	10	Jameer	123	70
Akaria	92	75	Thomas	157	80
Brittany	110	20	Ramon	118	56
Angellis	137	71	Nandi	101	23
Apryl	98	27	Kenneth	171	80

Their retell scores are below 50% of their oral reading fluency scores, with most below 25%, indicating additional signs of possible comprehension problems. These students will need to be assessed further in comprehension. Finally, note that the oral reading fluency score for Akaria is well below benchmark, bordering on at risk, yet her retell score was much higher than many students in the class who were able to read more words. She is likely to be a slow but accurate decoder with a high level of oral language, reasoning skills, and background knowledge.

Assessing kindergartners and first-semester first graders for comprehension when these students are not reading, or assessing older learners with limited decoding skills, presents problems. For these students, the best option is to assess listening comprehension. You can assess listening comprehension in two ways. For younger students you can use a specifically developed listening comprehension measure, such as the Texas Primary Reading Inventory (TPRI) described in Chapter 6, in which students listen to a passage and then answer explicit and implicit comprehension questions about what they heard. Early Reading Diagnostic Assessment (ERDA) is a similar listening comprehension instrument. In the ERDA, students in kindergarten listen to the teacher read passages, answer questions about the passage, and then retell the story in their own words; first-grade students look at a picture, listen to the teacher read a passage, and then answer comprehension questions about main ideas and supporting elements from the passage. For older students with limited decoding skills, take the comprehension assessment you are giving to the rest of the students and give it orally. Read the text to the students and then ask the questions. While most tests haven't been standardized to account for oral administrations, giving the test orally should still provide you with an adequate basis for screening potential comprehension problems.

Diagnosis

Once you have determined that there is a comprehension problem, the next step is to identify the specific problems that contribute to poor reading comprehension. Since there are many kinds of comprehension problems, this part of the assessment process can be challenging. For example, as described at the beginning of the chapter, some students may be unable to decode accurately and fluently enough to think about what they are reading. Other students may lack the background, semantic, and/or syntactical knowledge needed to make inferences or glean information from the text that is not explicitly stated. Still others may be able to read accurately and fluently but don't think about what they are reading; they may need to learn how to ask themselves questions about key vocabulary and other story components as they read. Some students may have trouble monitoring their comprehension; these students cannot determine whether or not they are attaining the appropriate level of understanding, and, if not, employ fix-up strategies to improve their understanding. Finally, students may not understand how to use the organizational structures of both narrative and expository text. Described below are assessments that can be used to assess student strengths and weaknesses in the above areas.

Reading Accuracy and Fluency   As described in Chapter 5, student oral reading accuracy and fluency is strongly related to reading comprehension and can be measured using the DIBELS Oral Reading Fluency measure.

Oral Language   A number of assessments used to screen and diagnose oral language problems were described in Chapter 6, including the Peabody Picture Vocabulary Test-3rd Edition (PPVT-3), Texas Primary Reading Inventory (TPRI) Listening Comprehension, Iowa Test of Basic Skills (ITBS), Test of Word Knowledge (TOWK), and the Wechsler Individual Achievement Test-II WIAT-II).

Background Knowledge   While there are some standardized tests that assess students' general level of background knowledge, background knowledge required for comprehension varies so much from text to text that it makes most sense to assess student background knowledge at the beginning of each instructional activity. A strategy for determining how much knowledge students already have about a topic so that you can decide how much background information to present in class prior to a reading assignment is called the PReP (PreReading Plan) strategy (Friend and Bursuck, 2006; Langer, 1984). The PReP strategy has three major steps.

1. Preview the text or lesson and choose two to three important concepts. For example, for a science lesson, Mr. Amin, the teacher described in Step 2, chose the concept of photosynthesis and the key words *cycle* and *oxygen*.

2. Conduct a brainstorming session with students. This process involves three phases. In Phase 1 of brainstorming, students tell you what comes to mind when they hear the concept. This gives you a first glance at how much they already know about the topic. In Phase 2, students tell you what made them think of their responses in Phase 1. This information can help you judge the depth and basis for their responses and provides a springboard for students to refine their responses in Phase 3 of brainstorming. In Mr. Amin's class, two students mistakenly thought that photosynthesis had to do with photography because of the presence of *photo* in the word. This error provided an opportunity to build on students' knowledge. Mr. Amin explained that *photo* means light and that in photography, a camera takes in light and combines it with certain chemicals on film to make pictures. He then said that plants take in light, too, and when the light combines with chemicals in the plant, carbohydrates and oxygen are made. This process is called *photosynthesis*. In this way, Mr. Amin used what the students already knew to teach them a concept they did not know. In Phase 3, students can add to their responses based on the discussion in Phase 2.

3. Evaluate student responses to determine the depth of their prior knowledge of the topic. During this step, you can decide whether students are ready to read the text and/or listen to a lecture on photosynthesis or whether they first need more information. In Mr. Amin's class two students continued to have trouble understanding that photosynthesis was something plants did with light to make carbohydrates and oxygen. They needed more

information before they were ready to read the chapter. Mr. Amin accommodated these students by showing them a video illustration of photosynthesis including concrete examples that weren't necessary to use with the rest of the class (p. 321).

Basic Literal and Inferential Comprehension

You can diagnose basic literal and inferential comprehension skills using the assessments listed below.

Gray Oral Reading Test IV (GORT IV)

This assessment for students ages 6.0–18.11 years is given individually. The test consists of 14 developmentally sequenced reading passages that are read orally and followed by five content-specific comprehension questions.

Iowa Test of Basic Skills (ITBS) Form M

This assessment for grades K and up can be given individually or in groups. Comprehension starts with Level 6, and the tasks require progressively more independence in reading as the test level increases.

Texas Primary Reading Inventory (TPRI)

In this individually given assessment for grades 1 and 2, students read developmentally appropriate passages and answer five comprehension questions, three of which are explicit and two implicit.

Test of Reading Comprehension-Third Edition (TORC-3)

The *TORC-3* measures comprehension in four ways: syntactical similarities, paragraph reading, sentence sequencing, and reading directions.

Woodcock Reading Mastery Test-Revised (WRMT-R)

In this individually-administered assessment, students read silently a passage that has a word missing and then tell the examiner a word that could appropriately fill in the blank space. The passages are drawn from actual newspaper articles and textbooks.

Assessing Text Structure: Narratives

One way to assess student knowledge of narrative text structures is to turn information about story grammars into comprehension questions. Using story grammar questions to assess narrative comprehension skills has a number of advantages. First, focusing on story grammars assures that the focus of the assessment is on the big ideas of stories as opposed to less important details. Second, writing clear comprehension questions that accurately measure the intended comprehension skill can be difficult. In our experience, when writing your own questions it is often difficult to discern whether students have a comprehension problem or whether the comprehension items simply weren't written clearly enough. For your primary readers, try these more basic story grammar questions (Carnine et al., 2004).

Who is the story about?
What is he/she trying to do?
What happens when he/she tries to do it?
What happens in the end?

For more intermediate readers, select among these possible questions for each essential story grammar (Carnine & Kinder, 1985).

Theme

What is the major point of the story?
What is the moral of the story?
What did _____ learn at the end of the story?

Setting

Where did _____ happen?
When did _____ happen?

Character

Who is the main character?
What is _____ like?

Initiating Events

What is _____'s problem?
What does _____ have to try to do?

Attempts

What did _____ do about _____?
What will _____ do now?

Resolution

How did _____ solve the problem?
How did _____ achieve the goal?
What would you do to solve _____'s problem?

Reactions

How did _____ feel about the problem?
Why did _____ do _____?
How did _____ feel at the end?
Why did _____ feel that way?
How would you feel about _____?

When assessing story grammars, first have the students read a story that they can read with at least 95% accuracy (Gunning, 2002). Older struggling readers benefit from reading the story silently, then orally. For older skilled students the story can be read once silently. Younger students should only read the story orally (Klingner, 2004). For students with significant decoding problems, read the story as they listen. After students have heard or read the story, ask the story grammar questions and record student answers.

There are times when you might not wish to ask questions about a story. Specific questions can give students clues to the answers, and they especially help students identify the information you think is important to remember or the way you organize this information. One way to solve this problem is to have students retell stories after they read them but without a time factor as in the DIBELS retell. Students then must organize the information they think is important, so you can evaluate the completeness of their recall. Two requirements are necessary for effective evaluation of story retells to occur: a standard set of criteria to evaluate the completeness of the **retelling,** and the opportunity to evaluate each student's retelling individually. In the Effective Teacher at Work feature on page 280, Ms. Padilla used a Story Grammar Retelling Checklist to evaluate the story retelling for Chantille, a student in her class. While in this case Ms. Padilla had Chantille read the story, if Chantille had been unable to read the story with 95% accuracy, Ms. Padilla could have read it to Chantille before having her retell it.

Look at Chantille's scores shown in Table 7.7. As you can see, she had a good idea of who the main characters were and received a + for this component (Characters). Chantille named two problems in the story: Dora making a farola that her family laughed at and Dora's brother and sister getting lost. Chantille identified the problem of the lost kids without being prompted, and the problem of the funny farola with prompts; thus a + and a ✓ were scored for Goal/Problem. It was unclear from Chantille's response exactly how the characters tried to solve their problem, so she received a – for Attempts. Chantille did say the problem was solved when Dora's brother and sister saw the frog; she received a + for this element of Resolution. However, she did not say how this resolved the problem of her family laughing at the farola, so she received a –. Chantille's reaction to the story was appropriate, so a + was scored. For Setting, Chantille received a ✓; Ms. Padilla prompted her. Finally, Chantille received a – for Theme. This response was lacking, even after prompting.

Effective Teacher at Work

Using Story Grammars

Ms. Padilla's second-grade students have just read the story *The Funny Farola,* by Ann Miranda and Maria Guerrero. The story is about a girl and her family participating in an ethnic festival in their city. The girl, Dora, makes a farola, which is a type of lantern people carry while marching in a parade. Dora's family laughs at her farola, because it is in the shape of a frog. However, her unusual farola saves the day when it helps Dora and her parents find Dora's lost brother and sister. Ms. Padilla is assessing Chantille's comprehension of the story using the story grammar retelling format.

Mrs. Padilla: Chantille, you have just read the *The Funny Farola.* Would you tell me in your own words what the story is about?

Chantille: The story is about a girl named Dora who made this funny frog that she carried in a parade. You see, her brother and sister got lost at the parade 'cause they were having such a good time, but they got found again 'cause they could see Dora's frog.

Mrs. Padilla: Chantille, where does this story take place?

Chantille: It took place in a city and the people were having a big festival. That's why they were having the parade.

Mrs. Padilla: Chantille, what was the problem with Dora's frog?

Chantille: Well, it was called a farola, which is a kind of lantern. Everyone was making them for the parade. Dora's family laughed at her farola 'cause they had never seen a frog farola before.

Mrs. Padilla: You said that Dora's sister and brother got lost. What did they do to solve that problem?

Chantille: They saw Dora's frog, so they knew where to find them.

Mrs. Padilla: How did you feel at the end of the story?

Chantille: I felt happy.

Mrs. Padilla: Why did you feel happy?

Chantille: 'Cause Dora's borther and sister found their mom and dad.

Mrs. Padilla: Chantille, what lesson do you think this story teaches us?

Chantille: Not to get lost from your mom and dad.

A score sheet that Ms. Padilla completed for Chantille is shown in Table 7.7. A plus (+) means that Chantille responded accurately to that element without any prompting to questioning; a check mark (✓) means that Chantille mentioned the element after she was questioned or prompted; a minus (–) means that she failed to refer to the element even after questioning or prompts.

Source: Friend, M., & Bursuck, W. D. (2006). *Including students with special needs: A practical guide for classroom teachers* (4th ed., pp. 128–129). Boston: Allyn & Bacon.

Notice that Ms. Padilla's prompts included explicit references to the various story grammar components. For example, she asked, "You said that Dora's sister and brother got lost. What did they do to solve that problem?" as opposed to asking a more general question, such as, "What happened to Dora's sister and brother?" This use of specific language makes

TABLE 7.7   Story Grammar Retelling Checklist

Student Name	Story Elements Evaluated											
	Theme		Setting		Characters		Goal/Problem		Attempts		Resolution	Reactions
Chantille	−		✓		+		+	✓	−		+	−	+	

Source: Friend and Bursuck, *Including Students with Special Needs: A Practical Guide for Classroom Teachers* (4th ed.), pp. 128–129.

the story grammar components more clear, a necessary structure for younger, more naïve learners.

Assessing Text Structure: Expository Text   Student knowledge and use of expository text structures can be assessed by having students read passages from one or more of their content-area textbooks. The passages should be at the students' independent reading level and should reflect common text structures that you want to assess. Passages from students' science or social studies books work well for this purpose. As with story grammars, students can read the passages orally, silently, or both, depending on reading skills. If students are unable to read the book with at least 95% accuracy, read the passages to them. Following reading, the student answers questions developed to assess text structure comprehension. For example, here is a brief passage from an eighth-grade social studies text (Buggey, Danzer, Mitsakos, & Risinger, 1987).

> **Striking Workers**
>
> As prices rose, labor unions demanded higher wages. Although many of these demands were met, some companies refused to give their workers adequate pay increases. The result was a number of strikes that soon threatened the stability of the American economy.

This passage represents an example of a cause and effect text structure. Note the presence of the word *result* to signal the cause and effect relationship between high prices, demands for higher wages, and the occurrence of labor strikes. The following questions could be developed for this passage to assess different aspects or levels of student knowledge and use of text structures.

To assess knowledge of signal words, after the students read the passage, ask them to "identify the word that signals a cause and effect pattern" (*result*).

To assess knowledge of text structures, after reading the passage, have students "identify the relevant text structure" (*cause and effect*).

To assess overall comprehension of text, ask a main idea question based on the text structure. Here are two possible examples for this paragraph.

Why were there a number of union strikes after the war?

What happened as a result of a rise in prices after the war?

You can also use retells to assess knowledge of text structures. Ask the student to, "tell me in your own words as much information as you can remember from the selection you just read" (Gunning, 2002; Klingner, 2004). If the student does not tell you enough information, ask, "Can you tell me anything more?" While the student is engaged in the retell, note whether critical features are present in the recall. For example, you might note whether the student demonstrated knowledge of the cause and effect relationship between rising consumer prices, demands for higher wages, and strikes.

Metacognitive Skills   **Metacognitive skills** in reading involve an awareness of one's thought process while reading and the ability to plan, monitor, and select effective strategies when there is a problem with comprehension. Despite their importance, most formal and informal reading assessments tend to ignore metacognitive skills, stressing pure recall or low-level inferences instead (Applegate et al., 2002). Fortunately, you can assess metacognition by adding a metacognitive component to the assessment strategies just discussed. One way to add a metacognitive component to your assessments is to ask students what they do to help them understand what they read before, during, and after reading. You can then use the following checklist to record strategies that the student used (Gunning, 2002).

Before Reading
___ Read the title and headings
___ Looked at the pictures
___ Predicted what the passage might be about
___ Asked self what already knew about the topic

During Reading
___ Thought about what reading
___ Stopped sometimes and asked what read so far
___ Pictured in mind the people, places, and events that reading about
___ Imagined talking with author while reading

When came to a word didn't understand:
    ___ Looked for clues and tried to figure it out
    ___ Used a glossary or dictionary

When came to part of text that was confusing:
    ___ Read it again
    ___ Kept reading
    ___ Tried to get help from pictures or drawings

After Reading
___ Thought about what read
___ Applied information learned
___ Compared what read with something already known

At first, students may engage in few or none of these metacognitive skills. However, over time, they will learn to use them as you model these metacognitive skills using **think-aloud** teaching strategies described later in the chapter.

Another way to assess student metacognitive skills is to add a think-aloud component to your comprehension assessment. In think-alouds, students are asked occasionally to stop and voice their thoughts about the reading process while reading a text (Klingner, 2004). These questions for think-alouds have been suggested by Gunner (2002).

Before Reading the Entire Selection
What do you think the selection might be about?
What makes you think so?

During Reading Each Marked-Off Segment
What was going on in your mind as you read this section?

What were you thinking about?
Were there any parts that were hard to understand?
What did you do when you came to parts that were hard to understand?
Were there any hard words?
What did you do when you came across hard words?

After Reading the Entire Selection
Tell me in your own words what this selection was about.

As the student "thinks aloud," note the use of strategies and whether any of the following are performed (Klingner, 2004):

Makes predictions prior to reading
Revises predictions while reading based on new information
Thinks about information read previously
Makes inferences
Draws conclusions
Makes judgements
Visualizes or creates mental images
Paraphrases
Summarizes
Constructs questions
Reasons about what was read
Monitors understanding
Uses context to figure out the meaning of difficult words
Rereads difficult sections
Uses illustrations to help with comprehension (Klingner, 2004, p. 65)

Paris (1991; cited in Catts & Kamhi, 2005) suggested using a Think-Along Passage (TAP) to assess the strategies students use during reading to identify topics, predict what will happen next, monitor meaning, make inferences, and summarize. The kinds of questions that could be used in a Think-Along Passage assessment are shown in Figure 7.9.

When your students are able to read accurately and fluently, as well as understand what they read, you will have given them a powerful tool to increase their learning over a lifetime. Still, reading is only empowering insofar as students do it. That is why it is so important for teachers to motivate their students to read widely to further their own learning. Strategies for motivating your students to read widely are described in the following section.

How Do I Motivate Students to Read Widely?

Provide daily opportunities for students to read self-selected and teacher and peer-recommended texts. All teacher-selected material should be at the students' independent level so they can be read with at least 95% accuracy. See pp. 185–186 in Chapter 5 for guidelines on how to select the appropriate reading material for students. Convey enthusiasm for the books your students are reading and talk about reading you are doing. One week Mrs. Rice told her class about a book she was reading about magnets because she would be teaching that subject and wanted to learn more. Another week she described the exciting mystery novel she was reading and the adventures the main character had in the deserts of the Sahara. If students' parents aren't modeling recreational and informational

Present child with book or reading passage (Example: *Too Many Tamales* by Gary Soto).

Identifying the Topic

1a. Look at this page. What do you think the story will be about?
  Ex: A surprise party; lots of tamales

1b. How do you know this?
  Ex: Their eyes look like this (points)

1c. If you don't know, how could you figure it out?
  Ex: Turn the pages; read the book

Possible Strategies

Scans text
Looks at title
Refers to pictures
Refers to prior knowledge
Points out words
Other

Predicting
After a significant event in the story, stop the reading (e.g., after Maria tries on her mother's ring).

2a. What do you think will happen next?
  Ex: Her mom'll get mad

2b. Why do you think that?
  Ex: 'Cause she shouldn't wear her mom's ring

2c. If you don't know, how could you find out?
  Ex: Read more of the story; look at the pictures

Possible Strategies

Predicts based on prior knowledge
Predicts based on text cues
Rereads
Looks forward in the text
Uses context cues
Other

Monitoring Meaning
Choose a word that you think will be unfamiliar to the student.

3a. What do you think "masa" mean in the sentence you just read?
  Ex: Dough

3b. How could you tell?
  Ex: From the pictures; it's in a bowl
  Ex: They kneaded it. That's what you do with dough

3c. If you don't know, how could you find out?

Possible Strategies

Uses context cues
Substitutes something that looks or sounds similar
Mentions other resources
Mentions dictionary as resource
Relates personal experience
Other

Making Inferences
Select something that is not made explicit in the story.

4a. Why do you think they put the masa on corn husks?
  Ex: Cause they wanted to
  Ex: To keep all the stuff together

4b. How did you decide this?
  Ex: I just thought it
  Ex: I know cause I help gramma make tamales

4c. If you don't know, how could you figure it out?

Possible Strategies

Infers based on text cues
Infers based on prior knowledge
Relates personal experience
Gives analogy
Scans forward
Rereads
Other

Summarizing
After you or the student has finished reading the book, ask for a summary.

5a. If you wanted to tell your friends about this story, what would you tell them?

5b. How did you decide what things to tell them?

5c. If you don't know, how do you think you could decide?

Possible Strategies

Retells mostly main ideas
Retells mostly details
Organizes ideas in recall
Summaries are disorganized
Expresses opinions or reactions
Connects to personal experiences
Uses genre structure to help recall
Other

FIGURE 7.9 Think-Along Passage Protocol for Assessing Strategic Reading

Source: Based on information from Paris, S. G. (1991), cited in Catts, H. W. & Kamhi, A. G. (2005). Language and reading disabilities (2nd ed., p. 187). Boston: Pearson Education.

reading at home, the teacher can pass along the purpose of and excitement from reading outside of school.

Teachers who allow students to select books from a classroom library when they have completed their work not only minimize behavior problems that can arise from waiting but also provide more opportunities for students to self-select books of interest. To meet the needs of all students, the classroom libraries should contain a wide range of books from easy decodable books to challenging chapter books without pictures. As recommended in Chapter 6, 50% of the books should be nonfiction. Teachers can honor and encourage students' outside reading in many ways. Some schools have motivational plans developed to encourage students to read a certain number of books in order to earn awards. Be a book detective and notice what your students are reading so you can use short moments to comment on their selections. Students will do more reading if it leads to more attention. When Mr. Bayer was teaching the continent of Africa in social studies, he turned to Lydia and asked her to tell the most interesting thing she had learned about Africa in the book about pyramids that he had noticed her reading last week. When the lunch line was backed up in the hall, Mr. Bayer turned to Shelley and said that he noticed she had been reading *Little House on the Prairie,* which was always a favorite book of his students.

How Can I Give Struggling Readers a More Systematic, Explicit Approach to Learning Comprehension Skills?

A key theme of this book is that some students struggle to acquire reading skills, despite receiving Tier 1 instruction that is enhanced and reasonably well executed. For the reading components of phonemic awareness, alphabetic principle, and fluency, struggling students were provided with extra support in Tiers 2 and 3. You may find that some of your students also struggle with reading comprehension. Described below are four reading comprehension programs designed for students who can benefit from more explicit, systematic instruction delivered within a smaller instructional group.

Corrective Reading (Engelmann, Hanner, & Johnson, 2002) is an intensive direct instruction reading program for students in grades 4–12 who are reading one or more years below grade level. The program has two tightly sequenced strands—decoding and comprehension. At specified times in the connected text activities, students are asked literal and inferential questions that are scripted in the teacher presentation books at specified times in the connected text activities. Throughout the program, students learn key comprehension strategies to help them understand what they read including thinking operations, information skills, reasoning skills, sentence-writing skills, as well as strategies for organizing information, operating on information, using sources of information, using information for directions, and communicating information (Marchand-Martella, Slocum, & Martella, 2004).

Reading Success: Effective Comprehension Strategies (www.classicallearning universe.com) is an 80-lesson reading comprehension program designed to supplement your regular reading program. It can be used with students of any age who decode at a mid-second-grade level or higher, but who struggle meeting state standards in reading comprehension. Lessons take approximately 15 to 20 minutes each and can be taught daily, or three times per week. The authors recommend scheduling the lessons to ensure that students finish the program before any spring testing in reading comprehension. The program teaches key comprehension skills using the scientifically based components of explicit strategy instruction, scaffolding, and review. The principal outcomes of *Reading Success* are related to: inference, main idea, fact and opinion, literal comprehension, author's purpose, paraphrasing, rewriting passages, word meanings, and figurative language. The program includes placement tests as well as quizzes or tests every five lessons to test mastery of key program skills.

Text Talk, a curriculum for grades K–3 (Beck & McKeown, 2001) focuses on comprehension and vocabulary development through the use of read-alouds and open-ended questions. The teacher reads stories that contain challenging vocabulary and enough complexity of events for children to build meaning. Throughout the read-aloud sessions, the teacher asks questions designed to encourage children to elaborate on their initial answers and draw on their background knowledge to gain understanding from the text. After students have responded to the text, pictures are discussed and a variety of activities relating to the new vocabulary words are completed.

In the *Language!* program (Greene, 2004) comprehension is taught through the use of decodable connected text containing phonemic/graphemic concepts, vocabulary, and words that have been directly taught in the program. Reading comprehension instruction is also coordinated with instruction in expressive writing. The program stresses two key comprehension strategies within a before, during and after reading instructional routine: answering comprehension questions that correspond to Bloom's taxonomy and story grammars. Each story is followed by questions related to different levels of Bloom's taxonomy; the levels are introduced gradually, beginning in Unit 3. Students are directly taught the signal words for each of the six levels of the taxonomy so they can recognize what is being asked of them and can respond accordingly. They are also taught to create questions using signal words from the taxonomy. Story grammars are introduced gradually through Level 1 and into Level 2. While the Bloom questions and story grammars are stressed, *Language!* incorporates other comprehension strategies into its teaching routines including brainstorming to build background knowledge, paraphrasing/summarization, and the use of graphic organizers to recognize story parts.

How Do I Prepare My Students to Pass High Stakes Tests in Reading?

While the most important job we have as teachers of reading is to teach our students to read for their own enjoyment and learning, the realities of today's culture of school accountability dictates that we must also prepare our students to perform well on high stakes reading assessments. In our estimation, the best way to prepare students for high stakes tests in reading is to have an effective reading program in place when children start school. Scientifically based reading programs, much like those described in this text, enable students to pass state tests by providing them with the phonemic awareness, phonics, fluency, vocabulary, and comprehension skills needed to read a wide range of text with understanding. That said, your students can still benefit from teacher-directed instruction and practice geared specifically toward your particular state test. Here are some steps to assure that the practice you provide your students is effective.

Analyze Your State Test

a. What types of passages are students required to comprehend? Most high stakes tests in reading use narrative, expository, or functional material from everyday life such as application forms, recipes, or advertisements.

b. What levels of understanding are measured? Usually there is a mix of literal and inferential questions. Questions also test student ability to analyze and evaluate information as well as use metacognitive strategies.

c. What kinds of information are tested and how are the questions asked? Educational Resources Inc. (2004) has compiled a list of key question types as well as typical questions for each type. These are shown in Figure 7.10. Additional items and questions related to narrative prose and poetry adapted from Goudiss, Hodges, and Margulies (1999) are also included.

Teach Students to Recognize the Various Question Types They Will Encounter on High Stakes Tests

The ability to determine what a question is asking is an important first step in answering it correctly. That is why students need to be directly taught the information shown in Figure 7.10, along with other question-answering comprehension strategies like the QAR. When Travis was able to recognize that a question was asking about sequencing, he was then reminded to look for key words to help answer the question such as *beginning, last, next* and *before*. When Abdul recognized a vocabulary question, he automatically looked at the words around the word in the passage to figure out what it meant.

Teach Strategies for Answering Question Types Systematically and Explicitly Using My Turn–Together–Your Turn Think Alouds

Just as in teaching the reading comprehension strategies described earlier in this chapter, systematic, explicit instruction works best when teaching your students to answer items on high stakes tests. You can be systematic by working on the various question types one at a time, gradually introducing new types of questions as other types are mastered. You can be explicit by adding think-alouds to your My Turn–Together–Your Turn teaching routine. Examples of how to use think-alouds for a main idea/summarization question and a metacognitive question are shown below.

Main Idea/Summarization

I bought my car seven years ago. I haven't driven it for a year because I've been away. Yesterday I thought I'd get it ready to take out on the road again. I had a real shock when I looked at it.

The back window is cracked. Two of the lights won't go on. The motor needs a lot of work. The rear door won't open. I don't think I can afford to fix it. It's a shame. I liked my old car.

What is this passage mainly about?

A. New cars are expensive.

B. The car lights don't work.

C. The car is in very bad shape.

D. The writer has been away. (Goudiss et al, 1999, p. 105)

Think-Aloud *Let's see. I need to figure out what this whole passage is about—not just one thing that is in the passage. Let me try the first choice, A, "new cars are expensive." That wasn't even mentioned in the story, so that can't be right. Choice B says the car lights don't work—that was in the story but it's only one thing in the story, not what the whole passage is about—so the answer can't be B. Choice C says the car is in very bad shape—that's what a lot of the sentences in the passage talked about, so it would make a good choice here. I'm going to pick C.*

Metacognitive Question

Pretend that in 2 minutes you will take a test on this story, which means you don't have time to reread the whole story. Which of these strategies would help you understand how all parts of the story fit together?

A. Making a list of all the most difficult words

B. Asking yourself what are the main ideas in the story

C. Rereading the part of the story where it tells about days and nights

D. Reading the second sentence in each paragraph (Goudiss et al., 1999, p. 131)

Main idea/Summarization	Author's Purpose	Moral
▪ This *story* is mostly about _____? ▪ What is this *story* mainly about? ▪ What is another good name/title for this *story*? ▪ Another title/name for the *selection* might be _____?	▪ This story was written mainly to _____? ▪ The writer wrote this *story* mainly to _____? ▪ The *article* was written in order to _____? ▪ _____ was written in order to _____?	▪ The important message in the *story* is _____? ▪ What lesson can be learned from this *selection*? ▪ What lesson did _____ need to learn? ▪ This story suggests _____?
Mood/Feeling/Emotion	**Fact and Opinion**	**Sequencing**
▪ At the end of the story, _____ probably felt _____. ▪ What made (character) feel _____?	▪ Which of these is a fact in the story? ▪ Which of these is an opinion in the story? ▪ Which of the following is NOT _____? ▪ All of the above except _____? ▪ Which of these is a fact stated in the article?	▪ The boxes show _____. ▪ Which belongs in box _____? ▪ What must be decided before _____? ▪ In the beginning of the story _____? ▪ Which of these happens last? ▪ After _____, what must happen next?
Prediction	**Vocabulary**	**Sources of Information**
▪ What will probably happen the next time _____? ▪ What will probably happen next? ▪ What probably happened after the story ended? ▪ Which of these happens last? ▪ In the future?	▪ In this story, _____ means _____? ▪ In this story, a _____ is a _____? ▪ What did the author mean when he said _____? ▪ In this story, a _____ is like a _____? ▪ In this article the phrase _____ means _____? ▪ What words in the story show that _____?	▪ If you wanted to find out more information you should _____. ▪ Look in a (source) ▪ Look in a book called (title) ▪ You would most likely find this story in a _____? ▪ What is the best way to learn more about _____?
Metacognitive Questions	**Miscellaneous Stems**	**Character Analysis**
▪ To skim this passage the reader would _____? ▪ In order to answer question _____, the reader would _____?	▪ Which question does the first paragraph answer? ▪ If the author added a sentence in the story, _____ ▪ This story is a _____?	▪ The most important character in the story is _____? ▪ How would you describe _____? ▪ How are _____ and _____ different? ▪ What is the best word to describe _____?

FIGURE 7.10   Common Question Types on High Stakes Reading Tests

Setting Analysis	Plot Analysis	Author's Point of View
■ The story takes place _____? ■ Where is the story set? ■ What time do you think _____ takes place? ■ Where is _____ at the end of the story? ■ Where do you think _____ lives? ■ How much time passes in the story?	■ What is the problem in the story? ■ How is the problem resolved?	■ What does the author think of _____? ■ What does the author think people should do if _____?

Poetry and Poetic Language
■ Which lines rhyme?   ■ What does the author mean by _____?   ■ Why do you think the author wrote that?   ■ What do the words _____ describe?   ■ What point is the author trying to make when she _____?

FIGURE 7.10 Continued

Source: Adapted from Educational Resources Inc. (2004). Unpublished materials; and Goudiss, M., Hodges, V., & Margulies, S. (1999). *The ISAT coach: Grade 3 reading.* New York: Triumph Learning—Coach Books.

Think-Aloud *This is the kind of question where I have to tell what I would do in a made-up situation. Usually it's about how I would think to solve a problem; how I would learn about something. In this situation, I'm going to take a test on a story in 2 minutes and don't have time to read the whole story. How can I best get the hang of the main idea of the story? Making a list of the most difficult words, choice A, isn't going to help with the main idea. Asking myself what the main ideas in the story are might work because it deals with main ideas. So the answer might be B. Rereading a part of the story, choice C, wouldn't really get at what the whole story was about—I'd only be looking at a part. Reading the second sentence in each paragraph wouldn't work either. I don't think that sentence would have the most important information. So, I think B is the best choice.*

How Do I Teach Comprehension to Older Learners?

Reading instruction should increasingly emphasize comprehension strategies once students are reading at a fourth- or fifth-grade level (Moats, 2001). Some students who are at risk will continue to increase their reading skills if they are in content classes with teachers who routinely weave the comprehensive strategies discussed earlier in this chapter into their instruction. A biology teacher who teaches his students to ask questions to check their understanding of the chapter on plant life, who uses think-alouds to show how to apply comprehension strategies, and who accompanies reading assignments with graphic organizers is teaching expository reading comprehension strategies along with biology. An English teacher who teaches students to answer inferential questions based on the novels they are studying, who models ways to differentiate between major events and added details, and who demonstrates how to summarize sections of the story is teaching students narrative reading comprehension strategies.

Other students who are at risk can benefit from a separate class of study skills where comprehension strategies are taught more explicitly and the teacher provides the opportunity to systematically apply those strategies to course material from their content classes. Unless they spend more time learning comprehension strategies, these students will not acquire higher reading levels. A third group of students is comprised of those who still need support in beginning or advanced word reading, some of it intensive. Because they are still advancing in their word reading skills, a smaller proportion of their instruction will include learning comprehension strategies. To help these students make the most progress, teach them to apply comprehension strategies to narrative and expository text at their independent or instructional reading level.

One of the greatest challenges for teachers of older struggling readers is finding text that is at the students' instructional level but still is interesting and content rich. In selecting text for comprehension instruction with these readers, teachers have several options. Spadorcia (2001) recommends that books be examined through many different lenses, recognizing the particular skills that less skillful students need to learn to become better readers. If the student has established alphabetic principle, Spadorcia recommends using balanced literacy books having a combination of many high frequency words combined with some decodable words. Her analysis showed that these books had higher levels of sentence-level sophistication. *Swamp Furies* (Schraff, 1992) is an example of this type of book. Another type of book, the "high interest—low reading level decodable book" is also often appropriate for comprehension instruction. A science fiction book, *Deadly Double* (France, 1998), is a typical high–low book that falls into this category (Spadorcia, 2001).

Because your older readers must learn subject matter content in many of their classes, and because they are more likely to read expository text as adults, look for content books that are written at students' independent or instructional reading levels. Content books written at a lower readability or for students at a lower grade level can be used to teach comprehension strategies for expository text. If used for teaching content, the teacher has to be sure that all state standards for that content area are included or taught.

As mentioned earlier in this chapter, if the readability of a book is above the older student's instructional level, teacher read-alouds become an important instructional strategy. Using read-alouds with books or taped CDs enables older struggling readers to participate in the equivalent comprehension strategy instruction as peers. Older students will eventually need to practice using these strategies when reading text, but in this way the teacher can at least model the reasoning she uses in strategically approaching a book. The following example demonstrates dialogue a teacher might use during a read-aloud with the book *Max the Mighty* (Philbrick, 1998).

> "The title is *Max the Mighty*. On the cover there is a picture of a big guy, almost a giant, carrying a much smaller girl, who is holding a book. She doesn't look younger than him, just smaller. He must be Max the Mighty because he's huge. He's running away from something, but she looks like she's holding on, not trying to get away from him. Now I'm going to read. [Teacher reads aloud.] 'My name is Maxwell Kane and the thing you should know about me is this: even though I'm a big dude with a face like the moon and ears that stick out like radar scoops and humongous feet like the abdominal snowman, inside I'm a real weenie. A

yellow-bellied sapsucker. A giant wuss. A coward.' [Teacher thinks aloud.] Maxwell is Max the Mighty, from the cover, because Max is a nickname, and the way he describes himself, you know he's big. I don't think he's a ferocious giant, because he described himself as a coward. He makes me think of that character in *Willy the Wimp* [Browne, 1989] who becomes a body builder but in the end turns out to be a wimp on the inside. I've read stories like this before, so I think he's going to tell about a time when he acted like a coward. But sometimes in books and movies cowards turn out to be heroes. When I look back at the cover, he looks more like a hero than a coward. I predict that he'll do something heroic." (Ivey, 2002)

Ivey also recommends that teachers combine read alouds with directed listening-thinking (DR-TA) activities. First the teacher shows students a book asking them to predict what it might be about from clues on the cover or in the title. The teacher reads a portion of text before stopping to ask students if their predictions were correct and if not, what their changed predictions are. This cycle of reading, checking, and adjusting predictions continues as the teacher periodically pauses to ask more questions at logical stopping points (Ivey, 2002).

How Can I Teach Reading Comprehension to English Language Learners?

Comprehension of narrative and expository text can be challenging for English language learners who have no real-life experience with common story themes. A story that involves a typical children's birthday party in the United States or one that takes place while family members are watching an after-Thanksgiving dinner football game might be unduly confusing unless the teacher has explained the larger context before the reading. Eskey (2002) provides an example of five questions that might be confusing for students who have no experience with the type of party described in the following paragraph:

> It was the day of the big party. Mary wondered if Johnny would like a kite. She ran to her bedroom, picked up her piggy bank, and shook it. There was no sound. (p. 6)

Eskey describes that without discussion before reading the passage, the following questions would be difficult for students who have no cultural experience with such birthday parties:

1. What is the nature of the party in the text?
2. Are Mary and Johnny adults or children?
3. How is the kite related to the party?
4. Why did Mary shake her piggy bank?
5. What was Mary's big problem?

Expository text presents other related challenges. Even students who have developed fluent social language in English still find that academic language, the formal language of textbooks and lectures, requires different skills. Academic language has longer sentences, more complex grammar and more technical vocabulary than social language. Also, topics in academic contexts are often more abstract and the clues that English language learners gain from gestures and expressions are absent. A student who is proficient with social language can take up to five more years to develop academic language. That is why English language learners have to be more assertive with their teachers, because cues such as raised eyebrows or puzzled looks are usually inadequate to convey confusion in situations in which academic language is used. Of course being assertive can raise additional problems for English language learners. Some of these students may be from cultures whose respect for teachers precludes their need to be assertive.

As you learned earlier in the chapter (see Table 7.2), signal words in text provide clues to indicate relationships among ideas and clarify content. However, signal words provide additional challenges for English language learners. Signal words such as *for example, because, like,* and *first* link sentences and paragraphs together. They are essential for comprehension because they give the reader an indication of what will be happening. In the following sentence, the signal word *as* indicates a time relationship, letting the reader know that the makeup of wood changed at the same time as the mud and sand of the swamps slowly turned to stone.

> "As the mud and sand of the swamps slowly turned to stone, the makeup of the wood changed." (*DK Science Encyclopedia,* p. 238)

Explicit teaching of the signal words and their function enables English language learners to use them as a strategy for increasing comprehension (Short, 1994). Teachers can use think-alouds to demonstrate how signal words provide clues for understanding, ask students to locate specific signal words in text and describe how the words provide clues to the meaning of a passage, and construct writing activities that require students to use specified signal words.

Teaching English language learners comprehension strategies needs to be accompanied by careful instruction in comprehension monitoring. The ability to carefully monitor their comprehension and apply fix-up strategies is crucial, because additional linguistic obstacles routinely impede their comprehension. However, Yu-fen Yang (2002) cautions that the focus of reading comprehension instruction first must emphasize language knowledge when he writes:

> However, the truth is that if readers do not possess sufficient language skills, then no matter how many diversified reading strategies they are equipped with, and how much training in metacognitive strategy usage they receive, the process will turn out to be fruitless if they have no basic resources to access when attempting to solve problems. They must have extensive resources to monitor whether their understanding of the text is coherent and logical. (p. 37)

What Games and Activities Will Reinforce Reading Comprehension Skills?

Some of the following games can be adapted for younger or older students. Other games are more appropriate for older groups.

Find the Hot Spots

Give students several stick-on notes to use as they read a text. Ask them to mark the described hot spots. For example, ask students to do one or a combination of the following:

- Place pink stick-on notes on pages where there is a vocabulary word they do not know or where the text is confusing.
- Place green stick-on notes on pages where they were excited about what they were reading and thought that the author was exceptionally interesting.
- Place orange stick-on notes on pages where the author makes a claim that is not substantiated by facts or valid, reliable sources.
- Place blue stick-on notes on pages where the author writes about a problem.
- Place purple stick-on notes on pages where they wish they could write like that.

Technology

Reading for Understanding on the Internet

The lack of valid research investigating the different skills needed to read text in books versus Internet text has fueled ongoing debate. Teachers wonder whether their students need to substantially retool and learn additional skills to derive meaning from Internet text. When MacArthur and colleagues (2001) reviewed studies comparing reading on paper to reading unenhanced text on screen, they found no indication that reading text on screen affected students' comprehension either positively or negatively. Other studies they investigated in which students read text containing enhancements such as hyperlinks providing definitions of difficult words or main ideas showed mixed results.

Since students increasingly use the Internet in place of or in addition to a library, teachers are responsible for critically evaluating claims about best methods to improve reading comprehension online. Unique features of Internet text may place different demands on the reader. In the course of reading, students often have to make decisions about the large volume of information instantaneously available to them. Becoming overwhelmed with these decisions, many students have been observed to "snatch and grab" the information. Rather than taking the time to evaluate critically which information is most valid and related to their research needs, students quickly hyperlink without much thought (RAND, 2002).

A second challenge of reading Internet text results from the increased number of questionable sources found online compared to those from sources in a conventional library. More of a burden rests on the reader to apply critical thinking skills and evaluate the source of the text, the validity of the information, and the bias of the author. In the process, multimedia distractors and advertisements can draw the reader's attention from reading the actual text selected by the reader.

Finally, the reader must be skilled at comprehending expository text since it comprises the majority of reading on the Internet. Students who have not learned or do not apply expository strategies to paper reading, cannot be expected to use them when reading on the Internet. Because estimates indicate that 90% of what students read in elementary school is narrative, students will be unable to fully utilize Internet sources unless teachers have explicitly taught and expected students to read expository text. When Schmar-Dobler (2003) compared reading strategies used in reading books to those used on the Internet, they found no differences in how readers:

- Activate prior knowledge
- Determine important ideas
- Synthesize to sift important from unimportant details
- Draw inferences, reading between the lines and using background knowledge to help fill in gaps

Differences that they noted included how readers:

- Relied more on skimming and scanning techniques because of the volume of text.
- Placed more emphasis on using guiding questions to stay focused to avoid getting lost in the text options
- Used Internet basic skills in order to perform tasks such as downloading appropriate text and avoiding pop-up ads that interfere with text reading

Provide Evidence

Divide students into small groups and give each player six cards. Three cards are adjectives used to describe the personalities of a character and three cards are characters from books recently read in class. Students take turns taking and discarding cards until they have a character and adjective that match. Once a student has a match, he names the story his character is in, describes why his character has the specific personality trait, and provides evidence from the story supporting that opinion. For example, a student might explain that Mr. McGregor in *The Tale of Peter Rabbit* was mean "because he chased Peter around the garden" (Richards & Gipe, 2000).

What Would Your Character Do?

Divide students into small groups. Each student selects a card designating a character from a recently read story. The teacher then presents a situation and asks the students to think about what they know about their character from the story and describe how he or she would respond in the situation. The following is a sample situation described by the authors of this game:

> Your character is transported to a foreign land for two weeks. No one speaks your character's language. English is the only language your character speaks, reads, and writes. Your character needs food, a place to sleep, and money. What would your character do? (Richards & Gipe, 2000, p. 77)

Students should explain what their designated character would do and what evidence from the story leads them to predict that action.

Try Out Your Test-Making Skills

Divide the class into four groups. After students read expository text about social studies or science, ask them to write a specified number of questions about the main ideas of the text. Design a rubric to evaluate their test, making sure to award each team extra points if every question is about a main idea. Once students are finished writing their tests, give each group another group's test and see how well they remember the information they read. Award team points for questions answered correctly.

Research to Practice

Begin Writing with Kindergarten

Beginning in kindergarten many of the Project PRIDE teachers integrated writing activities into lesson planning to further enhance their students' reading comprehension skills. Teachers found that because students had such strong phonemic awareness skills and had learned to sound-spell, their writing was readable even when they used words that they had not yet learned to spell. Some of the writing activities that teachers planned in connection with comprehension activities were:

- Writing summaries of stories or expository text in their own words
- Retelling a story from another character's perspective
- Writing several sentences connecting the theme of the story to something they have personally experienced
- Using a key sentence from a story as the story prompt for their writing
- Using the same graphic organizers used for reading comprehension as prewriting organizers before writing stories or informational text
- Completing charts or workbook pages requesting more information about text just read

Effective Teacher at Work

A Model Comprhehension Lesson

Ms. Cowen's second grade class was going to read *It's Probably Good Dinosaurs Are Extinct* by Ken Raney (1993). Before they read the book, students practiced reading the new morphemes they had recently learned and were now frequently applying to more difficult words they encountered in their reading: *age, tion, ish,* and *dish.* Next they decoded the new words that were in this story. Because students did not know the meaning of the words *extinct, roamed, existed,* and *herd,* Mrs. Cowen directly taught them as vocabulary words. Three dinosaur names, *Apatosaurus, protoceratops,* and *stegosaurus,* initially presented decoding challenges. Ms. Cowen knew that if students couldn't read the story with adequate accuracy, they would not understand it, so she planned her reading lessons so that students did not read the story until the second day after they had more practice with these and other new words.

On the day that students read the story, Ms. Cowen told everyone the title and, pointing to her large flip chart, asked everyone to tell her what information they already knew about dinosaurs. She wrote the students' answers on a graphic organizer (see Figure 7.11) and extended discussion through questions.

When students pointed out that some dinosaurs ate just plants, Ms. Cowen linked this story to a previous one by reminding students that several weeks ago in a different story they

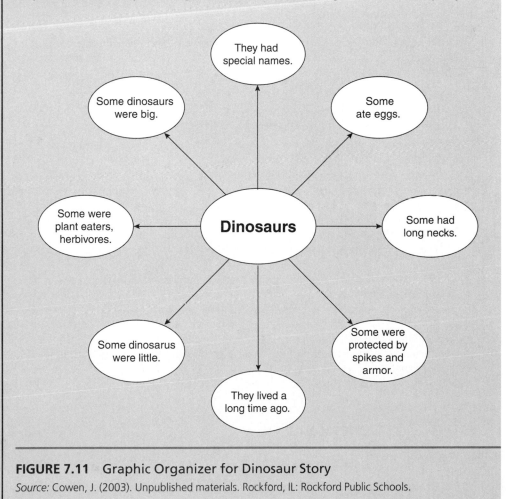

FIGURE 7.11   Graphic Organizer for Dinosaur Story

Source: Cowen, J. (2003). Unpublished materials. Rockford, IL: Rockford Public Schools.

Continued

had learned a word that they could use for animals who only ate plants. After a hint, someone excitedly remembered, "herbivore." After the chart was completed, Ms. Cowen asked, "Where did the dinosaurs live?" That question stumped the class and so she drew everyone's attention to a large dinosaur picture on the wall. "Caves, they lived in caves," a girl shouted out. Ms. Cowen expanded that answer and said, "Yes, they lived everywhere on Earth. They lived in every country. They've even found dinosaur bones in ice. Some lived in water. Where did others live?" Several students chimed in and explained that some lived on land and others in the air. Ms. Cowen used the moment to expand everyone's knowledge and pointing to the globe told the students that scientists believe that the continents were all connected at one time.

Looking deep in thought, another child asked the teacher, "How did the scientists discover the dinosaurs?" Ms. Cowen explained how they found the bones and came up with the name, "Terrible Lizard," which is what dinosaur means. "But they only found the bones—nothing else," she explained as everyone nodded their heads. At that, a student volunteered information about how her dad had bought her a computer CD about dinosaurs. One of the dinosaurs on the CD had a hard skull. Another student asked Ms. Cowen if dinosaurs were alive when she was a girl. At first Ms. Cowen joked about all the dinosaurs she would see outside the school at recess, but then she switched into a more serious mode and admitted that dinosaurs lived so long ago that there were none even when she was a baby. Most of the class seemed to enjoy the humor in this exchange.

After all the students had opened their books, Ms. Cowen explained that the new story was a fantasy story, and she asked what that meant. When one student replied, "not true," Ms. Cowen expanded the answer and explained that "Yes, the story was make-believe." Next everyone orally read the title in unison. Ms. Cowen asked students what "it's" was, since they had been studying contractions and the class answered, "it is." One student then read two or three sentences while everyone else followed along with their fingers. At the end of that passage, Ms. Cowen asked several questions that the students enthusiastically answered:

"How does the boy feel about dinosaurs?"
"What does he wish he had?"
"How many of you wish you had a dinosaur for a pet?"

After the entire class raised their hand, one student explained why he wanted a dinosaur to help him. Then a second student read another two sentences. This time Ms. Cowen stopped and asked, "Now the book says, "It's probably good that dinosaurs are extinct." What exactly does extinct mean?" Even though she had taught that word for two days, it took several hints for the class to remember what the difficult word meant. Wanting her students to use this word more, Ms. Cowen asked, "What would happen if dinosaurs were no longer extinct?" The students were appalled. "But they'd tear up our houses and eat our food," one answered. "They'd eat up our relatives," said another. A third girl chimed in, "They'd be very noisy at night and I couldn't sleep."

The first story reading continued with students reading passages followed by teacher questions. Information was clarified, connections drawn, understanding checked during this enjoyable story. Later, students would write and illustrate their work before it was displayed in the hallway. Two more dinosaur stories followed this one, one a narrative and the other expository. Decoding, oral language expansion, writing, fluent reading, graphic organizers, storybook structure, and frequent questions all worked together to develop these students' reading comprehension.

How Well Do I Understand?

As you read short pieces of expository text to students, ask them to raise one finger if they understand the text being read and two fingers if they do not understand it. Stop when the majority of students have two fingers raised and discuss strategies to clarify understanding of the text.

The Text Detective

Before students read an assigned text, give them short-answer worksheets with key *wh-* questions you want them to answer. Some questions might include: "In what period of time is this biography set?" "What was the main problem this character encountered growing up?" "Where did this character live most of his life?" "Who was the most influential person in this character's life?" and "Why do people say that this character is a leader?"

> Visit the Cultural Literacy Rocks website at: **www.aft.org/pubs-reports/american_educator/ spring2004/literacyroacks.html.**

Fact or Fiction

1. **While the research on developing phonemic awareness, alphabetic principle, and reading fluency is conclusive enough to guide teacher practice, we don't know have a comparable knowledge base for reading comprehension.**

   Fact   **Fiction**

   Fiction: There is enough research on reading comprehension (National Reading Panel, 2000; Rand Report, 2002) to provide teachers with strategies for teaching comprehension systematically and explicitly in their classrooms. The challenge is teaching students "*when* to apply *what* strategy for *which* particular students" (National Reading Panel, 2000, pp. 4–47; Duffy, 1993), using a multiple strategy approach as described in this chapter.

2. **Teaching reading comprehension requires that children first have a book in their hands that they are able to read.**

   Fact   **Fiction**

   Fiction: Teachers can and should emphasize reading comprehension from the beginning rather than waiting until students have mastered basic decoding skills (Armbruster et al., 2001). Until students have acquired enough word identification skills, teach comprehension orally, through listening, using the same teaching strategies described in this chapter for teaching reading comprehension.

A P P L I E D   A C T I V I T I E S

1. Shown here are DIBELS Oral Reading Fluency and DIBELS Retell scores for Ms. Redmond's grade 3 class in May. Identify which children may be experiencing difficulty with reading comprehension. Go to the DIBELS website or Table 5.1 in Chapter 5 and determine whether any of these students are also below benchmark in ORF. Why do you think students who read slowly are more likely to have trouble with comprehension?

Student	ORF	Retell
Alex	115	62
Bruno	70	10
Celia	100	49
Alicia	110	60
Aquanetta	93	38

2. In this chapter you learned that the ability to comprehend is influenced by the person reading the text, the text being read, the task the reader is trying to accomplish, and the context in which the reading is being done. For each of the following reading problems, discuss the factor(s) that are contributing to the problem.

   a. Sharif is impulsive and when given a reading assignment tends to rush through the text and not think about what he is reading.

   b. Margaret could not understand her library book because she always selects books that are too difficult for her.

   c. The reading assignment was difficult for Darren, but by trying extra hard he was able to get through it and answer the questions. Darren needed a good score on the assignment to get a passing grade for the marking period.

   d. Rinaldo refused to read in class because his classmates are critical of anyone who does what the teacher wants.

3. Think of a recent reading assignment for one of your classes. What metacognitive skills did you exercise in completing that assignment? How helpful were these skills for the successful completion of the assignment? How could you teach these skills to students unable to do them?

4. Shown here is a fable relating how slow and steady wins the race. Develop a graphic organizer that could be used to guide students as they read to comprehend the passage. Write a script showing what you would say if you were using My Turn–Together–Your Turn think-alouds to teach your students the key story grammar elements.

   One day the Rabbit made fun of the short legs and slow pace of the Turtle. The Turtle replied, laughing, "Though you may be fast as the wind, I will beat you in a race." The Rabbit, believing that to be simply impossible, agreed to the race. They agreed that their mutual friend the Fox should choose the course and fix the goal. On the day of the race the two animals started together. The Rabbit began running as fast as she could and soon got tired, lying down by the side of the trail. She fell fast asleep. The Turtle plodded along as he always did and never stopped for a moment, but went on with a slow but steady pace straight to the end of the course. Rabbit, at last waking up and moving as fast as she could, tried to catch up. Arriving at the end of the course, she saw the Turtle had reached the goal, and was comfortably resting. The Fox who had helped them laughed out loud and said, "it is true . . . slow but steady wins the race!"

5. Read the following passage taken from an eighth-grade social studies book. Identify the key text structure in the passage. Tell how you would use My Turn–Together–Your Turn think-alouds and a graphic organizer to teach students to recognize the text structure and understand the passage.

Striking Workers

As prices rose, labor unions demanded higher wages. Although many of these demands were met, some companies refused to give their workers pay increases. The result was a number of strikes that soon threatened the stability of the American economy.

The rail strike was probably the most serious. The huge semitrailers and interstate highways we know today didn't exist then. Most of the nation's goods moved by rail. President Truman, who had worked feverishly to end the coal and auto strikes, was angry when the railway workers announced their strike. He said that he understood their problems, but that he couldn't allow a rail strike at the time. (Buggey, Danzer, Mitsakos, & Risinger, 1987)

6. Select a children's fiction story and generate 12 questions that you could ask students. Your questions should reflect story grammars as well as important vocabulary. Indicate which questions reflect explicit or implicit information in the text.

R E F E R E N C E S

All America Reads (literature circle). Retrieved on November 17, 2005 from: www.allamericareads.org/lessonplan/strategies/during/litcirc3.htm

Applegate, M., Quinn, B., & Applegate, A. (2002). Levels of thinking required by comprehension questions in informal reading inventories. *The Reading Teacher, 56*(2), 174–180.

Armbruster, B., Lehr, F., & Osborn, J. (2001). *Put reading first: The research building blocks for teaching children to read.* Washington, DC: Partnership for Reading.

Beck, I., McKeown, M., Hamilton, R., & Kucan, L. (1997). *Question the Author: An approach for enhancing student engagement with text.* Newark, DE: International Reading Association.

Beck, I., & McKeown, M. (2001). *Text talk.* New York: Scholastic.

Browne, A. (1989). *Willy the wimp.* New York: Knopf.

Buggey, L., Danzer, G., Mitsakos, C., & Risinger, C. (1985). *America! America!* (2nd edition) Upper Saddle River, NJ: Prentice Hall.

Carnine, D., & Kinder, D. (1985). Teaching low-performing students to apply generative and schema strategies to narrative and expository material. *Remedial and Special Education, 6*(1), 20–30.

Carnine, D. W., Silbert, J., Kame'enui, E. J., & Tarver, S. (2004). *Direct instruction reading* (4th ed.). New Jersey: Merrill Prentice Hall.

Chall, J., & Jacobs, V. (2003). Poor children's fourth grade slump. *American Educator, 27*(1), 14–15.

Chall, J., Jacobs, V., & Baldwin, L. (1990). *The reading crisis: Why poor children fall behind.* Cambridge, MA: Harvard University Press.

DK Science Encyclopedia, The. (1998). C. Beattie, H. Dowling, L. Martin, M. Patria, L. Pritchard, J. Wilson, and Charles A. Willis, (Eds.). New York: DK.

Duffy, G. (1993). Rethinking strategy instruction: Four teachers' development and their low achievers' understanding. *Elementary School Journal, 93*(3), 231–247.

Dunston, P. (2002). Instructional components for promoting thoughtful literacy learning. In C. Block and M. Pressley (Eds.), *Comprehension instruction research-based best practice* (pp. 135–151). New York: Guilford Press.

Educational Resource Inc. (2004). *Strategies for taking high-stakes tests.* Unpublished materials.

Englemann, S., Hanner, S., & Johnson, g. (2002). *Corrective reading.* Columbus, OH: SRA/McGraw-Hill.

Englert, C., & Mariage, T. (1991). Making students partners in the comprehension process: Organizing the reading "posse." *Learning Disability Quarterly, 14*(2), 123–38.

Englert, C., & Thomas, C. (1987). Sensitivity to text structure in reading and writing: A comparison between learning disabled and non-learning disabled students. *Learning Disability Quarterly, 10*(2), 93–105.

Eskey, D. E. (2002). Reading and the teaching of L2 reading. *Teachers of English to Speakers of Other Languages Journal (TESOL Journal), 11*(1), 5–9.

France, M. (1998). *Deadly double.* Novato, CA: High Noon Books.

Friend, M., & Bursuck, B. (2006). *Including students with special needs: A practical guide for classroom teachers.* Boston: Allyn and Bacon.

Greene, J. F. (2004). *Language! A literacy intervention curriculum.* Longmont, CO: Sopris West.

Goudiss, M., Hodges, V., & Margulies, S. (1999). *The ISAT coach: Grade 3 reading.* New York: Triumph Learning—Coach Books.

Gunning, T. (2002). *Assessing and correcting reading and writing difficulties* (2nd ed.). Boston: Allyn & Bacon.

Hirsch, E. (2000, Spring). You can always look it up . . . or can you? *American Educator, 2.*

Idol, L. (1997). *Reading success: A specialized literacy program for learners with challenging learning needs.* Austin, TX: Pro-Ed.

Ivey, G. (2002). Building comprehension when they're still learning to read the words. In C. Block and M. Pressley (Eds.), *Comprehension instruction: Research-based best practice* (pp. 234–246). New York: Guilford Press.

Jones, R. (2000). Reading Quest: Strategies for reading comprehension history frames/story maps. Retrieved on November 17, 2005 from: http://curry.edschool.virginia.edu/go/readquest/strat/storymaps.html

Keene, E. (2002). "From good to memorable": Characteristics of highly effective comprehension teaching. In C. Block, L. Gambrell, and M. Pressley (Eds.), *Improving comprehension instruction: rethinking research, theory, and classroom practice* (pp. 80–105). San Francisco: Jossey-Bass.

Kinder, D. (1990). *A reciprocal teaching example.* Unpublished materials.

Kletzien, S., & Szabo, R. (1998). *Information text or narrative text? Children's preferences revisited.* Paper presented at the National Reading Conference, Austin, TX, 1998.

Klinger, J., Vaughn, S., Arguelles, M., Hughes, M., & Leftwich, S. (2004). Collaborative strategic reading: "Real-world" lessons from classroom teachers. *Remedial & Special Education, 25*(5).

Kozloff, M. (2005). Tips for effective teaching of language for learning. Retrieved on November 17, 2005 from: www.educationation.org/languageforlearning tips.DOC

Luft, D. (1980). *Robert Musil and the crisis of European culture: 1880–1942.* Berkely: University of California Press.

MacArthur, C., Ferretti, R., Okolo, C., and Cavalier, A. (2001, Jan.). Technology applications for students with literacy problems: A critical review. *The Elementary School Journal, 101*(3), 73–301.

Marchand-Martella, N. E., Slocum, T. A., & Martella, R. C. (2004). *Introduction to direct instruction.* Boston: Allyn & Bacon.

Marliave, R., & Filby, N. N. (1985). Success rate: A measure of task appropriateness. In C. W. Fisher & D. C. Berliner (Eds.), *Perspectives on instructional time* (pp. 217–235). New York: Longman.

McEwan, E. (2001). *Raising reading achievement in middle and high schools.* Thousand Oaks, CA: Corwin Press.

McNeil, J. D. (1992). *Reading comprehension: New directions for classroom practice* (3rd ed.). Los Angeles: University of California.

Moats, L. C. (2001, March). When older students can't read. *Educational Leadership, 58*(6), 36–40.

Moats, L. C. (2005). Language essentials for teachers of reading and spelling Module 6: Digging for meaning: Teaching text comprehension. Boston: Sopris West.

Philbrick, R. (1998). *Max the mighty.* New York: Scholastic.

Pressley, M. (2000). Comprehension Instruction: What Works. Retrieved on December 14, 2005 at reading rockets: www.readingrockets.org/articles/68

Pressley, M. (2002). Metacognition and self-regulated comprehension. In A. E. Farstrup & S. Samuels (Eds.), *What research has to say about reading instruction* (pp. 291–309). Newark, DE: International Reading Association.

RAND Reading Study Group. (2002). Reading for understanding: Towards an R&D program in reading comprehension. Retrieved August 10, 2004 from: www.rand.org/publications/MR/MR1465

Raney, K. (1993). *It's probably good dinosaurs are extinct.* Seattle, WA: Green Tiger Press.

Reading Success Network, Southeast Comprehensive Assistance Center. (n.d.). *Implications for Teaching Reading to English Language Learners: Participant Materials.* Retrieved August 7, 2004 from: www.sedl.org/secac/rsn/ELL.pdf

Reich, J. R., & Beiler, E. L. (1988). *United States history.* Austin, TX: Holt, Rinehart & Winston.

Richards, J., & Gipe, J. (2000). Reading comprehension games for young students in mainstream settings. *Reading & Writing Quarterly, 16,* 75–80.

Robinson, F. P. (1961, 1970). Effective study (4th ed.). New York: Harper & Row.

Runelhart, D. (1984). Understanding understanding. In J. Flood (Ed.), *Understanding reading comprehension* (pp. 1–20). Newark, DE: International Reading Association.

Schmar-Dobler, E. (September, 2003). Reading on the internet: The link between literacy and technology. *Journal of Adolescent & Adult Literacy, 47*(1), 80–85.

Schraff, A. (1992). *Swamp furies.* Costa Mesa, CA: Saddleback Publishing, Inc.

Shankweiler, D., Lundquist, E., & Dreyer L. (1996). Reading and spelling difficulties in high school students: Causes and consequences. *Reading and Writing, 8*(3).

Short, D. (1994). Expanding middle school horizons: Integrating language, culture, and social studies. *TESOL Quarterly, 28,* 581–608.

Smith, M. (1999). Teaching comprehension from a multisensory perspective. In J. Birsh (Ed.), *Multisensory teaching of basic language skills.* Baltimore: Paul H. Brookes Publishing Co.

Spadorcia, S. (2001). Looking more closely at high-interest, low-level texts: Do they support comprehension? *Perspectives, 27*(2) 32–33. Retrieved on December 15, 2005 from: www.resourceroom.net/index.asp.

Yang, Y. (2002, April). Reassessing readers' comprehension monitoring. *Reading in a Foreign Language, 14* (1). Retrieved from: http://nflrc.hawaii.edu/rfl/April2002.

A How Do I Make a Progress Graph for One Student?

1. Open the *Excel* spreadsheet program.
2. Type *Month* in cell A1; Type *Score* in cell B1.
3. Type the name of the month in which you will give the first ORF assessment in cell A2; the second month in cell A3; the third month in A4; and so on. Your final column should list each month in which you plan to give the assessment.
4. Type the first ORF score for the student in B2. Type the second ORF score in B3. Repeat this for each score and complete for column B.
5. Select the entire section—A and B columns should be selected down to the last month you typed in.
6. Click on the chart wizard and select *line.*
7. Select the chart labeled, *line with markers displayed at each data value* and press *next.*
8. Accept the given *data range* and make sure that *columns* is selected. Press *next.*
9. Type Oral Reading Fluency Chart followed by a semicolon and the student's name in the Title section; type *month* in the *x axis* section; type *words correct per minute* in the *y axis* section. Press *next.*
10. Select *as object in* under the Chart Location section and press *finish.*
11. Format graph: In order to disconnect data points between the line, click once on the line. Then, right click on the same place again. FORMAT DATA SERIES menu will appear. Selct *None* in the line secton and click OK.
12. Double click on the shaded background of the graph. You will see FORMAT PLOT AREA menu. Under th Border section, select *None.* Under the Area section, select *None.* Click on the OK button. This will remove the gray background color and the right border from the graph.
13. Right click on any gridline and select *format gridlines.* Select *scale.* Type in the following values: *minimum = 0; maximum =* (type in a number higher than highest ORF score you expect your most advanced student will be reading by the end of the year; for second grade you might type in 140*); major unit = 10; minor unit = 5; category x axis crosses at = 0.* Make sure that none of the boxes under the *auto* column are checked.
14. Left click on the outside frame of the graph and pull out until it is the size you want.
15. Select *line* on the *drawing* toolbar. To draw an *aim line,* start the line at the point representing the first ORF score and pull the line up to the data point for the final month. The aim line will be at a slant.
16. You are now finished and can save the graph.

B Signals Used in Formats

1. Fingers Raised and Rainbow Arc Signal:

2. Finger Snap Signal:

3. Hand Clap Signal:

4. Loop Signal:

5. Sounding Out Regular Words Signal:

Part 1:   Part 2:

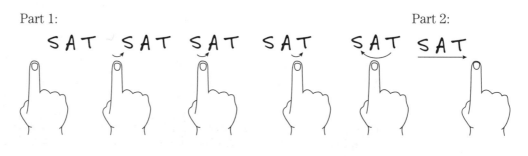

C Teaching Formats

Phonemic Awareness

Segmenting 1: Format for Segmenting First Sound

Instructions	Teacher	Students
	1. Advance Organizer	
	2. My Turn	
	"It's time to play the *first-sound* game. I'm going to say a word, and you'll say the first sound in the word. My turn. First sound in *sat?*" "/s/."	
	3. Together: The teacher answers with students this time:	
	"Together. First sound in *sat?*" (signal) **"/s/. Yes, /s/."**	/s/
	4. Your Turn:	
	"Your turn. First sound in *sat?*" (signal) (answer) **"Yes, /s/."**	/s/
	5. Individual Student Checkout	
	"Individual turns. First sound in *sat?*" Jontrell." (signal) (answer) **"Yes, /s/."**	/s/
	"First sound in *mop?* Corinne." (signal) (answer) **"Yes, /m/."**	/m/
	Call on several individual students to check accuracy.	
Error Correction	If students make an error, immediately return to a My Turn–Together–Your Turn pattern. Later present the word that was missed two more times during the lesson.	

Blending 2: Format for Blending Individual Phonemes

Instructions	Teacher	Students
	1. Advance Organizer	
	2. My Turn	
	"Today we're going to play *Say It Fast*. I'm going to say a word slowly, and then fast. My turn. /n/-/ă/-/p/. The word is *nap*."	
	3. Together: The teacher answers with students this time	
	"Together." (extend fingers) **"/n/-/ă/-/p/. What word?"** (arch palm) **"nap. Yes, *nap*."**	nap
	4. Your Turn	
	"Your turn." (extend fingers) **"/n/-/ă/-/p/. What word?"** (arch palm) (answer) **"Yes, *nap*."**	nap

Continued

5. Individual Student Checkout

"Individual turns" (extend fingers) **"/m/-/ŏ/-/p/. What word? Mary."** (arch palm) (answer) **"Yes, *mop.*"**   mop

(extend fingers) **"/r/-/ŭ/-/n/. What word? Telly."** (arch palm) (answer) **"Yes, *run.*"**   run

Call on several individual students to check accuracy.

Error Correction	If students make an error, immediately return to a "My Turn," "Together," "Your Turn" pattern. Later present the word that was missed two more times during the lesson.

Segmenting 2: Format for Segmenting Individual Phonemes

Instructions	Teacher	Students
	1. Advance Organizer	
	2. My Turn **"I'm going to say a word, and you'll say all the sounds in the word. My turn. Take apart *leg.* /l/-/ĕ/-/g/. The sounds in *leg* are /l/-/ĕ/-/g/."**	
	3. Together: The teacher answers with students this time **"Together. Take apart *leg.*"** (extend finger) **"/l/"** (extend finger) **"/ĕ/"** (extend finger) **"/g/. Yes, the sounds in *leg* are /l/-/ĕ/-/g/."**	/l/-/ĕ/-/g/
	4. Your Turn **"Your turn. Take apart leg."** (extend finger) (answer) (extend finger) (answer) (extend finger) (answer) **"Yes, the sounds in *leg* are /l/-/ĕ/-/g/."**	/l/-/ĕ/-/g/
	5. Individual Student Checkout **"Individual turns. Take apart men. Sharnicca."** (extend finger) (answer) (extend finger) (answer) (extend finger) (answer) **"Yes, the sounds in *men* are /m/-/ĕ/-/n/."**	/m/-/ĕ/-/n/
	"Take apart win. Bryan." (extend finger) (answer) (extend finger) (answer) (extend finger) (answer) **"Yes, the sounds in *win* are /w/-/i/-/n/."** Call on several individual students to check accuracy.	/w/-/i/-/n/
Error Correction	If students make an error, immediately return to a My Turn–Together–Your Turn pattern. Later present the word that was missed two more times during the lesson.	

Alphabetic Principle

Format for New Letter-Sounds Introduced in the Curriculum: Part A

Instructions	Teacher	Students
	1. Advance Organizer	
	2. My Turn (examples given for continuous and stop sounds) Write a lower case letter s on the board and point to the letter: *continuous sound:* (finger to the left of letter) **"Here's our new sound for today."** (loop signal) **"/sss/."** (loop back to starting point) **"This letter says"** (loop signal) "**sss/.**" (end signal). *stop sound:* (finger to the left of letter) **"Here's our new sound for today."** (loop signal and bounce out) **"/t/."** (back to starting point) **"This letter says"** (loop signal and bounce out) **"/t/."** (end signal).	

3. Together

The teacher answers with students this time.

Signal for *continuous sounds:* (finger to the left of letter) **"Together. What sound?"** (loop signal) **"/s/."** (loop back to starting point) **"Yes, /s/."** /s/

Signal for *stop sounds:* (finger to the left of letter) **"Together. What sound?"** (loop signal and bounce out) **"/t/."** (back to starting point) **"Yes, /t/."** /t/

Repeat this sequence several times.

4. Your Turn

Signal for *continuous sounds:* (finger to the left of letter) **"Your turn. What sound?"** (loop signal) (answer) (loop back to starting point) **"Yes, /s/."** /s/

Signal for *stop sounds:* (finger to the left of letter) **"Your turn. What sound?"** (loop signal and bounce out) (answer) (back to starting point) **"Yes, /t/."** /t/

Repeat several times.

5. Individual Student Checkout

Signal for *continuous sounds:* (finger to the left of letter) **"Individual turns. What sound? Marissa."** (loop signal) (answer) (loop back to starting point) **"Yes, /s/."** /s/

Signal for *stop sounds:* (finger to the left of letter) **"Individual turns. What sound? Tonia."** (loop signal and bounce out) (answer) (back to starting point) **"Yes, /t/."** /t/

Call on several individual students and check accuracy.

Error Correction   If students make an error, immediately return to a My Turn–Together–Your Turn pattern. You may need to refocus students to your mouth position as you say the letter.

Format for New Letter-Sounds Introduced in the Curriculum: Part B

Instructions	Teacher	Students
	1. Advance Organizer	
	2. Your Turn	
	The teacher uses an alternating pattern to teach the new letter sound by writing the new lower-case letter on the board followed by one previously taught letter, followed by the new letter, followed by two previously taught letters. This pattern is continued until five letters separate the last two new letters (for example, **s** t **s** a t **s** m t a **s** h m t a **s** a t h m f **s**). The teacher provides more practice identifying the more difficult previously taught letters and vowels by including them in the list every day.	/s/, /t/, /s/, /a/, /t/, /s/, /m/, /t/
	Signal for *continuous sounds:* (finger to the left of letter) **"Your turn. What sound?"** (loop signal) (answer) (loop back to starting point) **"Yes, /s/."**	/s/ . . . .
	Signal for *stop sounds:* (finger to the left of letter) **"Your turn. What sound?"** (loop signal and bounce out) (answer) (back to starting point) **"Yes, /t/."**	
	3. Individual Student Checkout	
	Signal for *continuous sounds:* (finger to the left of letter) **"Individual turns. What sound? Kyle."** (loop signal) (answer) (loop back to starting point) **"Yes, /s/."**	/s/
	Signal for *stop sounds:* (finger to the left of letter) **"Individual turns. What sound? Lynnette."** (loop signal and bounce out) (answer) (back to starting point) **"Yes, /ă/."**	/ă/ . . . .
	Call on several individual students to check accuracy.	

Continued

Error Correction	If students make an error, immediately return to a My Turn–Together–Your Turn pattern. Then alternate between the missed letter and familiar letters until students identify the missed letter correctly three times.	

For example, if you are working on *a, m, r, s,* and *i,* and the students missed *s,* say, (finger to the left of letter) **"This sound is /s/"** before asking, **"What sound?"** (loop signal and end) **"Yes, /s/."**

Then ask the students to identify letter sounds using the following alternating pattern: a **s** m i **s** r i m **s.**

Sound Writing Format

Sound Spelling Activity: Children write /t/ and /r/.

Teacher: You're going to write some letter sounds.

> **"First sound /t/. What sound?"** (signal) (answer) **"/t/. Yes, /t/."**
> **"Write /t/."** Check children's answers and give feedback.

> **"Next sound /r/. What sound?"** (signal) (answer) **"/rrr/. Yes, /r/."**
> **"Write /r/."** Check children's answers and give feedback.

Format for Reading Regular Words—Stage 1: Orally sounding out regular words

Instructions	Teacher	Students
	1. Advance Organizer	
	2. My Turn (Note: See Ms. Elizondo's fourth tip on page 93 in the text to determine whether to start at Step 2, 3, or 4.)	
	(finger to the left of the first letter) **"My turn sounding out this word."** (loop from letter to letter) **"/f/-/ă/-/n/"** (loop back to starting point) **"What word?"** (side-slash signal) ***"fan."***	
	3. Together	
	The teacher answers with students this time:	
	(finger to the left of the first letter) **"Together, sound out this word."** (loop from letter to letter) **"/f/-/ă/-/n/."** (loop back to starting point) **"What word?"** (side-slash signal) ***"fan."*** (loop to starting point) **"Yes, *fan.*"**	/f/-/ă/-/n/ fan
	4. Your Turn	
	(finger to the left of the first letter) **"Your turn to sound out this word."** (loop from letter to letter) (answer) (loop back to starting point) **"What word?"** (side-slash signal) (answer) (loop to starting point) **"Yes, *fan.*"**	/f/-/ă/-/n/ fan
	Repeat step 4 for every word in the row.	
	5. Individual Student Checkout:	
	Point to the first regular word written on the board (*fan*) and place your finger slightly to the left of the word.	
	"Individual turns. Sound out this word. Grant." (loop from letter to letter) (answer) (loop back to starting point) **"What word?"** (side-slash signal) (answer) (loop to starting point) **"Yes, *fan.*"**	/f/-/ă/-/n/ fan
	"Sound out this word. Leila." (loop from letter to letter) (answer) (loop back to starting point*)* **"What word?"** (side-slash signal) (answer) (loop to starting point) **"Yes, *sip.*"**	/s/-/ĭ/-/p/ sip
	Call on several students to check for accuracy. When students' correct answers show you that they know all of the words in the row, move to the second row of words.	
Error Correction	If students make an error, immediately return to a My Turn–Together–Your Turn pattern, always requiring them to sound out the word. Then return to the beginning of the row and have students reread words the fast way.	

Format for Reading Regular Words—Stage 2: Subvocal Sounding-Out

Instructions	Teacher	Students
	1. Advance Organizer	
	2. My Turn (finger to the left of the first letter) **"My turn sounding out this word in my head."** (loop from letter to letter and silently mouth the letter sounds /f/-/ă/-/n/) (loop back to starting point) **"What word?"** (side-slash signal) ***"fan."***	
	3. Together The teacher answers with students this time: (finger to the left of the first letter) **"Together, sound out this word in your heads."** (loop from letter to letter and silently mouth the letter sounds /f/-/ă/-/n/) (loop back to starting point) **"What word?"** (side-slash signal) ***"fan."*** (loop to starting point) **"Yes, *fan.*"**	fan
	4. Your Turn (finger to the left of the first letter) **"Your turn. Sound out this word in your heads."** (loop from letter to letter) (students mouth sounds) (loop back to starting point) **"What word?"** (side-slash signal) (answer) (loop to starting point) **"Yes, *fan.*"**	fan
	5. Individual Student Checkout (finger to the left of the first letter) **" Individual turns. Sound out this word in your head. Maria."** (loop from letter to letter) (student mouths sounds) (loop back to starting point) **"What word?"** (side-slash signal) (answer) (loop to starting point) **"Yes, *fan.*"** Call on several individual students to check for accuracy.	fan
	6. Read the Row: Reading the row of words the fast way. Note: If you provide three seconds of think time before signaling for an answer, students should be ready to read the row of words the fast way. Use the Part 3 format for this section: **"Let's read all four words the fast way this time."** (think time) **"What word?"** (side-slash signal) (answer) (loop to starting point) **"Yes, *fan.*"**	fan
	(think time) **"What word?"** (side-slash signal) (answer) (loop to starting point) **"Yes, *sip.*"**	sip
	(think time) **"What word?"** (side-slash signal) (answer) (loop to starting point) **"Yes, *let.*"**	let
	(think time) **"What word?"** (side-slash signal) (answer) (loop to starting point) **"Yes, *cat.*"**	cat
Error Correction	If students make an error, immediately return to a My Turn–Together–Your Turn pattern requiring them to sound the word out loud. Then return to the beginning of the row and have students reread words the fast way.	

Format for Reading Regular Words—Stage 3: The Fast Way

Instructions	Teacher	Student
	1. Advance Organizer	
	2. My Turn (use for first word only, and only for the first day or two using this format) (finger to the left of the first letter) **"My turn to read this word the fast way?"** (side-slash signal) ***"fan."***	

Continued

3. Your Turn

   Note: For new words that you anticipate your students misreading, use the Part 1 sounding out format the first time the word is introduced in the list.

   "Your turn to read the rest of the words."

   (point and pause) **"What word?"** (side-slash answer) (loop back to starting point) **"Yes, *fan.*"** — fan

   (point and pause) **"What word?"** (side-slash answer) (loop back to starting point) **"Yes, *hat.*"** — hat

   (point and pause) **"What word?"** (side-slash answer) (loop back to starting point) **"Yes, *sit.*"** — sit

   (point and pause) **"What word?"** (side-slash answer) (loop back to starting point) **"Yes, *Pam.*"** — Pam

4. Individual Student Checkout

   (point and pause) **"Individual turns. What word? Ali."** (side-slash answer) (loop back to starting point) **"Yes, *fan.*"** — fan

   (point and pause) **"What word? Toni."** (side-slash answer) (loop back to starting point) **"Yes, *sit.*"** — sit

   Call on several individual students to check for accuracy.

Error Correction If students make an error, immediately return to Part 1 sounding-out aloud using a My Turn–Together–Your Turn pattern. Then return to the beginning of the row and have students reread words the fast way.

Regular Word Spelling Format

Spelling activity: **Students write *in, pin, pat.***

Teacher: **"You're going to write the word *in.* Listen. *In.* Say the sounds in *in.*"**
Signal for each sound by using a fingersnap, clap, or extended finger as the children say /ĭ ĭ ĭ/ (pause) /nnn/. Repeat until firm.

Teacher: **"Everybody, write the word** (pause) **in."**
Check children's answers so you can give feedback.

Repeat for ***pin*** and ***pat.***

Format for Reading Sight Words

Instructions	Teacher	Student
	1. Advance Organizer	

Part 1: Introduction of new words.

2. Write the new sight words from the daily story in a column on the left side of the board: for example, *today, father, strange.* Write four review sight words in a column on the right side of the board: for example, *was, isn't, should, great.* Teach the first new sight word written on the board (*today*).

   a. (finger to the left of the first letter) **"This word is"** (side-slash while saying **"*today.*"**) (loop back to starting point)

   b. **"What word?"** (side-slash-answer) (loop back to starting point) **"Yes, *today.*"** — today

   c. **"Spell *today.*"** (point to each letter as students answer) (loop back to starting point) — t-o-d-a-y

   d. **"What word?"** (side-slash-answer) (loop back to starting point) **"Yes, *today.*"** — today

   e. (finger to the left of the first letter) **"This word is"** (side-slash while saying **"*father.*"**) (loop back to starting point)

f.	**"What word?"** (side-slash-answer) (loop back to starting point) **"Yes, father."**	father
g.	**"Spell** *father."* (point to each letter as students answer) (loop back to starting point)	f-a-t-h-e-r
h.	**"What word?"** (side-slash-answer) (loop back to starting point) **"Yes, father."**	father
i.	Return to the top of the list and point to the left of the first word. Pause and ask, **"What word?"** (side-slash-answer) (loop back to starting point) **"Yes, today."**	today
	Quickly point to the left of the second word. Pause and ask, **"What word?"** (side-slash-answer) (loop back to starting point) **"Yes,** *father."*	father
j.	Repeat steps e–i with the remaining words until students can read all of the words in the column without errors.	
k.	Individual Student Checkout: Call on between one and three students to check for accuracy.	

Part 2: Students sight read new words and review words.

3. Point to words randomly.

   a. **"When I signal, read the word."**

(finger to the left of the first letter) **"What word?"** (side-slash-answer) (loop back to starting point) **"Yes,** *father."*	father
(finger to the left of the first letter) **"What word?"** (side-slash-answer) (loop back to starting point) **"Yes,** *was."*	was
(finger to the left of the first letter) **"What word?"** (side-slash-answer) (loop back to starting point) **"Yes,** *should."*	should

   b. Individual Student Checkout: Call on between one and three students to check for accuracy.

Error Correction — If students make an error, immediately return to a My Turn. Tell students the word, ask them to spell the word, and then ask them to read the sight word (Part 1: Steps a–d).

Format for Reading Stories in the Curriculum and Decodable Books:
Pre-Alphabetic Principle

Instructions	Teacher	Students
	Advance Organizer	
	Steps to reading stories and books (Pre-Alphabetic Principle):	
	First Reading(s)	
	1. Suggested wording for focusing students to follow along: **"We are first going to sound out each word and then we will read it the fast way. When I clap, say the sound of the first letter. When I clap again, move your finger and say the next sound. When you are at the end of the word, move your finger back to the beginning of the word so you can read it the fast way. Watch me do it first."** (You will need to use a finger snap with your nondominant hand as you show students how you follow along to the signal, sounding out and reading the words.) **"Everybody, put your finger under the first letter of the very first word."**	Students touch under the first letter of the word
	2. Focus students to accurate reading and tell them the goal you've set: **"Our goal is to miss no more than one word today."**	

3. First Story Reading—Sounding-Out: Pause 1 second and then say, **"Sound it out"** and clap for the first sound. After 1 to 1½ seconds, clap for the next sound. After 1 to 1½ seconds later clap for the last sound. When students have said the last sound correctly, make sure that they move their finger back to the left of the word. Ask **"What word?"** and clap. Students side-slash their finger as they read the word the fast way. Then they immediately move their finger to the left of the next word.

Students say sounds, pointing under the letters as they say them; they move their finger back to the beginning of the word before orally reading the word at a normal rate.

4. Pause 1 second and then say **"Sound it out"** and clap for the first sound. After 1 to 1½ seconds, clap for the next sound. After 1 to 1½ seconds later clap for the last sound. When students have said the last sound correctly, make sure that they move their finger back to the left of the word. Ask **"What word?"** and clap. Students side-slash their finger as they read the word the fast way. Then they immediately move their finger to the left of the next word.

5. For sight words, avoid sounding out. When students move their fingers to the left of a sight word, say, **"What word?"** and clap to signal students to say the word.

Students read the whole word without sounding it out.

6. Continue using this format to the end of the story or to the end of the page.

7. Wrap Up: Have students reread the story, sounding out each word until the error limit is met. When the error limit is met give individual turns. Do not move on to the second reading format until the error limit is met.

Second Reading(s)

1. Repeat Steps 1–5, but have students subvocally sound out the words as in Stage 2 regular word reading (Table 3.6). Provide 5 seconds of think time before asking **"What word?"** At the end of the story have students practice reading any missed words. Do not move on to third reading format until the error limit is met.

Students subvocally sound out, before saying the word at a normal rate.

Third Reading(s)

1. Repeat Steps 1–5, but have students read words the fast way as in Stage 3 (Table 3.7) word reading. Provide 5 seconds of think time before asking **"What word?"**

Students read the words in the story the fast way.

2. Use individual checkouts to determine whether students are solid on reading the story. Have each student read one sentence.

Error Correction

- When students make a sounding out error, immediately say, **"My Turn,"** and sound out the word correctly. Move into a Your Turn and ask students to sound out the word before always going back to the beginning of the sentence. Any error (missed word, plural ending left off, etc.) is treated as an error.

Advanced Word Reading

Format for New Letter Combinations and Affixes Introduced in the Curriculum

Instructions	Teacher	Students
	1. Advance Organizers	
	2. My Turn (Examples given for continuous and stop sounds.)	
	Point to the new letter combination or affix.	
	continuous sound: (finger to the left of letter) **"My turn. Here's our new sound for today."** (loop signal) **"/ar/."** (loop back to starting point)	/ar/
	stop sound: (finger to the left of letter) **"My turn. Here's our new sound for today."** (loop signal and bounce out) **"/ch/."** (back to starting point)	/ch/
	3. Your Turn	
	continuous sound: (finger to the left of letter) **"Your turn. What sound?"** (loop signal) (answer) (loop back to starting point) **"Yes, /ar/."**	/ar/
	stop sound: (finger to the left of letter) **"Your turn. What sound?"** (loop signal and bounce out) (answer) (back to starting point). **"Yes, /ch/."**	/ch/
	4. Individual Student Checkout	
	continuous sound: (finger to the left of letter) **"Individual turns. What sound? Inez."** (loop signal) (answer) (loop back to starting point) **"Yes, /ar/."**	/ar/
	stop sound: (finger to the left of letter) **"Individual turns. What sound? Shan."** (loop signal and bounce out) (answer) (back to starting point). **"Yes, /ch/."**	/ch/
	5. Your Turn to Read the Row (new plus previously learned letter combinations and affixes)	
	Starting at the first letter combination/affix move through the row of letters on the list, signaling for each letter combination/affix just as you did in Step 3. As you move through the list say, **"What sound?"** for each letter combination/affix.	/ar/ /ea/ /ar/
	6. Individual Student Checkout	
	Point to random letters. Starting at the first letter combination/affix, move across the row of letters on the list, signaling for each letter combination/affix just as you did in Step 6. As you point to random letter combinations/affixes on the list say, **"Individual turns. What sound? Carmella."**	/ing/, /ar/, /ent/ . . .
Error Correction	If an error occurs at Step 3, immediately return to a My Turn–Together–Your Turn pattern.	
	If an error occurs at Step 5 or 6, immediately return to a My Turn–Together–Your Turn pattern. Then alternate between the missed letter and familiar letters until students identify the missed letter correctly three times.	

Format for Reading One-Syllable Regular Words with Letter Combinations

Instructions	Teacher	Student
	1. Advance Organizers	
	2. Your Turn with Sound Prompting	
	a. (finger just to the left of underlined sound) **"Your turn. What sound?"** (loop signal) (answer) (loop back to starting point). **"Yes,** (loop signal) **/sh/."** (loop back to the left of the word)	/sh/
	b. (pointing to the left of the word.) **"What word?"** (side-slash-answer) (loop back to starting point). **"Yes, *ship*."**	ship

3. Your Turn without Sound Prompting

After the first three or four words on the list, omit the sound prompting. Remember to use a longer think time the first or second time students read words on the list.

"What word?" (side-slash-signal under the entire word–answer) (loop back to starting point) **"Yes, *shall.*"**	shall
"What word?" (side-slash-signal under the entire word–answer) (loop back to starting point) **"Yes, *wish.*"**	wish

4. Individual Student Checkout

"What word? Bethany." (side-slash-signal under the entire word–answer) (loop back to starting point) **"Yes, *wish.*"**	wish

Call on between one and three students to check for accuracy.

Error Correction	If students make an error reading the new sound combination, ask them to tell you the sound and then read the word again. If students still make a mistake, move into a My Turn–Your Turn pattern. Then return to the beginning of the row and have students reread the words.
	If students make an error reading another sound they have previously learned, immediately have them sound out loud and then read the whole word. If they still make an error, return to a My Turn–Your Turn. Once the error is corrected, return to the beginning of the row and have students reread the words.

Format for Reading One-Syllable Words That End with VCe

Instructions	Teacher	Student
	Note: The first few times you read VCe words, use a My Turn to show students how you apply the rule and read the words.	
	1. Teach students the rule for one-syllable words that end in VCVe. **"When it's vowel–consonant–vowel, the first vowel says its name."** Don't move on to Step 2 until students can say this rule.	When it's vowel– consonant– vowel . . .
	2. Point to the first word and ask, **"Does this word have a vowel–consonant–vowel?"** (pause) (finger snap) (answer) (point to VCV letters as you affirm) **"Yes, this word has a vowel–consonant–vowel."**	yes
	3. Point to the first vowel and ask, **"So does this letter say its name?"** (pause) (finger snap) (answer) **"Yes, this letter says its name."**	yes
	4. Point to the first vowel: **"Say the name of this letter."** (finger snap) (answer) (point to the first vowel) **"Yes, /ā/."**	/ā/
	5. Point your finger to the left of the first letter in the word, pause and ask, **"What word?"** (side-slash-signal under the entire word–answer) (loop back to starting point) **"Yes, *name.*"**	name
	6. Repeat this pattern for all of the words.	
	7. After students read all of the words on the list, start at the beginning and read all of the words the fast way.	
	(point and pause) **"What word?"** (side-slash-signal under the entire word–answer) (loop back to starting point) **"Yes, *name.*"**	name
	(point and pause) **"What word?"** (side-slash-signal under the entire word–answer) (loop back to starting point) **"Yes, *gate.*"**	gate
	(point and pause) **"What word?"** (side-slash-signal under the entire word–answer) (loop back to starting point) **"Yes, *sale.*"**	sale
	Gradually fade out your prompts. On day 2 or 3, you might begin omitting Step 4. If students are not successful, add that prompt for several more days. Once students can read the long vowel words when you omit Step 4, also omit Step 3 during the first time through the words.	

8. Individual Student Checkout

    (point and pause) **"Individual turns. What word? Austin."** (side-slash-signal | gate

        under the entire word–answer) (loop back to starting point) **"Yes, *gate.*"**

    (point and pause) **"What word? Chan."** (side-slash-signal under the entire | sale

        word–answer) (loop back to starting point) **"Yes, *sale.*"**

    Call on between one and three students to check for accuracy.

| Error Correction | If an error occurs at any step, immediately repeat Steps 2–6. Repeat the rule as in step 1 if necessary. |

Instructions	Teacher	Student
	1. Ask students to tell you the vowel–consonant–vowel rule (signal 1).	When it's vowel–consonant–vowel . . .
	2. Point to the first word and ask, **"Does this word have a vowel–consonant–vowel?"** (pause) (finger snap) (answer) (point to letters as you affirm) **"Yes, this word has a vowel–consonant–vowel."**	yes
	3. Point to the first vowel and ask, **"Do we say /a/ or /ă/ for this letter?"** (pause) (finger snap) (answer) (point to letter as you affirm) **"Yes, /ā/."**	/a/
	4. Point to the left of the word, pause, and ask, **"What word?"** (side-slash-signal under the entire word—answer) (loop back to starting point) **"Yes, *tame.*"**	tame
	5. Point to the second word and ask, **"Does this word have a vowel–consonant–vowel?"** (pause) (finger snap)	no
	6. Point to the first vowel and ask, **"Do we say /a/ or /ă/ or for this letter?"** (pause) (finger snap) (answer) (point to letter as you affirm) **"Yes, /ăăă/."**	/ă/
	7. Point to the left of the word, pause and ask, **"What word?"** (side-slash-signal) (answer) **"Yes, *cat.*"**	cat
	8. Repeat Steps 1–4 for each of the words on the list.	
	9. After reading all of the words on the list, start at the beginning and read all of the words the fast way.	
	(point and pause) **"What word?"** (side-slash-signal under the entire word–answer) (loop back to starting point) **"Yes, *tame.*"**	tame
	(point and pause) **"What word?"** (side-slash-signal under the entire word–answer) (loop back to starting point) **"Yes, *cat.*"**	cat
	(point and pause) **"What word?"** (side-slash-signal under the entire word–answer) (loop back to starting point) **"Yes, *sap.*"**	sap
	(point and pause) **"What word?"** (side-slash-signal under the entire word–answer) (loop back to starting point) **"Yes, *gate.*"**	gate
	Gradually fade out your prompts. On day 2 or 3, you might begin omitting Step 3. If students are not successful, add that prompt for several more days. Once students can read the words when you omit Step 3, omit Steps 1 and 2 the first time through the words.	
	10. Individual Student Checkout	
	(point and pause) **"Individual turns. What word? Glynnis."** (side-slash-signal under the entire word–answer) (loop back to starting point) **"Yes, *sap.*"**	sap
	(point and pause) **"What word? Dyron."** (side-slash-signal under the entire word–answer) (loop back to starting point) **"Yes, *tame.*"**	tame
	Call on between one and three students to check for accuracy.	

| Error Correction | Repeat Steps 1–4. |

Continued

Instructions	Teacher	Student
	1. Advance Organizers	
	2. Your Turn with prompting of word parts	
	"First you're going to read the parts of the word and then you'll read the whole word."	
	a. Place your finger to the left of the first underlined part of the first word written on the board (<u>read</u> <u>ing</u>). **"First part?"** (scallop signal under the underlined part)	read
	b. Point to the left of the second underlined part of the word. **"Next?"** (loop signal under the underlined part)	ing
	c. Loop your finger to the left of the word. **"What word?"** (side-slash-signal under the entire word–answer) (loop back to starting point) **"Yes, *reading*."**	reading
	Repeat this pattern for all of the multisyllable words on the list.	
	3. Your Turn without prompting of word parts	
	After reading all of the multisyllable words on the list, start again and read the words the fast way without prompting the parts.	
	(point and pause) **"What word?"** (side-slash-signal under the entire word–answer) (loop back to starting point) **"Yes, *reading*."**	reading
	(point and pause) **"What word?"** (side-slash-signal under the entire word–answer) (loop back to starting point) **"Yes, *shelter*."**	shelter
	4. Repeat 3, even faster.	
	5. Individual Student Checkout	
	(point and pause) **"Individual turns. What word? Johnny."** (side-slash-signal under the entire word–answer) (loop back to starting point) **"Yes, *candle*."**	candle
	(point and pause) **"What word? Greta."** (side-slash-signal under the entire word–answer) (loop back to starting point) **"Yes, *tailor*."**	tailor
Error Correction	If students make an error reading the individual parts, immediately have them first orally sound out that part of the word and then read the entire part as a whole. Ask students to read the whole word one more time. Finally return to the beginning of the row and have students reread all the words to that point.	
	If students make an error reading the whole word the fast way, immediately tell students the word; then ask them to read the word parts again before reading the whole word. Once the error is corrected, return to the beginning of the row and have students reread all of the words.	

Reading Fluency

SAFER Reading

Instructions	Teacher
	Advance Organizers: When you tell students your behavior expectations, remind them that they must use a pointer finger to follow along with the reading.
	Steps to reading stories in the curriculum and decodable books:
	1. Call on individual students randomly and have them read between 1–3 sentences of the story.
	2. Expect the other students to follow along with their fingers.

3. Call on students quickly and avoid unnecessary tangential teacher talk by focusing comprehension questions to key ideas, vocabulary, and supporting details. (Refer to comprehension and vocabulary strategies in Chapters 6 and 7.)

4. Write missed words on the board. At the end of the story have students sound out each missed regular word and read it. If the word is a sight word, use the initial sight-word teaching format to review the word, having students orally spell it.

5. Move on to the next story when students read the story with between 97–100% accuracy. The error limit is based on the number of words in the story. Before reading tell students what the error limit is. When children exceed the error limit, discontinue reading and have students practice the words they missed and reread the story.

Error Correction

a. When a student makes an error, let the student read several more words, then say, **"Stop."** Do not use an abrupt or loud voice. By waiting you are giving the student a chance to self-correct.

b. Point out to the student what error was made, indicating whether he misidentified a word, skipped a line, or omitted a word.

c. Model the correct pronunciation of the word, or have the student sound it out. Then, ask the student to read from the beginning of the sentence. Treat omitted words as errors.

d. Remember to write the missed word on the board for later practice, as described in Step 5 above. Use the list of story errors as an opportunity for extra word reading practice.

Vocabulary

Teaching Vocabulary Through Modeling

Instructions	Teacher	Student
	1. Advance Organizers	
	2. My Turn	
	■ If modeling a word, show students three positive examples and three nonexamples of the word. If teaching the word *eyebrow,* point to your eyebrow and say, "This is an eyebrow." For a nonexample, you might point to Jason's foot and say, "This is not an eyebrow."	
	3. Your Turn	
	Ask students direct questions about the vocabulary word related to positive and negative examples. Intermix your type of questions. Students should answer 6 questions correctly before moving on to the next step.	
	■ If modeling the word *eyebrow,* you might point to Shondra's chin and ask this nonexample question, **"Is this an eyebrow or not an eyebrow?"** You might point to Kendra's eyebrow and ask this example question, **"Is this an eyebrow or not an eyebrow?"**	not an eyebrow an eyebrow
	4. Review of previously learned words (example- and nonexample-based questions) interspersed with questions about the new word.	
	5. Individual Student Checkout	
	Ask two or three students to answer questions about the new word and/or review words.	

Error Correction

If students make an error, immediately return to a My Turn–Your Turn pattern. Later in the lesson ask students about the word they missed to provide more practice. Only use a "Together" if students have difficulty pronouncing the vocabulary word and could use the practice saying it with you.

Synonyms: Examples and nonexamples for teaching the word *timid*:

1. Before presenting example and non-examples, have students look at the word and repeat the synonym after you until they can easily say it:

   timid **"*Timid* means easily frightened or shy. What does *timid* mean?"**

2. Ask students questions based on examples and non-examples of *timid*.

   - The new student was shy on the first day of school. Was the new student timid or not timid? How do you know?
   - Gabriel enjoys making everyone laugh. Is Gabriel timid or not timid? Why?
   - Sara is not afraid to give presentations in front of the class. Is Sara timid or not timid?
   - Marissa became easily frightened during the play and forgot her lines when she saw all the people in the audience. Did Marissa become timid or not timid? Why?
   - William is very friendly and outgoing. He can make friends with anyone. Is William timid or not timid?
   - A deer is a shy animal. Is a deer timid or not timid?
   - (Teacher makes a scared face with matching body posture.) Do I look timid or not timid?
   - On the first day of camp, Jorie was so afraid that she could hardly talk. Was Jorie timid or not timid? How do you know?
   - Lionel always raises his hand in class because he likes to explain the answer. Is Lionel timid or not timid? Why?
   - Sara is afraid to give presentations in front of the class. Is Sara timid or not timid?
   - (Teacher swaggers around the room with an "I am cool look" on his face.) Do I look timid or not timid?
   - A robin will fly away as soon as a person comes close to it. Is a robin timid or not timid? Why?
   - A grizzly bear will growl and run after a human who is trying to escape from him. Is a grizzly bear timid or not timid? Why?

3. Ask students to tell you the definition for the word timid one more time. Ask review questions about previously learned words.

   - What does *timid* mean? What does *nonsense* mean? Kendra moved from Swan Hillman School to Lewis Lemon School when she was in first grade. Would you say that Kendra *transferred* or *did not transfer* schools?

Direct Teaching: Definitions

Teaching Definitions: Examples and nonexamples for teaching the word *permanent*

1. Before presenting examples and nonexamples, have students look at the word and repeat the definition after you. Say the definition slowly and with emphasis so students can easily repeat it. With more difficult definitions, you may need to inject some "Togethers" when teaching the definition. You and the students will repeat the definition together until they are able to say it by themselves.

   - "*Permanent* means 'meant to last for a long time.' What does *permanent* mean?"

2. Ask students questions based on examples and nonexamples of *permanent*.

   - Molly bought an ice cream cone on a hot day. Is an ice cream cone permanent or not permanent? Why?
   - The Mayor of Chicago paid the artist, Pablo Picasso, to build a large concrete sculpture that sits in the plaza. Is the sculpture permanent or not permanent? Why?
   - Patrick put his old plastic action figures into a box when he left for college. The action figures are made out of strong plastic and will probably last until his grandchildren are old enough to play with them. Are these action figure toys permanent or not permanent? Why?

- Stuart wrote a secret spy note to his friend on paper and told his friend to destroy it after reading the message. Is the note permanent or not permanent? Why?
- After Maria's baby teeth fell out, new, larger teeth grew in her mouth. Maria's mother told her that if she brushed these new teeth every day, she would have them for the rest of her life. Were the new teeth permanent or not permanent? Why?

3. Ask students to tell you the definitions for the word one more time. Ask review questions.
   - "Tell me one more time what *permanent* means?"

Indirect Teaching: Context Clues

1. Give students a short reading passage of several sentences. Select a passage that contains a vocabulary word you have decided to teach where context clues are provided in the text.

   Example: It was while he was serving in the Illinois legislature that Lincoln decided he'd like to study to become a lawyer. He had a lawyer's *logical* mind, and he had a special knack for proving his side of an argument. Step by step, he could lay out the facts in a clear and uncomplicated way until soon enough he'd have everyone convinced.

2. Ask one student to read the passage before identifying the underlined word.

   Teacher: **"Kyle, read this passage about Lincoln."**

3. Ask another student(s) to find either the synonym or the definition of the underlined word in the passage.

   Teacher: **"How did Lincon prove his side of an argument, Cyndie?"**

   Cyndie: "Step-by-step he laid out the facts in a clear and uncomplicated way."

   Teacher: **"Yes, Lincoln explained all of the facts of a case *step-by-step in a clear and uncomplicated way.* That is how his mind worked. Everybody, let's read that last sentence together."**

   Class: "Step by step, he laid out the facts in a clear and uncomplicated way until soon enough he'd have everyone convinced."

   Teacher: **"Greg, what is a logical mind?"**

   Greg: "A mind that lays out the facts step-by-step in a clear and uncomplicated way."

4. Ask students to reread the sentence and substitute the synonym or definition for the vocabulary word

   Teacher: **"So I could read, 'He had a lawyer's *mind that laid out the facts step-by-step in a clear and uncomplicated way.'* That's how a logical mind thinks. Everyone let's read the entire second sentence together but instead of reading *logical,* use the definition."**

   Class and Teacher: "He had a lawyer's mind that lays out the facts step-by-step in a clear and uncomplicated way and he had a special knack for proving his side of an argument."

   Teacher: **"Kwame, it's your turn to read the second sentence with the definition for *logical."***

   Kwame: "He had a lawyer's mind that lays out the facts step-by-step in a clear and uncomplicated way and he had a special knack for proving his side of an argument."

Notes:

- Synonym context clues are easier to teach than definition context clues. You will need to provide more support through questions and Togethers for longer definitions.

- Use regular error correction strategies when students make an error. Often students who are at-risk will have difficulty with verb tense and pronouns when substituting a definition for the vocabulary word. In these cases, use more Togethers, and model the way to say the revised sentence before asking students to do the same

Teaching Multiple Meanings Using the Dictionary

Teacher	Students

1. The teacher reads the word in context.

   "The doctor gave the sick boy a *shot* of very strong medicine."

2. The teacher asks students to find word in their dictionaries.

   "Let's see if we can figure out the meaning of the word *shot* using the dictionary. Everyone, find the word *shot* in your dictionaries and raise your hand when you have found it."

   Students raise hands

3. The teacher helps students think through selecting the correct definition.

   "There are 3 definitions in the dictionary. We know that dictionaries often have more than one definition for a word. Let's see if we can figure out which one fits our sentence from the story.

   I'm going to read each definition and we'll try to figure out which one fits our sentence about the sick boy.

   1. The sound of firing a gun.
   2. A kick, throw, or hit in some games to score points.
   3. Medicine placed under the skin by a needle.

Let's talk about the first one. The sound of firing a gun. Does that fit what the doctor is doing to the boy?"

Everyone: No

"Why doesn't it fit, Simone?"

Simone: The doctor isn't shooting a gun or something at the boy.

"Let's look at the next one. A kick, throw, or hit in some games to score points. Everyone, does that fit what the doctor is doing?"

Everyone: No

"How do you know, Latese?"

Latrese: The doctor isn't playing a game with the boy, he's trying to make him feel better.

"Let's look at the last definition. Medicine placed under the skin by a needle. Everyone, does that fit what the doctor is doing?"

Everyone: Yes

"Manny, how do you know?"

Manny: He's putting medicine in him to make him feel better.

"So, everyone, what definition fits our sentence?"

Everyone: Medicine placed under the skin by a needle.

"Yes. Now, when we talk about the old west in social studies today, we'll talk about a different definition for shot. Which one do you think will fit into that story, Garth?"

Garth: The sound of firing a gun.

Strategies for Answering Vocabulary Questions on High Stakes Tests

Question Type 1: Using Context Clues to Determine Meaning

Example	Alonzo thinks the stars are beautiful. He likes to _gaze_ at them for hours. When he is in the country, the sky is very black so he can see the stars well.
	A person who _gazes_ at the stars—
	A. dislikes them B. draws them C. looks at them D. talks to them
Strategy	Read only the underlined vocabulary word and try to pick out the correct definition based on what you already know.
	If you can't figure out the correct definition, go back and read the sentence. Underline the clue words that can help you find the definition and try again.

Strategy (Continued)	If you still can't find the definition, substitute each of the choices into the sentence and pick the one that makes sense.
	If you still can't answer the question, guess one of the answers you think might be right.
Applied Strategy	**"Let's see. The underlined vocabulary word is *gaze*. Let's see if any of the choices means *gaze*. Hmm . . . Dislikes them? Draws them? Looks at them? Talks to them? I'm not sure what the answer is."**
	"I'm going to read the sentence and see if I can find words that might give me a clue about the meaning of gaze. I think the words see the stars well are important, so I will underline them in the sentence. But I'm still not quite sure of what the answer is."
	"OK. Now I'm going to substitute each choice word in the sentence and see which makes sense.
	He likes to dislike them for hours? That doesn't make sense at all. He likes to draw them for hours? I don't think he would be able to draw the stars at night. It couldn't be that one. He likes to look at them for hours? That one seems to make sense since it talks about being able to see the stars in the dark. I'll check the last one out just to be sure, but I think the answer is *look*. He likes to talk to them for hour? That doesn't make sense. So, I think the answer is C, *looks at*."

Question Type 2: Multiple Meaning Formats

Example	When Dashika finished the 10 mile race, she was <u>dead</u>.
	In which sentence does the word <u>dead</u> mean the same thing as in the sentence above?
	A. The roses in my garden are <u>dead</u>.
	B. The beach is <u>dead</u> in the winter time.
	C. The soldier was a <u>dead</u> shot with the rifle.
	D. The camper was <u>dead</u> after climbing uphill for 2 miles.
Strategy	Read the underlined vocabulary word.
	Read the bolded sentence containing the word and think of a simple definition or words that means the same thing.
	Read each of the four possible answer sentences substituting your definition instead of the word.
	After each sentence, ask yourself, "Does this make sense?" If not, cross out that choice and repeat for the other choices.
	If you still can't come up with the answer, take a guess by picking one of the choices you think might be right.
Applied Strategy	**"The underlined word is *dead*. Dead has many meanings. I need to figure out what it means in the bolded sentence. First I'll read that sentence. When Dashika finished the 10 mile race, she was *dead*. Well, even though a 10 mile race is very long, I don't think Dashika is likely to die from it. I think she would be *very tired*. So I think *dead* here means *very tired*. Let me put very tired in each sentence and see which one makes sense."**
	"The roses in my garden are very tired. That doesn't make sense. Roses don't get tired. I'm going to move to the next one. The beach is very tired in the winter time. That doesn't make any sense either. How about then next one? The soldier was a very tired shot with the rifle. That doesn't make sense either. Let's try the last one. The camper was very tired after climbing uphill for 2 miles. That makes sense. The camper would be tired after that climb. So the answer is D."

Question Type 3: Synonyms

Example	An <u>incredible</u> story is:
	A. boring
	B. unbelievable
	C. unhappy
	D. long

Continued

Strategy	Ask yourself what the word means without looking at the definitions given below.
	See if your definition is one of the four choices.
	If your definition is not one of the four choices, try to put each choice in a sentence and ask yourself, "Is that **incredible?**"
	If you still can't come up with an answer that makes sense, make a guess on one of the choices you think might be right.
Applied Strategy	"What does *incredible* mean? I think it means *funny.* Let's see if that is a choice. Hmm . . . It isn't. Now I'm going to try to put each of the choices into a sentence and see if I can figure out the meaning of *incredible* that way."
	"An incredible story. A boring story? Incredible and boring don't mean the same thing."
	"An incredible story. An unbelievable story? That seems right. I remember my brother talking about an incredible band. He said they were so good, he couldn't believe it. I'll look quickly at the other two choices, but I think B is the right answer. Let's see—*unhappy*? No—*long*? No, that isn't right either. I'm going to answer B for this question."

Glossary

acquisition stage of learning First stage of learning when the goal is learning to perform a skill accurately.

affixes Morphemes attached before or after a base word or root to modify its meaning.

aim line A graph line drawn from a student's current level of performance to a fixed benchmark score. The slope of the line depicts ongoing progress scores needed to meet the final benchmark score.

alphabetic principle The understanding that there are systematic and predictable relationships between written letters and spoken sounds. Students who have attained the alphabetic principle can identify regular words accurately and automatically, as well as acquire and remember sight words more readily.

assistive technology Any of a wide variety of technology applications designed to help students with disabilities learn, communicate, enjoy recreation, and otherwise function more independently by bypassing their disabilities. Also called *adaptive technology.*

at risk Students who require extra support learning to read because they are raised in poverty, have not been read to as children, were premature babies, have a primary language other than English, or have a learning disability.

automatic word recognition To decipher words effortlessly; to read regular words without consciously blending the sounds of letters or letter clusters into words.

base word The part of the word that establishes the basic meaning of the word. A base word can stand alone. In the word *undone, done* is the base word.

blending The ability to say a spoken word when its individual phonemes are said slowly.

closed syllable A syllable ending in a consonant as *pan* in *pancake (pan cake).*

comprehension The reason for reading, comprehension is the active process of getting meaning from written text. Comprehension is influenced by the person reading, the text being read, the task the reader is trying to accomplish, and the context in which the reading is being done (Rand Reading Study Group, 2002).

comprehension strategies Consciously planned procedures that readers use and adapt to understand text. Examples of comprehension strategies include predicting, summarizing, and generating questions.

consonant blends Two or more successive consonants sounded out in sequence without losing their identity. Examples of consonant blends include *str* as in *street, sl* as in *sloppy,* and *nt* as in *ant.*

context The words and sentences around an unknown word that, along with the reader's background knowledge, help to identify it or explain its meaning. Contextual clues can be semantic, involving meaning, or they can be syntactical, involving word order.

continuous sounds With continuous sounds, also known as *continuants,* the airflow does not stop as the sound is pronounced, so the sound can be held as long as some air remains in the lungs. Therefore, continuous sounds can be held for several seconds.

cumulative review The method of selecting teaching examples whereby the teacher adds previously learned material to newly learned material. Cumulative review teaches students to discriminate between new and old learning and helps students retain previously learned material.

CVC variants The first words introduced in phonics-based beginning reading programs in which all the vowels and consonants say their most common sounds. For example, the word *cat* is a CVC word; the word *mist* is a CVCC word; and the word *stump* is a CCVCC word.

decodable books Books in which at least 70% of the words can be sounded out because the letter sounds and combinations comprising these words say their most common sounds. Decodable books also contain a relatively small proportion of previously learned, high-frequency sight words. A decodable book is readable or appropriate for instruction when on a first read the student can read the text with at least 90% accuracy.

decode To decipher unfamiliar regular or irregular words.

diagnostic assessments Longer and more in-depth assessments that provide detailed information about a student's skills and instructional needs in order to help the teacher plan effective instructional support if needed.

differentiated instruction   A range of instructional options that meets the diverse needs of students.

digraphs   Two successive letters articulated as a single phoneme. Examples of digraphs include /ch/ as in *chop*, /th/ as in *this*, and /oo/ as in *book*.

diphthongs   Vowel blends in which the first sound appears to glide into the second sound. Examples of diphthongs include /ou/ as in *mouse* and /oi/ as in *boil*.

explicit instruction   The unambiguous, clear, and direct teaching of skills and strategies. Explicit instruction includes clear instructional objectives, a clear purpose for learning, clear and understandable directions and explanations, adequate modeling, demonstration, guided and independent practice with corrective feedback, and valid assessments for instructional decision making.

expository text   Text that is written to inform, persuade, or explain. Nonfiction writing. Examples of expository text include content-area textbooks, newspapers, reference books, journals, brochures, and the majority of online writing.

expressive vocabulary   Oral expressive vocabulary means using words in speaking so that other people understand you; written expressive vocabulary is communicating meaningfully through writing.

figurative meaning   A meaning that is not literal; the meaning is more picturesque implying something other than what is said on the surface.

fix-up strategies   Comprehension strategies that readers use when they are not fully comprehending text. Rereading, underlining text, and using a dictionary are examples of fix-up strategies.

fluency   The ability to read text accurately, quickly, and with expression.

fluency-based assessments   Assessments that measure both the rate at which students perform skills as well as their accuracy. Student scores on fluency-based assessments are often reported on a per-minute basis such as words read correctly per minute or letters identified correctly per minute.

fluency stage of learning   Second stage of learning when the goal is accuracy plus speed.

grapheme   A written letter or letter combination representing a single speech sound.

graphophonemic strategies   Strategies for identifying words that involve looking at the letters, breaking the word into parts, and/or matching letters and letter combinations with the sounds they make; phonics strategies.

high-frequency words   Words that appear most often in written language. They may be regular words or irregular words. Some high-frequency words are *in, of, the,*

that, was, when, and *where.* Dolch and Fry have published the most common lists of high-frequency words.

hypertext   With hypertext, the software designers link designated words, usually indicated by a different text color, to a database. Readers can select the words and bring on screen the information in the database. Pressing a designated word might link the reader to a definition of the word, to a picture of the word, to a clue for figuring out the word, or to a video of someone describing the word.

idiom   A speech form or expression that cannot be understood from the meanings of the separate words comprising it, but instead must be learned as a whole. "In the same boat" is an idiom that means two or more people are in the same situation. "As fit as a fiddle" is an idiom that means "very healthy." Also called *figurative expression.*

inference   A logical conclusion or educated guess arrived at by reasoning from evidence rather than relying on direct observation. Readers make inferences by drawing on their own background knowledge or finding clues in the text when the author has not provided information directly. For example, readers make inferences to determine character motivation, analyze the behavior of the character, look for clues from the author, and think about why they or someone they know would have done the same thing.

intonation   The rise and fall of the voice pitch on a scale extending from high to low. The pitch of the voice rises, falls, or remains relatively level during the pronunciation of words and sentences. Different patterns of pitch changes convey a range of meanings from the speaker's emotional state to the difference between statements, questions, and exclamations.

irregular words   Also called *sight words.* Words that cannot be conventionally sounded out and are learned as whole words.

keyword method   Method of teaching vocabulary directly that uses visual imagery to help students understand and retain word meanings.

letter combinations   A cluster in which two or more adjacent letters form one distinct sound. Examples of letter combinations include the digraphs *sh, ar,* and *ee,* and the diphthongs *oi* and *ou.*

lexical retrieval   The efficiency with which a reader can locate and apply to reading previously learned information about letters and words stored in long-term memory. Lexical retrieval is a strong predictor of reading success.

literal meaning   The primary meaning of a word. The actual meaning.

main idea   The central idea around which a piece of expository text is organized. It may be stated explicitly (written in a sentence) or implied (suggested without being explicitly stated). Each paragraph in expository text contains a main idea. In a paragraph when the main idea is explicitly described in a sentence, it is called the *topic sentence.*

Matthew effect   Early success in acquiring reading skills often results in later success in reading because a good reader becomes an even more highly skilled reader, acquiring more vocabulary and background knowledge as a result of reading more: also expressed as "the rich get richer, the poor get poorer."

median score   The middle score. If a student reads three grade-level passages at 40 words per minute, 76 words per minute, and 50 words per minute, the median or middle score would be 50 words per minute.

metacognitive skills   An awareness of one's thought processes while reading and the ability to plan, monitor, and select effective strategies when there is a problem with comprehension. Examples of metacognitive strategies include assessing what one already knows about a given topic before reading, assessing the nature of the learning task, planning specific reading/thinking strategies, determining what needs to be learned, assessing what is comprehended or not comprehended during reading, thinking about what is important and unimportant, evaluating the effectiveness of the reading/thinking strategy, revising what is known, and revising the strategy.

modeling   Demonstrating or directly telling; the My Turn phase of instruction.

monitoring text   Good comprehenders self-evaluate how well they understand while they read, and when problems arise they are able to use "fix-up" strategies to improve their comprehension. When readers are monitoring, they are consistently asking themselves, "Is what I am reading making sense?"

morphemes   The smallest parts of words that have a distinctive meaning. In the word *unladylike,* the morphemes are *un + lady + like.*

narrative text   Text that tells a story or that relates events or dialogue; fiction.

narrow reading   When students read several different texts about the same topic.

nonexample   The opposite of an example. Vocabulary nonexamples are items or concepts that are *not* representative of the specified word. When the term *ocean* is taught, nonexamples might include *desert, sky,* or *land.*

norm   A statistic describing the average or typical score.

onset   The beginning sound(s) that precede(s) the vowel in a syllable.

open syllable   A syllable ending in a vowel as *pa* in *paper (pa per).*

outcome assessments   End-of-the-year assessments that identify whether students achieved grade-level performance in the area tested.

overgeneralize   Draw too general a conclusion. For example, if all of the examples used to teach the concept of *red* are balls, students can draw the conclusion that something has to be a ball to be *red.*

PDA   Also called a personal digital assistant. PDAs are small handheld digital devices that store information, analyze data, and chart progress.

phoneme   The smallest unit of sound that is heard in spoken language. Phonemes are represented by back slashes; for example, /c/ + /a/ + /t/ = *cat.*

phonemic awareness   The ability to hear the smallest units of sounds in spoken language and to manipulate them.

phonics   The study of the relationships between letters and the sounds they represent. This term has become shorthand for describing instruction that establishes the alphabetic principle by teaching students the relationship between written letters or graphemes and the 41 to 44 sounds of spoken language or phonemes.

plot   Fictional stories have plots composed of a sequence of events that inform the reader what happened. Typically, the plot consists of a central problem or conflict that the main character(s) has to resolve, the steps the character(s) takes to solve the problem, and the resolution of the problem.

prefix   A morpheme that precedes a root or base word and modifies its meaning; also called an *affix.* In the word *submarine, sub* is the prefix.

prior knowledge   The sum total of what the individual knows at any given time. Prior knowledge includes knowledge of content and specific strategies.

progress monitoring assessments   Brief assessments given during the school year that inform the teacher whether students are making adequate progress toward grade-level reading ability.

pronoun referant   The noun that a pronoun refers to; the pronoun referant can be difficult to figure out for struggling readers. In general, the closer the pronoun is to its referent, the easier it is to understand.

prosody   The ability to read text orally using appropriate phrasing, intonation, and attention to punctuation.

r-controlled   An after a vowel always changes the sound of the vowel. Examples are *or* as in *portrait* or *ar* as in *partial.*

reading fluency   The ability to read text accurately, quickly, and with expression.

receptive vocabulary   Oral receptive vocabulary involves understanding the meaning of words when people speak; written receptive language concerns understanding the meaning of words that are read.

regular words   Words that contain previously taught letter–sound patterns enabling the reader to sound the words out.

retelling   The process of telling a story that one has read or heard. Teachers can use retelling to gather information about a student's reading comprehension, because when students retell a story, they must synthesize and organize information, make inferences, and draw on prior knowledge.

rime   The rest of the syllable that contains the vowel and all that follows it.

root   The part of the word that contains the basic meaning of the word. A root cannot stand alone. The words *diction, dictate, predict,* and *contradict* all have the common Latin root *dict,* which means *to say.*

round-robin reading   A method of reading in which all students in the class read aloud from the same book, regardless of their reading levels. The teacher calls on individuals to read, usually following a predetermined order.

screening assessments   Brief tests conducted at the start of the school year and designed as a first step in identifying students who may be at a high risk for delayed development or academic failure in the tested skill area. Further diagnostic evaluation is needed for students who have difficulty with a screening assessment in order to determine whether they need extra or alternative instruction.

scripted lessons   Teaching formats that specify what the teacher says when presenting information or skills to students. The purpose of the scripts is to ensure that instruction is uniformly clear, efficient, and effective.

segmenting   The ability to break apart words into their individual phonemes or sounds.

semantic mapping   Visual representations of vocabulary that help students establish relationships among new and old words by having students categorize, label the categories, and discuss concepts related to a target word.

semantic strategies   Strategies for identifying words that focus on meaning. Semantic strategies focus on whether or not a word makes sense in a sentence.

setting   When and where a story takes place. The setting can be specific or indefinite and can change within the text.

sight words   Also called *irregular words.* Words that cannot be conventionally sounded out and must be learned as whole words. Words that contain letter sounds that students have not yet learned in isolation and must be learned as whole words.

signal words   Signal words such as *for example, because, like,* and *first* link sentences and paragraphs together and are essential for comprehension because they give the reader clues about what will be happening.

sounding-out   Students first say each sound in succession, moving from left to right. Students then blend the sounds together quickly to say a word. Sounding-out can occur orally or subvocally.

stop sounds   With stop sounds, the air is completely blocked before it is expelled, either because the lips come together as with /p/, or because the tongue touches the upper mouth, as when saying /d/. Therefore, stop sounds can be held only for an instant.

story grammar   A story's grammar is the structure that the story follows. Typical story grammar elements include setting, characters, a problem or problems, plot, resolution, and theme.

story map   This type of graphic organizer portrays the story grammar of narrative text. Completing one helps students focus on the significant elements in a story as well as the relationship among these elements.

subvocal sounding-out   Deliberate sounding-out that is characterized either by lip movement unaccompanied by audible sounds or by conscious thought unaccompanied by audible sounds.

suffix   A morpheme added to the end of a root or base word; also called an *affix.* Some suffixes influence the grammar of a sentence like *s, ed, ing;* other suffixes change the part of speech; for example, *er* meaning, "one who," as in *singer.*

summarization   A monitoring strategy that helps readers evaluate their understanding of a passage they have just read. Periodically, the reader stops after having read a passage and first rephrases the main ideas before recalling key details. Summarization can be done orally or in writing. Students are often asked to summarize as one way to demonstrate their understanding of what they read.

syllable   Basic unit of speech, formed around a vowel or group of vowels that has one or more consonants preceding or following it. The word *bat* consists of one syllable; the word *spin ner* consists of two syllables.

syntactic strategies   Strategies for identifying words that focus on the conventions and rules related to sentence structure; grammatical strategies. Syntactic strategies involve figuring out whether a word sounds right in a sentence as if someone were talking.

synthetic phonics   This explicit phonics approach first teaches students individual skills (blending, segmenting, letter–sound identification, word reading) before providing practice applying these skills to carefully coordinated reading and writing activities. Student success and independence are emphasized through the use of carefully supported teaching strategies and curriculum.

systematic and explicit phonics   Phonics instruction characterized by the careful and thorough teaching of a planned, sequential set of letter–sound relationships. Systematic and explicit phonics incorporates materials that provide students with practice applying these relationships, including decodable books and other carefully coordinated reading and writing activities. Curricula that emphasize the teaching of phonics through literature or other materials, without a deliberate sequence of letter sounds and coordinated word reading activities, are not systematic or explicit phonics programs.

systematic error correction   A method of providing immediate corrective feedback to students by modeling the correct answer or skill, guiding the student to the correct answer as needed, asking students to give the answer independently, and asking students to repeat the correct answer later in the lesson.

systematic instruction   Instruction that clearly identifies a carefully selected and useful set of skills and then organizes them into a logical sequence of instruction.

theme   The subject or message that the author of narrative text wants to convey.

think-alouds   A technique by which teachers or students model a metacognitive skill and verbalize their thoughts about a strategy they are using. This process enables students to see a skill that could not otherwise be observed.

unvoiced sounds   Sounds that are produced when the vocal cords do not vibrate.

VCe words   Words having the vowel–consonant–silent *e* pattern. Examples include *cake, mine,* and *pole.*

voiced sounds   Sounds that are produced when the vocal cords are vibrating.

WCPM   Words correct per minute.

Index